COTTON ROW
TO
BEALE STREET

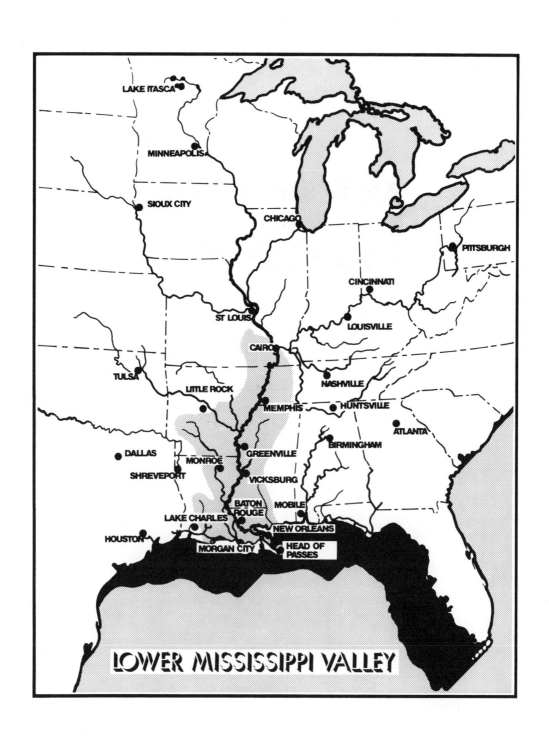

LOWER MISSISSIPPI VALLEY

COTTON ROW TO BEALE STREET

A Business History of Memphis

Robert A. Sigafoos

MEMPHIS
Memphis State University Press

Manufactured in the United States of America

International Standard Book Number: 0–87870–068–4
Library of Congress Catalog Card Number: 79–89884

Library of Congress Cataloging in Publication Data

Sigafoos, Robert Alan, 1923-
  Cotton Row to Beale Street.

  Bibliography: p.
  Includes index.
  1. Memphis—Economic conditions. 2. Memphis—Commerce—History. 3. Business—History. I. Title.
  HC108.M417S56   330.9′768′19   79-20117
  ISBN 0-87870-068-4

Acknowledgments

Among the great resources of Memphis are its dedicated historians and archivists who are paving the way for academic scholars, students, and the general public by building in depth the information sources needed to interpret the city's past correctly. I am personally indebted to the talented and thoroughly professional History Department of the Memphis/Shelby County Public Library and Information Center for their generosity and interest in assisting in this project from start to finish.

This outstanding municipal library literally has dozens of professionals and assistants who were constantly helpful and courteous. Many offered valuable suggestions, worried along with the author when information gaps emerged, and gave encouragement. These librarians went the full distance by actually taking time to understand the objectives of the research so they could be of maximum help. Needless to say, I am very grateful.

Particular credit goes to Dan Yanchisin, Head of the History Department, and James R. Johnson, Assistant Head of this Department. These two professionals gave me the benefit of their outstanding grasp of American history, and guided me to valuable source material that I would have overlooked. They have been helpful and friendly critics.

Other History Department members who were constantly helpful were Joe Brady, Stephen Findlay, David G. Feinberg, Delanie Ross, and Joan Cannon. John Norris, former City Archivist, and Frances French, Sallie Johnson, Reba Orman, Barbara Shultz and the entire combined staff of the Business-Technical and Sciences Departments assisted me in gathering a multitude of source materials.

Of the Brister Library staff of Memphis State University, I would like to thank Reference Librarian Mary Edith Walker; Interlibrary Loan Head, Deborah W. Brackstone; and Curator Eleanor McKay and her assistant, Marcy W. Kinkennon, of the staff of the Mississippi Valley Collection for their cooperation.

Memphis has not been overlooked by historians. The city is fortunate to have had many talented individuals during the past two centuries to record and analyze various aspects of the life of this city. J. M. Keating was probably the outstanding historian of the nineteenth century. Contemporary historians who have made significant contributions include Paul R. Coppock, Gerald M. Capers, James E. Roper, William D. Miller, Charles W. Crawford, David M. Tucker, and Bette Baird Tilly. Numerous articles on Memphis history appear in the journal, *West Tennessee Historical Society Papers*. I acknowledge these valuable sources.

Special thanks for assistance are directed to Carol Ann Seitz, administrative secretary of the Department of Finance, Insurance and Real Estate, College of Business Administration, Memphis State University; to Shirley Stanphill and Pat Still of the Bureau of Business and Economic Research, Memphis State University. Technical assistance was provided in the preparation of graphics by Edward B. Ebbing of the University's Center for Instructional Service and Research; and by two of my former graduate students, Jeff Rodd and Steve Williams. Thomas A. Wofford of the University's Photo Services staff copied the bulk of the photographs and helped improve the quality of many for reproduction here.

Contents

Tables

Preface

Complexity and confrontation are woven into almost every facet of the colorful history of Memphis. It is a city which has managed to survive innumerable crises. Starting with pioneer hardships, it has witnessed war, disease, economic discrimination, race conflict, national depressions, agricultural depressions, political bossism, and adverse technological change. Nothing came easy for the old Memphis of the nineteenth and early twentieth centuries. Nor has it come easy during the contemporary period of its city-building process. Even 160 years after its founding in 1819 it is still searching for its own special identification as an urban social and economic entity. Its story, therefore, is worthy of examination by students of urban history.

The city's fascinating economic history underlies all of these matters of urban concern. It has influenced events and people, and been influenced and directed by the vicissitudes of outside events and by legions of personalities representing a variety of interests and causes. This book attempts to capture the essence of changing economic or economically-related events, and to synthesize this history with the equally rich social and political history. Without some reference to the latter any economic history of Memphis would lack cohesiveness.

Contemporary life in other parts of America must be considered if one is to be objective in analyzing Memphis' development at different periods. An economic analysis of Memphis would be difficult to prepare if no consideration were given to other cities and regions, and their corresponding status of development. Memphians are usually harsh on their forebears when interpreting the city's past history. Seldom do they attempt comparisons with other competitive or regional cities during the same time periods to observe similarities and differences. Memphis, for example, was not the only disease-plagued city during the nineteenth century. New Orleans was far worse off. Some other cities were at least the equal of Memphis in an almost total lack of regard for sanitation and public health. Yet Memphis has almost alone carried this shame. Most Memphians are unaware that other cities also disgraced themselves by their callous disregard for matters of community sanitation.

Similarly, other cities and regions suffered at times from technological change, economic depression, natural disasters, and from pervasive political machines and bosses. Modern day Memphis may, or may not, be better off knowing it was not totally alone during dark periods of its existence. To assist the reader, then, at appropriate points comparisons are made to relate Memphis to its urban counterparts.

This research of Memphis' economic history covering almost two centuries started from an initial interest in exploring the process of urbanization and the shaping of the physical environment of this city since World War II. Faced with a battery of land use controls and policies concerned with city planning, the logical step was to review the origin of these regulations and the intent of civic leaders when framed. Suddenly I was stepping back into the period of the 1920s. This whole retracing exercise opened up to my unsuspecting eyes a sequence of new and intriguing subjects which included Mister Crump, the Memphis Chamber of Commerce, port development on the Mississippi River, commercial aviation, street car systems, annexations, and electric utilities.

Further, being of inquisitive mind, a certain fascination with some of these subjects and people thrust me back in time to the nineteenth century in a further search for facts. The time spent in the reading of nineteenth century published histories of Memphis, the State of Tennessee, and the United States, private papers of historical figures, and archival material reaped benefits totally unanticipated at the outset. At a certain point in this probing, the city's history suddenly came alive, aided and abetted by countless personalities from all walks of life in the past, and from a seemingly endless number of dramatic events. At that moment an outline was drafted designed to deal with people—the wealthy, the ordinary, the poor, Beale Street denizens, Madison Avenue bankers, Front Street cotton factors, roustabouts, City Hall politicians, merchant princes, entrepreneurs and promoters, scalawags, slumlords, and social outcasts. This outline also included organizations and institutions—business, political and social—the Mississippi River, railroads, King Cotton, Main Street, suburbs, as well as land speculators and developers carving out and building a city.

All of this information formed the basis for a comprehensive economic and urban land history. Heretofore, most historians writing about Memphis have not singled out economic growth and change as a special subject for interpretation. Collectively, they have not overlooked these specific subjects. Most of the good local histories allude to economic and business matters and land development; yet with few exceptions their basic theme is the political and social development of the city. These materials have been invaluable aids in the preparation of this more specialized type of history. There is an abundance of good historical writing covering a multitude of general and special topics. Probably the most serious gaps in the literature of Memphis, however, concern twentieth century urban development. This book attempts to fill part of that gap.

My approach was to write to a variety of audiences who might be expected to have an interest in urban economic history, and in Memphis' economic history in particular. Part of the intended audience were businessmen, urban planners, political and civic leaders, students, and professional or lay historians. In particular, it was the hope that the larger group of readers would be present and future residents of this city who might find it interesting and beneficial to learn more about the economic and urban land evolution of this city and region. It is a book meant to be both instructional and enjoyable.

Robert A. Sigafoos
Memphis State University

COTTON ROW
TO
BEALE STREET

1

Pioneer Origins

When Hernando De Soto landed in Florida in 1541 for his trek west, he was apparently looking for gold, not a new town site, as he ventured near the Mississippi River. If special land acquisition and speculation had been his objective, the fierce Chickasaw warriors would not have waited for fever to dispose of this great Spanish explorer a year later. But when Andrew Jackson and General Isaac Shelby came to negotiate the cession nearly three centuries later, the Chickasaws' hospitality had mellowed considerably. The friendly tribal chiefs had learned the value of the American dollar and manufactured goods. They had also realized the inevitability of encroachment by the white race drifting from the more urbanized Eastern shores. They knew that time was running out on them.

Poor De Soto and his hapless emaciated army actually did not accomplish much of anything. In all probability, he and his band did not even enjoy the benefits of viewing the mighty Mississippi from the heights of the Fourth Chickasaw Bluff, site of present day Memphis. Apparently, his crossing of the river was many miles below Memphis. De Soto's only accomplishment seems to have been a symbolic one. His men, to impress the Chickasaws, interred their dead leader into the mighty river they called Rio del Espiritu Santo. Not even in the wildest dreams of these Spanish soldiers could they have realized that they were placing De Soto's mortal remains in what would become in the nineteenth century one of the world's great commercial rivers and the spinal cord of a powerful nation.

Later explorers appear to have been equally luckless. Joliet and Marquette explored the river in the 1660s. La Salle ventured almost the entire length of the river in the 1680s, whereupon he formally claimed the entire Mississippi Valley for the King of France. On his return trip in 1684, his luck ran out completely, as he and his men fruitlessly searched for the entrance of the Mississippi from the Gulf of Mexico. Nevertheless, these visitations and those to follow in the next two centuries were to lead to territorial disputes among the European powers, and to involve the young United States government in the final years of that period in claims for territory in the Mississippi Valley broadly encircling Memphis and the Chickasaw bluffs.

France lost its claim of ownership to Great Britain in 1763. The Treaty of Paris which ended the French and Indian War awarded Britain all land east of the Mississippi River. Twenty years later Britain lost its control to the United States.

The Spaniards, however, were still a political and military force in parts of the lower Mississippi Valley. They had claims over the western and southern boundaries of the United States. Spain expressed hostility to the idea of free navigation into and out of the Mississippi River from the Gulf of Mexico.[1] This particular concern precipitated the first major historical event at the present day site of Memphis. On 30 May 1795 Spanish military forces occupied the Fourth Chickasaw Bluff—downtown Memphis today—and began construction of a fort. Another concern of the Spaniards were American land speculators moving into the region. The Georgia state legislature had conveyed several million acres of that state's western territory to three different private land companies.[2] Two of these huge land grants bordered the Mississippi River between Natchez and the Chickasaw Bluffs. The Spaniards under General Gayoso held on to Fort San Fernando de las Barrancas until 1797 despite Pinckney's Treaty, which was signed by Spain and the United States on 27 October 1795.

This treaty, negotiated by Thomas Pinckney, United States minister to Great Britain, settled the dispute over the southern and western boundaries of the United States and the matter of free navigation on the Mississippi River. President Washington put pressure on the Spaniards to withdraw. They dragged their feet, and did not officially exit until 1797. Because of the military importance of the Fourth Chickasaw Bluff, the Americans quickly constructed Fort Adams, and soon after that Fort Pike. The latter was subsequently renamed Fort Pickering in honor of Timothy Pickering, Secretary of War under George Washington.

Nothing of importance occurred at the Fourth Chickasaw Bluff from 1797 to 1819, concludes one Memphis historian.[3] But during this same period, St. Louis, Louisville, and Cincinnati were developing as urban commercial centers on the banks of either the Mississippi or the Ohio rivers. The bluff, nonetheless, was recognized by early visitors as having good locational characteristics for urbanization. The site was elevated above the flood stages of the Mississippi. The bluff extended practically to the river's edge, which permitted direct access to the water. With the topographic features of the bluff and the contiguous land area, the general higher ground appeared to have excellent natural drainage. The bluff also had military significance insofar as controlling activity on the river. Only Vicksburg and Natchez along the route of the river as it meandered through the vast alluvial valley from near Cairo, Illinois, to the Gulf had such natural advantages. The Fourth Bluff also had a potentially excellent natural harbor at the confluence of the Wolf and Mississippi rivers. In later years, an additional advantage to the site of Memphis would be the narrow width of the Mississippi. It was only 2,800 feet from the Memphis side to the top of the bank on the Arkansas side during periods of normal flow.

LAND GRANTS

The end of the eighteenth century and the first part of the nineteenth century was a period of great opportunity for citizens to share in the nation's young economy. Land ownership was equated with wealth and substance. Thus, when lands were opened for settlement, large numbers of people from the Atlantic seaboard followed the land speculators into the western lands of the period. North Carolina's western claim included almost all of the present state of Tennessee; statehood did not come to Tennessee until 1796. Georgia's western territory included the present areas of Alabama and Mississippi.

Similar to the generosity of the federal government and some state governments in awarding twentieth century war veterans certain monetary and nonmonetary benefits, Revolutionary War veterans and some state militiamen received military bounties for their service.[4] North Carolina was particularly generous. By 1791 her veterans held claims to over eight million acres of land. Many of these veterans did exercise their options, but unused warrants in areas of present day Tennessee, including the Chickasaws' hunting ground west of the Tennessee River to the Mississippi, fell into the hands of opportunistic land speculators.[5] These early land promoters bought warrants entitling them to vast land holdings. Interestingly enough, one of the principal beneficiaries of West Tennessee land was the University of North Carolina. Early land maps of Memphis indicate that that institution owned land just south of the present-day campus of Memphis State University and elsewhere in the region.

JOHN RICE—PROMOTER

Profit-oriented John Rice conceived a land promotion scheme in the early 1790s on a 5000-acre grant of land he had received from North Carolina. Mr. Rice bears the distinction of being Memphis' first real estate speculator even though his dealings were in absentia. His ads, placed in Eastern papers, carried information about the opportunity for the public to buy "town lots" in a settlement to be developed at the Chickasaw Bluff and the Mississippi River. His ads had a certain appeal. As bait, Mr. Rice offered buyers of his lots a bonus. They would be given the opportunity to acquire 100-acre sites at the mouth of "the Big Hatcha" River on payment of $33.33 at the time of landing. Rice's promotion called for one lot per family to be determined by a drawing. He was indeed a forerunner of the modern day recreation-retirement lot promoters. If dinnerware and electrical appliance premiums had been in existence, doubtless Mr. Rice would have offered these lures. His ads cited liberal terms, and permission to till and cultivate the adjacent land for a period of five years rent free. Rice further guaranteed prospective buyers that the Chickasaws were a friendly, peaceable and humane people. Unfortunately for Mr. Rice, he did not live to carry through his land venture. Reports of the day say he met an untimely death at the hands of Indians in 1791. It is unlikely that the murderers were Chickasaws. Would Mr. Rice have lied in his ads?

Rice apparently took no notice of the matter of the legality of his town lot promotion. The Chickasaws owned these lands until purchased by the federal government. Formal transfer of title did not occur until 1818. John Overton apparently did not care either about the legality of his title to the Rice tract which he purchased from Rice's brother for $500 in 1794.

This latter sale was to lead eventually to the settlement of Memphis in 1819. Overton sold half interest in the Rice tract to Andrew Jackson in 1796. They were friends and business partners, and over many years these two Nashvillians were to team up in land speculations throughout the South.[6]

The Chickasaw Cession

The purchase of the Chickasaw lands, called the Western Purchase or the Chickasaw Cession, was the final event leading to the formal founding of Memphis. In what may be one of the all-time real estate rapes of the American Indian, the 6,848,000 acres of fertile land lying west of the Tennessee River to the Mississippi River was purchased by the Federal government for four and one-half cents per acre. Andrew Jackson and General Isaac Shelby were appointed negotiators to deal with the Chickasaw leaders. Accounts of the actual negotiations indicate that Jackson took the leadership role and applied tremendous pressure on the Chickasaw chiefs to capitulate to the cash offer he was making on behalf of the United States government. The methods employed, according to one analyst, would be embarrassing for either a chamber of commerce or a council of churches to endorse.[7]

A softening up process was employed prior to the opening of formal negotiations. Presents were sent to the Indians before the arrival of Jackson and Shelby. Then at the formal session Jackson applied the strategy of inferring that the federal government might appropriate the lands.[8] Jackson opened with an offer of $150,000. The Indians refused. Then it was raised to $200,000, followed by an offer of $250,000. Meanwhile Jackson and General Shelby were at odds over the offers being made; Shelby seemed distressed at Jackson's bargaining manner and his failure to be forthright. The ill General Shelby was also aware of Jackson's ownership with Overton, General James Winchester, and William Winchester of the Rice tract on the Chickasaw Bluff.

Negotiations ended on 19 October 1818 and the treaty was ratified on 7 January 1819. Jackson had raised his offer to $300,000 to be paid to the Chickasaws in 15 annual payments of $20,000 each. The Indians not only received what might be considered a ridiculously low price, but they had to wait some 15 years for full payment.

MEMPHIS AND ITS PROPRIETORS

The way was paved to start a community on the Bluff. John Rice's original plan to sell town lots in an urbanization scheme was to become a reality 28 years later. Fortunately for Jackson, Overton, and General James Winchester, the town's original proprietors, the land warrants granted by the State of North Carolina in Tennessee were honored by the latter's land offices. The Chickasaw Cession cleared the last hurdle. Shortly after the treaty was signed, Jackson sold another one-eighth undivided interest in the 5000-acre Rice tract to General Winchester for $5,000. This action again created suspicion of Jackson's motivations in pressuring the Chickasaws for a quick settlement.

The three partners moved rapidly after the treaty. Jackson told General Winchester that they must act quickly to get a head start on other promoters considering settlement schemes on the bluffs north of Memphis.[9] Also, some 160 miles to the west in Arkansas a colonization scheme by Stephen F. Austin was in the planning stages.[10] On 12 January 1819 Jackson, Overton and Winchester agreed to lay out a town site. Legend has it that this agreement was worked out in Memphis' famous Bell Tavern. Unfortunately, this story lacks substance since Paddy Meagher's famous saloon was not in existence at that time.[11]

Surveyor William Lawrence was hired. His finished product was a rectangular town site containing 362 lots, lying parallel with the river bank. None of the Proprietors had any intention of residing in the settlement, so they hired Marcus B. Winchester, the General's son, to act as their sales agent. The younger Winchester became Memphis' first on-the-scene real estate agent and entrepreneur. He became the town's leading citizen and held this position for the next 20 years.

The sales strategy approved by the Proprietors was much more sophisticated than John Rice's earlier approach. An ad placed in the *Nashville Whig* stated: "It is the intention of the proprietors not to offer the lots at public sale, but to induce, and make it the interest of the prudent and discreet adventurer of all classes to settle and improve the place."[12] And the ad went on to describe Memphis as the handsomest place on the Mississippi below St. Louis.

One Benjamin Fooy was awarded the first deed, on the condition that he build a commercial structure on the site. So the first sale was a noncash arrangement. The Proprietors wanted to show some activity to future prospects.

Memphis grew very slowly and was a disappointment to its developers. In 1820 there was a population of 251 whites and 103 slaves. At the time of incor-

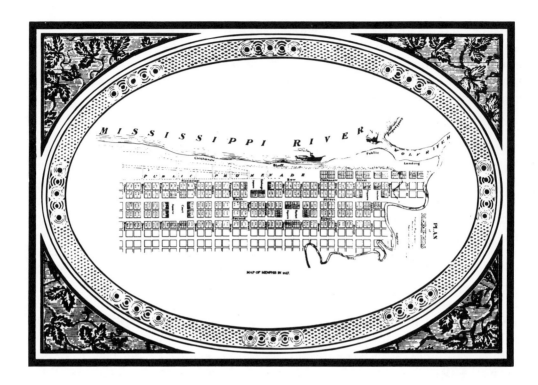

Fig. 1. *Above.* Plan of the original town site of Memphis. *Below left to right:* Memphis founders General James Winchester, Andrew Jackson, John Overton; and the agent of the three Proprietors, Marcus B. Winchester, son of General Winchester. (Courtesy of Memphis Room, MPL)

poration in 1826 it had 309 citizens. Not much is known about most of these early settlers except that they soon developed a hostility to taxes. The majority felt that incorporation was purely in the interests of the Proprietors. "Why should we pay taxes when it would be the Proprietors who would benefit from growth?" was the argument of these settlers. Apparently no ill-will was extended to Marcus Winchester. He was elected an alderman in 1827, then chosen Mayor by his fellow aldermen.

Lot sales were unspectacular during the first decade. Only 122 lots had been conveyed in 1829. Andrew Jackson had long since sold his remaining interest; and a new and powerful real estate investor named John C. McLemore entered the development venture of the Rice tract. McLemore also became for many years a successful promoter and developer of land contiguous to the Rice tract before he went broke in the late 1840s and departed for California.

ANDREW JACKSON PROFITS FROM MEMPHIS INVESTMENT

Jackson's investment of $100 made in 1796 when his friend and business associate, John Overton, sold him a one-half interest proved to be a good one. For some 27 years Jackson held a partial ownership position in the Rice tract. In 1797 Jackson sold to the Winchesters for $625 his interest in 1,250 acres for which he had paid only four cents an acre when acquired from John Overton the year before. In today's investment world, a financial analyst would say that Jackson had made an annual rate of return of 1,150 percent. Jackson bought it for four cents an acre and sold it for 50 cents an acre. In 1818, he sold another 625 acres of his Rice tract holdings for $5,000. Considering that Jackson had held this particular acreage for 22 years, his annual rate of return on his investment on these 625 acres was an impressive 23 percent. Jackson traded his remaining one-eighth interest, or 625 acres, to McLemore in 1823 for some 1,140 acres of rural land in present day Madison County, Tennessee.

Gerald Capers in his excellent history, *Biography of A River Town,* pointed out that Jackson found it expedient to sell out to McLemore in 1823 to draw the public's attention away from its belief in his fraud in the Chickasaw Cession matter.[13] In 1824 Jackson was to make his first bid for the Presidency. Tennessee gave Jackson a resounding vote of confidence, but he lost the election to John Quincy Adams.

Shelby County was created by the Tennessee legislature in 1819. It was named after General Isaac Shelby, a former governor of Kentucky, a prominent military figure of the Revolutionary War, and, along with Jackson, a negotiator of the Chickasaw Cession. For the next 60 years after 1819 the pattern of present day West Tennessee counties was taking shape. Some counties formed after the 1820s were carved out of portions of old counties.[14] Shelby County managed to retain most of its original territory in this political jurisdictional adjustment process.

A boundary dispute between Tennessee and Mississippi was settled in 1837.

Shelby County and other counties in West Tennessee bordering the state of Mississippi acquired additional land in this settlement.[15]

PUBLIC SPACE IN TOWN PLAN

To their everlasting credit, the original Proprietors insisted that the town plan contain adequate public areas to help make it more livable. When Surveyor Lawrence drew his plans, he included one full city square and three half squares; he also set aside an area bordering the river as a public promenade. These lands were dedicated by the Proprietors for public usage. In later years, however, some encroachments were made by private interests under long term leasing arrangements for all or portions of various public sites.

Court Square, still a prominent landmark, was the target of private developers. Proposals were made around 1900 to build a skyscraper office building on the site. In the immediate post–World War II years, proposals were made to turn Court Square into a parking facility to accommodate the increasing volume of automobile traffic coming into the downtown area. Auction Square and Market Square have also been preserved as open space. Exchange Square, however, has been occupied almost continuously since the mid nineteenth century. Since 1924 the site has been occupied by the publicly-owned Ellis Auditorium.

The area designated for the Public Promenade bordered the Mississippi west of today's Front Street, north of Union and south of Jackson. The Proprietors designated it as a place for walking and leisure. The tract contained some 36 acres when deeded to the City in 1828. Over the years the question of the Proprietors' intentions in setting aside the land was debated. One court in 1834 was of the opinion that the City had the right to use or dispose of the site as it so chose, and that this land should never be a deterrent to progress.[16] Apparently this latter view prevailed. The federal government acquired the Custom House site in 1877. The city dedicated a site for the construction of Cossitt Library in 1888. Railroads were permitted to traverse the Promenade area with their tracks, and to build switching yards and stations on this land. In contemporary times additional facilities, including a fire station and parking garages, have been built on this original Promenade area. Today, only a few open areas for leisure use remain, including the one-block square Confederate Park at Front and Jefferson and the equally small Jefferson Davis Park at Riverside Drive and Jefferson. Until the post–World War II period there were few preservationists in Memphis to fight for the maintenance of these open areas originally set aside by the Proprietors for community social and recreational usage.

EARLY STREETS

Street names honored former U.S. Presidents and the three Proprietors. There were also streets named to coincide with the four public squares, and some streets were given standard names such as Main Street, Second Street and

Third Street. Mississippi Row was the original name for Front Street between Union and Jackson. Chickasaw Street was that part of Front Street between Jackson and Sycamore.

Main Street was the spine of the street system. In later years this name was considered by some civic leaders too provincial for a growing city and various suggestions were offered for a more euphonious name.[17] It took local legislators another 70 years to get around to a name change. Recently, that portion extending from Exchange to Gayoso was designated the Mid-America Mall and given over exclusively to pedestrians. Thus, the founding fathers were partially compensated for the earlier losses of the Promenade with this new emphasis on public, open area in the downtown.

Front Street prior to the Civil War became the center of the region's cotton business and wholesale trade. North of Beale it was Front Street. Until 1906 the extension south of Beale was called Shelby Street. Shortly after the birth of Memphis, Union became the political boundary between the city and the rival village of South Memphis. The two towns merged in 1849, and Union continued to grow into one of the city's principal east-west thoroughfares. Spanish Governor Gayoso, prime mover in the construction of Fort San Fernando in 1795, was honored with a street name during the early settlement days. Beale Street, listed on nineteenth century maps as Beal or Beale Avenue, was named about 1840 by wealthy entrepreneur-promoter Robertson Topp. That street like Union was a residential street with homes of wealthy Memphians during the greater part of the nineteenth century.[18] Unfortunately for historians, Col. Topp never identified the background of his honoree, his first name or the correct spelling of his surname.

Central Avenue was in existence as early as 1845. Active real estate agent Marcus Winchester was promoting the sale of country lots "out Central." Pigeon Roost Road (renamed Lamar) was once a Chickasaw trail.[19] A private investment group received a charter in 1853 to operate this early thoroughfare as a turnpike. The Civil War disrupted the operation and maintenance of this private venture, and the charter was lost. Chelsea Avenue, one of the city's oldest streets, took its name from the early small community of Chelsea. This particular residential enclave was absorbed by Memphis in the latter nineteenth century.

The first street identified with the raucous and rowdy nineteenth and early twentieth century Memphis reputation as a wide open city was really little more than an alley. Whiskey Chute was the name given to the shortcut passageway extending from Main to Front Street between Court and Madison. Within this one block enclave was a string of saloons. Today this alley in the heart of downtown Memphis bears the very respectable name, Park Lane.

Memphis had great difficulty establishing for itself a position of urban dominance in Shelby County prior to 1840. Not many residents or visitors to West Tennessee were impressed by this small town on the bluff overlooking the

Mississippi. In 1827 the county seat was moved from Memphis to the tiny hamlet of Raleigh located some 10 miles away. Memphis had to wait until 1866 before full county government functions were transferred back to it. The first real home for the Shelby County Courthouse was not provided until 1874, when the county acquired the former Overton Hotel which was located at Main and Poplar. When the county government outgrew that facility it moved into its present facility on Washington between Second and Third streets in 1910.

Memphians took pride in new public buildings regardless of their functions. The dedication of an ornate jail soon after the Civil War, for example, sparked a great civic celebration. This new publicly-owned building for the moment at least was the architectural pride of Memphis. *The Public Ledger* stated editorially that ". . . this jail is an ornament to the architecture of Memphis though its inmates are anything but creditable to society."[20]

Throughout most of the nineteenth century the lack of a public library was lamented by the civic leaders. Occasionally private, specialized reading rooms were opened, but these in no way would be called general libraries. This community-wide cultural and educational lag continued until the opening of Cossitt Library at Front and Monroe in 1893.

SCHOOLS AND CHURCHES

The free school movement in the city beginning in 1848 was somewhat ahead of other American cities. As early as 1852, Memphis had a number of schoolrooms in operation. These were one-room, one-teacher schools covering instruction in the primary, secondary and senior grades. One problem was the difficulty finding suitable rooms in rented buildings.[21] Surprisingly, by 1860 the city schools were operating with an enrollment of 1,700 pupils from a school age population in the city of about 3,600. For that period, this was an exceptionally good enrollment.

Among the most imposing early community structures were the churches constructed by Protestant and Catholic congregations. Several survive today to give evidence of the boldness of the architecture. These facilities brought substance to the small river town which had drab, inadequate housing for the ordinary citizen.

TOWN GROWTH AND PERIPHERAL DEVELOPMENT

Town growth was slow through the 1820s and 1830s. The hopes of the land speculators that in-migration into West Tennessee and to the banks of the Mississippi would yield handsome returns through price escalation were dashed when the Panic of 1819 and subsequent poor national economic conditions slowed arrivals.[22] Memphis town lots were inexpensive enough. Prices were $30 to $100 a lot depending on location. Typical lot sizes were 37⅛ feet by 148½ feet, or about 5,500 square feet. One acre lots adjacent to the eastern boundary of the original town site were $10, while lots abutting the Promenade were $500.[23]

Competitors operating land subdivisions just south of Union Street threatened sales in the Rice tract. John Overton worried that Robert Fearn's plan for a new town adjacent to his investment, and John McLemore's land development venture at Fort Pickering would hurt Memphis. Working against the interests of the Proprietors was their own sales agent, Marcus Winchester, who became an investor in McLemore's land settlement venture called the South Memphis Company.[24] This particular subdivision was appended to Memphis. Its developers extended Shelby (Front Street south of Union) and Main streets into their land holdings to tie in with early Memphis. The Proprietors received another blow to their development efforts when the decision was made to move the courthouse to Raleigh despite their intensive lobbying against such action of the State Capitol in Nashville.

McLemore's Fort Pickering, near present-day DeSoto Park, land venture extended well into the 1840s. His primary objective was to build there the region's first railroad-river terminal facility. Residential lots were part of his plan, but they were a secondary land use to his commercial projects. The failure of the La Grange & Memphis Railroad Company in the 1840s and lagging sales in the residential development eliminated this competitive urbanization threat to Memphis. Heavily indebted, McLemore left for California in 1849, doubtlessly turning his attention from land speculation to gold. He returned to Memphis on the eve of the Civil War and died here in 1864.

The ever-active Mayor and Postmaster Marcus Winchester had another venture going to the east of early Memphis. His newspaper announcement, as follows, would still appeal today: "A number of country lots on the great Central Avenue are now available. These are not too far from the city and are distinguished by their healthful situation, convenience to five springs, good schools, churches and upright neighbors."[25]

The urbanization process gained momentum when the community of South Memphis merged with Memphis in 1849, contributing some 67 city blocks to its area. Robertson Topp, a young attorney, then just starting his flamboyant career as a promoter and investor in real estate and railroad ventures was South Memphis' leading business figure. Topp obviously saw advantages in this annexation. He had extensive real estate holdings in South Memphis, including his brand new Gayoso House described as the grandest hotel in the tri-state area. Topp at the time was in the early stages of his planning for the Memphis & Charleston Railroad. With the terminus in one consolidated city, the combined economic strength would justify City of Memphis financial grants to this railroad venture.[26] Mr. Topp was an astute strategist, and the premier stock and bond salesman of his time.

This first expansion created the impetus for civic improvements. Memphis issued $119,000 in bonds in 1850 to celebrate its growing importance. Population had increased to 8,800, and property valuation to $4.6 million. Additional portions of the original Rice 5000-acre tract started filling up. The Greenlaw Addition was a partial northern extension of the original town plan. In 1856 this area was called Chelsea.[27]

Elsewhere in Shelby County there were just small pockets of urban development. Agriculture, however, was becoming economically significant. The hamlet of Raleigh was the county seat and the town in the late 1820s had hopes of becoming the region's principal center of trade. Meanwhile, in the vicinity of present-day Germantown, Frances Wright, a newly arrived human rights activist, was attempting to create her utopia, the Nashoba Experiment. This 30-year-old Scots woman, characterized as a "radical thinker and a free enquirer" by her contemporaries, interested herself in the American slave question. She bought a 1,940-acre tract in the Germantown-Ridgeway area bordering the Wolf River on which to conduct her radical, communal experiment. She named her holdings "Nashoba," an Indian word for wolf. Frances Wright's plan was to purchase a number of slaves and to help them through formal education and training to achieve the tools of life required to survive emancipation.[28] The plan was akin to "on-the-job training." Slaves through their work at Nashoba would earn something for themselves and at the same time earn enough to pay for their freedom. But the Nashoba Plan ended in failure in 1830. The illness of Frances Wright, together with an impractical concept at that time, brought to an end Shelby County's opportunity to observe a utopian society. Elsewhere, in New Harmony, Indiana, English industrialist Robert Owen's communal social experiment which he had founded in 1825 failed after only two years. Owen's followers were white, working-class people, and not slaves as in Frances Wright's venture.

The early impetus to develop came from the land speculators. Their perception of Memphis and Shelby County was as a place to earn a quick profit by getting in on the ground floor of expected in-migration and changing transportation technology, which was soon to bring the steamboat and railroads on a large scale. Memphis would be a terminus. But from the time of Fort San Fernando in the 1790s to the Civil War urbanization on the Bluff was little more than a minor ripple in the nation's growth. The seeds were here nevertheless for dramatic change, due largely to locational advantages on the Mississippi River, which was just assuming its role as an economic pivot in the young nation.

2

Emergence

Spain closed the Mississippi to the British and the Americans during the Revolutionary War to prevent settlements. When the Spaniards capitulated in 1794, free navigation came to the river. A transportation artery for hauling goods and people was born and cities and towns sprang up on the river's banks or in the interior regions near the river. Western settlement received its greatest stimulus when pioneers and early day merchants started moving west and south on the Mississippi and its major tributary rivers. Memphis owes its origin to the river. So does St. Louis, New Orleans, Natchez, Vicksburg, and countless other towns. Their early economic growth was totally dependent on the river. Not until the 1850s, when the era of railroads began, did the river begin to lose some of its dominance as the generator of economic development for the city.

The Mississippi River and its total contribution to Memphis over its 160 year history involve both economic and psychological matters. Memphis built its early commerce around the river. People and goods came up the river from New Orleans; or down the river via the Ohio River from Louisville, Cincinnati or Pittsburgh; or from St. Louis and points on the upper Mississippi or Missouri rivers. Cotton, the principal commodity handled in Memphis, was assembled there from various points in the Mid-South prior to being transshipped via the river in the nineteenth century. Psychologically too, the river has been pivotal. The romantic appeal of the Mississippi throughout its colorful history has increased the fame of the city. The scenic attractions, the traditions of music and talented entertainers associated with the river have all contributed to Memphis' development.

This mighty river has also been a cantankerous and lethal force of nature. It has not only challenged river pilots since before the days of Mark Twain because of its traps and snares and meanderings, but it has also wrought havoc on thousands of people and on urban and agricultural property through its periodic floods. The Mississippi, born at Lake Itasca in Minnesota, travels some 2,340 miles south to Head of Passes, just above the Gulf of Mexico. It drains one and one-quarter million square miles. The Lower Mississippi Valley from near Cairo, Illinois, to below New Orleans is an alluvial plain varying in width from 20 to 80 miles wide, and extending 954 miles. Memphis lies in this huge alluvial valley 735 miles upstream from Head of Passes and 219 miles below Cairo.

RIVER TRAFFIC

Prior to the railroads, the Mississippi and its tributaries served exclusively as the long distance north-south route, and as the east-west route via the Ohio, Missouri, Arkansas, and other feeder rivers. Agriculture has long profited from the Mississippi. Only in the twentieth century did heavy and medium industry come to enjoy equal economic benefits.

Ante-bellum Lower Mississippi Valley commerce was first transported by primitive flatboats; then later by the slightly more mobile keelboats and finally by the steamboat. Railroads were to start their challenge in the 1850s. Flatboats had the disadvantage of only being able to head south on the river. At their ultimate destination they were dismantled for firewood. Keelboats eventually replaced them. These were shallow freight boats. The keel design aided in sailing into the wind and made two-way trade possible. But both flatboats and keelboats proved primitive. The new technology of the early nineteenth century was about to create a new economic era for Memphis and the Mississippi River. Fast, two-way traffic demanded change.

Memphis did not receive much notice as a port of call in the 1820s and 1830s. Rafts and flatboats stopped to take on provisions. Flatboatmen, a rough and hardy bunch, "raised hell" in Memphis and helped create the town's early reputation as a center of sin and lawlessness. Hodding Carter has described the perils of travelers in Memphis running afoul of gamblers, prostitutes and belligerent flatboatmen.[1] Pinch, a waterside neighborhood just north of the present day Cook Convention Center, was the principal scene of violence in the early days. According to historian Francis B. Simpkins, Memphis was dismissed outright as a place to live by the Southern aristocracy, because the city failed "to segregate its 'flatboat folk' and its numerous gambling dens and bawdy houses from more respectable districts."[2] In the compact, early urban form of Memphis it was hardly possible to create isolated residential neighborhoods.

The introduction of the steamboat gave Memphis its first economic reason to grow. River trade was growing and faster and larger vessels were needed to meet the demands of commerce. Whereas flatboats found difficulty maneuvering in the swift river currents in front of Memphis, the new steamboats found it advantageous in the early years.[3] Steamboats plying the Mississippi and Ohio rivers between New Orleans downstream and fast developing Ohio River cities like Cincinnati, Louisville, and Pittsburgh, could easily add Memphis to packet service. By the 1830s great advances had been made in the speed and size of steamboats. Boats especially designed for Mississippi River trade had flat bottoms and paddle wheels instead of screw propellers. Shallow waters, tricky currents and much river debris causing snags were considerations in designing the Mississippi steamboat.

Steamboats despite improved engineering and navigation technology were often referred to as fancy firetraps. Between 1810 and 1850 over 4,000 people were killed or injured in Mississippi steamboat disasters. Commonplace catastrophes were boiler explosions, fires, and destruction on snags or sandbars. Many lurid accounts of accidents were reported in early Memphis newspapers. Memphians and Memphis-bound cargo were often involved. Because steamboats were becoming numerous on the river, the accident rate accelerated. In 1834 there were 230 packets on the river. By 1850 there were over 1,000 on scheduled service.

Steamboats on the Mississippi have always carried colorful names. Such names as *Belle of the Bends, Grand Republic, Georgia Lee, Goldenrod Showboat, Robert E. Lee, Chickasaw Princess, Kate Adams,* and *Molly Able* were typical. Each seemed imbued with a distinctive personality and a loyal following of merchants and travelers. Before the Civil War the larger vessels were built in Pittsburgh and Cincinnati. Those built in Tennessee were mostly small boats and under 50 tons in weight. Memphis appeared to have all of the natural resources to engage in shipbuilding, but it did not try to compete in steamboat construction although the region had unlimited hardwood forests for timber, and the Wolf River provided a sheltered area where large scale construction could have taken place. The crest of steamboat building was in the 1850s although hundreds of vessels were built after that period.

Although cargo was the principal commodity carried, the lore of the Mississippi steamboat is generally involved with the passenger and entertainment aspects. Gamblers such as the legendary George Devol, who travelled on the river in ante-bellum days, perhaps have received an undue amount of attention.[4] The work of the steamboats in the early and middle years was hauling cotton bales by the millions. Occasionally a big event, such as competitive races between rival boats, would capture both rivertown and national attention. The great upriver race from New Orleans to St. Louis between the *Robert E. Lee* and the *Natchez* came in July 1870, near the end of the glory years of the steamboat. This race, watched by thousands along the way, was won by the *Robert E. Lee* in the record time of 3 days, 18 hours and 14 minutes. National attention was focused on the river for that brief period.

The first scheduled trip from Memphis to New Orleans was in 1834. A local company financed by Memphis businessmen were behind this venture. From this limited start of river front activity, the volume of steamboat traffic was to increase to about 2,300 arrivals and departures just prior to the Civil War. Port activity accelerated in the 1850s. The city came to the attention of entrepreneurs in the thriving cities of Cincinnati and Louisville on the Ohio River. Merchants in Cincinnati in particular saw advantages of enlarged trade with Memphis.[5] This was a boost to Memphis' commercial ego. After all, Cincinnati was then known as "Queen City of the West," and had steamboats serving such diverse places as Omaha, Minneapolis, and St. Paul and the Mississippi River towns. Memphis' alliance with New Orleans was also growing stronger. As cotton production increased in the 1840s and 1850s, it was moved down the river to New Orleans to be transshipped to New England or to Europe. In the 1850s Memphis assumed an importance in river transportation next to New Orleans on the Lower Mississippi.[6] St. Louis on the Upper Mississippi was substantially ahead of Memphis at that point. On the eve of the Civil War, Memphis showed signs of making its first move for economic recognition.

Navigation improvements supervised by the Corps of Engineers began as early as 1824. Federal responsibility for the Mississippi was to become a major effort in later periods of American history. Memphis business leaders recognized early the need for maintenance of clear channels. One of the major topics brought before the Commercial Convention held in Memphis in 1845 was that of improving the Ohio and Mississippi rivers. Well-known South Carolina politician John C. Calhoun, president at this convention of 600 delegates from every southern state, also made a plea for flood control on this river.[7] Subsequent trade conventions in the 1840s focused on river improvements. Memphis recognized that it would be a beneficiary of additional federal interest.

THE NAVY YARD

The Memphis Navy Yard announcement in 1844 set off a wild celebration in Memphis. "This will be the making of the city" was the consensus of Memphians. This city and its good friend, Lt. Matthew Fontaine Maury, then a 38-year-old United States naval officer, had been petitioning Congress for consideration of Memphis as the site for an inland naval depot and dock yard since 1841.[8] That year Congress appointed a commission to recommend a site somewhere on the Mississippi River. Memphians argued through a series of memorials directed to Congress and to the Navy that this city was an ideal location for a defensive position protecting both the South and the West. They pointed out that the Mississippi at Memphis and below was navigable year round. The city's geographic position would be ideal to draw the Navy Yard's supplies from the Ohio and Mississippi Valleys. In a further argument, reminiscent of contemporary "pork barrel" legislation by Congress, Memphis supporters felt that this part of the nation should be given the same consideration as the Eastern seaboard states. They argued that millions had been spent on the East Coast for defense, so why not on the Mississippi.

Born in Virginia but raised near Franklin, Tennessee, Maury later became a distinguished officer in the United States Navy, and during the Civil War in the Confederate Navy. He gained world renown for his scientific contributions in oceanography, hydrography, and meterology. Maury was effective in helping Memphis win Congressional approval of the Navy Yard plan. The federal government paid Memphis $25,000 for a waterfront site between Auction and Market streets.

Maury's position was that an inland facility on the Mississippi would avoid the possibility of a blockade of the river "by some foreign power."[9] Memphis would fit into his plan for fortifications at Key West, Florida, and in the Dry Tortugas. Tension was building for a potential all-out conflict with Britain over the Oregon Territory, and with Mexico. A naval boat yard on the Mississippi, argued Maury, would save time and expense. Rather than have ships stationed in the Gulf repaired in New York or Boston, it would be far more convenient to have them sent to Memphis.

Construction began in 1844 and was completed in 1846. Despite the fanfare not much happened at the Memphis Navy Yard in the ten years of its life. A historical marker near the site today states tersely, "The USS Allegheny, only ship built in the yard, was a failure." In 1854, admitting that a Navy Yard in the nation's interior was a mistake, the federal government turned the site and its facilities over to the city. The bad news from the Navy Department was received indignantly by Memphians.[10] The installation sank into obscurity. Later it was pledged as security to back the city's $300,000 bond issue to support the building of the Memphis & Little Rock Railroad.

Until the 1850s Memphis was totally dependent on the river for commercial contact with the outside world. Local and regional roads and turnpikes did exist, but they were poorly constructed and often impassable. A military road was authorized by Congress in 1826 to extend from the west bank of the river at Memphis to Little Rock. The road was considered a vital link in opening lands to the west and tying together the Arkansas Territory. Construction was difficult, and the road languished. The first leg had to cross a swampy area extending some 38 miles into Arkansas. In the spring the road was often under water as deep as 18 feet. Water transportation was far more effective and reliable.

The Iron Horse

Railroads were the major conversation of business and political leaders beginning in the later 1840s in the southern states. There had been some recent success in the East. This new transportation technology was considered a tremendous opportunity for Memphis and its economic region. Memphis felt it had its biggest chance for greatness, although an earlier attempt, the Memphis & La Grange Railroad, had collapsed for lack of financing in 1843 after completing only a few miles. This was the railroad John McLemore had been counting on to spur his real estate venture at Fort Pickering.

The 1848–1850 period was one of particularly intense interest not only in the South, but in the East and Midwest. All eyes were on the Pacific. Nervous

Fig. 2. Lieutenant Matthew F. Maury, distinguished naval scientist and longtime supporter of Memphis development interests. (Courtesy of the Library of Congress)

excitement was rampant in a number of cities that wanted to be the eastern terminus of a route to the Pacific Coast. Most wanted to be one of the principal jumping off places for a transcontinental route. Sectional rivalries sprang up. Memphis, St. Louis, Vicksburg, and New Orleans became competitors. A series of railroad conventions were organized by promoters in Memphis, St. Louis, Little Rock, New Orleans, Iowa City, Philadelphia, Chicago, and Charleston. The Memphis and St. Louis conventions almost coincided in October 1849, and each city viewed the other apprehensively as a competitor.

Again, Maury spoke out on behalf of Memphis. The Memphis Convention convened on 23 October 1849 with Maury presiding over delegations representing 14 states. He told the delegates that a railroad was needed across the Isthmus of Panama and one was also needed from the Mississippi River to California for the protection of that new state and the national interest. Maury's remarks, carried in the 29 November 1849 issue of the *Daily National Intelligencer,* seemed convincing. He argued that a route to the Pacific via Memphis would avoid the snows in the winter and also open up the great commercial trade potential with the northern provinces of Mexico if the route traversed Texas. Memphis was the "most convenient point of departure" said Maury, since the city was 840 miles from Lake Michigan and 860 from the Gulf of Mexico.

The discovery of gold in California in 1849 heightened the interest of most citizens. The Mexican War had added California and the New Mexico territories to the United States in 1848. Commercial interests stressed the idea of trade with the Orient. Whatever the grand objective, the era developed a new coterie of speculators, including some state and city governments as well as private promoters and investors. Memphis was no exception. The city, through direct and indirect financial underwriting, and several of its business leaders were about to take the plunge which would take the city into great prosperity. During the 1850s there was no negative thinking in the Memphis centers of community power.

The Memphis Daily Appeal of 12 April 1852 summed up the community's economic development objectives. Its editorial, quoted in part below, sounded the call to greatness:

> By prompt and decided action we may make this the great imigrant line to the "far West" and alternately secure to ourselves the Pacific Railroad over which, when completed, the travel and costly traffic of the world will pass.

> Then let us not falter. Let us no longer doubt as to our true policy. Great issues are now at stake; and the most enterprising men of the valley, North and South of us, are earnestly at work, seeking the same object.

> We cannot stand still if we would. We must advance, or we must fall

back. If but true to ourselves now—if, instead of hazarding all, by a timid and contracted view, our City Council will accrue all by a wise foresight and liberal policy, in a few years, we may proudly say, "Memphis, is on the noblest of God's rivers, and the most gigantic of man's works."

Advocates for the Memphis terminus lauded the business and trade potentials. It would be the right stimulant to increase the city's population and property values. Enthusiastic support was given to the city's $500,000 underwriting of the eastbound Memphis & Charleston Railroad. At the time its tracks extended only 40 miles east of the city. But the power elite had no doubt that the benefits to be gained dwarfed the costs of participation. Railroads were considered great public undertakings with broad general benefits to the community, as well as profit-making enterprises for their promoters and investors.

Memphis got encouragement from rival cities. The Cincinnati *Railroad Record* of 1854 eulogized the potential of Memphis. It summed up its complimentary economic analysis with the statement: "If Memphis would be great she must make railways and build factories."[11] This is what Memphians wanted to hear.

Congress after 1850 was beseiged with formal memorials from competitive interests. The opening of trade with the Orient and the idea of encouraging emigration to the West had been promoted among Congressmen since the mid-1840s by Asa Whitney, a wealthy New York merchant.[12] His petitions to Congress were for a northern route between the 42nd and 45th parallels from Lake Michigan to the mouth of the Columbia River. The South opposed Whitney's route, and by the early 1850s was pushing for a route through its section. Most proposals to Congress included suggestions for financing construction.[13] The most popular method was to sell federally owned land along the routes of the proposed lines.

Sectionalism entered the transcontinental railroad debate in the decade preceding the Civil War. The North had its advocates and the South countered with its spokesmen. Memphis' longtime friend, Lieutenant Matthew Maury (who credited himself with originating the idea of a Southern route to the Pacific with its terminus in Memphis), was as successful then in attracting some Congressional attention to this proposal as he had been in 1841 and 1842 when he was promoting the proposal for the Navy Yard for Memphis.[14]

Congress in 1853 passed an act instructing the War Department to conduct physical surveys of several alternative routes from the Mississippi River to the West Coast. The survey teams undertook the study of five routes, including one extending from the general area of Fort Smith, Arkansas, to the Pacific,[15] but made no recommendation of one route over the others. The ultimate decision was to be made in the political arena of the day. The rivalries among the various sections of the nation made the route evaluation process an extremely sensitive one, and it was not the Army's intention to get in the middle of this debate.

Memphis, however, did find some encouragement in the findings, since the Army surveyors found no major impediments to the possible extension of a route from Fort Smith to Little Rock, then eastward to Memphis.

The outbreak of war eliminated Southern representation in Congress, and dashed whatever hopes the South in general, and Memphis in particular, had for a Pacific route in the near future. More than ten years of intensive promotion by Memphis entrepreneurs and their political representatives went for naught.[16]

The Transcontinental Railroad

In 1862 Congress authorized the construction of a transcontinental railroad. President Lincoln signed the Pacific Railroad Act on 4 July 1862. He wanted the eastern terminus to be Council Bluffs, Iowa; however, it turned out to be the Missouri River at Omaha. The decision to build the northern route was partially a war measure to help keep the Pacific Coast within the union, to provide a means of supplying troops, and to help in controlling the Indians. On 10 May 1869 at Promontory, Utah, the construction crews of the Union Pacific coming from the east and the Central Pacific coming from the west met and completed a continuous transcontinental line from Omaha to California.

Did the fact that Memphis lost out in the competition to become the eastern terminus of the Pacific Route change significantly the economic destiny of the city and region? Probably it did. Memphis would have matured as an urban economy much earlier. It might have garnered some of the commercial and industrial facilities which were located in the Midwest cities during this period. It might have become the "Queen City of the South" with potentially superior transportation facilities running east and west, and north and south. However, fate left it remote from the nation's population centers, which then extended from Illinois east to New England.

Pre-Civil War railroad trackage in the United States was 30,635 miles. In 1860 Tennessee had just under 1,300 miles. Most of this was built between 1855 and 1860. Mississippi had far less trackage than Tennessee and Arkansas had just a very few miles of track. The Confederate states at war's beginning had only one-third of the nation's total trackage, and it was more lightly constructed than northern railroads. Southern roads used five foot widths for track, northern roads used four feet, eight and one-half inch widths. Not until 1886 did the Southern railroads change over to the latter width to bring about nationwide uniformity.

Despite losing out on the potentially catalytic economic benefits a Pacific Route terminus might have had on Memphis, the city did attempt to capitalize regionally in economic development with its rail service. There is no doubt that some growth acceleration did occur because of the contribution of these early railroad ventures undertaken within the Mid-South region. Their promoters and those who helped finance these ventures felt these railroads were indispensible to Memphis' economic future. And this enthusiasm was essential to sustain public support. Constructing and equipping railroads required enormous amounts of capital and whipping up public enthusiasm was essential to raising capital.

Population in the South was widely scattered. In 1850 Tennessee had only 23 persons per square mile; Mississippi, 13; Alabama, 15; and Arkansas, 4. Up north, New York State had over 67; Pennsylvania, 49; and Ohio, about 50. The cargo of cotton and other agricultural products was seasonal. These conditions forced railroads to charge higher rates to compensate for their increased costs.[17]

There were often severe physical obstacles. Constructing the Memphis & Little Rock Railroad meant crossing several rivers in Arkansas and extensive swamps. Costs per mile were high. So these ventures had to be sold to the public by capturing their imaginations about future wealth from the nation's expansion and gaining accessibility to natural resources. Similar persuasive power had to be cast over Congress, state legislatures, and city councils or boards of aldermen. They held either gift land or cash funds necessary to underwrite these pioneer ventures. The Memphis & Little Rock Railroad was one in this region which received federal lands in Arkansas to help finance construction. In the 1850s over one-third of Arkansas was public domain.

EARLY PROMOTERS

Stock promotion flourished in Memphis and the region. Promoters excited the citizenry with their plans. Business leaders Robertson Topp and Robert C. Brinkley placed ads in the Memphis and regional newspapers announcing where shares could be bought. Editorials encouraged the public to invest.[18] Leading citizen, and perhaps the city's first major businessman, Marcus Winchester was selling stock. Topp, ex-Tennessee Governor and United States Senator "Lean Jimmy" Jones, Col. Sam Tate, Col. John T. Trezevant, and W. B. Greenlaw—all prominent citizens and businessmen—crisscrossed the region promoting railroad stock among all who would listen. No one mentioned risk. If there were doubters, they certainly were not conspicious in Memphis. Community attitudes were molded by its influential early business elite.

Promoter is an accurate term in describing Topp, Brinkley, Jones, and the others. But they were also entrepreneurs. They had an idea or concept, and the ability to generate action. Of course, they speculated with their investors' funds and the public's credit, but they believed sincerely that creating railroads across Tennessee, Arkansas, and Mississippi would make everyone a profit, including the overly generous City of Memphis. The latter certainly admired the enterprise of these early entrepreneurs. The city, with a resident population of little more than 8,800 people in 1850, backed the railroad ventures with over one million dollars. Considering the limited population and the limited wealth of Memphis, this was a tremendous financial burden to shoulder.

Why did the city have such confidence? It was the result of the enthusiasm which reached a crescendo at the time of the Pacific Route Convention held in Memphis in 1849. With transcontinental rail service through Memphis, the city's business and political leaders saw an opportunity for economic greatness. They felt strongly that a line extending eastward to the Atlantic seaboard would enhance Memphis' chances of winning a route to the west coast.

The city backed the Memphis & Charleston Railroad with $500,000. It guaranteed $350,000 in bonds to furnish funds to the Memphis & Little Rock Railroad, and pledged the Navy Yard property as a guarantee for bond repayment. The city also contributed $250,000 to the Mississippi & Tennessee Railroad.

Memphis was hardly an isolated case of a city financing railroads. Its miniscule size, however, did make it an exceptional case. Numerous cities were floating bonds and providing cash grants and noncash privileges. New Orleans, for example, did as well as many Eastern cities.

Perhaps the city and the many citizen investors in Memphis and throughout the South were naive, and pawns in the hands of free wheeling promoters, who were the respected business elite of the city. But none had built a railroad before. Later, this inexperience meant a huge waste of capital funds and stoppages of construction due to mounting debts. Stockholders and bondholders were largely kept in the dark and they had no control over the dispensing of their money.

The Memphis & Charleston was chartered in 1846. Construction did not start until 1852, and was not completed until 1857. In addition to Memphis investors the stock was sold throughout the South. At the height of construction some 600 men were at work building the line eastward. Before going to England to purchase rails Robert C. Brinkley negotiated for a 14-acre terminal site on Lauderdale. In 1854 rail service started on the completed sections. Passenger business was reported good and considerable cotton was being hauled to Memphis.[19] When the line was finally completed huge celebrations were held in Memphis, Charleston, and other cities joined together by this railroad. Memphis was truly in the railroad era. The line from Memphis reached Stevenson, Alabama, some 272 miles away, with connections at that point to the seaboard. *The Memphis Daily Appeal* of 2 May 1857 exhorted its readers with this capsule summary:

> The Great Railroad Jubilee at Memphis. Thirty Thousand People in Council. South Carolina, Georgia, Alabama, Mississippi and Tennessee cementing their union. Imposing procession of Military, Firemen, Councilmen, and Citizens. Eloquent Speaking and Immense Enthusiasm.

While the crowd count should be suspect, the city did glory in its success with a two-day celebration. Soon after, the M&C would proudly announce a schedule of two trains daily between Memphis and Charleston.

Moderate financial success came at the start. Gross earnings in fiscal 1859–60 were $1.6 million. The Civil War was a setback for the young line. And the postwar years were unspectacular before its ultimate takeover by the Southern Railway Company.

The Mississippi & Tennessee, chartered in 1852, was also completed in 1857. It was a 100-mile line south from Memphis to Grenada, Mississippi. In 1889 it became part of the Illinois Central system. The M&T received not only $250,000 from Memphis through a stock subscription, but also a $97,500 loan from the State of Tennessee.

The Memphis & Ohio, also chartered in 1852, was completed in 1860 to the Tennessee-Kentucky state line, where it connected with the Louisville & Nashville in 1860. The irrepressible Robertson Topp was president of the Memphis & Ohio and Col. Trezevant, its secretary and treasurer. Later it became part of the L&N system. Louisville entrepreneurs had an intensive interest in linking the L&N to Memphis, an additional market for coal being mined along the L&N's route in Kentucky.[20] There were others favoring an overland rail connection between the two cities to avoid the Ohio and Mississippi rivers which were considered unreliable. Countering this support were some Memphians who feared that Memphis would be cast under Louisville's influence, and that business would be drained away from Memphis.[21] Memphis nevertheless committed $100,000 to this project.

Another railroad with the same name was chartered in 1842, and rechartered in 1858. It became the Memphis & Paducah in 1871, before being absorbed first into the Chesapeake, Ohio & Southwestern in 1883 and then into the Illinois Central system in 1896.

The chartering of the Memphis & Little Rock in 1853 was the beginning of the struggle to complete an economically sound railroad from the west bank of the Mississippi River to Little Rock. Again, urgency prevailed in the minds of the promoters and the financial backers. With the Pacific Route question still in debate nationally, endorsers of the M&LR felt the need to get under way quickly to gain access to Texas and beyond to the Pacific.

Once more the prominent names leading the drive were Trezevant, Brinkley, and Topp. Memphis aldermen were put under pressure to provide partial financing. When the aldermen approved the $350,000 allocation, the *Memphis Daily Appeal* commented: "Memphis has learned that, in order to achieve greatness, she must be willing to vote herself taxes."[22] Additional pressure was applied to Tennessee state legislators and the Governor of Arkansas to approve financing plans necessary to capitalize the venture. The pressure was relentless.

An 1856 memorial signed by 56 prominent Memphis civic and business leaders was presented to the Legislature in Nashville. The list included Topp, Brinkley, Eugene Magevney, Sam Tate, Seth Wheatley, John Trigg, Isham Harris and other leaders. They requested that the State of Tennessee endorse the $350,000 Memphis bond issue to finance the M&LR. The endorsement, they claimed, would prevent any deep discounting of the Memphis bonds by New York lenders. The Memphians lamented the lack of knowledge of "distant lenders" in the quality of the city's bonds. The legislators were assured there was no risk. The bonds would have the support of the wealth of the City of Memphis, the security of the Navy Yard and other city assets. And again, the legislators were reminded of the advantages which would accrue to Memphis and Tennessee if it should gain the Pacific Route terminus.

One counterargument that did not hold up was the inadvisability of the State of Tennessee endorsing bonds to aid the construction of a railroad entirely within the boundaries of the State of Arkansas. Supporters of the venture sent several more memorials to the State Legislature before endorsement was secured.

In 1853 the M&LR had gained title to 438,647 acres of public lands in Arkansas. Two years later Little Rock and its surrounding Pulaski County invested $100,000 in the venture. In 1861 the State of Arkansas loaned the same amount. After the Civil War, in 1866, the railroad received 365,539 acres along its route as a federal land grant.

Construction began in 1854. The first leg, from the west bank of the Mississippi to Madison, Arkansas, opened in 1859. Service was anything but convenient. Passengers and goods were ferried to the west shore from Memphis; then train service to Madison; then stagecoach; then train again for another 48 miles; and finally ferry service on the Arkansas River to Little Rock. The second leg of the route, from the St. Francis River to the White River, was completed in late 1865. The entire route was finally opened in 1871. At that time Robert C. Brinkley was the M&LR's president. In the 1870s and 1880s the line was in deep financial difficulties on several occasions.[23] It really did not achieve financial stability until it became part of the Choctaw Line in 1898, and later part of the Rock Island Line in 1902.

The dreams of getting a competitive edge into Texas and the southwestern region were dashed by financial crises, inept management, and war. The exhilarating spirit of the Memphis business elite and its cooperative city aldermen in the early 1850s was largely broken by the end of the decade, as realism began to replace exhilaration. Memphis did achieve rail service. Perhaps it was not of the dramatic and profitable type it had wished for; but it was complementing the strong packet boat activity and bringing more transportation flexibility.

The Mississippi River was the early city's great highway to the Midwest and to New Orleans and the Gulf of Mexico. And during the 1850s it was the dominant means of transportation despite the public's newfound excitement in railroad building. Railroads were still very much in the trial stages in the South.

The new technology created for Memphis a colorful era in its economic history. Despite its diminutive size the city was quite bold and brash in its drive for early greatness and seemed on the verge of achieving its goals. Never again in its history was Memphis in quite the same position to attain so quickly urban economic prominence.

MEMPHIS
AND
LITTLE ROCK

RAIL ROAD!

THIS ROAD IS OPEN

And in operation from Memphis to the town of Madison, Arkansas, a distance of thirty-eight miles, and from Duval's Bluff, on the White River, to

LITTLE ROCK.

A distance of forty-eight miles. The two divisions of the Road are connected by

Chidester's Line of Stages.

The time from Memphis to Little Rock is thirty-four hours, and will soon be reduced to thirty hours.

ACTIVE OPERATIONS

Will soon be commenced on the Middle Division, and it is confidently expected that the Entire Line, one hundred and thirty-one miles, will be in operation within twelve months.

S. B. BEAUMONT,
Superintendent.

Fig. 3. Poster of November 1858 announcing the opening of the first two sections of the line from Memphis to Little Rock. Uninterrupted service was available by 1871. (Courtesy of Memphis Room, MPL)

3

Ante-Bellum Growth

Paddy Meagher's Bell Tavern, center of early business deals and social life, provided liquid refreshments and lodging.[1] Legendary Paddy probably was the town's first merchant. His counterpart, one Joab Bean, the town's blacksmith and gunsmith, operated the first primitive manufacturing enterprise. Mrs. Fooy was the first lady of commercial transportation. If someone wanted transportation to the west bank of the river in Arkansas, the Fooy-operated ferry service was available. And for lot sales and other real estate matters, Marcus Winchester was the person to see. Some Memphis historical writers have created interesting folk tales about their lives, and have made them into folk heroes. The truth is that there was nothing particularly romantic about these early years of commerce, or about the drab lives of early residents.

In the 1830s and 1840s economic activity was simple. River traffic gave Memphis its business life. Early Memphians sold various services to denizens of the river and provided fuel for the boats. The occupational skills were in the hands of various artisans and tradesmen. Mr. Bean was soon joined by other blacksmiths, as well as shoemakers, tanners, brewers, woodworkers, and printers. With the possible exception of its excellent geographic position on the Mississippi River, there was not much to distinguish Memphis from hundreds of other small, isolated towns of the early nineteenth century. Its trade area was small and insignificant. Later, when cotton emerged to provide the giant underpinning for the economy, Memphis' economic influence expanded to cover much of the Mississippi Valley. The steamboat and railroad by the 1850s provided the technological spur to a more advanced form of development. These transportation improvements helped connect Memphis with important outside markets, and in the 1850s it became the principal river city between St. Louis and New Orleans. But, despite its growing reputation, Memphis with under 10,000 whites was hardly a threat to either of these two rapidly growing cities.

EARLY ENTREPRENEURS

Messers. Meagher and Bean, and Mrs. Fooy, were resourceful citizens, but were obviously not the catalysts for growth and change. Fortunately, for the sake of community survival, the small river town attracted an unusual group of bold city builders and business entrepreneurs to bring Memphis into Phase II of its economic history. In the 1840s and 1850s the names of Robertson Topp, William Bickford, F. H. Cossitt, Eugene Magevney, J. Oliver Greenlaw, William B. Greenlaw, John T. Trezevant, Sam Tate, Robert C. Brinkley, Henry A. Montgomery, and James C. Neely were to become identified with new enterprises which contributed to the economic development of the city and region. The business leadership ratio to population size seemed unusually large for a city so small in population.

Ubiquitous businessman Robertson Topp plunged into real estate, railroads, cotton plantation operations, and politics. He became the most influential and flamboyant speculator and investor Memphis was to witness in the ante-bellum economy. It did not take Topp long to surpass the business exploits of Marcus Winchester and John McLemore after he arrived in Memphis in 1838. For the next 38 years Topp was a dynamic and innovative business leader. He accumulated money from many of his ventures, though occasionally he lost spectacularly. Although he lived until 1876, most of his successes were prior to or during the Civil War.

Topp's initial interest was real estate. His first acquisition was 414 acres south of Union Avenue in South Memphis. Here in the present-day area of Beale Street he started his lot sales program in 1841. Before he was finished, Topp had written hundreds of deeds. Commercial real estate was also part of his plan. In 1844, in a joint venture with William Vance, Topp opened the first Gayoso Hotel on a site which today is occupied by part of Goldsmith's Department Store. Topp was a developer, not an operator, so he leased the hotel to one D. Cockrell for an annual rent of $12,000. This particular Topp venture enjoyed only marginal success in later years. Several times it closed, reopened and closed again. Topp, as he had done so successfully in financing railroad promotions, received financial help from the city. The City of Memphis held a $38,000 mortgage on the hotel at the time of its failure in 1868.

Robertson Topp was undoubtedly the master of creative financing. He appeared to have learned early in life a valuable lesson. That lesson was to use other people's money to finance his projects. Throughout his spectacular business career Topp inspired confidence and his overall influence as a citizen was great. Railroads were Topp's interest in the 1850s. During the Civil War he was a successful trader and negotiator of business deals between enemy lines. Later, he suffered heavy financial reverses and died in 1876 largely broke. Politically, Topp was a major leader in the Whig Party in West Tennessee. This conserva-

Fig. 4. The only known photograph of Robertson Topp, an extraordinary promoter of railroad ventures and real estate projects. Active civilian trader with both the North and South during the Civil War. (Courtesy of Memphis Room, MPL)

tive political party, a forerunner to the Republican party, was composed largely of men of property and wealth.

Bickford, Cossitt, the Magevney brothers, the Greenlaw brothers, and Trezevant were all associated at one time or another with real estate development. The early Chelsea section was a Bickford development. The original Exchange Building, built in 1847, was also a project of this business leader. F. H. Cossitt, after whom the Cossitt Library is named, spent 18 years in Memphis in the wholesale dry goods business. He developed commercial property on both Main and Front Streets. His projects contributed to the early growth of retail business on Main Street. In 1861 he moved to New York. After Cossitt's death his daughters provided the funds to build Memphis' first public library.

The Magevneys proved to be very astute real estate investors. They had the knack of acquiring property in the path of urban growth, and then capitalizing on the appreciation in value of these holdings. Irish-born Eugene Magevney, who died in the yellow fever epidemic of 1873, was a prominent schoolteacher prior to his entry into the real estate business in 1840. His brother, Michael Magevney, also from Ireland, successfully bought and sold property in the Beale Street area both before and after the Civil War.

William B. Greenlaw and his brother, J. Oliver, were also early figures in real estate development and investment. One of their projects, the Greenlaw Opera House, was built by the enterprising brothers in the 1860s. The brothers also began a residential subdivision, the Greenlaw Addition, in 1856 just to the north of downtown Memphis in an area between Auction and Chelsea. William Greenlaw also had extensive interests in railroads and insurance. Losses from the latter Greenlaw's investments in the Memphis & Little Rock Railroad brought his business career to a tragic end in 1875.

John T. Trezevant, who was an associate of Robertson Topp in railroad promotion ventures, was an investor in South Memphis real estate. Another venturesome individual in railroad projects was Sam Tate. At one time he was president of the Memphis & Charleston, and a principal in the Memphis & Little Rock line.

Rivaling Topp both in flamboyance and influence was Robert C. Brinkley who had come to Memphis from Nashville in the early 1840s. He was as energetic as Topp in promoting stock ventures. One of his first promotions was the Memphis and Germantown Turnpike Company which absorbed his attention in 1850. Brinkley was a major force in the Memphis & Charleston and Memphis & Little Rock railroad ventures. He was president of Planters Bank of Memphis and developer of the original Peabody Hotel. In addition to the Peabody, he had extensive real estate holdings in the city. He tried to secure patent rights for a telegraph line between Nashville and Memphis in 1856. Brinkley married Annie C. Overton, daughter of John Overton, one of the founders of Memphis. From this union were born Annie and Hu Brinkley. Annie Brinkley married Robert Bogardus Snowden merging two wealthy families. Hu Brinkley, following in his father's footsteps, became a leading businessman and real estate developer.[2]

Another Ireland-born Memphian with a strong entrepreneurial spirit was Henry A. Montgomery. His vast activities transcended the war period; but his major prewar interests involved building telegraph lines in the Mid-South. He organized companies to build lines from Memphis to Little Rock; from Memphis to Cairo, Illinois; and from Memphis south toward New Orleans. One of the highlights of his development of telegraph lines was the laying of a cable across the Mississippi River in 1860. The war, however, interrupted service on Montgomery's lines. At war's end, Montgomery was unable to regain control of his system west of the Mississippi River from the federal military telegraph department. He sold his remaining interests to the Southwestern Telegraph Company prior to the latter's merger into the Western Union system. In 1867 Montgomery entered the cotton compress business and started a new business career.

James C. Neely was operator of a prominent wholesale grocery firm and a bank president. His descendants, the Neelys and the Mallorys, have long been part of the business elite of Memphis and activists in the development of real estate and in the cotton business.

ENTER KING COTTON

"King Cotton"—an expression repeated throughout the South for generations to symbolize the economic importance of this single commodity—was coined by David King in his 1855 book, *Cotton is King: or Slavery in the Light of Political Economy.*[3] It was to become a rallying cry for Southerners despite periodic severe declines in price or crop failures that caused despair among planters and brokers. In periods of good markets King Cotton was called a benevolent monarch. In depressed periods it was often called a despot and a whimsical ruler. However characterized, this semitropical plant, which required some 200 frost-free days from planting to harvesting, did control the economic destiny of Memphis and large portions of some 18 states in a zone called the Cotton Belt.

In the 1870s, this belt was defined as the area lying between the 35½° parallel on the north and the 31st° parallel on the south. Memphis was near the northern limits, and the confluence of the Red River with the Mississippi was about the southern limits in this region. Below the Red River the climate and soil were considered more suitable for sugar cane.

Cotton planters emigrated into the Memphis region in the 1830s. They were moving west from Virginia, the Carolinas, and Georgia into the Mississippi Valley. The cotton belt was expanded to obtain more land, and at lower acreage prices. The first crops started coming into Memphis by wagon and by small boats which plied the little rivers and creeks in the region. The earliest commerce was slight; only 300 bales came in 1825. By the late 1830s it had increased to 35,000 bales, and on the eve of the Civil War to almost 400,000 bales. By that time most of the cotton came by packet boat or by rail. Roustabouts, usually blacks, unloaded the cotton on the levee opposite Front Street and then by mule drawn carts hauled the bales to nearby warehouses for temporary storage.

Starting about 1850 Memphis first claimed the title, "Biggest Inland Cotton Market in the World." Thereafter Memphians spoke or wrote this phrase with a great sense of pride. To denote changing competitive conditions in the twentieth century Memphians laid claim to the new title, "Largest Spot Cotton Market in the World."

Cotton was the independent variable in the Memphis economic base of ante-bellum times. The economic fortunes of real estate, local commerce, the railroads and steamboats, and the telegraph business were heavily dependent on this basic agricultural commodity. There was little industry in Memphis at the time to provide much underpinning of the local economy. Price fluctuations in cotton on the world and national markets created either exhilaration or despair depending on which direction prices were moving. Cotton sold for 12.3 cents per pound in 1850. One year later, it had fallen to 9.5 cents. Then in 1856 it was up to 13.5 cents. Overproduction one year, followed by crop failures the following year created great uncertainties in the Memphis economy. As early as the 1850s cotton merchants felt the need for organizations to discuss common problems in the industry. In later years this concern led to the formal organization in 1873 of the Memphis Cotton Exchange.

SLAVERY

Southern agriculture depended heavily on slavery, as is well known to historians and economists analyzing this period of American life. Less known is the role played by slavery in the development of urban economies and in the South's infrastructure—its railroads, roads, telegraph lines, levees, and public buildings.

Slaves played a major role in the economies of Memphis and Shelby County. As shown in Table 1, they represented a large share of the combined white and black population.

TABLE 1
SHELBY COUNTY POPULATION DISTRIBUTION

	1820	1830	1840	1850	1860
White	251	3499	7605	16,579	30,863
Free Colored	—	—	76	218	276
Slaves	103	2149	7040	14,360	16,953
Total	354	5648	14,721	31,157	48,092
Percent Slave	29	38	48	46	35

SOURCE: U.S. Census of Population, various years

In 1860 slaves represented just over one-third of Shelby County's population. The majority of these slaves were quartered in the County area rather than within the boundaries of Memphis. The percentage of slaves to total population in selected Southern cities in 1860 was Charleston, 34 percent; Richmond, 31 percent; Mobile, 26 percent; Nashville, 19 percent; Memphis, 16 percent; and New Orleans, 8 percent. In 1860 there were 15,473 slaves in nearby Fayette County; in DeSoto County, Mississippi, 13,987; and in Crittenden County, Arkansas, 2,347. Tennessee had a slave population of 275,719. The free black population was 7,300.

Part of the Memphis' commerical business structure was its slave markets. It was not a dominant market by any means, but it did have several operators. St. Louis was the largest supplier of slaves to the Southern states. Slave prices depended on an individual's skills, age, and sex. Memphis historian J. M. Keating reported that the highest prices were paid for carpenters.[4] Slaves with this trade brought $2,500. Other typical prices were blacksmith helpers, $1,114; painters, $1,005; field hands, from $750 to $1,000; 12-year-old boys, $700; and 12 to 18-year-old girls, from $600 to $800.

Memphis' best known slave market was operated by the firm of Hill and

Forrest. The latter was Nathan Bedford Forrest, who a few years later became famous as an exceedingly tough and gallant Confederate general. Byrd Hill was his partner in this venture. Later, they went their separate ways as slave dealers. Hill and Forrest's ads stated that the firm was in the business of "buying and selling mules, horses and slaves." Sale prices for slaves ranged from $800 to $1,000. The firm also bought slaves for resale. Ads in the newspapers of the 1850s pointed out that Hill and Forrest paid the highest cash prices for "all good Negroes offered."[5] One source reported that in the firm's best years it sold over 1,000 slaves. Forrest found selling slaves to be more profitable than selling farm animals or real estate.[6] Slaves were only one of several commodities offered by many enterprising merchants. One J. A. Denie ran this ad in the *Memphis Daily Eagle* in 1850: "50 Double Mattresses, 40 Single Mattresses; 1 Fine Centre Table; 200 Peach Trees. Also 2 Likely Negro Boys; 3 Likely Negro Girls. At Private Sale. Cheap, at No. 28 Front Row."

Town slaves worked as mechanics, draymen, assistants to various craftsmen such as carriage makers and blacksmiths, and as household domestics. Many owners would lease out their slaves on a monthly basis for use as construction laborers and levee workers. In the Montgomery Papers, in the Memphis Room Collection of the Memphis Public Library, there is a receipt which says: "Received of James Coleman eight dollars 35/100 in full of hire of boy Sam to H. A. Montgomery for month of March, 1857." Sam was leased out to work on Montgomery's telegraph lines. Extensive slave labor was used to build Southern railroads. Some railroad companies owned their own slaves. Others were furnished by slave employing contractors. Slaves were primarily laborers, but some were used as colliers.

One estimate is that in the 1840s and 1850s roughly five percent of all slaves were assigned to Southern factories.[7] Frequently, they were leased by planters in exchange for shares of stock. Some plantations often were willing to lease slaves to factory owners when cotton prices fell.

Slaveowners in Memphis were taxed. Watches, carriages, pianos, real estate and slaves were all assessed for tax purposes. In the tax assessment of 1860 in Memphis the range of assessment per slave was from $500 to $800.[8] The average on the tax assessment list was about $750 per slave. Entrepreneur R. C. Brinkley, for example, owned 9 slaves. His assessment on this property was $5000.

PLANNING FOR ECONOMIC DEVELOPMENT: 1830 TO 1860

Cotton was becoming "king." This commodity would soon be the predominant item in American commerce in the years before the Civil War. The southern states produced the crop and prepared it for shipment, usually by Yankee ships moving between Southern ports and the East Coast or Europe. On the European runs these ships would return with a cargo of manufactured items and immigrants.

Why did the South not engage in more intermediate and final processing and manufacturing of the crop? Opportunities were bypassed because of the disinterest of Southern planters and cotton factors in manufacturing and trade. Some historians might argue that the term "disinterest" is too weak to describe the Southern attitude. These analysts believe Southern agricultural interests were openly hostile to both industry and urbanization in the South.[9] A more moderate view is that the South's intensive preoccupation with agrarianism blocked out consideration of all else.

For whatever reason, Memphis and few other southern cities and towns had factories producing goods for sale beyond their immediate local areas. The rise and fall of cotton and tobacco prices was the controlling factor of the degree of urban prosperity. Coupled with disdain for industry, was the economic fact that the regional market for manufactured products was small in the South. Added to this was the problem of high transportation costs for manufactured goods moving from the South to the North.[10] Capital was available in the South for agricultural expansion, but not for urban industrial investment.

Economist and editor, J.B.D. De Bow, in his influential business journal, *De Bow's Review,* constantly warned the South that it was lagging far behind industrially. This authoritative publication which circulated widely from 1846 until De Bow's death in 1867 had an editorial philosophy that said in effect ". . . industrialization is not only good for the South, but is also the salvation of southern agriculture itself."[11]

De Bow, an occasional visitor to Memphis, and some Southern political leaders, including John C. Calhoun, firebrand South Carolinian, did have some influence. A bloc of Southern and Western state delegations attended the Memphis Commercial Convention held in 1845. The 600 delegates met to discuss ways of improving transportation and expanding manufacturing.[12] Although the main theme was improving and expanding railroads and facilitating river navigation, the delegates were well aware of manufacturing. De Bow in reflecting on the major economic questions being debated concluded that this Memphis conclave was the most important event since the Constitution was drawn up. He was then residing in Charleston, a city which was economically depressed and seeking ways to increase its trade. South Carolina's representatives felt strongly that the general prosperity of the South Atlantic states depended heavily on a railroad connection with the Mississippi River. Four years later when the 1849 Convention assembled in Memphis, railroads were the principal issue, but nonetheless delegates and key local promoters visualized industries coming to Memphis if it were to become the Pacific Route terminus.

Some direct action was taken in Memphis to initiate manufacturing. In 1852, for example, the Memphis Manufacturing and Navigation Company was incorporated. This enterprise was organized to produce steam engines and locomotives, build steamboats, and to operate and sell steamboats. The city did not follow through despite some obviously favorable conditions. Steam power by the 1840s and 1850s had been perfected for industrial use. Coal was available from Kentucky and Southern Illinois, and from Northern Alabama and East Tennessee. Wood was also available in abundance in the Lower Mississippi Valley for fuel to generate steam power, but the city's business entrepreneurs opted to remain a commerical and transportation center.

Ante-bellum business enterprises in Memphis were predominantly retail and wholesale outlets. An inventory of businesses in 1849 showed 31 dry goods merchants, 40 grocery and commission merchants, and two banks. In professional services, there were 44 attorneys and 25 physicians.

Memphis had a sphere of economic or trade influence extending in a 100-mile radius. Within this orbit in 1850 was a population estimated at 600,000 whites and free blacks. It was an adequate support population at least for a modest amount of manufacturing. The truly amazing thing in retrospect is that within this sea of cotton and cotton warehouses there were no manufacturing establishments taking advantage of the direct access to this raw material. Instead this cotton in bales was transferred hundreds or even thousands of miles to the New England cotton mills, or to Liverpool and other English ports, for distribution to British mills. And, rather absurdly, the finished product came back to the region to be sold to the local population by the multitude of wholesale and retail dry goods firms operating out of Memphis. The original Chamber of Commerce established in 1860 was primarily concerned with cotton and other commodity trade. There is no record indicating an interest in promoting industry.

Southern industry in 1860 contributed only one-tenth of the total American output. Southern consumers partially perpetuated the economic supremacy of the Eastern and Midwestern states. Pittsburgh, Cincinnati, and Chicago, for example, sold a large part of their manufacturing output down the Ohio and Mississippi River valleys. Tools, implements, and pig iron came from Pittsburgh and Cincinnati. Farm implements and machinery came from the Chicago region. In that area jobs in the factories producing farm implements increased from 2,000 to 10,600 between 1850 and 1860. At least some of these types of industries could have operated successfully out of a Memphis base, particularly after the railroads started operating in the 1850s. It would take another 100 years to bring in a large farm implements operation. International Harvester came to Memphis right after World War II. Manufacturers of farm implements should have come sooner.

In 1860 Memphis had 892 employees in 93 manufacturing businesses. Total capital invested was $830,000. Twenty-one of these firms produced boots and shoes; 9, wagons and carts; 9, machinery and steam engines; 7, tin, copper and sheet iron; and 6, saddlery and harnesses.[13] All were small, lightly capitalized enterprises serving primarily Shelby County. Up the river in St. Louis there were nearly 9,400 workers in manufacturing.

The point is that Memphis could have had a greater industrial base. Entrepreneurs like Robertson Topp, Robert C. Brinkley, Henry Montgomery and the other high profit seekers could probably have attracted the required investment capital and put together the marketing organizations to merchandise the finished products. They had the ability, but not the inclination.

GROWTH OF WHOLESALE TRADE

Memphis' first step toward becoming a major wholesale distribution center was in the 1840s. The construction of the Navy Yard and plans to build railroads in the region attracted Memphis' oldest wholesale enterprise, Orgill Brothers, in 1847.[14] Then called R. T. Lamb and Company, this pioneer firm, still a major Memphis-based institution, saw the locational advantages of Memphis and the market potential for distributing hardware products in the region. Its hardware inventory could be received or shipped by both water and rail transportation. It could also be a supplier of materials in the building of the railroads.

Other wholesale houses were equally discerning. They obviously saw the same locational advantages. When Benedict Lowenstein, an itinerant immigrant peddler tired of moving about the South selling his sundries, he chose Memphis in 1855 to build his wholesale dry goods and notions business. Later his three brothers, immigrants from Germany, joined him in building an important Memphis-based firm. The Lowensteins were soon followed by William R. Moore, an Alabaman, who came to Memphis in 1859. Along with two partners, Moore invested $6,000 to start a wholesale dry goods business which later expanded to become one of the largest firms of its type in the United States.

These enterprises were the immediate forerunners of a large influx of wholesalers and wholesale-retail firms that flocked to Memphis during and immediately after the Civil War.

FINANCING AGRICULTURE—FACTORS AND BANKS

Agriculture required a credit system to function. Very early in the South's plantation economy, the cotton factor became a vital part of the process of getting the commodity planted, harvested and sold. The factor was a financial intermediary. He rendered a form of banking service, by providing working capital through seed and other provisions including food to the plantation operator to sustain him until the crop was harvested. The terms "cotton factor" and "commission merchant" later were used interchangeably to describe this special type of service.

Memphis became a center for cotton factors. Following the Civil War cotton factors were to become a dominant part of the commercial life of the city. Fees earned for their factoring services, and the profits from the allied wholesale grocery and provisions businesses, made fortunes for many families associated with these enterprises. A large part of present day Memphis wealth is in the hands of descendants of these early pioneer merchants.

Private banks chartered by state governments emerged in the 1830s result-

Fig. 5. Prominent businessmen of the mid-nineteenth century. *Top left,* Robert C. Brinkley, early railroad promoter and investor; *top right,* Elias Lowenstein, head of the dry goods firm and active leader in the Memphis Jewish community; *center,* Napoleon Hill, banker, cotton factor, and real estate investor, often called "the merchant prince of Memphis"; *bottom left,* Henry A. Montgomery, promoter and operator of telegraph companies, cotton warehouses, and other interests including the Memphis Jockey Club; *bottom right,* David T. Porter, first president of the Taxing District. (Photos courtesy of Memphis Room, MPL)

ing in a choatic system with numerous failures. Memphis had its first bank in the early 1830s. The Farmers' and Merchants' Bank of Memphis, capitalized at $600,000, led a rocky life for the next two decades before failing in 1856.[15] Near its end, its bank notes were heavily discounted.[16] This first bank was located on the northeast corner of Jefferson and Front Streets when it closed its doors for good. Lowenstein's Department Store occupies this site now. Other pre-Civil War banks were the Bank of Memphis, the Bank of West Tennessee, Planters Bank, and Union Bank (both branches of Nashville banks), Commercial Bank of Tennessee, State Bank, Southern Bank, and Gayoso Savings Bank.[17]

The combined efforts of these early banks did not contribute much to the economic growth of the city. Their resources were modest, and inadequate to assist any major industrial or commercial development projects. They did play a role in supplying credit to the factors and to some plantation operators. Banking was practically eliminated during the war years.

EARLY HOTELS AND THEATERS

Memphis was a stopping place for many travelers in the Mid-South. These visitors provided support for about a half a dozen hotels in the 1840s. The premier hotel was Robertson Topp's Gayoso House. When war came the Overton, a new hotel built to challenge the Gayoso House, was not finished. During the Civil War it served as a military hospital; then for a brief period it operated as a hotel before being converted into the Shelby County Courthouse.[18] The original Peabody Hotel was built in 1869, and was located at Main and Monroe until torn down in 1923.

Throughout its early history, Memphis had theaters for variety entertainment, lectures and drama. Crisp's Gaiety opened in 1857. The name was changed in 1880 to Leubrie's Theatre, and later to the New Memphis Theatre. Fire closed out its life in 1891. The original New Memphis Theatre opened in 1859.[19] This 1,093 seat theater was at 82 Jefferson Street. It became a financial victim of the yellow fever epidemic years of 1873 and 1878 and closed in 1879. The Greenlaw Opera House was a well-known theater of the post-Civil War period.

Earlier in the 1840s and 1850s theatricals and lecture events were held in lodge halls and public buildings. Memphis did not lack entertainment at any time either before or after the Civil War. Events were well supported by the public.

IMMIGRANTS ARRIVE IN MEMPHIS

Major changes in the ethnic make-up of the city began occurring in the mid-nineteenth century. Immigrants, principally Irish and German, came to Memphis and Shelby County. Of the total white and "free Negro" population of 31,139 in Shelby County in 1860, some 8,251, or roughly one in every four residents, was foreign born. The Memphis area, however, had a lower percentage of immigrants than St. Louis, New Orleans, or Louisville. The percentage figures were Memphis, 26.5; St. Louis, 52.7; New Orleans, 41.5 and Louisville, 33.0.

Nevertheless, Memphis changed socially and politically as a result of these newly arrived citizens. The Irish were the predominant immigrant group. Within the city limits of Memphis in 1860 were 4,159 Irish-born residents; 1,412 German; 635 English and Scots; and 120 French.

The reasons for emigration to the United States by the Irish and the Germans were roughly the same.[20] Ireland suffered a potato famine in the late 1840s. In Germany it was also crop failure and famine that brought the first wave of Germans to the United States. Following the American Civil War the second wave of Germans were fleeing because of political discontent and wars. Both the Irish and the Germans were also responding to the demand for labor in the United States.

The majority of the Irish who settled in Memphis and elsewhere in the Lower Mississippi Valley entered the United States through the port of New Orleans. They were Catholic Irish on the ships which came from Liverpool to New Orleans.[21] Fares charged for passage ranged from $12 to $25.[22] Steerage class conditions were intolerable. Ship operators, mostly Americans on American ships, handled the immigrants like so much cattle.

Once in New Orleans a great number stayed there; but others migrated up the Mississippi. Some got jobs as firemen and deckhands, and left their steamboats to settle in places like Natchez and Memphis. In the southern United States the Mississippi was the great Irish immigrant route.[23]

Once in the Memphis area the Irish found jobs as laborers on railroad construction crews, on levee construction gangs, and on the steamboats and docks. A great number were attracted to the police and fire departments in Memphis. Prewar figures are not available, but in 1866 figures for the police department indicate that 167 of the 180 policemen were Irish.

The Germans were largely craftsmen, merchants, or professionals.[24] A large number of Germans and German Jews were active in the wholesale and retail business communities immediately before the war.[25] Names still recognized in Memphis business, such as Gerber, Lowenstein, Seessel, Gronauer, and Halle, were merchants of that day. Most of these early German citizens prospered in their new environment and contributed to the early business life of the city.

The Irish and the Germans retained their traditions through fraternal and social organizations. One of the earliest was the Hibernian Mutual Relief Society organized by Michael Magevney in 1848. Most of the other societies were to come right after the war. Social segregation existed in early Memphis. The Irish bore the brunt primarily because of their poverty and lack of education. Studies of the residential patterns of the 1860 period indicate that the Irish occupied an area referred to as the First Ward. This was an enclave bounded on the north and east by Bayou Gayoso, on the south by an alley between Exchange and

Market Streets, and on the west by the Wolf and the Mississippi rivers. In this area were the neighborhoods called Pinch and Happy Hollow.[26] Both were substandard, unsanitary areas and their residents were recipients of derision by the wealthier citizens of Memphis.

Other Irish lived in Fort Pickering. The Germans tended to scatter around the city. For the most part the latter were considered socially acceptable by the native American, white population.

Immigration in Memphis peaked in the mid-nineteenth century. As the century neared its close in 1890, there were 1,114 residents born in Ireland, 1,051 born in Germany, and 423 born in England or Scotland. There were just under 1,000 Memphians born in a scattering of other European nations and from Canada. Less than six percent were foreign born at that time.

THE PROGRESS OF FORTY-ONE YEARS

Memphis grew from a miniscule spot on the map in 1819 to a small city with an unusually high percentage of aggressive and able business talent. The business elite was not lacking for ideas or plans for the development of the city and region. Of course, these plans were not coordinated by any common leadership group. They were the plans often of self-serving entrepreneurs and exploiters. Nevertheless, with some luck Memphis could have become economically significant before the twentieth century if some national decisions had gone a different way.

The years before 1860 were not an easy period for the residents. The town was largely a frontier urbanization with a wonderful geographic location for commerce and contact with a vast portion of the interior of the nation. Memphis had disease and poverty. It had new citizens with skills and without skills. But it was not a handicapped town in any sense. It had no major catastrophes to weaken its will to expand. This was basically a simple period in the city's economic history. But its life was soon to become far more complex.

4

Civil War and Aftermath

Memphis looked forward to a promising decade in 1860. Though small in population, it had established itself as a center of commerce in the 1850s and had hopes of becoming a major transportation hub for the Southern and Southwestern states.

In 1860 Memphis had only 22,623 residents. The total count for Shelby County was just 31,139. In addition, there were 16,953 slaves. The local leadership was optimistic and felt population would soon increase and so would business and industry.

In politics Memphis appeared to be pro-Union on the issues which were boiling in other areas of the South. After all, Memphis had a heavy upriver economic allegiance with the Middle West, and was not a center of Southern firebrands.[1]

SECESSION

In an 1860 election Memphians had voted eight to one against secession from the Union. But in the election held in April 1861 there was a dramatic reversal of opinion. Memphians voted overwhelmingly for secession. In the statewide vote on 8 June 1861 on the question of staying in the Union or joining the Confederacy, the vote for separation was 104,913, and for no separation, only 47,238. Citizens in both Middle and West Tennessee were heavily in favor of separation, including both slaveholders and nonslaveholders alike. East Tennesseans with few exceptions were against separation from the Union.

What caused Memphis to change its mind and opt for the Confederacy? Historian Capers concluded in his analysis that it was concern for maintaining its way of life. Like other urban centers, citizens here feared changes and entrepreneurs from the outside. According to Capers' account of Memphis attitudes it was not in defense of slavery for, he said, "Four out of five owned no Negroes."[2] Capers speculated that the heavy vote of the immigrants for secession may have been either the result of terrorism or their fear of invasion.[3]

Influential business leader Robertson Topp had been a major leader of the Whig Party in Tennessee and pro-Union almost to the end.[4] When formal war broke out at Fort Sumter, all hell broke loose in Memphis. The *Daily Appeal* headlines screamed "The War Begun!—Fort Sumter Attacked." There were outcries at the perfidy of Lincoln among other fiery oratory, and the citizens resolved to unite to fight for the South. Topp went along with the community sentiment at that point. The war was also soon to add a new dimension to Topp's remarkable business career as a trader and intermediary between the Union and Confederate economies.

MILITARY AND NAVAL ROLE

Tennessee was a divided state in the war. East Tennessee remained loyal to the Union and some 31,000 of its residents joined the Union Army. On the other hand, the rest of the state, sympathetic and active in the Confederate cause, contributed nearly 187,000 to the Confederate forces.[5] The Memphis area sent over 4,000. At war's end, some 1,800 of these Memphians had died from all causes. Before war's end in 1865 Tennesseans were engaged in battles at Shiloh, Chickamauga, Fort Donelson and Fort Henry, Murfreesboro and Stones River. And there were numerous skirmishes beyond these major encounters.

Memphis, despite its strategic position on the Mississippi, was not fortified by the Confederates. Geographically, the city was considered a forward position and difficult to supply.[6] Nor did the Confederates want to expose Memphis to the possibility of destruction.[7] The Confederate fortifications at Island No. 10 in the Mississippi River near the Kentucky-Tennessee state line and at Fort Pillow on the river bluffs just north of Shelby County were considered adequate protection for the city. The Confederate strategy proved defective as Memphis was soon to find out.

The Battle of Memphis deserves special mention because it put the city into Federal hands early in the war. It is also recognized as one of the briefest and most inept naval engagements in American history. The Confederate Navy, courageous and daring, was all but annihilated in the river in front of Memphis by a blundering, but better equipped Union Navy. Each naval force appeared to try to outdo the other in comic tragedies in the aggressive battle commencing just after dawn on the morning of 6 June 1862. The event, which resembled a giant carnival, was witnessed from the bluff by an estimated five thousand people. Local citizens were hoping for a Confederate victory as they gathered in the predawn hours prior to the battle out on the river.

The Union ram fleet forces were commanded by Charles Ellet, Jr., a prominent civil engineer of the midnineteenth century. It was Ellet who had been an aggressive and vocal proponent of ram vessels in the North. At war's outbreak Ellet was assigned to supervising the conversion of Ohio and Mississippi river sidewheelers into ram vessels to form part of the Mississippi Flotilla. Ellet, the civil engineer, became Ellet, the commander of the rams, as the Union naval forces attempted to seal the Mississippi River and cut the Confederacy in half. The Union naval force met some resistance up river at Fort Pillow and Fort Randolph. This led the Confederate naval squadron under Commodore J. E. Montgomery to believe victory was possible at Memphis.

As the two forces began moving into position before dawn, both were aware that this would be the first naval battle in which ram would meet ram. Commander Ellet considered his four rams—*Queen of the West, Monarch, Lancaster,* and *Switzerland*—superior. He felt they would be particularly effective operating in the narrow river area in front of Memphis where Confederate ships could not easily escape. Both forces had rams and ironclad gunboats. As the battle began two Confederate ships, the *General Beauregard* and the *General Price,* maneuvered into an excellent position to attack the Union ram *Monarch* from two sides. As the Confederate ships approached for the kill, the *Monarch* slipped through, causing them to collide head-on and disabling both. The Union ram, *Lancaster,* which was expected to play a prominent role in the battle, did not get into action. Because of the inexperience of its pilot and mass confusion among its officers, instead of moving forward, they backed their ship ashore, wrecking the rudder.

Commander Ellet in an act of bravado at the height of the skirmish between his ship, *Queen of the West,* and two Confederate rams, was shot above the knee as he came out on the deck to rally his crew. The North's plaudits for Ellet's victory at Memphis were short-lived. The Commander died 15 days later from a combination of the gunshot wound, dysentery, and the measles.

The physical engagement ended about 7:30 a.m., having lasted barely 90 minutes. Much of the Confederate flotilla had been sunk or disabled. A few vessels were captured. Memphis had fallen. The city surrendered at 10:00 a.m. One month earlier New Orleans had been captured. The final major Mississippi river city to fall was Vicksburg on 4 July 1863. At that point the Union completely controlled the Mississippi.

FEDERAL OCCUPATION

Mayor John Park was ordered to surrender the city the morning of the Union victory out on the river. In a note responding to this request, Park wrote tersely: "In reply I have only to say that the civil authorities have no resources of defense, and by the force of circumstances the city is in your power."

A small band of Federal forces moved in following the Battle of Memphis and took command of the city. A larger occupation force arrived later. Memphis also was selected as a Naval Station for the Mississippi River Squadron. This latter facility served the Federal forces until 1865. That same year Memphis was bypassed by the federal government for the site of a permanent Navy Yard, which was set up at Mound City, near Cairo, Illinois. Memphis was just one of a dozen cities considered by the Federal government for this installation.

Major General William Tecumseh Sherman took command of Memphis on 21 July 1862. Creating stability in the Memphis area economy was an early priority. Blacks were recruited to pick cotton and harvest corn in deserted fields. Business codes were established and attempts were made to single out Confederate sympathizers for special surveillance.

Memphis became a haven for Northern merchants. One account stated that these traders "flocked into Memphis."[8] At first the Federal policy toward trade was liberal.[9] A certain amount of "between enemy lines" trade was permitted. The Union wanted cotton, then in extremely short supply. Cotton was bringing $1.00 a pound in early 1863. In mid-1864, it went as high as $1.44 a pound for a brief period. In 1860 cotton averaged about 13 cents a pound. This wartime shortage set off a wave of speculation and smuggling. Much of the trade was illegal, but was tolerated on occasion by a Federal policy of expediency, or by outright corruption of occupation officials. Occasionally, a get-tough policy would be implemented and some Memphis merchants and business leaders would be arrested and jailed for smuggling.

Newcomers and residents alike engaged in smuggling. General Grant when he took command temporarily of Memphis shortly after the initial Federal occupation commented on the disloyalty of some Memphians to their own cause.[10] Adventuresome Yankee and Southern traders alike and corrupt military officials were making fortunes in contraband goods.[11] Loyalty to the cause of either the Union or the Confederacy was a secondary consideration to these individuals.

One very successful and enterprising trader was Robertson Topp.[12] Topp acted as agent for other Memphis capitalists.[13] His effectiveness as a wartime trader was enhanced by his connections in Washington. Remember, Topp had been a loyal Union supporter until Fort Sumter and only joined the Memphis secessionist movement at the final moment. He was a man who could move freely in trading activities. He was a master opportunist.

During the war commerce largely ceased on the Mississippi River. Destruction of the railroads hurt overland commerce. For a time railroads did serve military needs. That portion of the Memphis & Little Rock Railroad completed at war's outbreak was used by the Confederate Army, and then later by the Union Army when it occupied Little Rock.[14]

Military rule in Memphis ended 3 July 1865. Occupation was over.

THE IMMEDIATE AFTERMATH

"No city suffered more from the effects of the war than Memphis" concluded an early Memphis historian.[15] He may have meant the early postwar years because Memphis came through the war unscathed physically and its business institutions were reasonably intact. Atlanta, Richmond, and several other cities were destroyed. They literally had to start from scratch in mid-1865.

The region was hard hit physically and economically.[16] The cotton plantations were in disarray, railroads torn up, and governments bankrupt. Memphis was far better off than its region. It did face the burdens of the heavy financial commitments made to the railroad ventures in the 1850s. But real estate values actually increased from $21.0 million in 1860 to $25.6 million in 1866. Wealth throughout the South fell 43 percent during the same period.

The abolition of slavery created the first postwar crisis for Memphis. Slavery was abolished in Tennessee when the legislature ratified the Thirteenth Amendment on 5 April 1865. During the war some slaves had congregated in Memphis and in 1866 the black population swelled to 15,000 despite the return of a large number of blacks to the plantation. These urban blacks were free, but largely destitute. Nashville, Knoxville and Chattanooga had similar influxes of former slaves. Great concern was expressed throughout Tennessee about the potential problems of thousands of blacks living in idleness. Whites were warned of possible depradations to be expected from these new residents.[17] *The Memphis Argus* commented: "Saturday night, Sunday and Sunday night were periods of unusual lawlessness among the negro population. Fighting, shooting and drunkenness were the general order."[18]

The Freedmen's Bureau, a federal agency to assist blacks in their transition from slavery to freedom, was established in March 1865. It had a variety of missions. The Bureau provided emergency food and shelter, helped blacks to work as contract laborers, assisted in establishing schools and colleges, and aided in voter registration. One of its first challenges was to discourage blacks from leaving the plantations. Here, the Bureau did have some early success in temporarily turning the tide. In the later 1870s, however, black farm labor shortages became a critical agricultural problem in the South as blacks were then migrating in wholesale numbers to the western states seeking to better themselves economically.

MEMPHIS RACE RIOT

The first of May 1866 was a tragic day in Memphis. A race riot, the worst in Tennessee during Reconstruction, was to run unabated for several days. When it was over 46 blacks and two whites had been killed. Houses and business properties were burned, principally in black neighborhoods. Some black women were raped. Many blacks were robbed and beaten brutally. Mob rule prevailed day and night. The attacks on the blacks were led by the police, several local politicians, and a group of town roughnecks.[19]

On 3 May Major General George Stoneman, commanding the Army's Department of Tennessee, declared martial law in the city and announced that any assembly of whites or blacks whether armed or unarmed was forbidden. Business leaders Robert C. Brinkley and William B. Greenlaw, obviously alarmed at the course of events, extended an offer of help to General Stoneman in patrolling the city to quell any additional outbreaks of violence. Prominent civic leaders were to comprise this force aiding the military authorities.

What precipitated the riot? The general crowding of blacks into Memphis was an overriding cause. The direct cause was an outburst of open hostility toward the blacks by the Irish who feared economic competition within the lesser skilled labor ranks. Some Irish complained they had been roughed up by blacks. A deeper reason was reputed to be a sense of bitter resentment by the Irish of Northern compassion toward ex-slaves and its indifference to the problems of the Irish.[20] The Memphis *Avalanche* blamed the riots on the teachings and practices of the Freedmen's Bureau's agents.[21]

Congress was quick to act, possibly fearing general outbreaks throughout the South. It authorized, on 14 May 1866, the formation of a Select Committee to investigate the Memphis riots and massacres. This was one of three investigations of the Memphis affair. The Select Committee came to Memphis on 22 May and examined 170 witnesses.[22] The principal findings were that both whites and blacks were at fault, but that the incident was made far worse by the abusive treatment of blacks by the Irish policemen. Mayor Park, drunk during the period of the riots, was severely criticized for doing nothing to end disorder.

The New Orleans riots occurred three months later, and the extent of violence and destruction was far worse than in the Memphis episode. In both cities heavy criticism was leveled against the Freedmen's Bureau. Northern reaction to these events was very emotional. The riots were the result of the high tension produced by Reconstruction politics and white frustration. Brother Maurelian of Christian Brothers College described the mood of white Memphians best in this letter:

> The carpetbaggers and scalawags that came South to hunt up a fortune, caused endless trouble. They formed a kind of alliance with the Negroes to keep the white people from voting and to get Negroes into the Legislature to control municipal matters. In this way they manipulated foisting huge indebtedness on cities. In Memphis these carpetbaggers issued bonds for one and a quarter million dollars, pocketed the money, and left the city in a bankrupt condition.[23]

RISE OF THE KLAN

The Ku Klux Klan emerged in West Tennessee in 1867, and it led a campaign of terror throughout the region. Its justification, stated its supporters, was to stop ex-slaves and renegade whites from their plundering.[24]

Memphis Klan leaders considered themselves patriotic with a mission to prevent the carpetbaggers and scalawags from manipulating the ex-slaves that were being thrust into political office. Through these illiterate blacks renegade whites had the power to bankrupt the city. Nathan Bedford Forrest and his

Fig. 6. General Nathan Bedford Forrest. Slave trader, Confederate Civil War hero, and postwar street and railroad building contractor. Active in early Ku Klux Klan activity. (Courtesy of Memphis Room, MPL)

followers interpreted conditions in a manner similar to Brother Maurelian's analysis. To stop the plundering of the city's treasury, the Klan's approach was to scare the ex-slaves sufficiently that they would not vote and elect blacks to public office.

Forrest bore the title of Supreme Grand Wizard. He is believed to have personally directed night riders in terror raids in West Tennessee and Eastern Arkansas.[25] Forrest was a violent man with strong convictions, who plunged into every undertaking with intensity whether it was military, business or Klan activities. He was particularly hostile to changes wrought by Reconstruction and reacted forcefully. Forrest had bought and sold slaves, and had owned slaves in his plantation operations before the war. He found it difficult to accept their new status.

THE FIGHT FOR THE RETURN OF CONTROL

Reconstruction was a bitter period in the history of Memphis and throughout much of Tennessee. The politics of Reconstruction in the latter 1860s involved a titanic struggle between the Radical Republican Party and its pro-Union followers and the Conservatives, a large group of ex-Confederates whose political strength centered in West Tennessee. The Radicals advocated strong measures granting political and economic power to blacks. The enfranchisement of blacks was a major objective of their reconstruction program. The Conservatives resented the harsh measures encouraged by the Radicals, and sought more leniency in treatment. The Radicals, with Governor William G. Brownlow as the titular head of the party, controlled the state until 1869 when they were defeated by the Conservatives. Brownlow moved on to the United States Senate.

The Radicals were detested in Memphis, where there was heavy resistance to their ideas and programs. The Memphis *Avalanche* and other conservative newspapers urged their readers to withhold jobs from those who supported the Radicals.[26] They also urged West Tennessee farmers to replace ex-slaves with white workers as a form of protest against harsh reconstruction policies.[27]

After 1869 the Radical Republicans lost their power base and control of Tennessee went to the Conservatives. This set the stage for a chain of events which led ultimately to the disenfranchisement and the total segregation of blacks by the turn of the century. The Tennessee Constitution of 1870 contained the poll tax provision for voting. Delegates to this historic constitutional convention claimed the poll tax would not disenfranchise the blacks.[28] The first effective enforcement occurred in 1891 when the poll tax receipt was made a requirement for voting. For the next 62 years this requirement stood. Throughout most of this period the poll tax in Memphis remained $2.00. Ironically, it was in 1870 that Amendment XV of the United States Constitution granting suffrage to blacks was added.

Separation of whites and blacks in the public schools was a provision included in the Tennessee Constitution of 1870. The original Jim Crow law was probably the 1875 Tennessee law which gave railroads, public places and inns the right to exclude anyone they so wished. In 1881 railroads were authorized to provide either separate cars, or sections of cars for blacks.[29] In 1905 Tennessee passed the Jim Crow law which imposed segregation on street cars. Prior to that time in Memphis blacks and whites were not separated on the street railway system. Segregated seating continued in practice until September 1960. Schools were desegregated beginning in 1961.

Blacks represented only a minor part of the political and economic life of Memphis during the aftermath of the war. Two blacks from Shelby County held seats in the state legislature for a brief period. A few other blacks held positions in Memphis city government between 1865 and 1905.[30] After 1905 blacks were no longer appointed to any public positions of responsibility or importance until the 1960s.

THE IMMEDIATE POSTWAR ECONOMY

Despite political turmoil and racial tension in the Reconstruction years, Memphis built its postwar economy on an urban physical and institutional structure that had not been seriously disrupted or destroyed by war. Response was immediate. River and rail transportation were quickly restored. Commercial business recovered. And the city grew physically. In housing, one estimate was that in January 1866 alone some 1,500 houses were under construction.

One of the first acts by Memphis business leaders following occupation was to raise $50,000 to reconstruct the Mississippi & Tennessee Railroad. The Memphis Chamber of Commerce led a subscription drive among local merchants to get these funds quickly. The leadership felt that Memphis needed to regain economic control over its prewar trade area. Restoration of rail service would provide the transportation needed to bring the cotton crop from the Mississippi Delta to Memphis, where it would be transshipped to the national and world markets.

The Chamber also took action in petitioning Congress to abolish the three cents-a-pound tax levied on cotton shipped out of the South. Throughout the region growers and brokers alike felt that this burdensome tax, passed in 1865, was inhibiting the economic recovery of the South, and that it should be repealed. Congress lifted the tax in 1868 when it appeared that American grown cotton might lose the competitive battle with cotton grown in India and other foreign areas.

Two other problems loomed large. First, Memphis had an acute shortage of capital for financing businesses and industries. And second, Memphis and its region were short of white labor. Both of these handicaps were to become longer term problems and linger on in the economy well after the Reconstruction era had ended. Credit was in short supply in Memphis throughout the nineteenth century. Local financial institutions did not have the resources to support much more than the immediate credit needs of the cotton planter and cotton factor. The bulk of the nation's capital for investment was held in the East. With the exception of railroads, capital invested in the South by Eastern interests was limited mainly to assist the young textile industry in Georgia and the Carolinas.

Bank failures in 1868 depressed the local economy temporarily. The failure of the Commercial Bank of Tennessee and the Gayoso Savings Bank were blamed on too liberal lending policies. The German Savings Bank suspended operations that same year. Banking business remained unstable in the 1870s and 1880s and liquidations were common. Mismanagement and national economic conditions were prime causes of failure. Union Planters Bank, organized in 1869, some 50 years later at its golden anniversary proudly announced that of the dozen or so institutions in competition with it in 1869 only one other bank, the First National Bank organized in 1864, had survived. Memphis' "Wall Street"—that area on Madison near Main—witnessed many changes during those turbulent years.

The shortage of white labor was a greater problem than just the immediate Memphis manpower requirement. It was considered a major Southern problem. One of the key committees of the Commercial Convention held in Memphis in May 1869 was the Committee on Immigration. This committee pointed to the need for populating the South "with an intelligent, peaceful, and prosperous population." Leaders in the South believed that one of the reasons the North was economically independent was the abundance of Caucasian manpower with its combination of intelligence and enterprise. The consensus was that there was only one source of manpower potentially available and this was Europe. The committee urged the convention to adopt a policy of trying to attract ships bringing immigrants to Southern ports and up the Mississippi. Memphis delegates to this major meeting of Southern businessmen included Robertson Topp, Sam Tate, John T. Trezevant, Nathan B. Forrest, William B. Greenlaw, S. B. Beaumont and Isham G. Harris.

Memphis again showed interest in promoting an all-weather route to the Pacific from the Mississippi River. And together with other cities located in the Ohio and Mississippi river valleys it was hoping to open up direct trade with Europe through South Atlantic seaports to give the region an economic boost. Agitation for more home-based manufacturing for Memphis was being expressed at the beginning of the 1870s.[31] Business leaders were expectant that the 1870s would bring greater population, new industry and Eastern capital to Memphis. Spirits were buoyed by commercial construction in downtown Memphis and the opening of upper middle class residential suburbs.[32] In 1870 the city had 40,230 residents and the urban fringe, an additional 6,450.

BLACKS IN THE URBAN ECONOMY

Beginning in 1866 blacks played a special role in the day-to-day business life in Memphis. Black labor was sought by the railroads and the levee construction firms. Local factories and trades employed blacks as common laborers or assistants.

Business proprietorships were organized by a handful of enterprising blacks. In 1866 there were about 20 black proprietors with small service businesses.[33] Records show that blacks owned and operated 500 drays and 50 hacks. Robert R. Church, who eventually became the most successful black businessman in Memphis through his real estate investments, came to Memphis during Reconstruction. In his early career he operated several saloons. At opportune times he acquired various properties in the general Beale Street area. Later he opened the first black bank. Another black to achieve success early was

Joseph Clouston. He started as a barber and then applied his savings to real estate investments on Beale Street.[34]

Black-operated businesses served only blacks and were located in black neighborhoods. They were therefore isolated economically and physically from the white dominated commerce of the city. Despite a few successes, such as Church and Clouston, the black share of community wealth was pitifully small then, and would remain so well into the twentieth century. Blacks would remain a hidden, unused economic resource.

Memphis had one of the more successful of the 34 branches of the federally-organized Freedmen's Savings Bank. It was a savings bank for blacks which had a brief 9-year life unitl it closed permanently in 1874.[35] The Memphis branch, which had deposits of $57,000 in 1874, was considered one of the strongest within the system. Questionable lending practices caused the system to collapse. Many blacks with savings in the Freedmen's Bank lost everything. In addition, it was a cruel blow to black pride.

RECONSTRUCTION'S CLOSE

The end of Reconstruction in 1870 gave Memphis an opportunity to govern itself and to plan its destiny as an emerging city. The city changed its form of government from Mayor and Aldermen to Mayor, Board of Aldermen and Board of Common Councilmen. Each of the city's wards was to be represented by one alderman elected every two years and two councilmen whose terms would be only one year. Combined, all of these representatives formed the Council. Memphis elected a new mayor, John Johnson, who took office in January 1870.

Generally, the city seemed more sure of its future than at any time in its history, yet it had financial liabilities overhanging local government, and an insecure banking economy. The city's burdens, however, did not appear insurmountable, considering the economic growth potential. Hidden from view of even the most perceptive of business and civic leaders were signs of calamities that would ravage Memphis in much the manner as an all-out military battle by opposing armies in its streets. The next phase of Memphis' life was to be very grim.

5

Debt and Disease

The Commercial Convention held in Memphis in 1869 seemed to echo the expectation of city leaders that the city was about to enter a period of growth and prosperity. With the worst of the Reconstruction period behind it, there emerged an air of optimism. This confidence was to last only a little more than two years before a succession of enormous problems were to envelop the economic and social well-being of the city. The first series of problems were financial and the second series medical.

Major John Johnson, in a message to the City Council in 1871, pleaded for austerity and lower taxes. Bonded debt of the city had reached almost $3.8 million. This did not include substantial floating debt. Major Johnson's request was hardly the first signal of probable municipal bankruptcy. Just four years earlier the city found it was incapable of financing badly needed sewerage and drainage services.[1] And Johnson's plea did not help stop debt escalation after his 1871 warning. By the end of 1878, the year of the city's greatest yellow fever epidemic, the city's credit was gone. It was bankrupt. Bonded debt, plus floating debt, had reached nearly $6.0 million. Its financial credibility, which the city had tried to maintain by overstating the real value of its assets, collapsed. On 31 January 1879 Memphis surrendered its charter. It was no longer a legally incorporated city.

CAUSES OF THE FINANCIAL CRISIS

What had caused this financial and pyschological disaster? Reconstruction waste and corruption were leading causes. Prewar financing of railroads and the debt burden created by these speculative ventures hung over city government like a black cloud. And, of course, the national economic Panic of 1873 and the yellow fever epidemics of 1873 and 1878 badly wounded the economic vitality of the city and destroyed a substantial portion of its wealth base.[2] Taxes were not collected. Bonds sold to Eastern investors carried deep discounts. Of course these investors were completely realistic and recognized the risks entailed. Memphians, however, spoke of them contemptuously as speculators and leeches.

The line between corruption and incompetence was obscure during the late 1860s and through the 1870s. The quality of municipal public administration as reflected through budgeting and planning for public works was poor. Good management controls simply did not exist. Favoritism in the awarding of contracts undoubtedly cost the city dearly, and there may have been payoffs via kickbacks. General Forrest and a partner went into the street paving business and bid on one of the large Nicholson pavement contracts against some experienced competition. The City Council rearranged two of the competing partnerships in order to give Forrest and another favorite this lucrative contract. As fate would have it, Forrest and his new partner did not realize any profit. City street paving contractors as a condition of the contract award had to buy the city's street paving bonds. When the city reneged on interest payments, the bonds declined drastically in value.

City expenditures were rising at approximately the same time that cotton prices were falling. Cotton sold for 29 cents a pound in 1868, 24 cents in 1869, and only 17 cents in 1870.[3] In most wards the city tax rate was $2.00 per $100 assessed valuation. In two wards, however, it was $1.50 in 1870. Tax collections started falling. It was the Panic of 1873, however, which probably was responsible for collections plummeting from about $1.0 million that year to only $435,000 in 1877. By the end of 1878 there were over $1.0 million in back taxes outstanding.

Mayor John Loague in his *Mayor's Message on the Question of Taxation,* read to the council of 12 May 1874, scored Memphis' banks and insurance companies for being indifferent to their tax liabilities. Loague pointed out that these institutions demanded police and fire protection, but did not seem to want to pay for these municipal services. Another target for Loague's attack was the railroads who were not taxed despite the fact that the city of Memphis had supported their ventures with thousands of dollars in capital. The fact that the city levied wharfage fees on steamboats yet exempted the railroads seemed unfair to Loague.

Assets listed in the 1873 report, *Financial Condition of the City of Memphis,* included a $38,000 mortgage on Robertson Topp's Gayoso Hotel. The hotel had closed in 1868 and had remained closed until it was remodeled in 1885, only to fall into receivership a few years later. This was illustrative of the financial plight of Memphis. The city had many paper assets listed on its balance sheet, but their actual market value was only a fraction of their posted value.

Robertson Topp, General Forrest, and other leading business and civic leaders also came under severe financial pressure. Topp had lost much of his fortune. He left his heirs the legacy of a $1 million war claim against the federal government.[4] This was the value, Topp claimed, of his cotton seized by federal forces during the war. General Forrest lost heavily in his ill-fated attempt in the early 1870s to build the Memphis & Selma Railroad.[5] And R. C. Brinkley also experienced financial misfortune. He lost heavily as a result of the financial troubles in the 1870s of the Memphis & Little Rock Railroad venture. The general public also suffered severe losses since their huge investments in these ventures went unrewarded.

THE YELLOW FEVER EPIDEMIC OF 1878

Memphis had previously experienced some major development setbacks, but undoubtedly the Yellow Fever epidemic was the city's greatest calamity. It took an awesome toll of human life. It caused panic, and disruptions to the community's economic and social life which would linger for years to come after 1878. And before it became a bad memory only in later years, the 1878 epidemic extracted from the survivors many penalties for the city's long term neglect of sanitation. It shocked the nation that such an epidemic could happen when modern public sanitation improvements and techniques were well known, and that a city callously disregarded their implementation. Memphis also was shocked into reality, and began assuming responsibility for modern public health measures.

Epidemics and plagues were commonplace in eighteenth and nineteenth century America. Many cities had periodic outbreaks of cholera and yellow fever. Philadelphia had over 4,000 deaths in 1793, and another 3,500 in 1797. Panic ensued there in this latter year and three-fourths of the city of 40,000 fled. New Orleans in 1853 had "the Great Epidemic," with 30,000 cases of yellow fever and 11,000 deaths. From the time of the Louisiana Purchase to 1900, New Orleans had 37 outbreaks of yellow fever, in addition to occasional epidemics of smallpox, bubonic plague, and cholera. Natchez, Vicksburg, St. Louis, and many Ohio River cities such as Cincinnati and Louisville had frequent visits of cholera and yellow fever. Nashville had serious cholera epidemics in 1866 and 1873. During the latter outbreak, the death rate ran from 60 to 100 per day. Nashville also experienced an epidemic of yellow fever in 1878. In the early twentieth century San Francisco had an outbreak of bubonic plague.

Memphis received the nation's designation as the most unhealthy city in the United States. The label might have been deserved, even though it appeared that New Orleans was a more unsanitary city and had more epidemics and loss of lives over the years than Memphis. Long after the threat of yellow fever and cholera had been eliminated, the city carried this albatross in the minds of much of the nation. Memphis was roundly criticized for its pre-1878 indifference to sanitation matters. The city's poor reputation was made worse by its threat in 1879 to renege completely on its public debt when it lost its municipal charter. Any pre-Civil War momentum for economic development which may have survived the war period and Reconstruction came to a halt. At least for a brief period, the local leadership may have had some doubts about the city's future. The 1878 epidemic cost 5,150 lives. The earlier epidemic in 1873 had cost 2,000 lives. The outlook was grim.

The cause of yellow fever remained a mystery until 1900, when proof that the aedes aegypti mosquito was responsible was established conclusively by the Yellow Fever Commission of the U.S. Army under the direction of Major Walter Reed. While the precise cause remained unknown in the 1870s in Memphis, public health officials knew there was some tie-in with filth, open standing garbage, polluted water, outdoor privies, and the like found in most parts of the city. In an investigation of the outbreak of cholera in the Mississippi Valley in 1873, the U.S. Surgeon-General referred to Memphis' sanitary conditions as "shameful and a disgrace."[6]

Some parts of Memphis were worse than others. The notorious slum, Happy Hollow, on the waterfront at the foot of Exchange Street was a low, marshy neighborhood. One visitor described it as a place Charles Dickens would have delighted to picture. Its pitiful shanties were built from old hulks found on the river bank after floods. The open Bayou Gayoso, long since eliminated by interceptor systems and huge underground drains, was then an open cesspool. Garbage, human waste, and other matter were dumped into this principal urban drainage channel. Unfortunately, Bayou Gayoso did not drain effectively, and it remained for many decades a foul, open sewer. The *Memphis Public Ledger* described Memphis streets as "huge depots of filth, cavernous Augean stables with no Alpheus to flow through and cleanse them."[7]

Memphis was not completely indifferent to its sanitary conditions. Happy Hollow could claim to be the city's first urban renewal project. It was demolished by the Board of Health in 1874. On 7 August 1878 Mayor J. R. Flippen gave a report on the status of city sanitation. He went on to explain that "our city is now cleaner than it has been for years, but no pains will be spared to keep it so."[8] He asked for each citizen to cooperate by cleaning his own premises and using liberal amounts of disinfectants. He also explained that a strict quarantine will be in effect against goods and passengers coming from New Orleans and Vicksburg.

On 13 August 1878, only six days after Mayor Flippen's report, there was news that Mrs. Kate Bionda, owner of a snack shop catering to riverboatmen, was dead of yellow fever. On 23 August 1878 an epidemic was declared. This epidemic was not confined to Memphis. It swept through Tennessee and several adjacent states. There was panic in Memphis and similar panic in other cities and towns of the Mid-South. The City Council urged Memphians to depopulate. Those who were able departed hastily to safe havens far beyond Memphis. Refugees, representing the upper classes and the business elite, went to St. Louis, Nashville, or sought the protection of rural areas. By mid-September Memphis was reduced to a city of just under 20,000. Seventy percent of those who remained were blacks. One writer said: "a great city which

Fig. 7. Workman shown burying in Elmwood Cemetery the latest victims of the 1878 Yellow Fever Epidemic. (Courtesy of Memphis Room, MPL)

escaped the rolling thunder of the Civil War's guns practically unscathed was brought to its knees by a mosquito."[9] Others, in looking back on this holocaust, have commented, "if the fever of '73 was sometimes called a plague, that of '78 was a veritable scourge. Out of a population of 45 to 50 thousand, more than half fled for their lives when the epidemic exploded. Of those who remained, most were stricken by fever and more than 5,000 died."[10]

"Bring out your dead!" was the morbid call from the wagon drivers and their helpers as they made their daily rounds of Memphis during September and October 1878. Hundreds of tragic stories unfolded. Major heroic acts by numerous ordinary people who stayed behind became part of the story.[11] Some who fled were accused of cowardice. The details of the 1878 epidemic are fascinating, and they give deep insight into the character of these citizens of a nineteenth century American city under stress.[12] The loss of life represented some 12 percent of the population that resided in the city as of 23 August 1878 when officials declared an epidemic. Of far less importance was the estimated $3 million Memphis lost in business volume during the period of the epidemic.

In Nashville, where yellow fever also abounded, the Board of Health in its 1879 *Annual Report* commented:

> We in the south have been fatally indifferent to our own best interests. With us it has been too much—"Come day, go day—Lord send Sunday." Happy in the present, we care not for the future. A mercurial people, we soon forget trouble; look on the bright side, hope for the best, and take a fresh start.

This analysis was particularly applicable to Memphis in the 1870s.

Yellow fever returned to Memphis in 1879. The toll was far less than one year earlier. Still, such influential newspapers as *The New York Times* gave almost daily reports on the epidemic in Memphis. The final epidemic was in 1897, and it was minor. Fifty cases were reported, and there were 13 deaths. No known cases appeared after 1900.

Memphis was the recipient of much outside direct aid in 1878 from all over the North. It had the sympathy of the nation. Attitudes by outsiders about health conditions and economic conditions lingered on for many years. This tended to be a development liability for Memphis into the 1880s, and well beyond the return to relative normalcy. Memphis was not a ghost town. It had been hurt badly, but it was not dead. It recovered most of its business leaders who had fled the city at the outbreak. It did face tremendous financial burdens. And it faced the task of implementing an effective sanitation system as quickly as possible.

CITY CHARTER SURRENDERED

Another landmark date was 31 January 1879 when Memphis forfeited its municipal charter to the State of Tennessee. The huge financial burden which had mounted over the years finally forced the city to succumb. The state legislature created a governing council of five members and a three-man Board of Fire and Police Commissioners. From the latter board, one of the three members was selected to serve as the president of what was legally designated the Taxing District of Shelby County. The Commissioners were granted judicial powers to enforce tax laws, but they were denied the power to create debt for the Taxing District.

Great furor emanated from Eastern financial institutions. They accused Memphis of a cruel trick to repudiate its outstanding debt. *The New York Times* carried in its 3 February 1879 edition a two-column editorial in which it accused Memphis of a "scandalous act of dishonesty." It went on to say that Memphis "is insensitive to shame." And it further added:

> Evidently, Memphis and Tennessee are worthy, each of the other. No state has more shamelessly disregarded its obligations and defied their holders, and no city has ever descended quite so low in financial infamy. From the decision of the state there is no appeal. We cannot suppose that the plan adopted to enable Memphis to rob its creditors will stand. . .

Like the national attitude that Memphis was a pest hole in matters of sanitation, the stigma of debt repudiation would linger on for the next 40 years. The New York financial community's violent reaction would cause Memphians and the State of Tennessee to do some soul searching and force them to come up with a compromise plan working out problems with their creditors. Memphis was the first to react to this harsh criticism. The Committee of Fifteen, representing the top business leadership of Memphis, was organized. Its first act was to prepare a memorial to the Governor stating that it repudiated repudiation and that as a group it would attempt to convince the citizens of Memphis that the bonds would be honored.[13] Among the committee's membership were prominent merchants Elias Lowenstein and William R. Moore, publisher Minor Meriweather, business financial leaders Robert B. Snowden and D. T. Porter, and prominent civic leader and attorney Luke E. Wright. The committee also concerned itself with developing a plan to improve sanitation conditions, and requested that the Governor call a special session of the Legislature to consider a sanitation plan for Memphis.

In 1881 the Supreme Court of Tennessee ruled that the Taxing District could be sued for the outstanding debt.[14] The legislature in the Act of 6 April 1881 authorized settlement of the debt at 33⅓ cents on the dollar. The debt would be funded with liquidating bonds at the rate of 33⅓ cents on the dollar with interest at three percent for the first five years, and six percent thereafter. In 1883 the refunding rate was raised to 50 cents on the dollar. And in 1885 the final $1 million in debt was liquidated at 70 cents on the dollar. The state of Tennessee also arranged a compromise with its creditors in 1883 in an attempt to get back in good standing with the nation's financial community.[15]

D. T. Porter, a prominent business and civic leader, served as the first president of the Shelby County Taxing District. Porter, who early in his career was a druggist, later became a successful operator of a grocery and commission house, and also head of the Planters Insurance Company. He served two years at an annual salary of $2,000. John Overton, Jr., grandson of one of the city's founders, served from 1881 to 1883. David P. Hadden, an equally prominent citizen, succeeded Overton. During the latter's tenure substantial efforts were made to get all eligible property on the tax roles, and to plug up the leaks. The tax rate was set at $2.35 per $100 assessed valuation. The tax rate for general purposes was $1.45, plus an interest tax of $.90 to help refund the "compromise bonds." Taxable real estate values had fallen from an all-time high of $33.4 million in 1869 to $12.6 million in 1880. During the life of the Taxing District, from 1879 to 1893, taxable values increased to $36.7 million during the final years.

THE CITY ACTS ON SANITATION

The announcement of the Memphis plan to install a sanitary sewer system brought forth the editorial comment in *The New York Tribune:* "Better late than never!"[16] It also went on to warn Memphis that if it expected outside asistance in the future, it had better make a serious effort to solve its problem once and for all. *The New York Tribune* could have given the same directive to Philadelphia, Baltimore, St. Louis, New Orleans and a number of other cities which were negligent on matters of public sanitation. City life in many sectors of late nineteenth century United States was quite disagreeable.

Dr. G. B. Thornton, longtime president of the Memphis Board of Health, deserved much credit for getting action on plans to sewer the city. For years prior to the 1878 epidemic he had been recommending underground sewers and modern surface drainage improvements. Thornton was a physician, not an engineer, so he did not have the experience to design an effective system. This was the assignment given to Col. George E. Waring, Jr., an engineer from Rhode Island. Waring was recommended by the special committee of the National Board of Health, which came to Memphis for an on-site inspection of sanitary conditions. Based on the gravity principle, Waring's system took full advantage of the city's natural drainage.

Sewer construction began in 1880. Thirty miles were built that first year. The initial lines bordered Bayou Gayoso, which was the natural drainage channel dividing the city's urbanized area. Soon after the system was operable, the city's promotion literature carried articles bragging about its public sewers. Waring achieved much acclaim for his work in Memphis, and went on to establish a national reputation as a sanitary engineer. Modifications were made to Memphis' system from time to time to improve its workability. In 1916, one of the greatest of all improvements was made when a large underground tunnel was built to replace the open Bayou Gayoso. Previous to that time flood waters from the Mississippi often backed up into this bayou causing considerable damages in the older, central part of the city.

Garbage collection and street cleaning services were added in the 1880s and 1890s. The Memphis Merchants' Exchange, a progressive business group, promoted better all-around sanitation for the city. By the early 1890s it proudly announced in its brochure that Memphis had over 50 miles of sewers, and a complete garbage and street cleaning service "consisting of carts, mules, street cleaning appliances, drivers, laborers, etc."[17]

PUBLIC WATER SUPPLY SYSTEM

The City of Memphis finally acquired ownership of the water supply system in 1903. It bought out a privately-owned company which had been providing service since the 1880s.[18] Prior to that company, Memphians had been subjected to inadequate or intermittent supplies, and more often than not to polluted water. A major part of the horrible sanitary conditions prior to the 1880s was lack of pure water. Where competitive cities like Cincinnati, Louisville, and Nashville had modern public supply systems, at least after the Civil War, Memphis was incapable of getting the city leadership to go along with plans or to provide the financing.

In the 1870s water was being drawn from near the mouth of the Wolf River. It was muddy, unfiltered, and often polluted from the human and industrial wastes dumped there. A private water company built water lines in 1873 and served its customers with more or less raw water. This group went bankrupt in 1875. The system ultimately was sold to its creditors in 1879, who in turn sold it to a Memphis group that included the successful real estate developer and investor, T. J. Latham. Mr. Latham later became a major factor in shaping the urban land pattern of the city. The city proded Latham to do something about the quality of the water supply. Whether the city had any premonition or not of what was soon to happen, dame fortune suddenly smiled on Memphis.

In 1887 an experimental artesian well was drilled near the heart of downtown Memphis.[19] Tests indicated that the water was pure, and of the highest quality. This was the best news the city of Memphis had ever received. Not only did it mean good water for the residents in 1887, but it would provide Memphis with a major long term asset for promoting and developing the city's economy. It was a catalyst for growth. Artesian wells were drilled and the water was found to be in ample supply. A new company was formed to challenge Latham's company temporarily, but then the two water companies decided to merge.[20] From that point forward, the city began eyeing this private utility for possible acquisition. The city knew Mr. Latham ran a very profitable operation and it was aware that Memphians were generally paying higher rates for service than citizens in Nashville, Atlanta, and some other competitive cities.[21] An audit of the firm in 1902 confirmed the city's suspicions that the management of the utility was milking the operation and had failed to reinvest much into the system. In 1903 Memphis issued bonds and bought out the company. The city moved into the water business as owner-operator.

The city did not have any sanitation problems from its public water supply after the early 1880s, but it did not have complete control over the system until the 1903 purchase. From that point on, it started gaining experience in municipal utility operations. Later, in the 1930s it would acquire control over electric power and gas utility operations and, in 1960, public transit operations.

FIRE PROTECTION

Between 1883 and 1904, Memphis had fire losses of $5.5 million.[22] The city was the scene of some spectacular fires in the downtown business and commercial districts. Many buildings were fire traps and susceptible to uncontrollable fires. Incendiarism also contributed to the toll. Insurance companies, showing great concern for the quality of the Memphis Fire Department, raised rates drastically in 1902 and forced reforms in this area of public safety.[23]

EFFECT OF EPIDEMIC AND SANITATION ON GROWTH

Memphians and Memphis organizations involved in business leadership in the early 1880s seemed preoccupied with self-pity when reflecting on the status of their community and economic development.[24] Historians writing in that era picked up that general mood and left subsequent historians with the view that Memphis' strength in leadership was sapped in the aftermath of the 1878 epidemic because many of those who fled never returned to the city. The truth is that most of the business and civic elite returned to Memphis immediately after the first frost in the fall of 1878.

Those leaders who sought refuge in St. Louis and Nashville formed "committees in exile" to meet and consider plans rejuvenating Memphis when they returned. A check made of the 33 business and professional leaders who formed the Executive Committee and the Committee on Legislation and Laws meeting at their refugee outpost in St. Louis indicates that 28 returned to Memphis, two stayed on in St. Louis at least until 1882 and three were unaccounted for. A check of the *Memphis City Directory,* editions of 1880, 1881, and 1882, confirms that these business leaders had returned. They were among the same influential group which had run the affairs of the city before the epidemic. The Nashville contingent also returned to Memphis to face the tough decisions of sanitation, fiscal solvency and growth.

Memphis did lose out in the growth competition in the 1880s and 1890s to St. Louis and Atlanta. Yellow fever was blamed for causing Eastern capitalists to direct their investments into these other cities.[25] This has been another myth perpetuated by Memphis historians. The truth is that Atlanta and St. Louis were developing very well in the 1870s before the epidemic. Atlanta was becoming a center of expansion because of its pivotal location for transportation, and because the regional area had water power to run the newly emerging cotton mills. The choice was not Atlanta over Memphis. The location decisions were economic ones for the most part, and not based on sanitation conditions. Atlanta had been physically destroyed in the Civil War. In the aftermath it developed a dynamic, progressive leadership that implemented plans for economic development. It held several expositions for the sole purpose of attracting industry.

St. Louis also had its sights set on industrial growth beginning shortly after the war. Business leadership there was making an all-out effort to catch rival Chicago.[26] Its major push was to develop the city as a great railroad hub.

Memphis was badly hurt by the 1878 epidemic. Similarly, it was hurt by its bankruptcy, and its loss of dignity when it surrendered its municipal charter in 1879. The emotional scars lingered on for years, but the city's growth did not stop. True, Memphis lost population from 1870 to 1880. But Shelby County gained some 2,000 in that decade, despite the fact that many blacks who had congregated in Memphis and Shelby County until the early 1870s had returned to more rural areas in Tennessee, Mississippi and Arkansas. And between 1880 and 1900 Memphis saw its population climb from under 34,000 to 102,000.

6

The Power Brokers of Front Street

Memphians were determined to build a sound economy in the 1880s. The work of building sewers, water lines, and streets would be paralleled by an aggressive push for greater business and business influence in the Mississippi Valley region. It was the start of an era of economic progressivism.

The city put the tragic 1870s behind itself. New leadership emerged to replace influential men like Robertson Topp, R.C. Brinkley and others who had died. The replacements were men of commerce and trade. Though lacking in the flamboyance and boldness of their predecessors, these new leaders nonetheless had a sharp eye for business and were aggressive. They set about the business at hand, and did not do much dreaming or long-term planning for Memphis.

The image of Memphis as a raw, chaotic frontier river town disappeared in the 1880s. The serious business at hand was to gain a greater economic identity with cotton, and to build Memphis into a place of dominance in cotton trading among Southern cities. The objective was not necessarily to downplay industrialization, but to concentrate on the comparative advantages of Memphis' central location and transportation networks, encompassing both river and rail facilities, to strengthen its cotton-based economy.

Memphis was not a completely agrarian and anti-industrial society. But the scarce financial resources were needed in the cotton and the wholesale trading sectors of the local economy so there was less than total commitment to factories. Industrial promotion did occur, though at best on a hit-or-miss basis with limited follow-through. This would change in the period 1890 to World War I.

The men of commercial influence, who operated both emotionally and physically in the atmosphere of the Memphis Cotton Exchange, tolerated the

Fig. 8. The city's total corporate area in 1888 contained only 4.6 square miles of land. (Courtesy of Memphis Room, MPL)

promotional efforts of other business associations and real estate brokers and developers, but their eyes remained fixed on the Exchange's quotation board. This, they considered, was the heart and the future of Memphis prosperity and growth. A tacit decision by these leading traders and financiers was that Memphis' prime areas of specialization would be cotton factoring, cottonseed oil, cotton warehousing, wholesale groceries and provisions, banking, and regional retail trade serving the tri-state region of Tennessee, Mississippi and Arkansas.

The stepped-up interest in a more extensive railroad network serving the city was reminiscent of the fervor of the 1850s. Memphians were not quite as romantic about railroads as their forebears had been, but they did realize the importance of good service in marketing cotton. The Mississippi River was declining in importance as a trade artery, but it still served as a commercial gateway for the city in the 1880s. Cotton brought to Memphis, after being warehoused, was moved North by rail or by river packet moving up the Mississippi and Ohio rivers. This was a reversal in flow. Before the war, cotton bales were sent south to New Orleans for transshipment elsewhere.

THE MEMPHIS COTTON ECONOMY

The rise and fall of the city's economy from year to year was the product of what was reflected on the quotation board of the Memphis Cotton Exchange. Here was the pulse of the Mid-South's cotton economy. Price rises and price falls were reactions to market conditions for this commodity. Constant nervousness permeated Memphis, since its wealth and growth hinged on a single agricultural product.

There was a desperate need to formalize the buying and selling of cotton and to provide the participants with accurate, up-to-date market information. One of the criticisms of the cotton growers in the immediate post–Civil War years was that market information on which they based their decision to sell was provided by the factor. They felt that this was one-sided, and that it penalized them. The Cotton Exchange was organized in 1873.[1] At the time Memphis occupied a position behind New Orleans in the importance of its cotton market. Soon after Memphis took the lead as the largest spot market. This type of market is one in which cotton is bought and sold on the spot in contrast to a futures market. The basic functions of the Exchange today are still the same as in 1873 when W. B. Galbreath became the first president. Throughout its life the Exchange has established and enforced trading rules and adjudicated differences. Generations of presidents of the Exchange have represented the city's business elite. Perhaps the most powerful nineteenth century president was the wealthy and influential Napoleon Hill who served in the early 1880s. Membership was limited to 175 individuals or firms.

The institution of the cotton factor is an indelible part of the economic history of Memphis. The function of the factor was to serve as a financial intermediary and a market catalyst. He was involved in the dynamic process of handling cotton from the hands of the plantation operator to the market. As explained in Chapter 3, he financed the operator's crop from planting through harvest with seed, provisions, and equipment. He then sold this crop and received a commission plus payment for all of the provisions furnished from the plantation operator. He was the planter's banker.

Most of the factors were also in the wholesale and retail grocery business. A major portion of the factor's profits came from selling provisions, since the normal commission for selling crops consigned to them by the plantation operators was two and one-half percent. Prominent factors represented the city's leading families. Many were bank presidents or board members of banks, so their economic influence was large indeed. Many of the prominent men in twentieth century business life of Memphis are descendants of these commission merchants and financiers. The cotton factor was a prominent part of Memphis business life for nearly half a century beginning in the 1880s.[2] The factor was a unique lender-merchant institution in Memphis and the South.[3] Factors were responsible for making Memphis in the 1880s one of the nation's leading distribution points for groceries and provisions. The Cotton Exchange was the center of trade in the Mid-South. The cotton factors and other members were among the region's most influential individuals and business firms.

Fig. 9. A turn-of-the-century view of the original Memphis Cotton Exchange Building at the corner of Second and Court Avenue South. It was replaced by the Exchange Building in 1910, which served as the home of the Cotton Exchange until 1924, when the move to Front Street was made. (Courtesy of the Memphis Chamber of Commerce)

The first and second Exchange buildings were at Madison and Second Street. The Cotton Exchange was moved in 1924 to its present location on Front Street in the heart of historic Cotton Row. This latter area is where cotton men made their fortunes, or on occasion lost them.

The colorful life on Front Street has been immortalized in W. J. Britton's poem:

FRONT STREET
You're not a very tidy place, Front Street,
And you have a dirty face, Front Street;
But in your buildings bleak and cold
There beats many a heart of gold.

And tho you're battle scarred and old
You're still our Front Street.

There's been many a gallant Knight on Front Street,
Who has fought a valiant fight, on Front Street,
There've been battles won and lost;
They've been clawed and gored and tossed
By bulls and bears at awful cost, on Front Street.

There's many a kindly deed done on Front Street;
They've helped many a one in need on Front Street.
There are hearts as soft as fluff
That assume a manner gruff—
Just to hide their real fine stuff, on Front Street.

Many have travelled far and wide,
Who have lived on Front Street
They have fought and bled and died on Front Street;
But with memories of the past
Crowding around me thick and fast
I want to stay until the very last on Front Street.[4]

Front Street, atop the Bluff, overlooked an endless sea of cotton bales, steamboats billowing black smoke, and teeming humanity—all involved in some function which got cotton bought, sold, stored, or transported efficiently. Front Street during the typical day was a mass of confusion with people and mule-drawn drays attempting to negotiate their way up and down the street. Colorful characters, sweating roustabouts, clerks, and specialists of all types were a part of the street scene. The black roustabouts did the manual labor. They moved the cotton from the packets to the levee, then to Front Street or nearby warehouses, and then back to the levee. Later, when railroads took over handling the transportation of cotton, these workers moved the goods between warehouses and rail cars. Quotation clerks or board markers handled the posting on the Exchange's quotation board. Cotton classers, a uniquely Southern specialty, determined the length, grade, and character of cotton samples taken from selected bales. Apprentice classers were called squidges. Many others played a role in getting the cotton processed and marketed. The heart of Front Street was "Cotton Row" where the leading factor and commission houses were located.

Front Street's activity was tied to the levee located down from the bluff to the river's edge. On this broad stretch of cobblestone, extending from Jefferson to Beale Street, cargo and passenger transfers between packet and levee created a colorful sight and massive confusion. The busiest period was between September and January when the bulk of the cotton was discharged or loaded. The old Memphis Levee varied in width from 100 feet to 500 feet. The heart of activity was at the foot of Jefferson Street.

Fig. 10. Late nineteenth-century scene of activity in the heart of Cotton Row, a 4-block area on both sides of Front Street between Monroe and Beale Streets. Ornate building at top left was the United States Custom House. (Courtesy of Memphis Room, MPL)

COTTON MARKET CONDITIONS

Memphis was basically a one product economy in the 1880s and 1890s. It was betting on cotton, a commodity with which it had become quite intimate since the first 300 bales were carted into the city back in 1825. Did this almost total reliance expose Memphis too heavily to great risks? Was it realistic for the businessmen of Memphis to think that the economy would remain sound and prosperous given the vagaries of the national and world markets for cotton? These leaders obviously concluded that it was worth the risks despite the potential of severe price breaks downward caused by a variety of economic conditions beyond their control. They felt cotton was the product to put the city on the nation's map as a vibrant urban center. Cotton men of this era believed that Memphis should continue to do what it did best—market cotton.

Cotton prices in the 1880s and 1890s were low compared with the 1870s and the early Reconstruction years. The very bottom was reached in 1894 when cotton sold for just over four and one-half cents a pound. The 35-year history of cotton production and prices from 1866 through 1900 (see Appendix B) shows the fluctuating prices faced by the planter and by the marketing intermediaries. The crisis of overproduction of cotton was the prime topic of the Cotton Growers' and Merchants' Association convention held in Memphis in 1892. Planters and political leaders from the Mississippi Valley region agreed that acreage should be reduced by 20 percent, and that farmers should consider seriously the development of a more diversified agricultural and manufacturing economy to keep the region healthy. But, despite long years of modest prices, Memphis and the region stuck to cotton and allied cotton businesses.

After the turn of the century, Memphis was warned that its future could not be supported solely by cotton, and for the economic good of the planter and cotton merchants, regional agriculture should be diversified. Editor C.P.J. Mooney of *The Commercial Appeal* was a leading crusader for diversifying agriculture as the only hope for the South. He spent two decades in this cause prior to his death in 1926.

RISE OF ALLIED COTTON INDUSTRIES

The cotton compress and warehouse facilities were a vital part of the industry. Cotton, after being ginned, was loosely baled and then brought to the compress to be formed into compact bales weighing approximately 480 to 500 pounds. The loose cotton fibers were put into compression chambers to create a density of 35 pounds per cubic foot, thus saving space in storing and shipping. Bales were wrapped with a coarse jute cloth and bound with wrought iron bands. Memphis got its first compress company in 1870. Contrary to usual practice in the South, it was not owned and operated by a railroad company. Henry Montgomery, who earlier in his business life put up telegraph lines in the South and who subsequently built Memphis' most prominent race track, was heavily involved in the compress and warehouse business shortly before his death in 1887. He headed the huge Merchants' Cotton Press and Storage Company which had a daily output of 6,000 bales. Business tycoon Napoleon Hill succeded Montgomery as head of this firm. Warehousing later became a giant industry in Memphis. In 1908 the city would brag, "There is not a bale of cotton exposed to the weather."

The cottonseed crushing industry, a major contributor to the Memphis economy, was then in the earliest stages of its history. By 1900 the city was the base for a dozen cottonseed oil firms. The rich oil, extracted from the seed once considered pure waste in the ginning process, became the principal ingredient in the manufacture of soap, salad oil, oleomargarine, and lard. Cottonseed cake was used as a cattle feed. Countless other products were developed after 1900 using the oil, cake, linters and hulls. The cottonseed was truly a versatile product for the initiation of new industries in Memphis.

A commodities market for the purpose of trading in grains, cottonseed oil and related agricultural products, except cotton, was organized in 1881. Called the Memphis Merchants' Exchange it became, in addition to a successful trading facility, the city's first organized business body known to promote the economic development of Memphis. It performed the valuable service of compiling statistics on the local economy and keeping track of commercial progress. Its first president was John K. Speed. Names such as Donelson, Mallory, Orgill, and Trezevant were prominent among the original membership. They were part of the business elite of that day.

The Merchants' Exchange promoted Memphis in the 1880s. It tried to impress upon the outside world that not only did Memphis have great rail and river transportation, but that it was located at the gateway of the West and Southwest. In its 1888 *Annual Report* it claimed, "all the West and Southwest is waiting for our merchants and businessmen to gather in its wealth and products." And it further added, "Alabama is close at hand with its exhaustless stores of mineral wealth." It was referring to the fact that the Kansas City, Memphis & Birmingham Railroad reached the coal fields and iron ore in North Alabama.

Others in promoting the city stressed this point of excellent location.[5] To this day all of Memphis' economic development promotions have featured the city's location and its transportation facilities in their list of attractions presented to potential outside investors.

THE HARDWOOD INDUSTRY

The production of hardwood in the Mid-South region was minor in the late 1880s, but within a short time considerable interest was being shown in the 80 million acres of virgin hardwoods in the Mississippi Delta. Memphis was the heart of this enormous inventory of hardwood forests. Lumbermen from the Midwest started moving to the South when such woods as white oak, poplar, walnut, and cherry became scarce in Indiana, Illinois, and Michigan.[6]

After a slow start, the hardwood industry became a major part of the Memphis and Mid-South economy at the turn of the century.[7] Memphis added the claim, "Hardwood Capital of the World," to its other claim as "Largest Spot Cotton Market in the World." The lumber and the wood manufacturing industries added industrial elements to a city which was largely a commercial center.

MANUFACTURING IN MEMPHIS

"The great want of Memphis is home manufacture" concluded the Memphis *Appeal* in an 1873 editorial.[8] From time to time after that the question was raised, "Why doesn't the city have manufacturing?" An occasional analyst would look at the list of goods imported into Memphis and find a variety of articles which he felt could be produced locally by Memphis artisans and tradesmen, creating many jobs in the city.[9]

Was Memphis losing opportunities as suggested? Probably the city could have supported some new home industries, and eliminated the necessity of importing certain articles. In all probability at least some small industries could have survived from their sales in the Memphis market area. Insofar as penetrating the broader regional or national markets, only a specialized few would have been capable of operating successfully from Memphis. The textile industry, at least on a modest scale, might have been economically feasible.

Several obstacles to industrial development faced Memphis. Even if the cotton barons and the grocery entrepreneurs had taken manufacturing more seriously as a component of the Memphis economy, it is doubtful if they could have controlled the external forces. Eastern capital was not much interested in

Memphis other than in railroad ventures. Local capital in Memphis simply was not available beyond the needs of the cotton economy. In 1890, for example, all banks combined had total assets of about $10 million. The combined loans and discounts of these banks were only $8 million. No single Memphis bank was dominant or in a position to commit scarce capital to a start-up type of manufacturing venture. Financial institutions of the 1880s were conservative. And wealthy plantation owners and Memphis cotton factors had little interest in stepping out of their traditional area of competence. Many, of course, did have interests in real estate, but not in manufacturing.

Bank resources were held down in the 1870s and 1880s as a result of the aggressive competition for the savings of Memphians from the emerging life insurance industry. Following the Civil War life insurance was enthusiastically accepted by the middle and upper middle classes both because of the protection offered and the savings potential of some policies sold. In Memphis firms representing national companies were actively selling policies to individuals who otherwise might have invested their savings in local banks and savings institutions. Thousands of dollars in premium payments were drained out of Memphis to be invested elsewhere.

Life insurance companies were extremely aggressive. They often used prominent public figures to front for their companies. Confederate hero Jefferson Davis came to Memphis in 1869 to become president of the Carolina Life Insurance Company of Memphis. As did many others, the company failed in 1873 as a result of questionable practices, insuring poor risks, and fluctuating national economic conditions. But life insurance did survive and grow as an industry and local savings placed into premiums continued to leave Memphis and the Mid-South region.

Raising capital through the sale of securities offered no answer. It was practically impossible to sell stocks or bonds. Too many potential investors with long memories recalled the Southern experience with prewar railroad securities and with Confederate bonds, and were not willing to risk their savings in unproven, new ventures. Transportation was another problem. Freight rates on manufactured goods moving by rail from the south to the north were discriminatory, favoring raw and processed commodities. This particular problem lingered on until modifications were made in the 1920s. Labor productivity, another locational consideration, was a known factor in the North. In the South it was untried and unproven. Outside industrial entrepreneurs were simply unwilling to move from the North, where they were convinced that total manufacturing costs were minimized, and markets for their products were more readily accessible.

The 1880 U.S. Census recorded 138 manufacturing firms in Memphis. They were small, locally-oriented operations for the most part. Total capital investment was just $2.3 million, and annual wages paid, $846,000. About 2,300 jobs were provided. The cottonseed oil industry employed just over 400. The rest of the jobs were in foundrys, lumber mills, printing shops, and in carriage and wagon makers establishments. The value of the output was $4.4 million.

By 1888, Memphis had 300 establishments with an estimated value of output of about $10 million. Later, in 1905, the city had 296 firms employing some 8,200 workers. Capital investment had increased to $14.1 million and value of products to $21.3 million. Still, the majority of the firms were of the type serving the local Memphis region. There were 46 printing firms or publishers, 27 bakeries, 16 lumber firms, and 15 foundrys and machine shops.

"Memphis should have a cotton mill," was another plea. Reacting to this suggestion, some local Memphis investors formed the Pioneer Cotton Mills in 1882, and began producing sheetings, sail, and wrapping and sewing twine. The plant in Fort Pickering had 5,000 spindles, 132 looms and 70 cards. Its work force consisted of 75 women and 50 men. After changing ownership, and its corporate name, several times, there is no report of this mill operating after 1905.

Northern industrialists overlooked Memphis as a location for cotton mills. They had gone to Atlanta on a limited basis before the Civil War, then on a larger scale in the 1880s with the aid of strong promotion from Atlanta and the Piedmont area. Atlanta was extremely aggressive in boosting its city. Industrial expositions to promote the city were held in 1881, 1887 and 1895. The Carolinas were similarly aggressive. After 1880 there was rapid development and by 1900 some $125 million had been invested in mills in Georgia and the Carolinas.[10] Broadus Mitchell, the Southern historian who examined this whole industrial revolution, quoted one speaker at the 1881 Atlanta Exposition as saying, "Here the cotton grows up to the doorstep of your mills, and supply and demand clasp hands."[11]

Hydroelectric power was considered a key locational consideration by the Northern industrialists moving south into Georgia and the Carolinas. But West Tennessee lacked the swiftly flowing small rivers and streams capable of being harnessed to provide hydroelectric power. The great Mississippi with its enormous potential power could not possibly be controlled. Memphis lacked what its Southern competitors in Georgia and the Carolinas were offering to the Northern mill operators. Still, Memphis, if it had had the inclination and the capital, could have provided textile mills with power from coal-burning steam engines. Coal had been used in large sections of New England to furnish power for the cotton mills, and Memphis had excellent transportation access to coal supplies. Although steam power was more expensive than water power, the differential probably was not a serious impediment financially.

Whether Memphis could have attracted Northern mill owners is uncertain. The child labor and cheap labor that drew Northern industry to other parts of the South also existed in Memphis. Wage rates of 8 to 10 cents an hour, and 55- to 60-hour work weeks were common. But, although cotton grew up to the doorstep of the mill in Memphis as in Atlanta, the business power structure just did not make the same effort as their counterparts in Atlanta. It is doubtful, however, that Memphis leaders were dissuaded from trying for fear that New Englanders would turn them down because of the city's public health problems of the 1870s.

The Tennessee Brewing Company, organized in 1885, became one of the early major manufacturing industries in Memphis. The founder, John W. Schorr, came from St. Louis and built his brewery on the bluff just south of present day downtown Memphis. The building still stands, but the plant closed forever in 1954. Schorr claimed that the artesian water in Memphis was the best in the world, and that it was a consideration in his decision to start the brewery. Schorr's operation was Memphis' only major brewery in history until Schlitz opened its giant modern regional plant in 1971. The Memphis Brewing and Malting Company, organized in 1906, struggled for a few years under several ownerships before closing in 1914.

Other early firms in Memphis were Pidgeon-Thomas Iron Company, whose predecessor the Manogue Iron Company was founded in 1872; Memphis Furniture Manufacturing Company in 1893; and True-Tagg Paint Company in 1896.

PROMINENT BUSINESS LEADERS

The economic power base was easily identifiable in the 1880s. A handful of influential men made most of the important decisions. These people were the ones who set the pattern for the city's economic structure for the next several decades. Surnames of the families who dominated the life of the times were the Brinkleys, Donelsons, Dunavants, Fargasons, Farnsworths, Farringtons, Fontaines, Galbreaths, Hills, Lathams, Mallorys, Neelys, Norfleets, Orgills, Overtons, Porters, Randolphs, Robertsons, Semmes, Snowdens, Toofs, Treadwells, Trezevants and a small group of other families. Not only did they control the successful cotton firms and the grocery houses, but they also controlled the banks and insurance companies. Their real estate holdings—both urban and rural—were extensive. These families comprised the city's social register of the late nineteenth century. Their economic positions and power were strengthened repeatedly by interfamily marriages, which perpetuated their influence for decades in Memphis.

Hu L. Brinkley, prominent in the 1880s and 1890s, was the son of Robert C. Brinkley and Anne Overton Brinkley, daughter of one of the original town proprietors. Brinkley, like his father, had railroad investments and real estate holdings. He held considerable stock in the Memphis & Little Rock Railroad before it went into receivership, and was active in promoting a belt line railroad in Memphis. One of Brinkley's other interests was theater ownership. He owned most of the stock in the famous Lyceum Theatre, a prominent cultural landmark in downtown Memphis.

John T. Fargason came to Memphis in 1879. He was described at the time as "capitalist, grocer and planter." His son also became prominent in business in later years. William M. Farrington was first president of the old Union & Planters Bank, builder and president of the Memphis Street Railway, a one-time Postmaster of Memphis, and first president of the Cossitt Library. Farrington married Robertson Topp's daughter.

Noland Fontaine was another pioneer businessman. He was a partner in Hill, Fontaine and Company, a major cotton and grocery concern. He was a director of several banks, and president of the Factors Insurance Company. William B. Galbreath led the drive to organize the Memphis Cotton Exchange and served as its first president. He was another prominent businessman and original member of an old Memphis business family.

The "merchant prince" of Memphis of that era and one of the wealthiest was Napoleon Hill. He moved to Memphis from Bolivar, Tennessee, in 1857 at the age of 27. His business interests and holdings in the city were extensive and always profitable. In addition to Hill, Fontaine and Company, he was involved in banking, cotton warehousing and downtown Memphis real estate. Hill lived ostentatiously in a mansion located until the 1920s at the present site of the Sterick Building.

Another enormously successful businessman was T. J. Latham. Not only did he operate the profitable Memphis Water Company prior to its purchase by the city in 1903, but he was also involved in banking and in large scale real estate development. Latham was heavily involved in the South Memphis Land Company which held extensive acreage in South Memphis.

Frank M. Norfleet achieved prominence in the cotton business. John Overton, Jr., grandson of the founder, was heavily involved in real estate, banking and insurance. D. T. Porter, best known for his services as first president of the Taxing District, was a successful businessman with interests in wholesale groceries, banking and insurance.

In 1870 Robert Bogardus Snowden arrived in Memphis from Nashville and became enormously successful in his investments in real estate, railroads, banks, and insurance companies. He married Annie Overton Brinkley, daughter of R. C. Brinkley, thus beginning a family dynasty of business and social prominence that controlled the economic life of the city and much of the region. The Snowdens were parents of R. Brinkley Snowden, Mrs. Lawson Treadwell, Mrs. Edward L. Boyle, Mrs. John T. Fargason, and John Bayard Snowden, all families still important in business and social circles today.

In the black community economic power was insignificant and did not in any way influence the economic development of the city. The only prominent figure to emerge was Robert R. Church. In the 1880s he was just starting to accumulate his wealth from a variety of real estate investments in the Beale Street area.

THE LABORING CLASSES

Work days were long, and wages were low not only in Memphis during the 1880s but throughout America. In about 60 percent of businesses and industries a 10- to 11-hour day prevailed. A few went as high as 13 hours a day. Those

Fig. 11. Robert R. Church, Sr., who came to Memphis following the Civil War, was the first black to become prominent in business. At the time of his death in 1912 he had accumulated great wealth, primarily through real estate investments in and around the Beale Street area. (Courtesy of Memphis Room, MPL)

employees with skills commanded the highest wages. Examination of the time records of the Memphis *Appeal Avalanche* composing room payroll shows weekly wages ranging from $19.50 for a six-day week to $38.75. Linotype operators were paid for the amount of lines they composed. The average paycheck was about $28 a week.

School teachers received $72 a month, and principals, $100 a month. Policemen and firemen received $60 a month; ordinary laborers earned $7.50 to $10.00 a week. On Shelby County farms life was even more austere for the hands. Those who boarded on the farms averaged $9.00 a month, while those working but not receiving board averaged $14 a month.

The Memphis labor force's composition was 20,000 males between 10 and 65 years and older, and 8,200 females. Of the males, 7,200 were blacks, and of the females, 6,000 were blacks. Leading occupational breakdowns were as follows in 1890:

Male	*Number*	*Female*	*Number*
Bookkeepers & clerks	2,105	Servants	3,291
Laborers	1,924	Laundresses	2,352
Merchants, dealers & peddlers	1,623	Dressmakers & seamstresses	1,024
Draymen, hackmen & teamsters	1,298	Teachers	256
Carpenters	1,165	Physicians & surgeons	7
Servants	1,098		
Steam railroad workers	1,012		
Lawyers	166		
Physicians & surgeons	147		

A few isolated organizations of skilled workers arose in Memphis prior to the 1880s and 1890s. Prior to the 1850s Memphis printers were loosely organized. In 1852 the arrangement became a formal one when Memphis printers joined the International Typographical Union through a local branch.[12] In 1860 Memphis had an arm of the International Molders Union. Renewed interest in trade unions occurred in 1885 when the Sheet Metal Workers International Alliance was organized, and in 1886 when the Carpenters and Joiners Union came into existence. Local carpenters were reacting to their 12-hour working day and wages of 25 cents an hour or less. The carpenters were not particularly effective, however; it took until 1897 to get their wage scale up to 30 cents an hour and their work day reduced.

In 1889 the Memphis Trades Council was formed. Its first principle of organization was "To lift our occupations from the degrading position of accepting a bare sustenance as a reward in life for a life of honest toil, and to elevate labor to a higher plane of respectibility." By 1894 it had 22 trade groups under its umbrella. Its organizational structure was patterned after the American Federation of Labor which was launched in the North in 1886.

Labor organizations remained largely confined to the skilled trades until the latter 1930s when the CIO brought on industrial unionism in Memphis. Labor was peaceful in Memphis and in the South, with a miniscule number of strikes and lockouts. The principal reason was the South had few manufacturing industries, which was where turmoil was most likely to occur.

RAILROAD VERSUS RIVER

The total economic contribution made to Memphis in its early history by the Mississippi River was enormous. No estimates have been made which have quantified its direct influence on the city's growth and wealth prior to 1880. What is known, however, is the strong dependence Memphis had on the river for its commercial ties to the outside world. Beginning in the late 1870s and into the 1880s, however, the river started to decline rapidly in importance. For example, in the 1880s less than 20 percent of the cotton shipments were being shipped by river. The Mississippi was to become less an economic asset and more a symbolic asset from that point until after World War II. Again, it was changing technology which caused the turning point.

The race of the *Natchez* and the *Robert E. Lee* in July 1870 rekindled interest in the river, which had been diverted by the dramatic railroad building following the Civil War. The Great Race did not do anything tangible to slow the economic decline, but perhaps it did focus greater attention on some of the physical problems associated with the river which had made it less competitive. Memphis leaders, although very absorbed in rail transportation as support for their businesses, did continue to take an interest in questions of harbor and general river improvements.

Annual port arrival statistics were one major economic indicator of the contribution the Mississippi River was making to Memphis. From 1870 to 1880, annual arrivals averaged about 2,250 a year. In the 1880s annual volume began to drop off. By 1890, when the yearly total was 1,557 vessels, the decline was well under way. The figure was only 1,100 in 1900, and 938 in 1910. Prior to 1890, an average of five to seven steamboats arrived in Memphis daily. In the 1890s, it was down to two to three per day.

A competitive response to the increasing inroads of railroads was the introduction into river commerce of the barge lines. In the mid–1880s four barge line companies, operating a combined 16 tow boats and 120 barges, were moving up and down the river between St. Louis and New Orleans. After 1900, however, barges all but disappeared until about the period of World War I.

Fig. 12. Unloading cotton on the Memphis levee at the turn of the century. (Courtesy of the Library of Congress)

Steamboats and barges could not compete with the aggressive railroads. Poor equipment and delays by navigational impediments within the unpredictable river system led to their demise.

Water transportation's competitive edge in the United States was its cheaper freight rates. Nationally water rates were lower in most instances, but in the Mississippi Valley railroads met this river competition head on. Starting in the 1870s, and picking up momentum in the 1880s, railroads grabbed a good portion of the cotton and general cargo business. Railroads had caused a major eclipse of the river. Memphis' commercial ties with the outside world moved to rail transportation.

The Mississippi River was referred to in the nineteenth century as "a natural highway of commerce." This description of the river came under challenge by those assigned the awesome responsibility of controlling its movement and channels for commercial trade purposes and for the protection of human life and property along the route. The costs of keeping the river an effective commercial route and providing flood protection have had to be measured by successive generations against the direct and indirect benefits derived.

In the latter 1870s representatives from cities and states dependent on the Mississippi River and its tributaries began convening to discuss strategies for pressuring Congress to appropriate funds for deepening channels and constructing a levee system on the Lower Mississippi River. Conventions were held through the 1880s in St. Paul; St. Louis; Quincy, Illinois; Washington, D.C.; and in Memphis. Cheaper transportation was the major concern of the agricultural states and territories.[13] Railroad interests were attacked on the matter of their high rates and their strong influence on Congress. Railroad companies and Atlantic Coast states fearful of the potential economic competition of the improved Mississippi River attacked these engineering and construction plans as wasteful and impractical. Accusations were made that the levee system would only benefit the plantation owners with land bordering the river.

At the Western Waterways Convention held in Memphis in 1887 the delegates were warned that Congress, through the Interstate Commerce Act, had not been able to bring down rates charged by the railroads and that the people of the South must help themselves.[14] The consensus was that improved waterways were essential to check the railroads.

But the problems of improving the Mississippi were not only economic and political. They also involved technical matters related to engineering. Engineers and scientists of the day were not certain about the recommendations proposed to harness the river. In the matter of flood control, for example, there was great concern whether the existing and proposed levee system would be able to prevent the river overflowing farm land and destroying crops and property. Engineers debated the effect of levees on the navigation channels.

Steamboat companies were advocating channel deepening below St. Louis to help keep the river navigable during low water periods. It was not until 1896 that Congress approved the dredging of a 9-foot channel, 250 feet wide between Cairo, Illinois, to Head of Passes below New Orleans. Proponents of creating an inland seaport at Memphis held the Deep-Water Convention in 1892 to promote the idea of opening the Mississippi from Memphis to the Gulf of Mexico to world, ocean-going commerce. *Harper's Weekly* commented: "The Deep-Water Convention . . . may be able to settle definitely whether the scheme is feasible and before long there may be a Memphis and Liverpool line of steamers, and the Memphis of the Nile overshadowed by her Tennessee namesake."[15] Memphis boosters were pushing again for an inland Navy Yard as part of the program of developing this world seaport.[16]

Congress had been appropriating funds for Mississippi and Ohio river improvements since the 1820s, but until the creation of the Mississippi River Commission in 1879 it had no official planning agency concerned with the Lower Mississippi Valley. In 1882 the actual engineering and construction work was assigned to the predecessor agency of the Army Corps of Engineers.[17] Almost a hundred years later this Commission was still responsible for improving the river for navigation and flood control. Millions and millions of dollars have gone into this program serving multiple purposes.

Memphis was one of the earliest direct beneficiaries of the work of the Commission. The Wolf River where it emptied into the Mississippi served as Memphis' harbor channel. In the 1870s and 1880s erosion and sandbars along or near the Memphis waterfront were impeding commerce, and causing losses of valuable property. The MRC and the Army Corps of Engineers undertook the engineering projects to help protect the waterfront from further attack. This was the start of extensive improvements to be made for the next century to protect the river bank and the Wolf River Channel. Sandbars were to become a nemesis to the city in later years. Today's prominent landmark in downtown Memphis, Mud Island, started as a small sandbar in 1909. That phenomenon of nature went on to create a major change in the Memphis Harbor, and some serious urban land use problems for the city.

Memphis at the beginning of the 1880s had five principal railroads serving it. The Memphis & Charleston connected Memphis to Chattanooga and the Southeastern states. The Memphis & Tennessee tied Memphis with Grenada, Mississippi, and the agricultural economy of that area. The Memphis & Little Rock, completed in 1871, joined Memphis and Little Rock. The L & N connected the city with Nashville and Louisville; and the Memphis, Paducah & Northern, with Paducah, Kentucky. Additional lines continued to come in later. Also, there were some consolidations and changes of ownership within the existing systems as the age of railroads descended full force on Memphis.

Optimism again prevailed in Memphis about the economic contributions railroads could make to the city. It was a repetition of the mood which prevailed in the 1850s when Robertson Topp, "Lean Jimmy" Jones, R. C. Brinkley, and their colleagues were promoting investment in their railroad ventures. In 1883 the Memphis *Avalanche* was telling its readers that railroads would make Memphis the future great city of the South.[18] Up river, however, St. Louis was fast becoming a major rail center for the Mid-Continent regions. James Eads, internationally known engineer, had finished construction in 1874 of the Eads Bridge across the Mississippi River at St. Louis. This major engineering feat was to attract new rail service to this city, which called itself "Queen of the Mississippi Valley," and precipitate a whole new industrial growth era. It was another 18 years before Memphis could complete its "Great Bridge" and eliminate rail-ferry service between Memphis and the Arkansas side of the river, which had been an obstacle to the smooth flow of rail service in and out of the city.

Railroads definitely became the popular choice of shipment by Memphis merchants and traders although not all were enamoured of their rate-setting policies on commodities moving in and out of Memphis and West Tennessee. There were incidents which caused much ill-will. The Memphis & Charleston, for example, charged a substantially lower rate for cotton shipped from Florence, Alabama, to Philadelphia than from Florence to Memphis.[19] The rate was 75 cents per 100 pounds to Philadelphia. Its regular rate, 95 cents per 100 pounds, was charged for the shorter haul to Memphis. A feeling of betrayal arose in Memphis particularly since its citizens and the city had poured so much capital into the building of this railroad.

Railroad pools and rebate practices did much to discriminate against Southern commerce. Agreements among railroads to maintain certain rates and to divide the business continued long after the Interstate Commerce Act of 1887 was to eliminate these practices. The ICC's original purpose was to adjudicate freight rate disputes. Tennesseans entered a plea to require railroads operating in the state to charge the same rate for local traffic as for interstate traffic. Railroads countered with the argument that regulation by Tennessee would discourage outside investors from putting their capital in the state.

MEMPHIS GAINS ECONOMIC PURPOSE

Memphis accomplished much in the 1880s. It recovered its dignity by taking the steps necessary to make it a habitable place. It subjected itself to financial austerity while working down the size of its municipal debt. But this austerity under the watchful eye of the Taxing District did not dampen the entrepreneurial spirit in any measurable way. Business activity was lively and those at the top prospered. Family wealth of the business leadership was greatly enhanced during the decade.

The city's population grew from 33,592 to 64,495. Shelby County increased from 78,430 to 112,740. Mercantile firms prospered. A sign of confidence was the heavy investment the cotton people and other merchants were putting into Memphis real estate.

No real commitment was made to manufacturing and it may have been a mistake for the city not to have gotten started before its competitors in the South. The combination river and rail system gave Memphis superior locational advantages.

The rank and file worker received only a modest wage for his toil, but it was not much different from the low wages paid anywhere in this period of American economic history.

Twelve years after the devastating 1878 epidemic the bulk of the citizens were optimistic about their future. This attitude had not really existed in Memphis since the 1850s.

7

Boosterism

"For Memphis! For A Bigger Memphis; For A Busier Memphis; For A Better Memphis!" exhorted a 1916 brochure of the Memphis Chamber of Commerce. In the same publication the Chamber enthusiastically proclaimed "things that are good for Memphis, it is for." These written pep talks for its membership were the outgrowth of the Chamber's promotional efforts to attract new industry to the city. Attempts to develop a civic pride and prosperity in the city had been under way since the 1890s. Business leaders and political leaders totally endorsed these objectives. Perhaps the best summation of the combined efforts of all the city's boosters was the following rallying cry of the Business Men's Club, predecessor organization to the Chamber of Commerce:

> Before the Dawn of Christianity
> The Boast of Man was
> > "I am A Roman"
> Today
> The Same Man Would
> Have Said
> > "I am A Memphian!"

The entire period from 1890 to World War I was one of intense effort to put Memphis in the mainstream of American urban economic life. Memphis leaders wanted for the city what they considered the progressive accomplishments of other large cities. They wanted new investment, jobs, higher incomes, parks and recreational facilities, quality suburbs, and effective transportation systems. Population growth was considered the best indicator of how things were going. One eye was always focused on growth rates in rival cities as a test of progress in Memphis.

The business leadership was greatly broadened. Merchants, small manufacturers, realtors, and bankers organized themselves into nonprofit development associations to concentrate their promotional efforts. Those prominent members of the business elite of the 1880s were still highly visible and influential in the decision-making process, and they would remain so during much of that 27-year period preceeding the entry of the United States into World War I.

Events and policy decisions made in the 1890s were to bear fruit after the turn of the century. Promotional programs, the opening of the "Great Bridge" across the Mississippi, land annexations, and new and imposing commercial construction in the heart of downtown Memphis changed the city's physical and psychological character. No wonder, then, that Memphians went wild when the federal census of 1900 reported a population of 102,320. It was a great emotional breakthrough for the wrecked city of 1878 whose population was down to about 30,000 and struggling for urban survival. Memphians were hopeful that the city would gain on New Orleans for urban supremacy in the South, and that it would pull ahead of the other major Southern cities. It seemed that during the first stages of this time span from 1890 to World War I matters of economic development and population growth would prevail over the ever-present political and social concerns. This chapter focuses primarily on the economic developmental efforts of Memphis during this period.

EARLY BOOSTERISM

Without anything to support its statement, Memphis in the early 1890s was calling itself, "The Manufacturing City of the South." Few factories or industrial concerns were in existence other than those with a direct market orientation to Memphis and its environs. The Young Men's Business League organized in 1892 with an objective of industrial development. One program of the Memphis Merchants' Exchange was to promote industries. In 1898 another group called the Industrial League had a similar purpose. Several of the major investors in the South Memphis Land Company, including T. J. Latham and B. Lee Mallory, served on the board of directors. The Industrial League languished, however, and its functions were later taken over by the Chamber of Commerce.

The Business Men's Club, forerunner of the modern Memphis Chamber of Commerce, first appeared in 1899. In 1916 it became for a brief period the Business Men's Club Chamber of Commerce, before changing its name to the Memphis Chamber of Commerce.

All of these organizations were attempting to attract industry and investment capital. Nationally, they publicized the outstanding locational advantages for distribution, and the cheap and abundant labor. They cited the ready access of Memphis to the Kentucky and Alabama coal fields via excellent rail service. It was pointed out that bituminous coal had a variety of industrial uses, including its principal attribute—the production of electric power. And, of course, the attraction of ample and inexpensive industrial land was featured in the promotional literature.

What specific types of industries were being promoted? A list prepared by the Business Men's Club, shown below, points out that it had done its work well by concentrating on those types of factories using the timber, cotton and grain resources of the region and those manufacturing farm implements.[1]

By-Products of Wood	Farm Implements and Products Using Iron and Wood
Furniture	Cotton Mills
Mantels	
Kitchen cabinets	Canneries
Sashes and doors	
Moulding, column and poles	Other Food Products
Boxes; barrel staves and	
heads	Feeds

Memphis advertised that there were 21 varieties of hardwood in the nearby region. It listed the following woods as lending themselves to manufacturing: white and red oak, black and red gum, cottonwood, poplar, ash, maple, tulip, mulberry, hickory, walnut, locust, dogwood, persimmon, ironwood, elm, pine, cypress, tupelo gum and redwood.

Promoters were optimistic that Memphis would be discovered by textile manufacturers. New England manufacturers would find that Memphis was in the center of the cotton economy. They would also find that Memphis was well positioned to serve the emerging Southern and Southwestern regions, the city's trade area for a variety of manufactured products.

SIZE OF THE TRADE AREA: MID-SOUTH AND REGIONAL

Memphis dominated a 105-county area that would be defined today as the Mid-South regional area. Within this geographic zone in 1900 were 3 counties in Alabama, 26 in Arkansas, 8 in Kentucky, 39 in Mississippi, 8 in Missouri, and 21 in Tennessee. The 1900 population was just over 2.1 million.

The 1900 population of the broader area including the entire states of Alabama, Arkansas, Louisiana, Mississippi and Tennessee was 8.1 million, about 11 percent of the total national population. Here, of course, were located New Orleans, Nashville, Birmingham, and other aspiring industrial cities. An additional impediment to establishing an effective trade area was the percentages of blacks and rural whites living on marginal incomes. Nor was there much market support in Texas and Oklahoma, which were just beginning to develop population concentrations.

The prospect of Memphis becoming a significant factory center for the most part depended on penetrating markets in the North. Success then depended on finding ways to compete on a cost basis. Transportation charges between Memphis and northern destinations became all-important in determining the degree of competitiveness that could be expected. Except for some products in which Memphis had a distinct comparative advantage in manufacturing costs, the city faced long odds in getting other types of industries when it had no particular competitive edge over northern cities.

COMPETING CITIES

Cities competitive with Memphis were also busy. Atlanta, which had held several industrial expositions in the 1880s, spent $2.0 million in 1895 promoting "the Cotton States and International Exposition."[2] St. Louis spent $42.5 million on its 1904 World's Fair.[3] Promoters of that enormously successful exposition considered it important that St. Louis present itself to the outside world. Leaders there considered St. Louisans self-centered people, and felt they would benefit from the exposure.

Birmingham came upon its own special brand of good fortune. By fortuitous circumstances coal, iron ore, and limestone were found at about the same time in North Alabama. This propelled Birmingham into becoming the principal industrial city in the South. Following its birth in 1871 the city became a boon town while establishing its iron, steel, cast iron, pipe, heavy machinery and textile industries.[4] New Orleans continued to grow as a port city and lead the South in population for a period well into the twentieth century. The decline of Mississippi River commerce prevented greater growth.

RESULTS

The tally of Memphis manufacturing establishments and their contribution to the local economy changed modestly in the 20-year period, 1899 to 1919. The federal census of manufactures showed these changes:

	1899	1919
No. of manufacturing establishments	223	379
No. of production workers	6,626	11,963
Value added by manufacturing	$6.4 mi.	$39.6 mi.

The principal growth industries were cottonseed oil and cake, and lumber and timber products. Even in these two major industrial categories, the number of workers was less in 1919 than in 1899, but the major change was in the dollar value of the production. Two-thirds of the total value of products of all Memphis manufacturing came from these two major categories by 1919.

Memphis had fallen behind some of its competitor cities by the World War I period despite the aggressive promotion campaigns by the nonprofit businessmen's organizations. Memphis' standing is shown in Table 2.

TABLE 2
COMPETITIVE POSITION IN MANUFACTURING ACTIVITY
MEMPHIS AND SELECTED CITIES, 1919

City	Number of Firms	Wage Earners	Value Added by Mfg. (millions)	Rank Among the Largest U.S. Cities
St. Louis	3,205	107,919	$330.9	6
Louisville	767	29,902	78.5	35
New Orleans	873	26,641	69.5	44
Atlanta	503	15,739	46.1	69
Birmingham	329	17,264	40.4	79
MEMPHIS	*379*	*11,963*	*39.6*	*82*
Nashville	391	10,666	25.7	100+

SOURCE: 1919 U.S. Census of Manufactures

The lag cannot be attributed to lack of effort in going after the types of industry with the greatest potential for success in Memphis. As a matter of fact, local effort was not just confined to brochures placed in the mail and sent up North. Memphis leaders did much to create a good physical and transportational environment. Well-located industrial land, rail facilities and port facilities were directed to best serving new industrial plants and warehouses.

SOUTH MEMPHIS LAND COMPANY

Planned industrial communities had been tried in Chicago and the suburbs of some other Northern cities, and by the 1890s had some success. Large acreage was set aside to provide sites not only for factories and warehouses, but also for workers' homes. These early industrial land planners pointed out to both industries and the host community the advantages of having a central industrial zone served by railroads and, in certain cases, by both rail and water terminal facilities.

Memphis developers were not far behind their Northern competitors. In the late 1880s the Chickasaw Land Company, in announcing its major "Industrial Community Plan," held out the offer of free sites to manufacturers. These firms were promised free water, low taxes, and river and rail connections to their plants. The developers expected to make their profit from the sale of residential lots to builders of modest-priced housing for factory workers.

Promoters of the 3,175 acre industrial-residential subdivision described it as "high rolling land just south of the city, and above flood areas." The tract was part of the Person Plantation, located just north of the Nonconnah Creek with its western boundary fronting for one-half mile on the Mississippi. Capital was raised through the sale of $900,000 in stock. Prominent businessmen and civic leaders, including E. H. Crump and Kenneth McKellar, were to become inves-

Fig. 13. Construction in 1891 of the "Great Bridge at Memphis," the first bridge crossing the Mississippi River south of St. Louis. The photo, taken from the Arkansas side, also shows the Memphis bluff south of the central part of the city. (Courtesy of Memphis Room, MPL)

tors in this venture over the years. The Person family received over $1 million in stock for contributing the land. But the company defaulted on its bond payment. T. J. Latham, representing the bondholders, forced the public sale of this huge tract. At the public auction, Latham was the highest bidder, paying $200,000 for the assets. He then formed a new company with several prominent Memphis investors to continue developing this major industrial subdivision. At the foreclosure proceedings in 1898, the Persons lost most of their investment.

Out of this early disaster rose the South Memphis Land Company, a new group with similar industrial development objectives. It hoped to get the project on a paying basis. In 1900, when it took over, not much industry had been developed there. Rail service was available at the time. Renewed promotion of the site was moderately successful. By 1906 the semblance of an industrial district was taking form. The principal occupants were cotton compress and warehouse operators, attracted mainly by the accessibility provided by the

Union Belt Line and the Illinois Central Railroad, both of which crossed this huge subdivision. Cotton warehouses had been in or near downtown Memphis prior to the advent of the South Memphis Land Company. Now cotton could be delivered by rail directly to the compresses, then stored in warehouses before reshipment by rail to the ultimate market. The Memphis Terminal Corporation was a consolidation of some 40 warehouses at one location.

The industrial site was ideally located and had excellent transportation services; yet it attracted little industry in the early years not directly related to cotton processing and storage. Much of the warehousing business was not new to Memphis, but these were firms relocating from other points in the Memphis area. With facilities such as those offered in South Memphis, the city was prepared to receive industry. The industrial planning was excellent, and no one could accuse Memphians of holding back in offering facilities to prospective new firms.

The Belt Line was operated by the Union Railroad Company and circled the northern, eastern, and southern boundaries of Memphis at the time of its construction in 1904. The principal financing came from George Gould, son of the famous financier Jay Gould. Hu Brinkley had organized and promoted the creation of this line encircling the city, but he died before its completion. The Belt Line gave the various railroads entering Memphis good accessibility to the South Memphis Land Company site. The Illinois Central system, moving north and south between the Midwest and the New Orleans Gulf Coast, placed the South Memphis Land Company's holdings in a strategic position to take advantage of this transportation contact with the outside world.

REGIONAL AND NATIONAL RAIL SERVICE

Memphis in 1890 was served by ten railroads, with 52 trains to and from the city daily. Nashville had two railroads and 50 trains a day; Atlanta, eight railroads and 62 trains; Birmingham, five railroads and 28 trains; Louisville, seven railroads and 156 trains; and St. Louis, 17 railroads and 291 trains.

At the time Memphis had reasonably good service, but it lacked a railroad bridge across the Mississippi and a union station serving most of the lines. The "Great Bridge," however, was about to solve this major barrier to fast, efficient service to and from states west of the river. In 1892 the "Great Bridge" at Memphis, the third largest in the world at the time, was opened. Later renamed the Frisco Bridge, it was the first bridge to span the Mississippi River below St. Louis.

Memphis would have had a bridge perhaps three or four years earlier if the private company authorized by Congress in 1885 to build the bridge had raised the capital. When nothing happened to move the bridge venture along, Congress in 1888 chartered a new group and imposed a requirement that the bridge be started within one year and be completed within four years.

The city celebrated for four days in May 1892. Huge crowds descended on

Memphis, including politicians from all over the nation, to join the formal ceremonies. The bridge was given a dramatic test of its strength when 18 locomotives, coupled together, were brought to its center. Fortunately for the celebrants and for Memphis, the "Great Bridge" took it all in stride.

George S. Morison, the Chicago bridge engineer who designed the Memphis structure, selected the site, picking the narrowest section of the Mississippi along the Memphis shoreline. The bridge was built by the Kansas City Railway and Bridge Company for the Kansas City, Fort Scott & Memphis Line. In 1903, when the Frisco line took over this other railroad, it was renamed the Frisco Bridge. The bridge gave Memphis access to the Missouri-Kansas regions to the northwest and to the Birmingham region to the southeast. The coal deposits in North Alabama now were accessible to Memphis and points west with this new service. After it opened, four railroads used the bridge. Early vehicular traffic also used it until completion of the Harahan Bridge.

The bridge gave a tremendous boost to Memphians concerned about economic development. Commented the *Appeal-Avalanche* on 29 April 1892, "She is at the crossing point of the commercial current flowing north and south and east and west, and is capacitated to draw tribute from both." St. Louis and Kansas City both derived huge economic benefits from their rail bridge crossings. Memphians expected the same.

Twenty-four years later in 1916 the Harahan Bridge was opened to both rail and vehicular traffic. Located just 200 feet north of the Frisco Bridge, this double-tracked rail bridge was authorized by Congress through the persuasive legislative skills of Kenneth McKellar. The bridge was named in honor of James T. Harahan, at one time president of the Illinois Central, who was married to the daughter of William B. Mallory, a wealthy Memphis wholesale grocer.[5] This new bridge was jointly owned by the Rock Island, Iron Mountain and Cotton Belt railroads. It cost $3 million for the bridge and $2 million for the approaches and bridge terminals. The master bridge builder in the United States, Ralph Modjeska, was the consulting engineer.

The Belt Line, which served industrial properties along its route, and the two Mississippi River bridges vastly improved rail service in the city. But one of the last stumbling blocks was the absence for many years of efficient passenger terminal facilities. For a period of time prior to the opening of Union Station in 1912, most of the railroads had their own individual terminals scattered throughout the city.[6] Agitation for a truly "union station" began in the city in the early 1890s. Various attempts were made to reach cooperative agreements among the lines. On occasion it seemed like the railroad managements would get together, and agree to operate passenger service under one roof. But there were jealousies, disputes over splitting the costs, and disagreements on proposed sites impeding total agreement.

The ultimate outcome was a separation of the individual railroads into two

Fig. 14. Union Station, on Calhoun between Second and Third, opened in 1912 and served Memphis for 55 years, before being torn down in 1967. This ornate terminal serving 5 railroads was just 2 blocks east of Central Station, which opened in 1914 and is still serving the public. (Courtesy of Memphis Room, MPL)

camps. The first group—some five lines—agreed to finance and operate its own terminal, Union Station. This ornate structure of Italian renaissance architecture opened in 1912, and the L&N; Southern; Iron Mountain; Cotton Belt; and Nashville, Chattanooga, & St. Louis railroads became tenants. The terminal was located at Calhoun and Third streets. In 1914, just two blocks away at Calhoun and Main streets, Central Station opened with its tenant group being the Illinois Central, Frisco, Rock Island, and Yazoo & Mississippi Valley railroads. This latter terminal was far less ornate architecturally than its competitor "down the street."

Union stations in American cities at the turn of the century were built as symbols of local progress.[7] The more grandiose or elegant the structure, the greater the community pride. It was the city's calling card extended to business and tourist visitors. Memphis lost its opportunity to build a really imposing terminal as a result of this rivalry and lack of cooperation among its lines. But the city did gain two superior terminals replacing the old pattern of crosstown stations.

Passenger and freight service was excellent in the period prior to World War I. With bridge service, rail lines came into Memphis from all directions. The quality of rail service was supportive of the industrial development programs. After the Panic of 1893 surviving railroads from the crisis became even stronger entities. Certainly after 1900 the lines operating in Memphis had strength and stability.

NEW MANUFACTURING OPERATIONS: PRE-WORLD WAR I

New entries among manufacturing firms included both home grown operations, that is, those started by Memphis entrepreneurs, and branches of national companies.

In 1892 R. G. Morrow founded the Memphis Furniture Manufacturing Company. This firm, still a major Memphis operation, soon after its opening referred to itself as "The South's Foremost Furniture Factory." The American Finishing Company started in 1905 as a finisher of cotton materials. The operation was phased out just recently in 1973. The Tri-State Dress Manufacturing Company started in 1911, specializing in ladies' wash dresses.

Abe Plough, Memphis millionaire industrialist, started a small drug business in 1908 in one room above his father's store at 83 North Second Street. Ten years later the Plough Chemical Company was incorporated at a plant at Second and Gayoso streets, and started bottling Plough's Antiseptic Oil. An ad in 1919 described Plough as "the sole proprietors and manufacturers of the Black and White Toilet Preparations and Prescription C–2223, a blood tonic relieving rheumatism and Purifies the Blood." Later this company grew into one of America's great corporations, merging in 1971 to become Schering-Plough, Incorporated.

Forest Products Chemical Company began in 1911 on Chelsea Avenue. It operated a major wood distillation plant, and later became the first company in the South to sell charcoal, a byproduct of its chemical business. Cudahy Packing Company built a plant on Chelsea in 1913 to produce margarine, shortening, and salad oils. Earlier in 1908, it had built a cold storage plant in Memphis.

Ford Motor Company built its first auto assembly plant in Memphis in 1913 at 495 Union. The building, later occupied by the Memphis Publishing Company, was vacated by Ford when it opened its large assembly plant on Riverside Drive in 1924.

This list, although modest, does show an attempt at product diversification in Memphis industrial activity in pre-World War I years.

PROGRESS OF THE COTTON MARKET PRIOR TO WORLD WAR I

Cotton prices continued to languish after 1900. At 7.03 cents per pound in 1901, prospects for those in the cotton business were bleak. From 1900 to 1910 the price exceeded 10 cents for only half of those years. From 1911 through 1918, as shown in Appendix B, the range from low to high was 7.35 cents in 1914 to 28.88 cents in 1918. The industry was beset with problems which cast dark clouds over Memphis and the rest of the cotton world.

The boll weevil began taking its toll after 1900. The weevil first appeared in the United States in 1892. It was found in some Mississippi counties in 1906, and appeared similar to the weevils infesting the Texas cotton crops. By 1914 it had became serious throughout the South, causing great crop losses.

Overproduction forced prices down and forced many farmers out of business. A group which called itself the Southern Cotton Association formed in 1905 to attempt to influence prices by limiting production.[8] The opening of new lands west of the Mississippi was increasing acreage and the size of the annual crop. This group faded in 1908, but it did generate interest in the South in discussing a wide range of problems besetting the industry.

The Great Southern Cotton Conference was held in Memphis in 1908. Representatives from planters, buyers, spinners, factors, ginners, warehouse proprietors and bankers discussed matters of low prices, the boll weevil menace, problems of financing cotton and stopping the menace of night riding. Dissident farmers were taking their hostility out on the ginners whom they blamed for the low prices. Nothing of a solid nature, however, came out of this well-attended Conference and no action proposals were apparent.

The sinking of the Lusitania by German submarines in 1915 caused a huge break in the cotton market. Fear of war in Europe cutting off the English market for American cotton drove the price down. Just the year before the South had experienced a huge glut of cotton. The 1914 crop was coming on the market in September, and there were few buyers. Memphis cotton dealers and those elsewhere in the South grew fearful that New England textile mills would take advantage of the South's surplus and drive the price down to a few pennies a pound. The 1914 crop was the largest on record. Out of this crisis came the "Buy-A-Bale of Cotton" movement in Memphis, Atlanta and hundreds of towns throughout the South. Citizens and business firms were urged as a patriotic gesture to buy this cotton at 10 cents a pound, and store it for at least a year, or to the point where the market price rose above 10 cents. The program was partially successful. In Memphis, for example, the Associated Retailers bought 1,168 bales to hold off the market. Many individuals bought a bale or two at about $48 to $50 each, depending on weight. The 1914 price was 7.35 cents. By 1915, it had moved up to 11.22 cents; so Southern investors in the program could sell out at a slight profit.

AGRICULTURAL DIVERSIFICATION IN THE MEMPHIS REGION

C.P.J. Mooney, the influential editor of *The Commercial Appeal* who had been advocating farm product diversification since 1910, stepped up his plea in 1914 for concerted action in the South. His point was that cotton was far too risky to place sole dependence on it for the region's economic livelihood. Mooney's editorial on 25 January 1914, titled "The South Can Solve the Supreme Problem of America," admonished his readers that the South had been overconcerned since the Civil War with politics and cotton, and that it had overlooked the great potential for growing food and raising cattle. Cotton production should continue, he added, but the land was capable of multiple agricultural uses. Mooney concluded: "The Southern people can make the South the chief food supply depot of the world. Will they?"

Mooney placed banner ads in *The Commercial Appeal* encouraging farmers to diversify. He pointed out the folly of the Memphis region being a one crop economy. Unfortunately, this rational suggestion by Mooney for farm diversification went unheeded. When the cotton market improved drastically on the eve of America's entry into World War I, cotton farmers and cotton merchants were not convinced of the validity of Mooney's convictions. Perhaps, if they had made the partial transition, Memphis could have developed as a food processing and manufacturing center for a variety of farm products.

SHELBY COUNTY'S AGRICULTURAL ECONOMY

Part of the immediate Memphis economic base was the farming going on outside the city's boundaries in Shelby County. Cotton was a big crop. In 1900 the output was over 39,000 bales; and in 1910, about 33,000 bales. Shelby County led all other West Tennessee counties in production. The total value of all farm crops in the county in 1910 was $4.3 million which lead West Tennessee and Crittenden County, Arkansas, and De Soto County, Mississippi. All of this Shelby County output came from several thousand small farm holdings. There were about 6,900 farms in 1900. This inventory increased to 7,900 in 1910. About four out of five were tenant operated, and only 628 farms in 1900 had more than 100 acres. The vagaries of the cotton market were very hard on these small operators. The low cotton prices of the general period from 1890 to about 1915 made most of these farms marginal operations. Memphis could not count on much contribution to its future economy from these area farms.

DEVELOPMENT PROGRESS, 1890–1918

Memphis organized itself quite effectively during this period to build a stronger and more flexible urban economic base. The leadership base widened considerably and more citizens felt a stake in programs to encourage more investment and more industry in the city. Political leaders joined businessmen in the cause. E. H. Crump, in his first campaign for Mayor in 1909, pledged he would do everything he could to induce more capital to come to Memphis. Undoubtedly he was reacting to the community's will that more activity than just cotton should underpin the Memphis economy.

The actual results in terms of jobs, factories and total capital investment were modest. The city did have pride in its efforts, and it deserved much greater recognition by the outside world as a place to do business.

8

Memphis' Greatest Day

"Third Among South's Cities" proclaimed *The Commercial Appeal* on 28 September 1900. Its headline continues: "Passes Three Southern Cities. In 1890 Memphis Was Smaller Than Nashville, Atlanta and Richmond, But in 1900 These Cities Drop to the Rear."[1]

The city proclaimed Friday, 5 October 1900 as Census Day, a giant civic celebration with a patriotic parade. This great day was for Memphis to honor itself for achieving an official census of 102,323 persons. The city had witnessed a 59 percent increase since 1890. Now the race was on to catch the two larger Southern cities, New Orleans and Louisville. From 1900 on, Memphis pushed for greater industrial and commercial development to try to meet this challenge.

Why did Memphis experience such a spurt in growth? The principal reasons were in-migration and annexation of contiguous suburban areas. The rural migrants came into Memphis to escape the grinding poverty of their areas. Although uneducated and unskilled, they considered their chances of economic survival better in an urban setting. Thousands in the rural South either moved to the North, to western states, or into the large urban centers of the South in search of jobs. Memphis drew heavily from Northern Mississippi, Eastern Arkansas, and West Tennessee and Alabama.

Popular observations of the day were that the State of Mississippi's major export product was "people to Memphis"; or that Memphis was the capital of North Mississippi. In later years, because of the economic influence of Memphis, it was claimed that the northernmost geographic point of the Mississippi Delta was the lobby of the Peabody Hotel.[2] In 1900 some 14,600 residents of Memphis were born in Mississippi. After 1900 thousands more Mississippians migrated to Memphis in search of economic opportunity.

The black population of Memphis increased by 21,000 between 1890 and 1900, an almost 60 percent increase. About half of Memphis' population in 1900 was black, and it was the greatest percentage of black population of the 38 cities with more than 100,000 people. Birmingham had a figure of 43 percent; Atlanta, 40; Washington, D. C., 31; and New Orleans, 27. Only six percent of St. Louis' population was black; only five percent in Philadelphia; and two percent in Chicago.

Ten years later, surprisingly, the black population had increased by only 2,500. This great drop off in black population growth caused a lowering of the percentage of blacks to 40 percent of the city's population. Throughout the South's urban centers, the black percentage figures declined from 1900 to 1910. One reason was the annexation by these cities of predominantly white fringe areas. The other was the renewal of the black migration out of the South. The forty percent figure for blacks in Memphis has remained relatively stationary since 1910. The 1970 figure was 38.9 percent.

The size of the population in Memphis in 1900 and 1910 did not represent any significant net contribution to the city's economic development or its potential to capitalize on this new manpower. Many had only limited labor skills to offer. They may have been acceptable workers for industries using cheap and unskilled labor, but they were incapable of contributing to more advanced industries. So while the population numbers were impressive in the promotional brochures, the quality of the labor force was quite low. This condition was a severe handicap to the promotional efforts of the Business Men's Club, as well as to its successor, the Memphis Chamber of Commerce, which had hoped to attract greater factory investment.

Population size was equated with success in Memphis and most American cities. Memphis grew to 131,105 in 1910; and shortly thereafter Mayor Crump contacted Kenneth McKellar, then serving as a Congressman in 1912, to see if something could not be done to have a federal census every five years. Crump told McKellar he wanted one in 1915, and perhaps extend the city's corporate limits "... so as to make us show up as the largest city in the South, outside of Louisville and New Orleans."[3] The Mayor was obviously distressed that Atlanta with a 1910 population of 154,839 and Birmingham with 132,685 had passed Memphis. It was a severe blow to the city's prestige to fall to fifth position in 1910.

Annexation was the device used by Memphis to expand its corporate limits and add to its population. It was a logical step for a city that was growing out physically from its historic central core. But annexation was also a device used in Memphis and many other aspiring cities in the competitive race for urban prestige. The 1899 annexation of more than 12 square miles gained 58,300 new residents. The timing was excellent for Memphis. It was just before the 1900 Census which would later report that Memphis had gone over the 100,000 mark. Again, in 1909 before the federal census takers made their count, Memphis annexed 3.32 more square miles and took into the city nearly 30,000 more people. Additional annexation occurred in 1913, 1917 and 1919.

Mr. Crump's efforts to pump up the city's population to escape ranking as fifth largest Southern city failed. When the 1920 Census was released, Memphis was still in fifth place. The actual spread in population between Atlanta and Memphis and between Birmingham and Memphis had widened. These competitor cities had out-annexed Memphis. Neither Atlanta nor Birmingham in 1919, when the federal Census of Manufactures was taken, had pulled that far ahead of Memphis in industrial development. Atlanta provided only 3,800 more factory jobs than Memphis, and Birmingham, 5,300 more jobs.

REAL ESTATE AND PHYSICAL GROWTH

The matter of prestige aside, Memphis' growth was evident by the increased absorption of previously vacant fringe acreage for suburban residential subdivisions, by development of land along the railroad corridors for industry and the more intensive development of commercial property in downtown Memphis. A major public park system was developed, a parkway system and improved streets replaced the primitive system which was a legacy of post-Civil War city governments. A street railway system was developed and extended to serve the new suburban population, and some industrial areas in South Memphis.

Real estate promoters had been optimistic about Memphis since the 1880s while the city was still under the protective eye of the Taxing District. When Memphis regained its charter in 1893 and resumed home rule once again, real estate agents were reporting solid gains in the annual volume of property sales. There was little speculation of the type seen in Birmingham and Chattanooga, but wealthy families were acquiring choice properties in anticipation of future growth. Most of the major cotton and wholesale merchant kings were men with extensive property holdings. The 1887 *Annual Report of the Memphis Merchants' Exchange* reported that good commercial properties were yielding six to eight percent returns on investment, and eight to ten percent on residential property. These were averages for the city.

A euphoria permeated the ranks of the realtors after 1890. They saw "the Great Bridge," which opened in 1892, as the key support for a healthy real estate market during the decade. The following type of ad began appearing, "Young men, now is the time for you, especially, to begin to save and stop paying rent by securing a home." Active real estate brokerage firms in the 1900 era included: Overton and Overton, George H. Glascock and Company, Cordes and Company, R. R. Church; and H. L. Guion Company (E. B. LeMaster, Proprietor). The growing interest in raising the standards of the profession created the need for a real estate board. In 1910, the Memphis Real Estate Association was formed by a small group of dedicated professionals. Edward B. LeMaster, a well-respected realtor, served as the Association's first president.

The Builders' Exchange of Memphis was organized in 1900 "to promote mechanical and industrial interests." This association of contractors, architects, builders and suppliers helped develop building ordinances for the city, pushed for building inspection, and for fair practices in contractual arrangements. This group revolutionized the Memphis building trades, and raised citywide construction standards at the early stages of a tremendous building period. In the latter nineteenth century unsafe buildings were prevalent, and fires or collapsing walls or roofs were commonplace. The new era demanded better construction technology in Memphis. Twelve years after the Builders' Exchange was organized, the city's first building code was adopted.

THE SHAPING OF THE CITY

The city's physical form in the 1870s was described as "close and compact, built in true Southern Style." The corporate area was only 4.6 square miles, and rectangular in shape. The 1899 annexation increased the area by four times, making its physical form square. This action did much to set the directional pattern for the city for the next half century. The city's spatial form was being determined in order to accommodate land developers in peripheral zones, and to protect the city's vastly improved public health and sanitation reputation. Improved transportation systems, namely the street railway, both influenced growth and reacted to growth, helping to tie the various parts of the city and suburbs together.

Mayor John J. Williams, elected to office in 1898, publicly led the drive (called the Greater Memphis Movement that year) to annex much of the outlying suburbs, including the communities of Idlewild, Madison Heights and Manila. Williams and a great number of Memphians were greatly concerned about sanitary conditions in these unincorporated areas, and they wanted to head off the possibilities of an epidemic. Opposition to annexation developed within the unincorporated areas. The main objection was the new residents' fear that they would be taxed to support previously incurred Memphis bonded debt. They willingly assumed the obligation to pay for their new sewers, streets and schools; but they asked for a 10-year moratorium on being taxed for the city's debt. Other charges by opponents of annexation were that it was encompassing considerable undeveloped land, and that Memphis was again endangering its credit rating by issuing additional bonds.

Mayor Williams was a progressive and during his regime the city developed much of its modern park system and parkway belt around the city. During this period Memphis began to look like a city physically, and began to enjoy the amenities which many citizens assumed to be part of the life in important cities.

ENTER THE LAND SUBDIVIDERS

In 1900 there were 5,000 real estate transactions and in 1901, 6,300. Building permits, an indicator of activity, increased from $1.9 million in 1900 to $6.4 million in 1910. The city was developing physically, and opportunistic promoters and developers saw land as a source of quick and substantial profits. The residential subdivision was their gold mine.

Memphis had seen housing subdivision promoters before. The aggressive lot sales promotion of the firm Donoho and Bulkley of "the Brinkley property" in the 1870s was a major one. This tract was in the vicinity of present day Jackson Avenue, Dunlap and the North Parkway. Messers. Donoho and Bulkley had vision, promising their prospective buyers that "Summer (later renamed North Parkway) ... must some day be adapted as one of the system of grand and fashionable 'boulevards'." In 1886 Edmund Orgill and W. P. Dunavant filed with the County Register a 55-acre subdivision on Mound Street beyond Gills Station to be known as the town of Magnolia. And there were some other subdivisions filed, but not heavily promoted.

The 1890s saw greatly increased subdivision activity. For the next twenty years land was merchandised in a circus-like atmosphere. Several thousand lots in a variety of subdivided tracts were offered for sale within the city and on its border. The biggest promoters were E. E. Meacham, Beaumont M. Stratton, M. M. Gilchrist, and V. C. Russell. Giant newspaper ads and leaflets announced "rare investment opportunities as well as good home sites were available for little down payment and convenient terms." One typical ad announced: "$100 Buys a Lot; $2.00 Down and $1.50 Per Month. No Lots Smaller than 50 x 150. Many Larger. Everybody Has $2.00. Perfect Title."[4]
Another ad in 1904 cajoled buyers:

> New subdivision, two blocks north of Brick Church, on Randolph Road and Thomas Avenue, on Main St. Car-line; nice, high, dry lots in a tony neighborhood. Think of it! Leave off smoking one cigar daily and that money will more than pay for your lot. Come quick if you want one. Will furnish you with money to build at 6 percent. $1.00 weekly; $400 per lot.[5]

An avalanche of ads appeared with about the same promotional appeal. Most firms provided prospects with streetcar fare to the lots, provided they came downtown to the real estate office before beginning the excursion.

Many abuses occurred in these subdivision promotions. Memphis first tried in 1901 to control the most flagrant abuses of these land developers. The matter of "pony lots" was the greatest menace to health and sanitation. Lots were being sold with 12½ foot frontages, with no alleys behind, and laid out in long and monotonous lineal fashion. The developers in many instances had no regard for the logical development of a city street system. Memphis had required developers to submit their plats and maps for approval in the early 1890s, but enforcement was lax. In an act of desperation in 1901 the city filed a subdivision suit against one of the city's biggest lot subdividers and was upheld in the United States Circuit Court. *The Commercial Appeal* editorialized:

In future there will be no more such unsightly places in the map of the
city as Eatontown, Meachamtown, Klondyke, New Chicago and like
subdivisions. The city has, therefore, every reason to congratulate itself upon the suit thus gained, and the public to thank the learned
jurist for his opinion, which means so much for the future good of
Memphis.[6]

Land planning was chaotic and much suburban Memphis land was raped
by profit-seeking opportunists who had no particular concern that improvements were lacking and that they were paving the way for squalid, slum conditions. The "quick-buck artists" of these earlier days have left Memphis with a
legacy inherited by the City's Office of Community Development in the late
1970s for correction.

Annesdale Park, however, was one of the first high quality residential
projects. Although promoted by developer R. Brinkley Snowden in flamboyant
fashion, this 1903 subdivision was the type which attracted upper middle class
buyers. The site was bounded by Bellevue (then called Raleigh Road), Peabody,
Harbert, and extending beyond Cleveland. The subdivision was near present
day Central High. Codevelopers were R. Brinkley Snowden, real estate investor
and banker, and his brother, J. Bayard Snowden, sons of wealthy businessman-
investor Robert Bogardus Snowden.

Newspaper ads placed by the Snowdens in *The Commercial Appeal* of 15
October 1903 announced the "Watermelon is Opened." It touted the big parade
for that afternoon which would feature wagons loaded with watermelons and
would follow a route from downtown Memphis at the old Peabody Hotel on
Main Street to the subdivision. The Snowdens sponsored a banquet before the
parade and invited 50 of the city's most prominent people. One account stated
that this luncheon gathering brought together "the blood, the brains, the wealth
and commercial sinew of the community." Mayor Williams gave the dedication
address at the subdivision.

Ads tempted the speculator. One in 1904 pleaded: "Invest your money for
best results. Why keep it idle when you can make it earn from 20 percent to 100
percent in a few months' time by buying Annesdale Park lots."[7] The Snowdens,
however, insisted that lot purchasers build. They also put the public on notice
that lots would only be sold to those whose position in society was such that their
presence in Annesdale Park would contribute to its social importance.

The Overton Park area in the era before World War I was considered
among the most desirable residential areas for the upper middle classes. Land
values had increased upon the opening and development of the Park. Investors
like R. Brinkley Snowden considered that land would appreciate in value near
Overton Park in much the same fashion as it had done adjacent to the re-
nowned Forest Park in St. Louis. Additional development impetus was given to
residential development with the completion of North Parkway. Originally this

prominent avenue was called both Summer Avenue and Speedway. Turn of the century automobiles raced on this thoroughfare. In addition to Snowden, prominent developers were Finley W. Faxon; Robert Galloway, prominent coal dealer and one of the original Park Commission members; and John M. Overton, successful realtor and businessman.

The greatest number of subdivisions being developed near the Park were to the north and west of Overton Park in the 1900–1915 period. Development companies called the Speedway Land Company and Union Land and Improvement Company were prominent developers. The most active developer was Finley Faxon. Early in his 50-year career as the city's leading developer and builder, he was responsible for much of the homebuilding in this newly emerging upper income section of Memphis.

Profits were to be made in land development and some of the city's oldest business families entered into the competition for profits with a new generation of builder-entrepreneurs. They assured the general public that land and home ownership was theirs if they would put their savings to work.

One development company, capturing Memphis' optimism about land values, made what might be called an offer the public could not refuse in the following newspaper advertisement:

> We are so sure of rapidly rising values that we will buy back at 90¢ on the dollar any property bought of us, at any time within a year from the date of purchase. You couldn't possibly lose over 10¢ on the dollar in any event.[8]

Memphis' area of urbanization was spreading out and creating a new distribution of the more affluent population.

MEMPHIS HOUSING PATTERNS

Except for the very lowest quality subdivisions, mostly located in North and South Memphis, the lots were developed as home sites. In 1890 Memphis had under 12,000 housing units. Thirty years later there were over 35,000 units. Shelby County, including Memphis, added nearly 30,000 units in that period. There was more family homeownership than ever before, but still Memphis and Shelby County families were predominantly renters rather than owners. In 1903 only 17 percent owned their own homes. The national average was 26 percent.

Low and modest income groups, including both whites and blacks, lived in the older, established sections of Memphis. Rental properties were prevalent in the geographic ring including downtown Memphis, and near the industrial areas, a pattern found in most U.S. cities.

Beginning in the 1890s Memphis experienced substantially greater separation of social and economic classes residentially. The wealthy cotton merchants, commercial classes and professionals started the trek "east" out of the traditional central Memphis area. The trend continued "east" through World War I to the present day. Some of the elite stayed close in until early in the twentieth century, but the majority built fashionable homes in Snowden's Annesdale Park, in the Overton Park area, and on such streets as Union, Peabody, Central and adjoining streets. Beale Street, at one time a residential street for the city's most prominent families, started its change to a commercial street in the 1880s.

Memphis, similar to the pattern in many Southern cities, did not entirely segregate itself by race even though this suburban movement was taking place before World War I. A large percentage of blacks lived in many of the 29 wards of the city. Only a few wards had a minimum of black residents, and could be called white enclaves. The highest percentage of blacks in any ward in 1911 was 68 percent in a ward near Elmwood Cemetery. Blacks were found living in the Overton Park area in significant numbers in 1911 and in the area later developed in the mid-1920s, Chickasaw Gardens. The heaviest concentrations of blacks were in neighborhoods on the south side of the downtown area. Fort Pickering and Orange Mound, near the Fairgrounds, had large black populations. Fort Pickering had many Irish as well as blacks.

The Street System

The Memphis streets were a shambles in the period 1870 to 1900. It took an effort paralleling that of the program modernizing the water and sanitary sewer systems to bring them to any kind of acceptable order. The notorious Nicholson pavements, which consisted of streets paved with a floor of small pine blocks six inches long and three inches square dipped in tar and cement, had been installed on the principal streets right after the Civil War. The construction of these streets was expensive and under a cloud of corruption in the awarding of contracts. For all intents and purposes, it was impossible for Memphis to maintain this type of street system; so right after 1900, work got underway to modernize the streets.

Citizens along the improved streets resented the front-foot assessment plan to pay for the construction, but work proceeded. Most of the streets were paved with asphalt in the downtown, although some were paved with brick. Granite blocks were used to pave Front Street from Linden to Poplar. The city used gravel for most of the other streets peripheral to downtown.

After 1900 one of the major problems was railroad grade crossings. This particular problem plagued Memphis throughout much of the early part of the twentieth century. Political leader E. H. Crump laid down a barrage against the railroads throughout most of his life on matters of grade crossings, viaducts and subways.

Poplar Pike, the principal highway route into the city from the east, was improved from the city limits to Collierville with a 55-foot right of way in 1910. The Harahan Bridge, which opened to motor vehicles in 1917, also improved access. Street lights were first introduced in 1892 with a system on Main Street.

Automobiles were still a novelty in 1908 when the Memphis Automobile Dealers Association held its first annual road endurance race. Some 21 cars started from Court Square on a cross country race through Shelby County. Only a portion finished this grind over the primitive and dangerous road network. Few could have anticipated at that time the changes this new technology would make on the daily lives of future Memphians.

STREETCARS AND SUBURBS

"Goodbye, hack drivers, your occupation's gone" commented the *Public Ledger* in 1866. Memphis had just been introduced to its first street railway car system running on Main, Jefferson, and Poplar. This was a horse railroad company that by the 1880s had 15 miles of track, 80 cars, 250 horses and mules, 150 men and charged a nickle for a ride. Not only in Memphis, but elsewhere, street railway technology was primitive until the introduction of the electrically-powered streetcars in the late 1880s and in the 1890s. The slow moving horse or mule drawn cars restricted mobility and forced the city to stay frozen in a more or less compact urban form. The spatial pattern changed dramatically when the electrically powered streetcars, with their higher speeds, made their appearance. Memphis now was physically opened up for land development on the periphery. Investors and real estate developers seized the opportunity and started the suburban movement which ran practically unabated until the Great Depression of the 1930s.

Hundreds of houses were built along or near the streetcar lines. Housing developers placed ads in the Sunday newspaper with maps indicating the streetcar route most convenient to their sale homes. Homebuilders and subdividers worked hand-in-hand with the management of the Memphis Street Railway Company in planning the route system. Obviously, there were advantages to both. The developers needed transportation to entice city dwellers to move to the suburban housing tracts. The Street Railway Company wanted the passenger volume to increase its investment return.

Memphis lagged a little behind competitive cities in electrifying its system. Richmond had a system in 1887 and Nashville in 1889. But once Memphis got started the system blossomed. By 1895 it had a route system extending over 70 miles. In 1910, it had increased to 110 miles; it carried 34.2 million passengers and it was profitable.

The streetcars helped keep the city physically unified. The new suburban areas were tied to the downtown and to the industrial areas. The system also had convenient service to the Fairgrounds, East End Park and other places of recreation.

One line ran to Raleigh, crossing the northern part of Overton Park, then out Jackson Avenue to National Cemetery and beyond. An interurban line of 12 miles from Memphis to Lakeview, Mississippi, operated by the Memphis and Lakeview Traction Company until taken over by the Memphis Street Railway Company in 1913, stayed in business until 1928 when it went bankrupt.

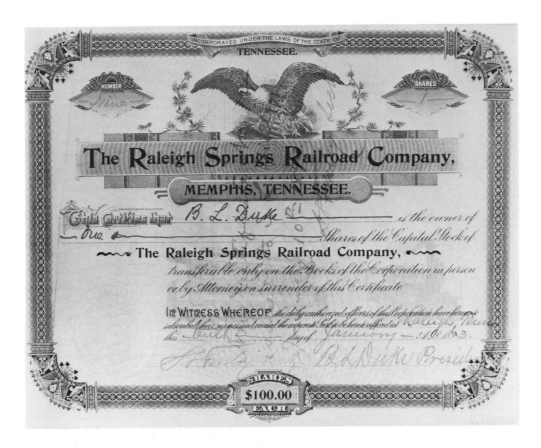

Fig. 15. Stock Certificate issued in 1893 to B. L. Duke, millionaire tobacco merchant of North Carolina, who financed the construction of the Raleigh Springs line and was its first president. (Courtesy of City of Memphis Archives)

The streetcar era was a colorful one in the history of Memphis. The system was functional, service was considered good, and the passengers obviously enjoyed themselves in that period from 1890 to the mid-1920s before the private automobile started making its claim as an important mode of urban transportation in Memphis. Today's land use pattern in the sections of the city developed prior to 1941 was heavily influenced by the streetcar network.

ELECTRIC AND GAS UTILITIES IN EARLY DEVELOPMENT

Like the streetcars, the contribution made by the utility companies in the city's growth is an important part of local economic history. While these early private companies provided the power and energy needed for the city to develop physically and industrially, they also became part of the day-to-day politics of Memphis, and during their long tenure from the 1890s to 1939 politicians and utility managements were embroiled in heated controversies over rates, service, and other operating practices. The classic confrontations between E. H. Crump and his political organization and the private utility companies from about 1914 to 1939 when the city-owned Memphis Light, Gas and Water Division was formed, were massive power struggles among strong adversaries. This important phase of local economic history is treated separately in Chapter 13 in the analysis of the development of the Tennessee Valley Authority and the entry of TVA power into Memphis in the latter 1930s.

The Memphis Light and Power Company, formed from a merger of two smaller companies in 1887, was the city's first important electric utility.[9] In 1890 this company received a ten-year charter. It was extended an additional 35 years in 1900. A company to provide gas service was organized in 1898, and five years later it merged with the electric company to become the Memphis Consolidated Gas and Electric Company. A rival company, the Merchants' Power Company, started operations in 1905, and had a 25-year contract to supply the city of Memphis with gas and electricity.[10] In 1917, the two utilities merged to become the Memphis Gas and Electric Company.[11] Later this company went bankrupt. New owners, principally out-of-town investors, took over in the 1920s and operated the utilities until Crump's stepped up battle against them led to the city's purchase of the system in 1939.

The utility companies saw increased profit potentials from serving the city's growth and so their services kept pace with the movement of surburban residential subdivisions. Although they were not as visible as the street railway system in directing urban spatial form, the utilities did contribute to the suburbanization of Memphis. Crump, however, felt that the utilities had a stranglehold on the city and that it should own the light company.

THE PARK SYSTEM AND CIVIC PROGRESS

Memphis, while considering itself progressive, was hopelessly lacking in 1900 in many of the urban amenities and civic-cultural facilities of the type that were being built and nurtured in most of the progressive cities of that day. Memphis had no major parks, no public zoo or art gallery, no ampitheatres or large public auditoriums, and no imposing monuments to provide for the recreational and aesthetic needs of its citizens. The city had just 6 acres of parks. Like the small Bickford Park, given to Memphis in 1869 by developer William Bickford, all of these compact parks were dedicated to the city, which had spent no major public funds prior to 1900 on recreational facilities.

Parks and boulevards were fashionable at the turn of the century. America's urban park acreage doubled in the years around 1900. Kansas City and Boston were the first cities to build encircling parks. St. Louis had its Forest Park of 1,300 acres which it acquired in 1876 for $885,000. Later, in 1904 it served as the site of the St. Louis World's Fair. Philadelphia had its extensive Fairmount Park which was the location of the 1876 Centennial. New Orleans had 450 acres in parks in 1890; Louisville had 400; and Atlanta had 153. Memphis was far behind its competitors.

The great need for public facilities and some civic ostentation became apparent about 1899 in Memphis. The city had sponsored a structure at the Tennessee Centennial in 1896 in Nashville that was in the form of a pyramid symbolizing Memphis' identification with the ancient city on the Nile. A group of public-spirited Memphians felt such a structure built on the riverfront would be appropriate for an auditorium seating some 15,000 people. The pyramid was to be 150 feet high and cost about $50,000. Robert Galloway was one of the originators of the proposal. Four years later the City Park Board, on which Galloway served, turned down the request of a private investment group seeking to build an exposition building on city-owned land near the riverfront. These proposals represented at least some interest in developing structural landmarks for local and tourist use. Memphis needed an attraction to symbolize both its breaking of the 100,000 population barrier and its desire for urban prominence.

Mayor Williams, Galloway, Hu Brinkley and other civic-minded leaders became interested in exploring the possibility of purchasing Lea's Woods from Overton Lea and his wife, residents of Nashville. Lea's Woods, which was renamed Overton Park when purchased by Memphis in 1901, was a virgin forest of some 342 acres east of the city's corporate limits. This potential park site cost the city $330 an acre, a bargain the city fathers may not have realized they were getting. The Leas had wanted more but settled when the City government suggested condemnation. Overton Park development planning was aggressively pursued by the Memphis Park Board after the sale was concluded. The Board's membership was Galloway, John R. Godwin and Judge L. B. McFarland, the first president. They were instrumental in obtaining consulting assistance from landscape architect John C. Olmsted, stepson of internationally famous landscape architect, Frederick Law Olmsted. The younger Olmsted did a site survey of Memphis in 1899 and helped convince the city of the wisdom of buying the site of Riverside Park, then south of the city, and tying both large parks together with a parkway system encircling the city. These were bold steps for a city which only recently had but six acres of parks. Olmsted was useful, but it was really the forcefulness of Galloway, and the influence of Hu L. Brinkley that got favorable decisions to proceed from city government.

The Overton Park design plan was prepared by a landscape engineer, George Kessler, who had come to Memphis from Kansas City. Construction of the Zoo started in 1905. The first arrival apparently was a bear; then in 1906 the Zoo acquired an elephant. Brooks Memorial Art Gallery opened in 1916. With the exception of some new buildings and monuments, like the E. H. Crump statue at the Park's entrance, the basic plan has remained relatively the same as it was in the early 1900s. It has been a highly useful public park for day-to-day pleasure and as a site for some of the city's greatest patriotic conclaves and picnics.

Riverside Park, which had 445 acres until it lost 29 acres to expressway

Fig. 16. Sunday afternoon in 1906 at the new bear pits of the Memphis Zoo in Overton Park. (Courtesy of the Library of Congress)

construction in 1965, was a well-used park until recent years, but this vast tract overlooking the Mississippi River was never able to challenge Overton Park for civic prominence and popularity. It was too remote, was located near middle and lower income residential neighborhoods, and abutted industrial land.

Construction began in 1904 for the Parkway on land that was largely donated by wealthy property owners along the right of way of the horseshoe shaped route encircling the urbanized sections of Memphis. These donors were undoubtedly civic-minded, but they also knew that land values would increase on completion of the system. The Park Board reported that land prices had actually quadrupled from 1903 to 1910 along the 12-mile route.

The Parkway was an early example of city planning at its finest. Over the years, this combination urban greenbelt and functional boulevard became a source of civic pride. It was one of the greatest land use decisions in the city's history. Although attempts at encroachment were made, particularly during the 1930s, many of the commercial interests wanting to dot the route with custard and barbecue stands and service stations were rebuffed by dedicated civic-minded groups protecting the intent of the original planners.

Memphis accomplished almost a civic miracle in going from practically no parks in 1900 to creating a park system befitting the progressive, more fully developed and sophisticated city that it desired to be by 1910. Although it was 1923 before the city acquired additional large acreage for recreational purposes, these two large site acquisitions in 1901 did much to reshape the city's urban form at a very propitious moment when the citizens needed desperately to develop more pride in the community and to present a showcase to the outside world.

THE ISLANDS—ASSETS OR LIABILITIES?

Population was drifting eastward in those years before World War I and it was still concentrated in subdivisions located south of the Wolf River and north of the Nonconnah Creek, two physical barriers which helped shape the city's development pattern. West of downtown Memphis was the Mississippi River, an obvious barrier to physical growth. Yet there were two land formations on the city's front doorstep that created troublesome problems for Memphis over the years as to the best use for these two "gifts of nature."

Presidents Island was an island in the Mississippi River some 8 miles long and 5 miles wide located about 3½ miles south of downtown Memphis. After years of mixed utility it was joined to the shoreline after World War II with the construction of a giant earthen embankment closing off the Tennessee Chute, that part of the Mississippi which ran between the Memphis shoreline and the Island. This physical connection made it possible to develop a portion of the island into a huge industrial district.

Partially flooded during the periods of high water on the Mississippi, the island had served as a cotton plantation, a quarantine station during the epidemics, a camp for liberated slaves run by the Freedmen's Bureau, a prison farm, and the location of pest houses. The latter were places where persons with communicable diseases were sent to be isolated from the public. For a time after the Civil War, General Forrest operated the convict work farm under a lease arrangement with Shelby County. Presidents Island was a haven for gamblers and bootleggers in the 1920s and a site for cock fights. So while the island served some useful social and economic purposes for certain elements of society, it was largely an unproductive resource until the 1940s when E. H. Crump and some others saw its industrial potential if improved by a major public works project which would close the Tennessee Chute and connect the island to the river bank.

Mud Island (denoted "City Island" on some maps), however, was a physical thorn in Memphis' side for decades after this downtown sandbar formed and expanded to jeopardize the future of the Memphis Harbor and general waterfront area. One account states that in 1876, some 23 miles above Memphis, the river changed its course. This shifted the direction of the current and created an eddy in front of downtown Memphis. As incredible as this story seems, it appears that Mud Island's origin was the direct result of the six-month anchoring in 1909 of the U.S. Navy gunboat, *Aphrodite*.[12] The eddy caused a small, submerged sandbar to form against the gunboat. When the gunboat left upon the return of high water, observers did not worry much about the small sandbar which now rose above the water at a point opposite Court Street. Quickly, however, the sandbar grew to a 40-acre tract and joined itself to the mainland. Soon it extended south to Beale Street.

Memphis had had continuous problems in the nineteenth century with river bank caveins and shoreline erosion. Its leaders had pushed for harbor protection to save valuable property and to keep the waterfront open for commerce. Mud Island, however, became the biggest threat yet seen, and local leaders feared its possible negative impact on river traffic and its spoilage of the aesthetic features of the harbor. Kenneth McKellar, in his campaign for a U.S. Senate seat in 1916, pledged his efforts to get rid of this huge obstruction. But the accretions continued, and the sandbar became a huge island directly in front of downtown Memphis. It created the necessity of continually dredging the Wolf River which had served as the main part of the Memphis Harbor. The Mississippi River Commission in 1917 authorized the removal of Mud Island by dredging the point of the bank at the mouth of the Wolf River.

Despite all of the planning, the island became a permanent fixture in the 1920s. City planning consultant Harland Bartholomew in his *Comprehensive Plan* for the city recommended that a grandiose park be built on Mud Island. Captain Eddie Rickenbacker, while a guest of the Chamber of Commerce in the 1920s, suggested that Memphis had a marvelous site for a municipal airport right downtown on its doorstep. In the 1930s the city zoned the island "A" residential to keep industry away. But despite concern dating back to about 1910, no major action was taken to develop the island until the 1970s, when construction started on Volunteer Park on that portion of the island south of the Hernando De Soto Bridge.

The flow of the Wolf River between downtown Memphis and Mud Island was cut off after World War II when the Corps of Engineers built a diversion channel which directed this river into the Mississippi north of the downtown district. This severance of the flow of the Wolf River through the Memphis Harbor created a still water area in front of the downtown. With the opening of harbor facilities at Presidents Island in the 1950s, the old traditional harbor area assumed a secondary role.

DEVELOPING DOWNTOWN MEMPHIS

Suburban growth reflected increased population growth and new urban transportation technology, as manifested by the streetcar. Downtown Memphis also reacted to the city's growth. The period from 1900 to 1915 saw a transformation of Main Street, Madison, Second, Union and a few other central streets from unimpressive commercial business structures to up-to-date office buildings, banks, retail sites, restaurants and hotels. There was a flurry of real estate activity and prices for prime sites rose substantially. Soon after 1900 investors saw potential business opportunities in the central business district. They realized that many existing buildings were obsolete, and that higher and better usage was necessary to support underlying land values. Many buildings were unsafe, particularly those predating the Civil War. New building laws were pushed after several units collapsed. Fires were also a problem.

But beyond this need to replace obsolete structures there was a pent-up demand for office space, retail space, hotel rooms, and other commercial real estate. Consider the market for office space: in 1898 there were 42 real estate brokers, 26 dentists, 140 physicians, 147 lawyers and 10 architects. In 1904, just six years later, there were 120 real estate brokers, 52 dentists, 225 physicians, 215 lawyers and 17 architects. These changes created a strong demand for centrally located office space. Developer response to the growing market came quickly.

Before 1905 the downtown commercial area was physically spread out and lacked unity. Business leaders and real estate investors both recognized the need to make downtown Memphis more compact and cohesive. The prime business location was Main and Madison. Rearranging downtown really began by using this "Number 1" corner as the central point. In 1904, an 11,026 square foot parcel sold for $30.84 per square foot, a very high price for commercial land in that day. The Luehrmann Hotel property, half a block south of the prime location, sold at auction in 1904 for $23.41 a square foot. The hotel was replaced by the Commerce Title Building. Another site located at the northwest corner of Union and Second sold for $5.08 a square foot. The land value pyramid was very steep in downtown Memphis at the turn of the century. The closer the property was to Main and Madison, the higher its value.

High rise office buildings were introduced to American cities in the 1890s, when a 10 or 12-story structure was called a skyscraper. Of course such a building was imposing when compared to the buildings it was replacing in the competitive market. Here new technology was having substantial influence on both urban land forms and the functions of buildings. The techniques of steel framing were created by an innovative group of architects referred to as "the Chicago School."[13] The steel framed structure replaced masonry bearing wall construction and freed developers from the traditional restrictions on height because of the safety factor. The use of steel framing permitted thinner and obviously lighter outer walls, and increased the speed of construction.

When excellent market conditions caused a surge of demand for new office space in Memphis, developers and investors took advantage of this new building technology. The D. T. Porter Building, originally the Continental Bank Building, went up in 1895. This 11-story steel frame building became an attraction because of management's policy of opening the roof for sightseeing. In 1905 a 15-story high rise, then called the Tennessee Trust Building, was completed. This building is now the 81 Madison Building. In the 1910–1911 period at Second and Madison near the heart of the financial district construction was completed on the 18-story Central Bank and Trust Building (later renamed the First National Bank Building and still later the Goodwyn Institute Building), and on the 19-story Exchange Building. The latter building became the home of the Memphis Cotton Exchange and the Memphis Merchants' Exchange for many years before both institutions departed for a Front Street location. Its sponsors advertised that this was the tallest and most expensive building in the South. Also constructed during this office boom period were the 15-story Memphis Trust Building (later renamed the Commerce Title Building) and the 10-story Falls Building. These buildings are all still standing.

THE COMPETITIVE BANKING BUSINESS

At all stages of Memphis' history banking has been competitive. At the turn of the century it was particularly brisk and many institutions fought for survival. Outwardly success was measured by a bank's annual volume of deposits. Using this as a measure the leading bank in the latter 1890s was the National Bank of Commerce with $2.4 million in deposits. This total gave it a slight lead over the State National Bank. The latter, however, took the lead in 1901 with deposits of $3.8 million. Third place was held by the First National Bank. In terms of the number of institutions the banner year was 1908 when the city was supporting 20 banks. Most were located on Madison, or on Main near Madison.

Bank mergers became commonplace as the competition grew keener. In 1906 Union Planters merged with the Tennessee Trust Company and moved into the latter's 15-story high rise at 81 Madison. Central Bank and Trust organized in 1906 merged with State National Bank in 1912 and became known as the Central-State National Bank until it merged in 1926 with the First National Bank. In 1918 Union Planters merged with the Mercantile National Bank. Somehow or other this latter institution had miraculously survived a defalcation of some $1.1 million in 1914 by its president, who had gambled away the bank's funds speculating in the cotton futures market.

At the time of World War I the combined deposits of the 17 Memphis banks were $65 million. Their total resources were $90 million. Bank activity had expanded considerably in the period 1900 to 1918.

DOWNTOWN RETAILING: LOWENSTEIN'S TO PIGGLY WIGGLY

In the growth period preceding World War I the city's major retail functions were consolidated on Main Street. Many of the prominent retailers of that day remain in the same leadership position more than a half century later. Main Street was synonymous with retailing until the 1950s and 1960s when the exodus to the suburbs began on a massive scale. Lowenstein's, Goldsmith's, the John Gerber Company, Bry's, Julius Goodman and Son, Oak Hall, Brodnax, Perel and Lowenstein, S. H. Kress and Company, and Julius Lewis were among the dominant retailers on this street.

B. Lowenstein and Bros., later known as Lowenstein's, had originally been a wholesale dry goods firm. In the latter nineteenth century it became one of Main Street's major retail department stores. Today Lowenstein's still operates one of its several stores on the city's Mid-America Mall, a pedestrian thoroughfare which replaced Main Street in the heart of downtown Memphis. The Goldsmith brothers relocated in 1895 from their small store on Beale Street to much larger facilities at Main and Gayoso. The John Gerber Company, started in 1880 by John Gerber and J. B. Wilson, operated a major department store at Main and Court for 95 years before going out of business in 1975. Another long time landmark was Bry's Department Store, founded in 1902 by Ike Block and Nathan and Louis Bry. The store was sold in 1956 to the parent company of Lowenstein's then demolished to make room for Lowenstein's downtown store on the Mall.

Traditionally the major retailers clung to the belief that the west side of Main Street was the best business location. Throughout the century or more of downtown retailing the major department stores stayed on that side of the street. The east side was the location of banks, office buildings, restaurants and some of the major movie theatres beginning in the 1920s.

On several other streets there were prominent businesses. On 16 September 1916 Clarence Saunders opened his first Piggly Wiggly grocery at 79 Jefferson, halfway between Main and Front Street. Henry Loeb's New Steam Laundry opened in 1887 at 282 Madison. And the well-known dry goods store on Beale Street, A. Schwab, opened earlier in 1876.

Most of these successful stores arose from very humble beginnings. Their original proprietors started from scratch. When business developed, they either built new stores or enlarged their original structures. By the time of World War I, Memphis had a solid retail tradition, and drew customers from the tri-state area to these aggressive and modern retail stores.

DOWNTOWN HOTELS

The best known hotels of the day were the Peabody, Gayoso, and Chisca. Memphis in the late nineteenth century had many small hotels. There was the historic Arlington at Main and Adams which survived until replaced in 1924 by the Claridge Hotel. The Fransioli was at Second and Union, the Clarendon on Madison, Gaston's between Main and Second on South Court, and Luehrmann's on Main near Madison.

The original Peabody, whose life span extended from 1869 to its demise in 1923, was a 75-room hotel at Main and Monroe. In 1906 it added 200 new rooms. Entrepreneur Robert C. Brinkley built the hotel, and reportedly gave it to his daughter as a wedding gift.[14] She had just married Robert Bogardus Snowden. The original Peabody, and its successor built in 1925, remained continuously in the Snowden family until 1953.[15] Brinkley named the hotel after his friend, George Peabody, a New England and New York financier who had once been helpful to the Memphian in his railroad ventures.

Fig. 17. In 1912 the corner of Main and Madison was the number one commercial corner in the city and it was crowded on this August day with shoppers and streetcars. (Courtesy of Memphis Room, MPL)

The Gayoso reopened in 1886 after being closed for years and became one of the principal hotels along with the Peabody. The hotel burned down in a spectacular fire in 1899, and caused great concern in the city over the future of Memphis in the competition for regional and national conventions. The business travel component of the market was also expected to suffer. *The Commercial Appeal* headline of 10 September 1899 was, "Needed, a Big Hotel." The city had only 500 rooms and many were second rate. The old Peabody with 75 rooms was only modest in size. Pressure was relieved when the new Gayoso opened in 1903 with 400 rooms. This landmark hotel survived until 1962 when Goldsmith's absorbed the hotel for additional retail selling area.

The 400-room Hotel Chisca opened in 1913, and proudly advertised that it was the "largest, most beautifully furnished hotel in Memphis." The real estate-oriented Snowden family, long identified with the Peabody, was the owner-developer of this hotel named after the famed town of the Chickasaws.

Hotel restaurants were popular attractions in Memphis. One of the most famous was Gaston's, owned by wealthy businessman John Gaston, who had started working in Memphis as a waiter. Part of Gaston's fortune was given to the city to build John Gaston Hospital. Henry Luehrmann was proprietor of Luehrmann's, a leading restaurant and meeting place on Main near Madison. Luehrmann's was described as: "A mecca for men who were epicureans of good foods and fine wines and liquors and a favorite haunt of actors and wealthy race horse owners."

THEATERS

Memphis had five major theaters competing for business in a city with just over 100,000 people. Although not all were financial successes, they did receive support from a city that enjoyed legitimate theater, variety shows, and public lectures.

The Grand Opera House, later known as the Orpheum, spanned the years 1890 to 1923 when fire destroyed this 2,200-seat theater. A syndicate of 25 investors had put up $3,000 each to build this structure at Main and Beale Street, which featured vaudeville. The first Lyceum was built in 1891 and burned down in 1893. The second Lyceum was built in 1894 at Second and Jefferson and became a prominent legitimate theater until 1919 when it turned to vaudeville, motion pictures, boxing and wrestling, and, just before its end in 1935, burlesque. Wealthy businessman Hu Brinkley was president of the Lyceum in its early life.

The Jefferson, later renamed the Lyric, was a 1,500-seat theater on Madison near Fourth. It remained a popular road show theater until converted to a movie house in 1933. Other theaters were the Tulane and the Auditorium. The latter, renamed the Bijou, was at Main and Linden on the site of the Chisca Hotel. It also fell victim to fire.

Movie theaters began making their appearance on Main Street after 1910. A theater operator named F. T. Montgomery opened four small theaters; another theater, the Princess Theatre, opened as a combined vaudeville and movie house in 1911. The large movie theaters did not make their appearance until after World War I when they gave Main Street a much more dramatic appearance as the Mid-South's business center.

BEALE STREET COMPLETES ITS TRANSFORMATION

Black business leader George W. Lee in his book, *Beale Street: Where the Blues Began,* called Beale in 1934 "the Main Street of Negro America."[16] Lee gives much of the credit for transforming Beale Street from a wealthy and upper middle class white residential street to a vibrant commercial street for blacks to businessman Robert R. Church, Sr. According to Lee, Church gained control of many of the businesses on Beale Street in the 1880s[17] when whites were leaving in heavy numbers. It was probably more like the 1890s when Church became the dominant owner of commercial properties.

Church was a man of enormous influence not only with Beale Street property, but with real estate contiguous to Beale. His monthly rent roll for his various properties was impressive. Church's Park and Auditorium on Beale near Fourth Street was built by Church in 1899. This was an imposing community center. Seven years later he entered the banking business when he opened the doors to his Solvent Savings Bank and Trust Company, the first black-owned bank in Memphis.

Beale Street became a mecca of fascinating businesses, colorful street characters and tragic social outcasts. Technically, a professional land economist would have described the street as "mixed commercial" after its pattern of businesses. Realistically, it was a polyglot street featuring dry goods and clothing stores, pawn shops, real estate and banking offices, saloons, gambling dens, theaters and houses of prostitution. Most of the latter were on nearby streets.

Lee in his book describes vividly the pulse of Beale Street during its height as the center of black business and social activity. In his portrayal of the typical weekend he wrote: "They bargain with the Jews for clothing, buy groceries from the Piggly Wiggly and fish and pork chops from the Greek, and sometimes moonshine in the 'blind pigs'." He goes on to say that on Saturday rural blacks came from the surrounding areas but they usually left by sundown. But Saturday night, Lee said, "belongs to the cooks, maids, houseboys and factory hands." This was the big night of the week for the urban blacks and Beale Street was lively.

Colorful characters abounded. There was Mac Harris, called the "King of Gamblers." In his obituary in the *Memphis Press Scimitar,* it was said of Harris that he "was known to have strutted down Beale Street in a cutaway coat, striped trousers and a wide felt hat, twisting his mustachios, his Vandyke beard trimly cut, his cane flashing in the lights."[18] Then there was Jimmy Turpin, the street's best poker player, who ran the gambling at the famous old Monarch;[19] and Estella Wiley, better known as "Ready Money," who was an easy touch for someone down on his luck. And hundreds more like these three were part of the Beale Street community. Whites operated many of the street's businesses, and they, too, were colorful characters in their own right.

Beale Street in its day was a very special part of life in Memphis. It was physically close to Main Street's commercial activity, but it was a street culturally detached from the white-dominated main stream of Memphis retailing and general business.

PENETRATION OF RETAILING BEYOND DOWNTOWN

After 1900 the tiny neighborhood grocery stores started to get major competition from aggressive chain food store operators. Duke Bowers, an active entrepreneur, opened his first grocery at Polk and McKinley in 1902 on a cash and carry basis.[20] He called the store the "Temple of Economy" and used as his emblem a St. Bernard puppy with the slogan: "You Won't Get Bit If You Buy of

Mr. Bowers." Bowers spread his stores all over the city. By 1912 he had 39. Later, in the 1920s he had his Mr. Bowers Stores, Incorporated at more than 100 locations at the time he sold out to the Kroger Company. The grocery business was following the people out to the suburbs. Clarence Saunders' biggest effort in the Memphis grocery store business came after World War I. Nevertheless, he had six Piggly Wiggly stores by 1917.

The advent of the private automobile brought forth the first drive-in service station at the corner of Poplar and Watkins in 1914. Soon two gasoline stations opened on Union Avenue and one on Mississippi Boulevard.

MEMPHIS ADDS OTHER FACILITIES

The physical renaissance of Memphis also included a variety of other public and private facilities which helped change the urban appearance. County political leaders in 1900 were urging that a new Shelby County Courthouse be built so local government could function more effectively. Despite some public concern about the tax rate in the 1909–10 period, construction was completed on the new $1.6 million courthouse covering the entire block bounded by Washington, Third, Adams and Second Streets. The architect was James Gamble Rogers of Chicago and New York, the same architect who later designed the Brooks Memorial Art Gallery in Overton Park. Of the new Shelby County Courthouse one promotional brochure referred to "its dignified Roman colonnades, its delicate bas-relief, and its heroic statuary, symbolizing the fundamental phases of municipal government."[21] One booklet described the building architecturally as the purest Grecian type. Another referred to it as partly Egyptian style. So while there was a difference of opinion as to its architectural style, the finished building was yet another symbol of civic pride to compliment Overton and Riverside parks and the Parkway system.

Sister Alexia and Sister Benedict of the Franciscan Order took charge of the newly founded St. Joseph Hospital in 1889, and by 1919 it had 300 beds. The University of Tennessee Colleges of Medicine, Dentistry and Pharmacy, founded in Nashville, transferred to Memphis in 1911 to take advantage of the larger clinical facilities available. This transfer helped strengthen substantially the medical economic base of the city, and to create a reputation for Memphis as a medical center in the South.

In 1912, when Crump was Mayor, the city purchased old Montgomery Park for $250,000 and established there the permanent home of the Fairgrounds. Political pressure was applied by real estate investors operating in the eastern fringe of the city. Robert Galloway of the Park Board felt that the old North Memphis Driving Park, near the present site of the Firestone plant, was a better park site. As it turned out, the city's selection was superior from the standpoint of location.

Both sites had been active race tracks at one time. Montgomery Park was built in 1884 by Henry A. Montgomery, businessman and founder of the New Memphis Jockey Club. Racing was popular in the 1880s at Montgomery Park and heavily patronized during the Spring racing season, which featured such stakes races as the Tennessee Derby, Gayoso Hotel Derby and the Peabody Hotel Derby. Racing ceased there after 1900. A new competitor, the North Memphis Driving Park, opened in 1901 only to close five years later when Tennessee outlawed pari-mutual betting. The latter park's biggest day was Saturday, 11 November 1905 when the legendary pacer, Dan Patch, set a world's record for the mile, one minute and fifty-eight seconds.

Colorful John D. Hopkins, a well-known amusement park entrepreneur, opened East End Park in 1904 and developed it into a successful private business venture featuring top flight entertainment and amusement rides.[22] Dancing and motion pictures were features along with a large artificial lake for boating. The Park closed in 1913 and went into receivership in 1914. The management claimed that its failure was primarily because of Tennessee's prohibition law and secondarily the new competition from amusements at the publicly-owned Fairgrounds and from the new downtown Memphis movie theaters. The Park remained open, but without vaudeville or movies, and of course, without alcoholic beverages. A 1916 ad read: "East End Park—The Cool Spot Where Your Dime Goes Furthest." This popular park was located near Madison Avenue and Morrison, just to the west of present day Overton Square.

Red Elm Bottoms was the home of Memphis' first professional baseball team beginning the 1901 season of the old Southern League. In 1915 the team's name became the Chicks. Russwood Park was built in 1921 at Red Elm Bottoms, and it was the home of the Chicks until the grandstand burned to the ground early in the 1960 season. The former site of Russwood Park is now occupied by Memphis Medical Center facilities.

The New Memphis

The urban land form changed dramatically in the 27 years from 1890 to 1917. The physical size of the urbanized area now dwarfed the compact city of the 1880s. Memphis began to get the physical improvements that characterized important American cities. Citizens were given more choices of places to live, to work, to entertain themselves or to be entertained. Commercial businesses matured, and offered Memphians and the regional population goods and services befitting a modern, progressive city. Adequate investment was forthcoming from the private utilities in order to provide the services when needed. But political leader E. H. Crump felt that their rates were excessive and that they were gouging the citizens.

Not all of the urban development was in the long-term best interest of the city. Land speculation and poor site planning in the suburban areas detracted from the efficient use of the land in many instances. The city did not act forcefully enough in demanding that developers adhere to coordinated planning, and thus for decades to come it was forced to pay a high social and economic cost for inefficiency in land use.

Still, the city did get into a healthy form of competition with rival Southern cities, and made decisions to build facilities that would not only serve local residents well, but would help the city attract new people and new investment. The next step then was to modernize its public administration and to turn its attention to concerns relating to the welfare of its citizens.

9

Mister Crump and Reform

Memphis was in a mood for a variety of reforms at century's end. The general public was demanding changes to improve the range and quality of civic and cultural amenities in the community. Although the rawboned days of the river-front and the tough fight to survive disease were over, citizens began to seek emulation of the civic reforms underway in other progressive cities. From various quarters in the city came demands to improve the quality of municipal public administration, the rights of the working man, women's rights, education, and the moral fiber of day-to-day life. Memphis had been experiencing great changes in its urban physical pattern and in its attitude toward a more diversified economic base. Now it also wanted to implement reforms of considerable political and social importance.

In many ways throughout the city's history economic decisions made by business leaders had been influenced by actions of local government. Similarly, many major business decisions of the power elite had done much to mold the local political process. At the most critical turning point in Memphis' history there seemed to be an interlocking of economic and political decisions. Memphis political leaders before the Civil War, through their generous extension of the public credit, supported all-out the most venturesome projects of the city's entrepreneurs. During the turbulent days of Reconstruction local government authorities, by their policies and budgeting practices, directly and indirectly controlled the city's business life. They rewarded their friends and punished their enemies. And during the 14 years when Memphis was without its charter the Taxing District and the State of Tennessee, in trying to get the sanitation system and other public works projects built while at the same trying to reduce overhanging public debt, had substantial influence on the climate of local business.

Both before and after the 1890s there is evidence of this strong relationship between local politics and business. City councils and boards of aldermen were usually for business despite the fact that many of these local legislators were not businessmen, and they were not identified directly with the prominent business families. With the exception of the Taxing District period seldom were any of the local public officials members of the old line, prominent families. There was a reluctance to serve. One exception took place in later years when in 1927 Watkins Overton was persuaded by the Crump organization to seek the Mayor's Office. Business leaders were interested in city and county government and demonstrated this interest by supporting major decisions to purchase and develop Overton and Riverside parks and the Parkway system. But prior to 1907, they did not appear to pay much attention to how their local governments were being managed.

Traditionally, the mayor had considerable influence over policy making and administration. Thus, a specific mayor's perception of management and his own management experience influenced the quality of local public administration. The three mayors preceding E. H. Crump were not businessmen, and this may have been one reason why Memphis was in such a state of disarray when the reformers moved into action. From 1893 to 1898 W. L. Clapp, an attorney and professional politician, was mayor. From 1898 to 1906, John J. Williams, who had been a County Trustee for three terms, served. Williams was succeeded by James H. Malone, a prominent attorney, who served until 1910.

The Memphis press from time to time questioned the integrity of these leaders, but much of it was done in the heat of mayoral campaigns. None of these charges amounted to any formal action. Of the three mayors preceding Crump, Mayor Williams was considered the most progressive mayor because of his work in accomplishing the huge land annexation in 1899, and for his promotion of sewer system extensions as a matter of protecting the city's public health.

During Mayor Clapp's regime the city issued $1.3 million in bonds. No bond issues were sold during Mayor Williams' eight years incumbency. But during Mayor Malone's four years, the city issued almost $2.3 million. On 1 July 1909 the city's indebtedness outstanding was $7.6 million. Over $3.0 million of this figure had been in water bonds. Great concern began to be shown at this point since the percentage of debt to the city's total assessed valuation for real estate was in excess of ten percent. This alarming financial status prompted an investigation of city government by a New York City nonprofit public administration organization brought into Memphis by the City Club, a Memphis "good government" body of civic leaders.

The City Club was organized in 1907 during the period of the municipal reform movement in America. Corruption had become commonplace in cities like St. Louis, Philadelphia, Pittsburgh, New York, Minneapolis, and San Francisco. Lincoln Steffens in his famous book, *The Shame of the Cities,* described vividly the corruption rampant in the major cities. The local City Club led by a prominent physician, Dr. R. B. Maury, became the standard bearer for clean politics. One of its first concerns was to undertake a study of the city's business methods and procedures. Since the City Club did not have the expertise to do this, it contracted with the Bureau of Municipal Research to make a reconnaissance survey of Memphis city government in 1909. This New York group undertook an exhaustive study of the status of municipal administration in Memphis, and prepared a comprehensive list of suggestions and reforms in administrative practices.[1] Concerning the status of the city's debt, the Bureau concluded: "The City has apparently decided to let the future take care of itself. It has hastened to assume obligations without formulating any definite fiscal policy looking to the retirement of the bonds issued, and it is today engaged in piling up debt without reference to consequence."[2] The Bureau staff was shocked that no provisions had been made for refunding the debt. No sinking fund had been set up, or serial bonds issued. The State of Tennessee had no statutory limit on the amount of municipal indebtedness at that time, but it did have the power to approve or reject a city's request for permission to issue bonds.

Strong support for the commission form of government was part of this reform movement in public administration. In 1909 business and civic leaders were convinced that a 5-person commission which would have combined legislative and executive powers could secure for Memphis far greater efficiency and control. A leading supporter of the movement was E. H. Crump, at that time a businessman as well as the City's Fire and Police Commissioner. Due to great pressure put on Tennessee legislators by Crump, Memphis secured approval from the state legislature through a charter revision. The changes approved by the legislature in 1909 implemented various fiscal controls. The new charter required competitive bidding on contracts exceeding $500.00 and voter approval of bond issues. It also allowed the city to set its own tax rate, not to exceed $2.00 per $100.00 assessed value. On 1 January 1910 the Commission form became a reality. For the next 56 years, Memphis was governed by this 5-member body. Birmingham voted favorably for the commission form in 1910, but one year later Atlanta voters rejected it as being too radical a change in the form of administration. Indeed, it was a radical change, and Memphis was considered very progressive for taking this revolutionary step.

In Memphis, each of the five elected members of the commission was given the responsibility for a specific administrative component of municipal government. The mayor also served as the Commissioner of Public Affairs and Health, and had certain appointive powers for special city boards. The other four members served as the Fire and Police Commissioner; the Accounts, Finance and Revenue Commissioner; the Streets, Bridges and Sewers Commissioner; and the Public Utilities, Grounds and Buildings Commissioner. This was the organizational format until the functions were reorganized in 1937. Shelby

County also adopted the commission form of government and it became effective in 1911.

Reformers had high expectations for commission government. Public sentiment was embodied in the strong campaign statement of E. H. Crump when he announced his candidacy for mayor in 1909. Crump explained:

> I desire to formally announce myself as a candidate for mayor of the city of Memphis at the November election.
>
> My chief reason for making this race is my profound interest in the success of the commission form of government which becomes effective on January 1, 1910.
>
> I have been a member of the legislative council for the city of Memphis for several years, and there had an excellent opportunity for knowing the wasteful, cumbersome, inefficient and unbusinesslike manner in which the large affairs of the city have been administered—even by those in authority who were both intelligent and faithful to their duties. I soon became convinced that the present form of government made anything like prompt and systematic business methods impossible, and therefore, although with no thought of becoming a candidate for mayor, together with other patriotic citizens, I aided in securing the election of a legislative ticket before our people upon a platform calling for a commission form of government, and earnestly advocated the same before the legislature at Nashville. I believed then, and believe now, that when properly and harmoniously administered, this form of government will be of inestimable benefit to our people if administered by those in sympathy with the ideas of an honest and progressive business administration.
>
> I had not originally contemplated running for mayor, as it involves considerable business sacrifice for me to do so, but I desire to see this form of government, which I aided in bringing about, and which I believe to be the best ever devised for an American city, wisely administered.[3]

In a hard fought election in 1909 Crump defeated former mayor John Williams by 75 votes. Crump got 5,894 votes and Williams, 5,819. The new mayor told the public in his victory statement: "I shall do all I can to make Memphis bigger and better." This was the start of Crump's power, and for the next 45 years he was the head of the Shelby County political organization which controlled the destiny of Memphis and the surrounding county area. He also became a powerful force and king maker in Tennessee politics, and a strong voice in the National Democratic Party. President Franklin Delano Roosevelt usually listened when Crump had a matter to discuss with him. Crump was elected mayor four times and served two terms in the U.S. House of Representatives. In his long career, he was elected to public office 25 times.[4] This was remarkable because most of the last 20 years of his life he held no public office.

William Miller in his book, *Mr. Crump of Memphis,* documents E. H. Crump's early life and rise to power after he arrived in Memphis in 1892 from his birthplace in Holly Springs, Mississippi.[5] Before becoming a bookkeeper for a carriage and saddlery firm in 1896, he was a clerk in a cotton brokerage firm on Front Street and in the office of the Galbreath Company, a prominent real estate firm. The partnership of Rehkopf and Crump was formed in 1903, but in 1906 Crump bought out his partner, and changed the name of the firm to the E. H. Crump Buggy and Harness Company. After the 1909 election Crump sold this firm. He did not enter business again until 1921, when he became a partner in the insurance firm of Crump and Trezevant.

Crump was urbane and socially suave, but politically he could be ruthless. A physically imposing figure, he was well over 6 feet tall, erect in posture, and dapper in dress. His hair was bushy and red, before turning snow-white in midlife. And his pink, smooth-shaven cheeks gave him a youthful look throughout most of his life. He always had a flair for capturing a popular public cause or attitude, and exploiting it politically. For instance, in addition to leading the way on reforming local government in 1909, he also jumped on the theme of loose living in Memphis. He promised the voters in 1909 he would rid the town of "easy riders," or pimps and gamblers. He commissioned W. C. Handy, then living in Memphis, to compose a lively, catchy song to serve as his campaign song. This was the origin of the song, "Mr. Crump," which contained the following great lines:

> Mr. Crump don't 'low no easy riders here
> Mr. Crump don't 'low it—ain't goin' have it here
> We don't care what Mister Crump don't 'low
> We gonna bar'l house anyhow
> Mr. Crump can go and catch his-self some air.[6]

This song played on downtown Memphis street corners during the campaign was later renamed "The Memphis Blues" and the words were changed in 1912. As far as the "easy riders" go, Crump did not run them off as promised. As a matter of fact he took a very tolerant position toward them, and only tightened their noose when he faced an unusual amount of public pressure during that period he served as mayor from 1910 to 1915.

Crump assumed a populist role in his attacks on the private utilities. In his later years Crump bragged about his standing up to the utilities. "When I went in office January 1, 1910, the utilities had a strangle hold on Memphis," he said, "the city was in shambles."[7] Crump did not like the railroads either. And later in his life he added the telephone company to his list. He blamed "the power trust" for trying to oust him from office in 1915.[8] When the Tennessee Supreme Court in a 1916 decision upheld the ouster of Crump from the Mayor's Office it was for his failure to enforce the state's liquor laws in Memphis.[9] Crump maintained it was the money barons of Wall Street, resentful of his attempt to have the City of Memphis purchase the light company in 1915, who manipulated his ouster from office.[10]

"Plan your work and work your plan," was one of Mr. Crump's many mottos which he adherred to in his long political and business life. After his ouster from the Mayor's office, he continued to tighten his hold on the political life of Memphis and Shelby County. He solidified his Shelby County political organization, while at the same time keeping a watchful eye on the matter of the efficiency of local public administration. Crump proved to be a very interesting reformer.

Labor Reform

Beginning in the 1890s conditions in workshops and factories came under close public scrutiny in Tennessee. Matters of concern were the hours of daily work, health and safety conditions in factories, child labor, and workmen's compensation. These were Memphis problems as well as statewide problems.

Regulation of work hours did not actually come under state law until the 1913–14 period. Tennessee imposed a limit of 57 hours a week for workers and prohibited a work day in excess of 10½ hours. Some trade occupations typically required as many as 60 hours a week. Many factory workers worked at least 54 hours a week.

The Tennessee Federation of Labor, the strongest force pushing for reforms of working conditions, was instrumental in pushing through the legislature in 1899 a factory inspection law to obtain cleaner air, better lighting, and adequate safety in factory buildings.

At this time child labor was a universal problem in the United States. It peaked about 1910, when nearly two million youths between 10 and 15 were working full time. There was great concern in the state that children were being exploited in mills and sweatshops. Again it was the Tennessee Federation of Labor which lobbied for protection of the very young. Prior to legislation in 1893 children under 12 years of age were found working in factories, workshops and mines. The Act of 1893 raised the age limit to 12 years of age, but exempted work in canneries. In 1914 the age limit was raised to 14 years, except in more dangerous occupations where there were heavy concentrations of dust, noxious and poisonous chemicals, or dangerous machinery. In Memphis this included paint and soap factories, cotton mills, woodworking industries, and dye rooms. Here the limit was 16 years. In 1900 the Bureau of the Census reported that in Memphis 15 percent of the nearly 11,000 children between the ages of 10 and 15 were family breadwinners.[11] Three out of four of these breadwinners were black children, and one out of every three was a female.

Tennessee adopted legislation in 1913 which made it compulsory for any child between 8 and 14 to be enrolled in public school for 80 consecutive days. And in the larger cities, the law compelled any unemployed child between 14 and 16 to attend school. Memphis had problems enforcing this new law because many of the rural migrants drifting into the city to seek employment were families with children who had been working, but were still below the minimum age permitted in Tennessee.[12] There were many conflicts with the child labor laws and the compulsory school attendance law.[13] However, there were many social benefits from the new child labor laws. A major economic consideration was the partial influence of the enforcement of these laws in lowering the illiteracy rate.[14]

Tennessee passed its first workmen's compensation law in 1919. Among Southern states Louisiana took action in 1915; Kentucky in 1916; and Alabama in 1920. Mississippi and Arkansas had no legislation as of 1920. Tennessee provided for a two-week waiting period, then a maximum weekly payment of $11.00 a week and a minimum of $5.00 a week.

Trade unions were numerous and well-organized in the pre-World War I period but strikes were infrequent. The greatest confrontation of the entire period was probably the strike called by the Retail Clerks Union against Bry's Department Store in 1917. Clerks at that time received an average weekly wage of $10.75 a week. Bry's competitors, Lowenstein's, Goldsmith's and Gerber's, paid their clerks slightly less. The Associated Retailers retaliated by closing all of the downtown Memphis stores on a Saturday to negate the clerks' plan to mass picket.[15] This action largely took the sting out of the union's plan to disrupt retailing.

"Equal rights to all; special privileges to none; justice, equity and the golden rule" was the motto of Brooks Local No. 1083, one of the 16 local units in Shelby County of the Farmers' Union. These chapters were at their height in 1914. They sought fairer credit practices, better methods of production and distribution, elimination of commodity speculation by boards of trade and cotton exchanges, and closer ties with all other labor unions.

TABLE 3
TIME BOOK—ALLEN ENGINEERING COMPANY—1910

Occupation	Wage Per Hour	Number of Hours	Weekly Pay
Pattern Maker	$.50	54	$27.00
Moulder	.39	54	21.06
Machinist	.37½	54	20.25
Machinist	.30	54	16.20
Carpenter	.30	54	16.20
Carpenter	.25	54	13.50
Laborer	.16⅔	54	9.00
Laborer	.15	55	8.25
Watchman	.17	70	11.90
General Foreman	($6.00/day)		36.00

SOURCE: City of Memphis Archives.

Wage rates in Memphis were not very different from prevailing wages paid throughout the United States. Jobs advertised in *The Commercial Appeal* in 1908 indicated that the following were typical wages: carpenters, $15 a week; laundry drivers, $15; grocery clerks, $12; watchmen, $12; and barbers, $10. Industrial wages were substantially higher as shown in Table 3.

The Business Men's Club in a 1910 publication, *Factory Facts and Figures,* advertised that labor rates in Memphis were 8 to 10 percent lower than prevailing rates in Pittsburgh and New York. In one example, it pointed out that common laborers earned 15 cents an hour in Memphis. An employer in Pittsburgh, however, would have to pay his laborers 16 cents an hour. In a testimonial, a manufacturer who had recently transferred his firm to Memphis cited the lower wage scale as one major reason for his decision.

Farm labor was paid an average monthly wage of $15.80 a month with board provided, and $22.30 without board. Blacks in the labor force were generally paid less than whites. Most black workers in this period were unskilled and were employed in menial jobs.[16]

THE STATUS OF WOMEN

Like women everywhere in the English-speaking world, Tennessee's women were struggling to gain the vote and upgrade their position. A fiery proponent of justice for women was publisher Elizabeth A. Meriwether, one of the most notable women in the city's history. She was the first Southerner to promote the cause.[17] As early as 1872 she was advocating the vote for women through her own newspaper and at public rallies. In 1897 Mrs. Meriwether organized the Tennessee Equal Rights Association to fight for equality of rights for both men and women.

One of the greatest demonstrations by the Memphis suffragettes was a giant parade and a rally at the old Lyric Theatre in 1916. Victory was achieved, at least as far as the vote is concerned, on 19 August 1920 when the Tennessee legislature ratified the 19th Amendment. Elizabeth Meriwether had died three years earlier, so did not see the fulfillment of her long crusade.

Women had made only token gains in business and the professions. In 1911 Mary Harry Treadwell and her sister, Georgia Harry, established a general insurance agency which became very successful. Very few women had entered the field of business prior to that time.

Two Memphians, Marion Griffin and Frances Wolf, were admitted to the Tennessee bar in 1907. They were the first women in Tennessee to gain this recognition after the State Legislature that year dropped the policy of sex discrimination in the legal profession.

PROHIBITION AND PROSTITUTION

Mayor Crump vigorously denied a claim that in 1912 Memphis had 1,700 saloons.[18] His estimate was about 500. Of course, this latter figure was a vast increase over the 131 saloons in 1890. It was not only the saloons that bothered a segment of the community. Gambling and houses of prostitution were also targets for their attacks on moral conditions in Memphis.

Saloons had played a big part in the business life of the city in the nineteenth century. The better establishments were patronized by businessmen and politicians. One saloon at 113 Madison was a particularly popular gathering place. One report says: "It was a meeting place of high class people. Cotton people from all over the South and as far away as England gathered there. Doctors, lawyers and even preachers used to come there."[19] There was also Tom Sullivan's on North Main "where judges, lawyers, and jurymen rubbed elbows as they tilted their glass."[20] But there were several hundred saloons not quite so fashionable, and many were centers of vice.

Opposition to these conditions spawned several major drives to mobilize public pressure against saloons, gambling, and prostitution. The Memphis Law and Order League in the 1890s brought in Sam Jones, a prominent Georgia evangelist, to rally public opinion. Subsequent drives were mounted. In 1912 a major study of vice conditions was undertaken by a New York crusader named Charles Steizle of the Men and Religion Forward Movement. In his report before a large assemblage of businessmen Steizle said:

> I've seen the names of your Memphis madames in bold letters on the doors of their houses. I recommend that the names of the owners be placed alongside them. These men are receiving exhorbitant rents; they are partners in the business. . . . You do not enforce your laws against the saloon. You must know that the non enforcement of law on one subject brings all law in contempt; and your young men will have the same contempt for all law that your officials have for this particular law.[21]

Memphis had looked the other way since 1909, when the Tennessee Legislature passed the Holladay Bill bringing prohibition to the State. The Memphis City Council, the Cotton Exchange, the Merchants Exchange, the City Club and the Businessmen's Club all protested this bill when it was before the Legislature.[22] When Crump became mayor he chose to ignore prohibition. This flaunting of the state's prohibition laws led ultimately to Crump's ouster from the mayor's office. Charges were brought against him in 1915 for violating a state law which provided for removal of any public official failing to enforce the state's edicts. In February 1916 the Tennessee Supreme Court upheld a lower court's finding that Crump had failed to enforce the law in Memphis. Crump had been legally elected to his third term, which was to have begun 1 January 1916. But pending the Supreme Court's decision, he did not formally take office. Once that decision was made, Crump took the oath of office then promptly resigned. For the moment prohibition had brought down the powerful leader.

"City's Underworld Wiped Out for Good," stated *The Commercial Appeal* headline on 17 July 1917. A subhead added, "Gayoso Avenue Panicky," and the story went on to describe how Chief of Police Hayes closed every house of prostitution in Memphis and that 1,000 prostitutes were planning to leave Memphis for St. Louis and Chicago.

These major demonstrations of law enforcement by the police, often staged for their publicity value only, did force the various vice operations into a somewhat more clandestine approach in their activities. Often, however, the political pressure being applied by City Hall on vice operators was temporary and lasted only until the uproar of church organizations and other moral forces died down.

VIOLENT CRIME

Public enemy Number 1 in Memphis for two decades before World War I was not a hardened criminal, but a New York statistician named Frederick L. Hoffman who annually in an insurance journal named *The Spectator* reported statistics on the murder rate in major cities. Year in and year out Dr. Hoffman's tables would show Memphis first in the number of murders per 100,000 population. According to Hoffman's measures for the decade from 1900 to 1910 Memphis had a rate of 47.1 murders per 100,000 population.[23] Charleston, South Carolina, was in second position with a 27.7 rate. A few years later Hoffman's statistics showed Memphis climbing to a spectacular murder rate of 89.9.[24] Atlanta was second with 31.8. The average for the thirty-one cities measured was 9.2 per 100,000.

Memphis was furious with Hoffman because of the bad publicity he was creating for the city. It questioned his statistics and his method of computation. The city leaders claimed that many victims who ultimately died in Memphis hospitals had been brought into the city for treatment following a violent act committed elsewhere.

The Commercial Appeal commented editorially that most of the killings were by blacks and that the bulk of the killing was attributed to "booze."[25] And it suggested that the remedy was to abolish the saloons, many of which were operated by unscrupulous white proprietors. *The Commercial Appeal* may have been referring to violent men like "Wild Bill" Latura, the hot-tempered, colorful, and notorious lawbreaker who was killed by Memphis police in 1916 outside of his saloon. Latura had executed a half a dozen or so blacks in local saloons and had escaped penalty. Another analyst claimed that murder in Memphis was the result of rural Southern migrants bringing with them rural mores which accepted the right of private vengeance.[26]

Memphis was understandably sensitive to the label "Murder Capital of the United States." Since Hoffman's figures were so widely disseminated through the popular magazine, *The Literary Digest,* it undoubtedly hurt the city's image and its appeal to industrialists considering relocation. Over the years Memphis received unfavorable publicity about its vice and violence in "exposé" articles in popular magazines of the day.

EDUCATION

Memphis did achieve good results in getting school age children into the public school system. In a city heavily populated by rural born people with a low priority on formal education, it increased enrollments from 40 percent of the school age population in 1890 to 71 percent in 1920. This was a rather remarkable showing considering also the large black population in Memphis and the handicaps these families faced in the day-to-day economy of that era.

In 1910, of those school age children between ages 6 to 14, some 80 percent of the white children and 60 percent of the black were in school. The percentage enrollment figure declined significantly after age 14, as many students left to join the labor force. The president of the Board of Education was concerned that so few boys remained in school to graduate and suggested adding an industrial or manual training program to hold them in school longer.

School buildings were built in response to this growing enrollment. In 1891 the city had seven schools for whites and four for blacks. Central High School, referred to then as "the capstone of the Memphis school system," opened in 1911.

The total school budget in the school year 1900–01 was $144,000. This was a modest budget and it was a prelude to a continuous history of underfinancing the public educational system. Teachers' salaries were very low. For example, the teachers received no salary increase from 1909 until they struck in the fall of 1918.[27] When 316 of the 400 teachers failed to report on 17 September 1918 the City Commissioners agreed to push the state legislature for permission to increase the school tax rate.

Despite growth of the public school system in enrollment and facilities, right after World War I it received a very poor evaluation from a federal government educational survey team. So, although the city did enjoy a reform in the public's attitude toward formal education after 1890 it did not achieve a quality educational system during this era.

Private education played an important role in Memphis in developing the educational resources of the community. In the 1890s the city had 31 privately-operated schools. The best known were Christian Brothers College, St. Agnes Academy and Le Moyne Normal Institute, a two-year school for blacks. Another school for blacks was Howe Institute.[28]

WORLD WAR I—END OF AN ERA

Memphis had witnessed many changes in the years immediately preceding the formal declaration of war by the United States on Germany on 6 April 1917. Its economy had diversified somewhat; its physical dimensions and its civic amenities had been greatly expanded; its municipal public administration for-

Fig. 18. Military aviation training at Park Field, near Millington, during World War I. (Courtesy of William Hatchett)

mat had been restructured; and its reputation as a open, vice-ridden city had come under severe public censure by large groups of indignant citizens. Memphis had seen many reforms as it matured into a more complex urban center in the South. The city appeared to be on the move in those years just before 1917.

War broke out in Europe in 1914. Not much notice was given to the war until the Germans brought submarine warfare to the Atlantic, disrupting American shipping. The torpedoing of the Lusitania on 7 May 1915 and the loss of 124 American lives caused a furor in the United States and created increased concern for what was happening in Europe. Memphis newspapers from that point on carried news of the war on page one. No effective attempts were made by Congress or President Woodrow Wilson to mobilize American industry prior to 1917 so there was little direct impact of the war in Memphis except for the matter of cotton shipments to England.

Memphis did take the war seriously from a patriotic viewpoint. On 3 June 1916 a huge "Preparedness Parade" was held to show President Wilson that Memphis was "first of all American and that Memphis is for preparedness first, last and always."[29] Some 20,000 were in the line of march, and thousands of others watched. When war was declared in 1917 a huge patriotic demonstration was held in Overton Park attended by a crowd of 35,000.[30] All-out war created a rush to the recruiting station to join up and another rush for marriage licenses to stay out.[31] The Selective Service Act, signed on 10 May 1917, inaugurated conscription in the United States. This inspired the "Registration Day" parade in Memphis on 5 June 1917 in which some 30,000 took part. Shelby County had 25,000 eligible men between the ages of 21 and 31. At war's end in November 1918 Memphis had 8,900 of its citizens in military service, and had lost 231.

Joseph B. Adkinson had been awarded the Congressional Medal of Honor. Memphians also supported the war through the purchase of $45 million in Liberty Bonds.

Memphis had indeed made a contribution to the war effort, but it did not receive many direct economic benefits from awards of wartime industries. The city was shortchanged in that department. One military base was established here. Park Field, near Millington, was briefly used as a pilot training center. Construction started in mid-1917 and the first students arrived in November 1917. All operations ceased after 13 November 1918 and the base was ordered closed by April 1919.[32] One of the few benefits of Park Field's brief appearance on the Memphis scene was that it stimulated interest in aviation locally, and many years later helped pave the way for the location during World War II of the Memphis Naval Air Station on part of this Park Field site.[33]

Nineteen May 1919 was declared Soldier's Day in Memphis and the last great World War I related parade climaxed the celebration. Officially, the citizens put the war behind them and prepared for a new era.

10

Memphis Only Yesterday

The veterans returned from World War I and the first act of the city was to help them get jobs. This was a high priority item for the Memphis Chamber of Commerce in 1919. The second item of business was to launch successfully the Memphis Centennial, a week long celebration in May 1919. Memphis wanted the world to know that it was the "Wonder City of the South" and that not only was it centered in the heart of the richest valley in the world, but it also had all of the advantages and conveniences of a metropolis.[1] One hundred years was behind it. And it had experienced traumatic moments. But now its leaders wanted to set their sights on the pursuance of greater economic well-being for its citizens and on the development of a greater physical city. The Centennial's celebrants eagerly anticipated the decade of the 1920s.

This chapter's title was inspired by historian Frederick Lewis Allen's book, *Only Yesterday: An Informal History of the Nineteen Twenties,* which portrayed vividly the great surge of urban growth and change in America.[2] It was the decade of the flood of automobiles; new streets and boulevards; traffic lights; car accidents; high rise apartments, offices, and hotels; land speculation; attractive suburban subdivisions; motion picture palaces; new factories; and other signs of material prosperity.

Memphians certainly felt the changes, although not all shared equally in the improved business climate and in the urban improvements which came in those relatively prosperous years prior to the Great Depression. The cost of living had started rising during the years preceding America's entry into World War I. Prices increased by more than two-thirds in the 1920s and made it imperative that Memphis attract new industries to help increase family income. Housing construction costs had increased 70 percent from 1914 to early 1921.[3]

Rents had been raised substantially, creating a storm of protests since 71 percent of Memphians lived in rental units in the early 1920s. The Civic Club undertook a study of the charges of rent gouging. Landlords retaliated by pointing out that rents in Memphis were 25 percent lower than in Atlanta and 50 percent under New York. The confrontation largely faded as the housing shortage of the immediate postwar years subsided.

PROMOTING BUSINESS

Memphis leaders made a commitment to stimulate greater economic development. Largely through the Chamber of Commerce in the early 1920s, a campaign was put on to focus greater national attention on Memphis.[4] *The Commercial Appeal* editorialized that thousands of people were ready to come if they could be convinced that Memphis would lower its homicide rate and enforce the law.[5] The Cotton States Life Insurance Company of Memphis sponsored an ad, captioned "Keep Southern Money at Home," which explained:

> The life companies of the East get more than $15,000,000 per year out of the Memphis Territory; why?
> Do you know if this money . . . were kept at home and deposited in our own banks, it would stimulate our trade in every line—seek investments in our resources—increase the Laborer's Opportunities and Earnings—make Financial Panics unknown and enable the South to take her rightful place in National Enterprise and Commercial Progress.[6]

Memphis leaders told the nation that the city had a good labor situation, and that it anticipated no trouble.[7] They pointed out that there were few foreigners here and that organized labor was not of much interest to the black working man in Memphis. Unionism in the South was on the rise as a result of labor unrest stemming from low paychecks and general industrial policies, but strikes in any number did not occur much before the late 1920s. Radicals were blamed for attempts to organize labor in the South. In Memphis industrial prospects were assured by business leaders that organized industrial labor had not made any challenges here, and probably would not try.

There was optimism in the city about the hardwood industry in the early 1920s but great concern about the future of the cotton market. Demand for hardwood from the North and Midwest regions was strong and the outlook for future markets looked bright. On the other hand, pessimism was rampant in the South toward the future of cotton because of serious overproduction stemming from World War I. In September 1920 a panic developed in the cotton market and prices plummeted downward. Memphis was the scene in December 1920 of a major conference of national cotton growers seeking ways to curtail production. One suggestion was to restrict credit to those failing to cooperate.[8] Stimulation of the export market was another recommendation. Prices fluctuated throughout the 1920s and production experienced wide swings, as illustrated in Appendix B. There was no sense of economic security in the crop on which Memphis had traditionally bet its future.

BLACK OUT-MIGRATION AND MEMPHIS COUNTERATTACK

The demand for laborers in northern industries attracted many blacks from Memphis and elsewhere in the South during World War I. Migration to the North and West by blacks had been underway for many years, but it became a major concern of the Memphis business community after the war. Blacks from Memphis had moved to Chicago and Detroit, then encouraged their relatives and friends to join them there. Slow industrial growth locally precipitated the outward movement. A special study of the problem was conducted by the Industrial Welfare Committee of the Memphis Chamber of Commerce. In its findings this group expressed concern over the adequacy of the Memphis labor supply and concluded "from an industrial viewpoint the negro labor is one of the best assets of this community."[9] The Committee appealed to Memphis businesses and industries to contribute funds to a program helping to improve living and working conditions for blacks. It promised seed money to help fund sound projects fostered by black organizations. Thus, Memphis business leaders tried to demonstrate to the local black citizens that they were very important to the city's economic future, and made a serious effort to reverse the outflow.

PUBLIC EDUCATION'S CONTRIBUTION TO THE CITY

The Memphis Board of Education, soon after the four-day teachers strike in September 1918, requested a study of the city's school system by the Bureau of Education, U.S. Department of the Interior. The team came in 1919 and after its study came up with this harsh conclusion:

> It is clear, then, when viewed from every possible angle, that Memphis is much below the average of American cities in the amount she expends upon the education of her children and far above the average in her financial ability to maintain her schools. Furthermore, it is perfectly clear that Memphis is well able financially, in comparison with other cities, to pay enough to make her school system the equal of any system in this country.[10]

It scored the low salaries, the poor methods of teaching, the poor facilities, and the fact that public schools were not only failing to meet the needs of the children, but also of the community. It blamed the city for being totally preoccupied with commercial growth and attempts to turn Memphis into a metropolis, while treating its schools as if it were a small village.

In a strange turn of events in 1923, despite the critical report by the Bureau of Education, the Memphis Board reduced the number of teachers and increased the number of pupils per teacher.[11] It had found that Memphis was below the national teacher/pupil ratio. Furthermore, the average per capita cost of instruction in Memphis was $57 while the national average for cities of 100,000 to 200,000 was $90. The superintendent, however, did not think Memphis looked so bad when compared with other cities.

The quality of education in the 1920s was definitely below the standards needed to provide for the training needs of a more complex and sophisticated industrial community which the city wanted to develop. It cost Memphis heavily in later years in the national competition for industry. Memphis lacked many of the desired job skills.

ROWLETT PAINE—BUSINESSMEN'S MAYOR

The business community scored a victory with the election of Rowlett Paine over former mayor John J. Williams. Paine was the handpicked candidate of the Committee of 100, a businessmen's group concerned about the turmoil in city government since E. H. Crump was ousted in 1915. In the brief span from 1915 through 1919 Memphis had seven mayors or acting mayors. The Paine-Williams contest was the first time women voted in a municipal election. Of the 10,000 women registered, some 6,000 voted. A total of 1,500 blacks voted.

Paine, a businessman, served two terms. He was defeated in the 1927 election by Watkins Overton, who had strong support from Crump's Shelby County political machine. It was during Paine's administration that Memphis implemented city planning and that downtown Memphis witnessed a huge construction boom of new commercial buildings, giving the city the look of a metropolis.

The 1923 election, however, was the highlight of Mayor Paine's political career. The Ku Klux Klan entered a candidate for mayor and also a slate of candidates for other local offices. At that time the KKK claimed 10,000 members in Memphis, the majority residing in the lower middle class white neighborhoods. Many of them joined when they felt threatened by the encroachment of black housing on their neighborhood fringes. With the strong possibility that the Klan might win, *The Commercial Appeal,* through its editor, C.P.J. Mooney, and political cartoonist, J. P. Alley, led an all-out attack on the Klan to expose them. Not until the final hour did the Crump organization commit itself to the election of Paine over the Klan candidate and a third candidate. Paine won 12,858 votes; Joe Wood, the Klan candidate, got 8,520 votes; and L. T. Fitzhugh, 3,892. When *The Commercial Appeal* was awarded the Pulitzer Prize in 1923 the citation read: "For its courageous attitude in the publication of cartoons and the handling of news in reference to the operations of the Ku Klux Klan."[12]

Paine had been a popular mayor with support from the Memphis Chamber of Commerce and other business groups. Why then was he soundly defeated by Watkins Overton in 1927? The answer lies in the decision of the Crump organization to put its total might behind Overton. Paine's political support of Governor Austin Peay in the 1926 gubernatorial primary alienated Crump. Also, the fact that Crump was unable to control the independent Paine the way he would have liked spelled doom for him.[13] It was a demonstration of total power by Crump carried out with military precision.

THE CRUSADERS FOR A MORE MORAL CITY

The 18th Amendment of the U.S. Constitution was ratified by three-fourths of the state legislatures by January 1919. Tennessee joined this group when it approved in early 1919 two amendments to prohibit the manufacture, sale, or transportation of alcoholic beverages. To enforce this new amendment Congress passed the Volstead Act in October 1919. After overriding President Wilson's veto, Congress put prohibition into force that same month. Of course, Tennessee had had its own prohibition law on the books since 1909, although it was frequently winked at in Shelby County. After the Volstead Act went into effect, illegal stills were operating all over the county, including operations on Presidents Island and in the North Parkway area near Overton Park. Similar to many other urban areas, bootlegging flourished in Memphis.

Opponents of bootlegging and vice invited fiery evangelist Billy Sunday to lead a massive revival campaign in Memphis in April 1924. A huge pavilion was built between Adams and Jefferson streets, called the Front Street Tabernacle, to serve as the center of revival. On opening day some 25,000 attended to hear Billy Sunday's assessment of moral conditions in Memphis. His opening statement of a particularly long sermon captured the prevailing mood of the community in the 1920s:

> Lord! I've been in old Memphis a week now. I got off a train and was glad-handed by the mayor, the preachers, and the businessmen. The key to the city is hanging in my room at the hotel. Lord, I want you to help me when I unlock the door and go after all the rottenness, meanness, filth, and vice in this town.
> Devil! You old scoundrel. You've had a pretty soft time of it in Memphis. You've had your own way a long time, but I'm out to get you. What have you ever done for this town, anyway? You've made all the rot gut liquor. You've been selling it to the people and making them drink the stuff. You've been filling the whisky cellars of the rich. You've been making moral lepers out of husbands. You've been robbing girls of their purity and young men of their decency and manhood.
> Now, it's time for a showdown; Come on, Devil! I ask for no quarter and I will give none.[14]

Business organizations, service clubs, and church organizations in Memphis joined in this revival. Mayor Paine had indeed given Billy Sunday the keys to the city as a token of appreciation for alerting the community to its condition.

Devastation in the Lower Mississippi Valley

Memphis and the Mid-South region felt the full impact of the flood of 1927—the greatest flood of record on the Mississippi to that point. The river went on a rampage that caused widespread loss of lives, damage to property, and mass suffering. Mississippi, Arkansas, and Louisiana were particularly hard hit when flooding inundated 2.3 million in valuable agricultural acres. Physically, Memphis was practically untouched; yet its economy, which was tied so closely with cotton and hardwood production in the Mississippi Valley, was seriously affected by the disaster.[15] Memphis was the center of relief work during and after the flood.

The nation's attention at the peak of this massive flood was not on the Lower Mississippi Valley, but on Charles Lindbergh's historic flight to Paris on the weekend of 21 May 1927. Yet the nation responded with an emergency aid program supervised by Secretary of Commerce Herbert Hoover. The latter, who was elected President the following year, proved to be a tough taskmaster in directing relief operations. One of his very strong suggestions was that R. Brinkley Snowden of the National Bank of Commerce take the lead in raising $5 million for low interest loans to landowners and sharecroppers.[16]

This devastating act of nature led to the passage of the Flood Control Act of 1928, which initiated a comprehensive protection plan including levees, floodways, channel improvements and new controls in tributary basins. The resulting work helped prevent Memphis from receiving the full brunt of the 1937 flood which was the greatest ever on the Mississippi River. The 1927 flood crested in Memphis at 46 feet. The 1937 crest was 48.7 feet at the Weather Bureau's gauge.

Memphis was probably fortunate that the 1927 flood brought new flood control planning; otherwise much of its industrial areas near the Nonconnah Creek and the Wolf River would have been destroyed in 1937. After World War II additional improvements were added by the Corps of Engineers to protect Memphis from any overflows into its low lying sections.

Population Increases—Industry Stabilizes

On Census Day in 1920 Memphis had 162,351 residents. Ten years later, the census count was 253,143. Shelby County's total population, including Memphis, increased from 223,216 to 306,482. Of the latter figure, blacks were 42 percent of the total.

Memphis provided more jobs to support this growing population, but the anticipated increase in industrial jobs still had not materialized despite new factories and other industrial activities which came in the 1920s. Industrial development in Memphis and in competitive cities of the South for the period 1921 to 1927 is shown in Table 4.

Atlanta and Birmingham experienced significant growth while Nashville and New Orleans had only a modest increase. Memphis retrogressed slightly.

Atlanta added numerous new industries and increased its numbers of jobs in the furniture category. Birmingham doubled its industrial jobs because of its blast furnaces, foundrys, and cast iron pipe industries.

TABLE 4

INDUSTRIAL GROWTH IN MEMPHIS AND COMPETITIVE SOUTHERN CITIES

City	Number of Establishments	Number of Wage Earners	Value of Products (millions)
MEMPHIS			
1921	311	10,174	$ 76.8
1923	258	10,508	95.5
1925	294	9,988	108.9
1927*	286	9,435	91.7
ATLANTA			
1921	490	12,660	79.8
1923	447	16,208	122.3
1925	429	18,208	131.2
1927*	428	18,583	115.8
BIRMINGHAM			
1921	258	8,778	45.2
1923	303	14,772	88.5
1925	295	16,054	100.2
1927*	321	16,611	109.0
NASHVILLE			
1921	279	11,120	73.3
1923	253	11,583	77.7
1925	224	10,549	79.3
1927*	221	12,975	94.4
NEW ORLEANS			
1921	708	20,288	117.5
1923	632	21,379	130.7
1925	661	22,118	155.1
1927*	679	22,289	151.9

SOURCE: Bureau of the Census, *Biennial Census of Manufactures,* 1921, 1923, 1925 and 1927.
*Data not available for 1929.

Memphis just could not seem to diversify its economic base, despite a clear recognition of its problem in being too wedded to the cotton and hardwood lumber industries. There was concern, too, that the city lacked both the labor skills needed to attract industry and modern management methods.[17] The Memphis Chamber of Commerce undertook a number of programs to try to develop interest in Memphis as a place to do business. It formed the Mid-South Development Bureau to promote the city within the region. It sponsored an industrial trade show, Made-in-Memphis Exposition, in 1928. The overriding theme of this one-week exposition was "more smokestacks and more payrolls."

Among the suggestions put forth were that Memphis attempt to attract cotton mills, iron and steel mills and automobile oriented industries. It was ironic that Memphis claimed title to being the greatest inland cotton market, yet did not have a complex of cotton mills. The Southern Railroad, in its annual reports of this era, pointed out that a source of its business was hauling coal from the Alabama coal fields to the cotton manufacturing centers of the Southeastern states. Since Southern served Memphis, this railroad could just as easily have moved the coal west.

Another proposal was that Memphis could be an ideal site for iron and steel industries. The reasoning was that the region had coal, iron ore, and limestone, and these raw materials could be hauled to Memphis much cheaper than to Pittsburgh, Chicago, or Birmingham.[18] This suggestion was made on several occasions, but nothing developed to bring the idea to fruition. The city did achieve some success, however, in attracting the auto industry to Memphis; and for a while the net contribution to the local economy was significant prior to the closing of those plants producing wooden spokes for wheels in the latter 1930s and the closing of the Ford Assembly Plant in 1958.

RETURN OF THE RIVER TO COMMERCE

Following World War I Memphis turned its attention once again to river transportation as an asset to its local economy. It began cooperating with St. Louis and New Orleans to popularize the use of the river. River commerce, which had practically dried up in volume after the 1880s, was more or less resurrected during World War I when the federal government established the Federal Barge Line-Mississippi-Warrior Service. Under government control, this service started with 40 steel barges moving between St. Louis and New Orleans. River tonnage at Memphis was only 411,000 tons in 1922, but had quadrupled by 1930.

Memphis floated a bond issue to build its Memphis River-Rail Terminal in 1923, and had high hopes that the benefits would stimulate additional business by offering shippers rates some 20 percent less than the railroads. Local officials believed that these rates might offset what they felt were the discriminatory class rates imposed on manufactured goods moving by rail from the South to the North.

The War Department operated the Federal Barge Line until 1924 when control passed to the Inland Waterways Corporation. Tonnage moved through Memphis continued to increase in the 1920s and 1930s; the bulk of the cargo hauled was agricultural products, coal, and other mineral products.

OTHER INDUSTRIAL ATTRACTIONS

Cheap industrial sites and the availability of natural gas were considered positive inducements to industry. In the early 1920s Memphis had an inventory of almost 3,500 acres of land in or near the city which it said could be utilized by industry. Prices ranged from $300 an acre for peripheral land to $700 per acre and up for land within the city. Much of the land zoned for industry was contiguous to the Belt Line system and some three miles of riverfront were available. Natural gas became available when a local company built a pipeline from the Louisiana gas fields to Memphis.

INDUSTRIAL ACCOMPLISHMENTS OF THE 1920s

Memphis added to its existing base. It solidified a strong position as a distribution center for agricultural products and steel products. It tightened its hold on the titles, "World's Largest Hardwood Market" and "The Hardwood Flooring Capital." In 1925 it had some 40 mills producing 300 million feet of hardwood lumber and it also had plants manufacturing furniture, hardwood flooring, boxes, and automobile parts from wood. E. L. Bruce Company began operations in 1921, and soon became the largest hardwood flooring manufacturer in the world. Other prominent companies utilizing wood were Anderson and Tully Company, Chickasaw Wood Products Company, Shannon Brothers, Chapman and Dewey, Memphis Furniture Manufacturing Company, and Fisher Tennessee Division of General Motors. All of these companies located in Memphis because of the nearby hardwood timber stands, the abundance of labor, and the transportation services offered to distribute their products.

Cottonseed oil manufacturing continued to grow. Thousands of tons of cottonseed were crushed in Memphis by such firms as Buckeye Cotton Oil Company, Perkins Oil Company, Southern Cotton Oil Company, Swift and Company, and HumKo Company. Locational advantages again were related to the ready supply of raw material—cottonseed—and the distribution facilities by water and by rail. Buckeye Cotton Oil, which became a subsidiary of Proctor and Gamble in 1930, added another reason. It saw a great advantage in having access to the huge underground water reservoir in Memphis.

The Memphis Packing Company, formed in 1919, called itself Dixie's largest home-owned packer. It operated from a 27-acre plant at Trigg and Riverside. This firm was acquired by Armour in 1935.

Kelsey Wheel Company, which opened in 1920, sold out to Fisher Body Company, a subsidiary of General Motors, in 1923. Kelsey retained its wheel division, but sold that operation to Fisher Body in 1934. Murray Wood Products Company came to Memphis in the late 1920s to manufacture wood parts for auto bodies. This company sold out to Fisher Body in 1935. All of these companies selected Memphis because of the nearby supply of hardwoods, the transportation network, and the large and stable labor supply. Changes in technology wiped out these automotive-related firms in the 1930s when auto manufacturers switched to all steel bodies.

Memphis had been a branch site for the Ford Motor Company since before World War I. In 1924 Ford moved from its small quarters on Union Avenue to a large single story assembly plant on Riverside Drive adjoining Riverside Park.

It was one of the 33 assembly plants that Ford had for cars and trucks. Ford operated here until it abandoned Memphis in 1958.

Cotton compresses and warehouses continued to expand. In 1922 this ad appeared in Memphis, placed by the Memphis Terminal Corporation: "The World's Largest Cotton Warehouse and Compress Terminal, Operating Approximately 250 Acres of Warehouses. All Cotton Handled Under Cover." The ad went on to claim that it was handling annually about 1,250,000 bales of cotton and that its storage rates were the cheapest. The location was part of the South Memphis Land Company tract where cotton warehouses were located right after 1900. The Federal Compress and Warehouse Company was formed in 1925 by a merger of 28 corporations owning 48 compresses and warehouses in the United States, including three in Memphis.

Again, the continued development of cotton warehouses in Memphis like the development of cottonseed oil, wood products, and steel distribution was an expansion of an industry already well established in the city.

MEMPHIS—THE MULE MARKET

The traction king on the cotton farm for generations was the mule. This great farm animal was ultimately "killed off" by the tractor—another technological change—in the 1950s. But during the mules' heyday they were in demand, particularly in the South. In the marketing of mules Memphis from the 1920s forward claimed the honor of being the "World's Largest Mule Market."[19] Other big markets were in St. Louis, Kansas City, Nashville, and Atlanta.

Sales took place via the auction market at the Union Stockyards on Kansas Street, Guyton Stockyards on West McLemore, the South Memphis Stockyards, Dixie National and several more mule commission houses. Colorful stories abound about the 51-year life of this Memphis activity that began around 1900. There were celebrities like Colonel M. R. Meals, the 350-pound auctioneer whose career spanned 31 years in the Memphis area. He claimed he once auctioned as many as 1,274 mules in one day and about 1.5 million in his career. The personable Meals presided every Monday and Tuesday at the Owens Brothers Horse and Mule Commission Company. As an auctioneer Colonel Meals had no equal; but as a prognosticator, he did not fare too well. In the 1940s he did not think the Jeep would replace the mule "down on the farm." But the mule was relegated to oblivion.

Memphis also served as an active market for other kinds of livestock. These markets were important as recently as the 1950s. But this component of the Memphis economy also vanished in the post-World War II years, leaving another void in the industrial makeup of the city.

ASSESSMENT OF INDUSTRIAL PROGRESS

No one could possibly accuse Memphis of not making an effort to grow, and to diversify its industrial base. The pity is that it achieved only a minor degree of success. What it witnessed unfortunately was a deterioration of its economic standing in the competition with rival cities of the South striving to become "metropolises." What went wrong to dampen the hopes of the city's business progressives for a stronger industrial community? Did any local action or policy in any way stifle growth?

Memphis did not have the labor skills to hold out as an inducement and this may have hurt the city more than it could have possibly realized at the time. But, it did have locational advantages, excellent water and rail transportation, a huge supply of artesian water, excellent industrial land, and a cooperative Chamber of Commerce to aid a newcomer industry. The reasons for its failure to attract a more diversified type of industry relates to the nation's image of Memphis as being only a cotton center and a hardwood center. In other words, Memphis' historic success with these two major industries may have been a promotional liability. Outsiders could not visualize the city as an industrial city like St. Louis, Birmingham, Louisville, or Cincinnati.

No evidence exists that E. H. Crump and his Shelby County political organization held back or discouraged new industries. Crump, as he demonstrated in the 1930s, was strongly anti-labor union, particularly industrial unions. But in the 1920s there was not enough cause to fear aggressive unionism as inevitable when outside industries moved in. Outwardly, Crump always appeared to favor industrial development for Memphis.

11

The Bartholomew Plan and the New Urban Land Form

Memphis streetcars were averaging 161,000 passengers a day on the 127-mile system in the early 1920s. The Chamber of Commerce called this transportation system the backbone of the city's daily commercial life and the chief contributor to the continual expansion of suburbia.[1] Downtown's Main Street was the heart of the system; and this focal point tied the city together physically and economically. A traffic survey by a consulting firm reported that four out of every five streetcars converged on Main Street between Jefferson and Linden.[2] Since Reconstruction days the streetcar had been a powerful force in influencing the city's land form. Residential, business and industrial locations were tied to the street railway system. Citizens in the compact 24 square mile city of the early 1920s had daily contact with this functional service.

THE AUTOMOBILE AGE

Once again as it so often had happened in Memphis a change in technology entered the scene and profoundly affected the character of daily life and the urban land form. The introduction of popularly priced automobiles and their ready acceptance by the consumer in the United States had an immediate impact in all large cities. Memphis was no exception.

Streetcar passenger volume dropped from 52.3 million a year in 1920 to 41.5 million in 1925. Automobile registrations increased from 19,000 in 1920 to 42,000 in 1925. By 1930, there were over 50,000 motor vehicles. This sudden surge of cars and trucks put an unusually heavy burden on an almost hopelessly inadequate street system. Easy access by auto from one section of the city to another was often prevented by the lack of crosstown streets, inadequate street widths, numerous street jogs, deadends, and railroad grade crossings inhibiting the free flow of traffic. Memphis, a city held together by a streetcar system, was a city poorly equipped to function with this new and popular form of transportation—the motor vehicle. It was obvious that something had to be done quickly to develop a more efficient network. Indifference to the uncoordinated pattern would seriously impair the daily commerce of the city and also destroy land values.

FRANK GIANOTTI AIDS THE CAUSE OF PLANNING

In 1920 the case of one Frank B. Gianotti versus the upper middle income residents of Union Avenue had much to do with alerting civic leaders to the growing problem of uncontrolled, mixed land uses cropping up throughout the city. Mr. Gianotti had been a thorn in the side of his residential neighbors because of the intrusion of his used car lot on their fine street. His displaying of cars under a blue canopy offended the homeowners. They called Gianotti's business a junk yard and an eyesore. Gianotti called his canopy a portable garage. He took offense at the accusation that he was running a junk yard, and claimed that his business was a combination used car lot and blacksmith shop. Justice prevailed. Gianotti was fined $50. A few years later he upgraded his property at Union and Lumpkin by constructing a greenhouse.

When the Gianotti episode first began, Memphis had no zoning laws to control development. This case, plus the spot encroachments of commercial businesses on Poplar, Union, and other traditional residential streets, created the climate for the acceptance of city planning in Memphis.

ADVENT OF CITY PLANNING

Direct pressure for action came from the city's principal civic organizations. The City Club, Engineers' Club, Rotary Club, Nineteenth Century Club, and the Chamber of Commerce all had active committees concerned with planning in 1919 and 1920. Members included the city's most influential citizens and property owners. Their collective voice was heard in City Hall. These organizations had a receptive mayor in newly-elected businessman Rowlett Paine in 1920. If there was one principal salesman for city planning, it was attorney Wassell Randolph, a distinguished citizen from before World War I until his death in 1970. Randolph carried the message for city planning to Memphis through extensive writing and speaking. His success was remarkable considering the fact that city planning was then only a recent innovation in American cities, and its effectiveness in aiding the development of more orderly, efficient cities was unproven as of 1920. Randolph was successful in his mission in Memphis because of affirmative support from the business and civic power structure. They bought the idea of planning to protect or enhance property values.

Mayor Paine established the City Planning Commission in early 1920. Wassell Randolph was appointed chairman and was joined by well-known architect Walk C. Jones and prominent realtor Edward B. LeMaster and five other citizen

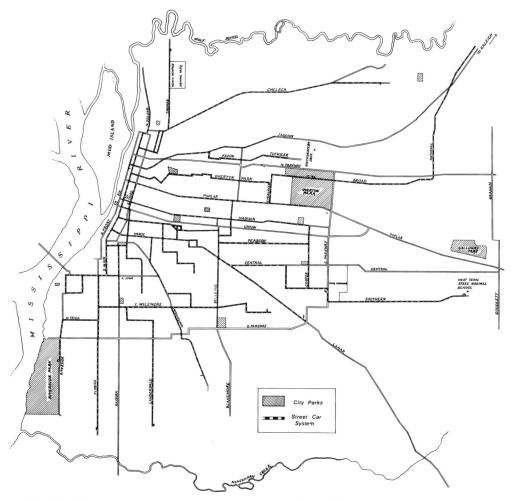

Fig. 19. The streetcar route system, as shown here for 1925, served most sections of the urban area. Service was frequent and convenient.

members, including two women. There were four ex officio members appointed from within the city government. Memphis had the first planning commission in Tennessee. Chattanooga and Knoxville created commissions in 1923, but by 1930 only Memphis and Nashville had active groups under powers granted by the state legislature.

State law also permitted zoning and subdivision regulations for Tennessee cities with at least 160,000 residents through 1921 legislation. So in its first two years of life the Memphis Planning Commission was given enormous powers and responsibilities that no other body had ever held in the regulation of how the city's land was to be used in the future. In the context of the early 1920s it was a radical step for Memphis.

The Bartholomew Plan

Memphis' first City Planning Commission was an extremely able body of dedicated citizens. They were sensitive to the city's problems and needs. They lacked, however, the technical skills to undertake the development of a formal plan for the city. Memphis leaders had been very interested in the planning efforts of St. Louis and had been aware of the 1916 *City Plan for St. Louis.* The planner-engineer of that city, who had done much of the technical work, was Harland Bartholomew, then a young professional just getting started in his long planning career. Mayor Paine brought Bartholomew to Memphis as a consultant and in 1922 he began work on the city's comprehensive plan.[3] This was the start of a consulting association with Bartholomew which would have a profound effect on land use changes in the city for the next half century. With some exceptions, the urban form of Memphis today is a product of the recommendations of the Bartholomew organization. Not all of their suggestions were followed over the years, so it would be unfair to attribute major planning flaws in the present-day city to this highly professional planning group.

Early city planning as a concept was oriented to physical planning, with less emphasis on economic and social planning of a city. Bartholomew personified this early approach to planning in his preparation of Memphis' first comprehensive plan. He directed his efforts to preparation of a zoning map and zoning law, a major street plan, and some recommendations on public improvements, such as viaducts, river-rail terminals, and public promenades, and on the perplexing problem of Mud Island.

Memphis reacted quickly by passing its first zoning ordinance in November 1922. Areas which were previously commercial were continued as commercial zones. Many of the major streets, previously residential, were zoned commercial in "strip" fashion. Third Street in downtown Memphis was zoned commercial and from the downtown the following streets were zoned commercial: Madison to Cooper, Union to Bellevue, Jackson to Trezevant, and Poplar in a broken pattern out to Overton Park. Lamar Avenue out to South Parkway was also zoned commercial, as was Cooper between Madison and the Southern Railroad. There were also many streets zoned commercial south of the downtown area. Land contiguous to the railroad tracks was designated industrial. The bulk of the city was given residential zoning designations.

The new zoning ordinance also included building height districts. Downtown Memphis was put under a height limit of 150 feet, or 12 stories. Bartholomew was adamant about his suggestions for building heights and undoubtedly influenced the city to go against a national trend at that time of building high skyscrapers. He felt that tall buildings in congested downtown areas were injurious to the city by compounding congestion and by shutting off air and light to pedestrians. Before Bartholomew's plan was printed in 1924 these height controls were compromised in the wake of high rise office building

PROPOSED TREATMENT
MEMPHIS RIVER FRONT &
THE ISLAND
CITY PLANNING COMMISSION · 1923

Fig. 20. This bold conceptual design was suggested in the early 1920s by the city's planning consultants for the development of the riverfront in downtown Memphis. (Courtesy of Memphis Room, MPL)

and hotel construction then underway in downtown Memphis in 1923 and 1924.

The comprehensive plan also concentrated heavily on problems related to the street system. Many streets were recommended for widening or straightening. Suggestions were made to eliminate many of the discontinuities. Bartholomew made major recommendations to increase traffic circulation, which when implemented later improved the matters of accessibility from one section of the city to another. Unfortunately, some of Bartholomew's suggestions for crosstown routes moving north and south between the Wolf River and the Nonconnah Creek were not implemented. This problem of the lack of adequate north and south crosstown routes persisted for the next 40 years and helped "force" development of the city ever eastward.

A schematic drawing appears in the Bartholomew Plan which portrays the downtown waterfront area and Mud Island as a grandiose "riverfront plaza" done in classical architectural style. He felt the city needed an elegant and dignified gateway as well as a functional promenade. Undoubtedly the City Planning Commission was aware that Bartholomew was including this concept in his report, and probably encouraged him to go all out for the idea. Good consultants usually gained clearance ahead of time before introducing "surprises" in their comprehensive plans. The plaza idea as well as the park recommended for Mud Island were not taken seriously by the city. This was unfortunate. It would have given downtown Memphis a major visitor attraction while clearing the area of the visual pollution and decay that was prevalent at that time.

Implementing the Plan

Union Avenue provided the setting for the first test of the city's then new zoning ordinance. In the case of *Spencer-Sturla Company* v. *City of Memphis,* decided in 1927 by the Tennessee Supreme Court, constitutionality of the city's zoning ordinance was upheld. Spencer-Sturla was operating a funeral home on the corner of Union and LeMaster Streets. The city had zoned this portion of Union Avenue a residential area and declared the mortuary was operating in violation of the ordinance. Spencer-Sturla contended that two blocks away on Madison a mortuary would have been permitted since that street was zoned commercial. The Court in its decision stated "that the similarity of the present development on Madison Avenue and Union Avenue two blocks apart, does not render arbitrary the action of the legislative council of the city in placing them in separate and distinct 'use' districts . . ." Since zoning was relatively new in the United States, this was one of the early test cases. It gave Tennessee cities the legal approval to proceed with their comprehensive plans.

Planning in Memphis in the early 1920s, supported by the work of Bartholomew, went far toward pushing the city into more orderly physical growth. The city had achieved another plateau in its efforts to build a very civilized urban society. The work of civic and political leaders during the Paine administration was as dramatic and as effective as the accomplishments of Robert Galloway and the Park Board in the early years of the century when the park and the parkway system were built. The product of Memphis' first city plan was a sound framework on which Memphis could build its future.

But the city was not quite through with its work in the 1920s. The city was concerned about air pollution and, for a period, it had the City Smoke Commission to oversee matters of air pollution. In 1929, through the promotion of E. H. Crump, Memphis created the City Beautiful Commission to help improve the physical appearance of the city. The work of that group began to show major results in the 1930s as the Commission successfully persuaded homeowners, businesses, and industries to improve the appearance of their properties and the city to clean up and improve the riverfront area. Memphis received many national awards for its work in keeping the city clean.

The Timeliness of the Plan

The Bartholomew Plan was implemented at about the height of the city's building boom of the 1920s. In 1924 some 2,400 housing units were built, the peak year during the decade. Downtown Memphis also experienced its top construction year in 1924. The timing was faultless. Zoning had already been implemented and the city was also operating under a 1921 state law permitting it to exercise control over residential subdivisions inside Memphis and within a 5-mile zone encircling the city.

The housing market was very strong beginning about 1922; and it remained strong until 1930 when the first effects of the Great Depression became quite apparent in the construction statistics. Throughout the decade some 18,150 units were built. Of this total 10,700 were single family homes, 2,850 duplex units, and 4,600 apartment units.

The majority of the single family houses built were in East Memphis subdivisions beyond the Parkway system. Higher priced homes were built in such exclusive residential developments as Chickasaw Gardens, Hein Park, and Red Acres.

Chickasaw Gardens was subdivided in the 1926–1927 period by an investment group from Louisville, Kentucky, called Garden Communities Corporation. The 463 lots in the original subdivision were laid out by planner Harland Bartholomew, author of the city's *Comprehensive Plan*. The tract was previously part of the Clarence Saunders estate, Cla-Le-Clare, which was sold in bankruptcy proceedings against the grocery chain king in the early 1920s. Advertisements proclaimed the subdivision as "the most exclusive" in the city, and that all applicants would be carefully screened to guarantee the high social standing of the community. The Pink Palace Museum building is on the site of the old Saunders estate. It was built to be Saunders' home, but it had not been completed at the time of his bankruptcy.

In 1921 Southwestern Presbyterian University (now Southwestern at Memphis) selected a 100-acre tract owned by the Fargason, Snowden, and W. A. Hein estates on the North Parkway opposite Overton Park for its new campus. Immediately adjacent on the eastern side of this tract was additional property owned by the family of Will Hein, a prominent businessman. This latter property was subdivided in 1923 and the development was given the name of Hein Park. Although the ads announced, "Lots at Popular Prices," the subdivision became an enclave of wealthier residents in fashionable homes. Red Acres, an exclusive subdivision surrounding Galloway Park near the northeast intersection of Poplar and Highland in East Memphis, was developed from a 136-acre tract by developer H. W. Brennan. To add to the appeal of his subdivision Brennan gave the city 120 acres of the original 256-acre tract to build a golf course and other recreational facilities. This permitted him to design his subdivision around the golf course. To maintain a high quality for his subdivision Brennan placed a minimum housing cost provision in his deed restrictions. Houses fronting on Galloway Park had to cost at least $10,000 (1923 prices); those fronting on Poplar or Highland, $8,000; and those on other streets, $6,000. A major lawsuit occurred when one owner with a house facing the park was challenged on the matter of the cost of his unit. Some of his neighbors reacted negatively to his architectural style and took him to court on the question of the cost of his house.

NONRESIDENTIAL FACILITIES

The 1920s was a period of building many types of nonresidential facilities. Russwood Park, home of the Memphis Chicks of the Southern Baseball League, opened in 1921 near the Baptist Hospital and, until its grandstand burned down on Easter Sunday 17 April 1960, it was the site of white professional baseball in Memphis. In the early years some college football games were played there. The Chicks won the pennant in 1921 and drew 253,000 fans that first year. They also won pennants in 1924 and 1930. The Memphis Red Sox of the Negro American League played at Lewis Park near Booker T. Washington High School in the late 1920s. Later the team moved to Martin Stadium at Crump and Lauderdale.

The exclusive Memphis Hunt and Polo Club in 1923 purchased a 70-acre site for about $400 an acre near Park Avenue and Cherry for its private facilities. It sold the property in 1953 and moved much further east to Shady Grove Road.

One of the most significant events of the decade was the dedication of the Memphis Municipal Airport in 1929. As early as 1919 the Chamber of Commerce had a committee exploring the potentials of a municipal airport. The Chamber felt that much business and many tourists would be coming to the city by plane. The air mail system had been started in the United States in 1919, and Memphis wanted an air mail route. In the 1920s there were a few airports in Shelby County for private planes, but they were inadequate. Armstrong Field near Woodstock, which opened in 1926, was the best local field available. Another field called New Bry's Airport was located on the north side of Jackson near Warford.

Perhaps the major impetus to building a municipal airport was supplied by two famed aviators who came to Memphis to make a plea for commercial aviation. Charles A. Lindbergh flew into Memphis in his *Spirit of St. Louis* monoplane in October 1927. At a banquet in his honor at the Peabody Hotel, Lindbergh made a special appeal to Memphis to undertake a progressive air program to keep the city in the forefront of American aeronautics.[5] He told his local audience that the nation's important cities were moving ahead in the development of municipal airports. A few months later Captain Eddie Rickenbacker told the Chamber of Commerce that Memphis was ten years behind in aviation progress. In alluding to Mud Island as a possible airport site, Rickenbacker said:

> Providence protects the weak. This is true in the case of Memphis. Here you have done nothing—comparatively speaking—for aviation,

and all the time you have the finest airport site in the world at your door—given you by this Providence.[6]

Rickenbacker's slap at Memphis' wrist worked. The Memphis Airport Commission was created soon after and began looking for a site. Mayor Overton and the new Commission stated that they were not necessarily committed to Mud Island if another site could be found at a minimum cost. Luck was with Memphis when after looking at 14 sites, the committee found a 200-acre site at Winchester Road and old Airways which it could lease. Later the city purchased the site for $250,000. Over the next half century Memphis added on to this original site and today it is the showcase Memphis International Airport, a complex of some 3330 acres.

The original airport handled four flights a day in 1929. Ten years later it had 30 flights in and out daily, and it was served by American, Eastern, and Chicago and Southern (now Delta) airlines.

THE CENTER OF BUSINESS

If downtown Memphis had a golden era of business prosperity and flamboyance, it would undoubtedly be the 1920s. It expanded enormously in the physical and economic scope of its commercial activities. Business expanded onto adjacent streets because of space limitations in the premier blocks of Main Street. This movement enlarged the physical area considerably as office buildings, banks, hotels, and some movie theaters selected locations near the heart of Main Street retail activity. A multitude of new buildings were constructed in a spate of activity by local and outside investors who saw opportunities for expanded retail trade and entertainment, and new offices and accommodations for business, tourist and convention visitors. It had been about 10 years since Memphis last had major additions to its downtown area. Changing times, population growth, prosperity and pent-up demand converged to give downtown Memphis impetus to expand in the '20s.

Property values reflected the economic strength of the downtown. Front foot valuations on South Main property from Madison to Union were $6,000 to $7,000. In 1920 the old Peabody Hotel, then an antiquated facility, was given the highest property valuation at $1,750,000 by the State Board of Equalization. The Exchange Building at Second and Madison was second, and the Gayoso Hotel at Main and Gayoso was third in valuation. A parcel at the southwest corner of Union and Front Street sold for $36 a square foot in 1927. Five years earlier this same site was purchased for $5 a square foot.

The old Peabody Hotel at Main and Monroe was considered the premier site for Lowenstein's new department store and the old hotel came down in 1923 to make room for a new eight-story building to house Lowenstein's. The new building was erected by the Snowden family, who owned both the land and the old hotel. Lowenstein's felt it had the very best retail site in the downtown area.

Woolworth's signed a 20-year lease in 1924 for $600,000. Kress renewed its lease for another 26 years in 1924. Both had Main Street locations. Britling's opened its cafeteria at 155 Madison in 1921 on the site of the old Clarendon Hotel. These commitments to downtown Memphis were typical of the faith major retail firms had in its future.

Memphis promoters claimed that the city had the longest "White Way" in the South. They were referring to the movie palaces which were opened on Main Street, and right off it in the 1920s. From North Main Street to the Beale Street area Memphis had a number of low priced, nondescript movie theaters as well as the elegant movie and vaudeville houses. Most of the major theaters were in the heart of the prime Main Street retail area.

Loew's State, a 2,235-seat theater, opened at 152 South Main in 1920. It had vaudeville and first run movies until 1932 when it dropped vaudeville. The theater survived until 1970 when it was razed for an urban renewal project. Loew's Palace, located on Union between Main and Front, opened in 1921. The theater featured a pipe organ with over 300 tone combinations. It was the first Memphis theater to show "talkies" in 1928. Loew's Palace closed in 1977 and it is currently being used as a church auditorium.

Pantages opened in 1921 and later changed its name to the Warner in 1929. This elegant theater with two balconies had an architectural style which its owners described as "symbolic of Italian Renaissance." It closed in 1968 to make way for the National Bank of Commerce's new facility, Commerce Square, on Main Street.

The Orpheum Theatre, a 2,800-seat facility, built at a cost of $1 million, opened in 1928 on the site of the Grand Opera House which had been destroyed by fire. It was originally part of the RKO circuit of theaters, and featured stage shows and movies. Opening night in 1928 brought out Memphis' society in full for the dedication. The theater struggled for economic survival during the 1930s and for several periods it was closed. RKO went bankrupt and defaulted on the lease in 1933. The management claimed vaudeville was dead in Memphis. M. A. Lightman, president of Malco Theatres, leased it in 1935 and struggled with it for a period before it closed again. It last operated as a movie theater in November 1976. The theater was purchased that year by the Memphis Development Foundation for use of the performing arts.

In 1924 when the jointly financed city and county Auditorium and Market House opened Memphis at last had a major public facility to serve as a cultural-entertainment complex and a convention center. This public center had been in the discussion and planning stage for 12 years prior to its opening. The prime mover in getting the complex built was Robert R. Ellis, after whom the facility was renamed in 1930. For many years this civic auditorium, which is now part of the Cook Convention Center, served as the site of circuses, trade shows, boxing, road shows, lectures, and convention meetings. Great entertainers and personalities appeared there on a frequent basis. Along with the movie houses, and their vaudeville entertainment, downtown Memphis had a strong entertainment economic base.

The construction of the Auditorium stimulated investor interest in several new hotel ventures which were under consideration at the time. The Chamber of Commerce was extremely helpful not only in attracting investor interest, but also in helping investors raise additional capital. The Chamber helped the promoters of the Claridge sell stock in the venture and was behind all of the projects because it felt Memphis urgently needed hotel rooms if it were to develop and prosper as a business center.

The Claridge opened in 1924, and looked toward increased convention business to support the new rooms it added to the city's inventory. The new Peabody opened in 1925 and the Elks Hotel, later renamed the De Voy and still later the King Cotton Hotel, opened in 1927. Other new hotels appeared to give the city still more guest rooms.

The Chamber of Commerce organized the Convention and Tourist Bureau in 1925 and with a budget of $26,000 announced to the world that "Memphis is ready for conventions" and that its operating funds were an investment in the future of Memphis. Over the 14-year span to 1939 an estimated 600,000 convention visitors came to Memphis. It was unfortunate for Memphis that the Depression years came so soon after the Chamber of Commerce launched its campaign to promote convention business. It was a very bad break for the city which had accomplished so much in building the basis for attracting conventions.

At the time of the announcement that the old Peabody Hotel was going to be demolished, R. Brinkley Snowden also announced that his Memphis Hotel Company was going to build a new Peabody Hotel on Union Avenue between Second and Third Streets. Two years later on 1 September 1925, this new 12-story, 625-room hotel opened. The construction cost was about $5 million. Its architect was Walter W. Ahlschlager of Chicago.

The new Peabody became the center of Memphis social life, and during its early years, a financial success. The Memphis Hotel Company which owned the Peabody, Gayoso and Chisca went into bankruptcy in 1934, but the Peabody Hotel was placed into a new corporation, the Peabody Hotel Company, owned largely by the Snowden family. The famous ducks and their daily ritual of parading through the lobby were introduced in the early 1930s and added to the wide reputation of the hotel. Of the Peabody Hotel, David L. Cohn in his book, *God Shakes Creation,* said:

> The Mississippi Delta begins in the lobby of the Peabody Hotel and ends on Catfish Row in Vicksburg. The Peabody is the Paris Ritz, the Cairo Shepheard's, the London Savoy of this section. If you stand near

Fig. 21. The well-known Hotel Peabody, shortly after its opening in 1925. (Courtesy of Memphis Room, MPL)

its fountain in the middle of the lobby, where ducks waddle and turtles drowse, ultimately you will see everybody who is anybody in the Delta.[7]

The major hotels were very competitive and continuously added entertainment facilities to attract a clientele. The Peabody had its famous roof and a typical summertime ad in 1928 announced:

The Hotter the Night—the More You'll Enjoy C–O–O–L Peabody Roof Where the Mississippi River Breezes Blow. Dance Tonight to the Sparkling Music of "Slim" Lamar and His Argentine Dons. $1 per Person.

The other hotels had similar night clubs offering dancing and entertainment.

Office Building Boom

Downtown's skyline changed dramatically in the 1920s as a result of a boom in office building construction. One million square feet of commercial office space came on the market between 1923 and 1929. The city's growth was attracting more insurance and real estate agents, more manufacturers' representatives, bankers and brokers, physicians and surgeons, dentists, attorneys, accountants and architects. The professional and business service individuals and firms created a huge demand for more leasable office space. Older, successful buildings like the Exchange Building at Second and Madison were full, and rental rates permitted the owners to make a good profit from their investment. The potential for new high rise office buildings looked very good.

In rapid succession the city saw the opening of the Shrine Building, the Columbian Mutual Tower, the Cotton Exchange Building, the Cotton States Life Building, the Dermon Building, the Farnsworth Building, the Medical Arts Building and the Sterick Building. Only the Columbian Mutual Tower (now the Lincoln American Tower) and the Farnsworth Building were built on Main Street. The others were constructed nearby on principal downtown streets. The physical design of the heart of the downtown commercial district more nearly resembled a square instead of its previous rectangular pattern.

When the 22-story Columbian Mutual Tower at Main and Court opened in 1924 it was advertised as the city's tallest building. Five years later when the 29-story Sterick Building was completed, it became the tallest building and remained so until 1964, when developer Harry Bloomfield completed the 450-foot 100 North Main Building. The Sterick Building, built on the site of the ornate Napoleon Hill mansion at Third and Madison, was described by its developers, former Texas Governor Ross Sterling and architect Wyatt Hedrick, as being "secular Gothic architecture executed in modern set-back style." This particular building became an instant landmark in Memphis, and its entry into the downtown landscape capped the final wave of construction there until well after World War II. Unfortunately, too, the Sterick Building was the first of the major buildings to go into bankruptcy. Two years after it opened officially in 1930 it went through the first of a series of financial crises in its 50-year history. The building is still one of the most distinctive high rise buildings in Memphis, and stands as a monument to the glory days of downtown Memphis when construction flourished and hopes ran high.

DOWNTOWN BANKING

The major event in downtown banking in the 1920s was the merger movement. Part of the growth in deposits, loans, and discounts in the principal banks was the result of merging with smaller banks. Union Planters merged with several smaller banks. First National Bank merged with the prominent Central State National Bank in 1927 and the Bank of Commerce merged with Commercial Trust and Savings in 1923. These mergers reduced the number of banking organizations operating in Memphis during the 1920s. As physical evidence of the growth of banking business, the Bank of Commerce moved into its new headquarters at Second and Monroe in 1929.

The building and loan associations, forerunner of today's savings and loan associations, were conspicuous in the residential lending field. Leader Federal, then called Leader Building and Loan Association, occupied the ground floor of the Porter Building at 10 North Main. It became Leader Federal in 1934.

The failure of the black-owned Fraternal and Solvent Savings Bank and Trust Company in 1927 sent shock waves through the black community. The 28,000 depositors received only about nine cents on the dollar in the liquidation proceedings. Not only was it a major blow to Memphis blacks economically, but it was also a jolt to the pride of the black business community. This bank was the result of a merger just two months before the collapse of the Solvent Savings Bank, which started in 1906, and the Fraternal Savings Bank, which was organized in 1910.[8] Both banks had been heavily involved in real estate loans and in the financing of ill-fated business ventures. Loose lending practices brought the banks down.

Suburbanization of Retail Stores

With all of the attention being directed to building in downtown Memphis, little attention was being paid to the first signs of a retail movement into the city's residential areas and its suburbs. It was not a significant occurrence in terms of dollar volumes of retail stores, and downtown merchants paid little attention to it.

The first inroads into downtown retailing, except for groceries, were in the latter 1920s. The following notice placed in *The Commercial Appeal* on 6 April 1929 more or less identified a problem for customers which seemed likely to get more serious as the number of automobiles increased:

> To relieve its customers of the inconvenience of parking in the Downtown congested area, the House-Bond Hardware Co. is opening neighborhood stores throughout the city. The locations ... are selected with the plan of offering the present day shopper a convenient spot to park her car without violating traffic regulations.

Sears Catalog Order Plant and Retail Store, which opened in 1927 at North Watkins near North Parkway, probably created the most dramatic challenge to major downtown department stores. Although this facility was in an older established neighborhood, it nevertheless could be classified as a suburban store. Downtown interests certainly must have taken notice of the opening day crowd of 47,000 people. The City of Memphis also assisted Sears by helping to get streetcar service to the facility.

Traditionally, grocery stores had located in the residential neighborhoods to be near their customers. But downtown Memphis also had food markets. Seessels had its first store downtown and so did Clarence Saunders with his initial Piggly Wiggly stores. After World War I, however, the chain store concept caught hold, and the food markets then entering the residential areas were bigger and much better equipped than the "Ma and Pa" type markets that at one time were predominant on many street corners.

THE CHANGING SCENE

The 1920s was a progressive decade for Memphis. It became a better developed city physically and it enjoyed a reasonably good business climate, although it did not attract a significant amount of new industry to underpin the local economy. Probably the biggest advancement the city made was in the field of planning and land use controls. It had succeeded in implementing a system of organization for controlling the type and the direction of growth, and for insuring a more functional city. Memphis pretty much had control over itself and the public's will decided how the land area would be used. Memphis wanted a planned city and was willing to use its police powers to implement it. The pity is that conditions changed in the 1930s and the public's priorities changed.

Memphis political leaders, ever sensitive to the population count, ended the 1920s by approving the annexation of some 88,700 people residing in a 24.5 square mile zone surrounding the existing boundaries. The action was completed in time for inclusion in the 1930 federal census count. Mr. Crump, Mayor Overton, and others in the Shelby County political organization wanted Memphis to continue in the competitive population race with rival Southern cities. The annexation was logical, and it conformed in its physical scope to the planning objectives outlined by the Bartholomew Plan.

As in other cities, grocery stores followed the city's expansion as Mr. Bowers' Stores and Piggly Wigglys spread throughout the residential portions of the city. Both operations had started before the war, but their major expansion came in the 1920s. Liberty Cash Grocers, a chain established by Fred Montesi, started about 1920; by 1931 there were 65 stores when Montesi sold out. The WeOna Food Stores, a cooperative buying organization, did not start operating until 1930. The Kroger Company entered the Memphis market largely through its purchase of 57 Piggly Wiggly stores soon after Clarence Saunders went bankrupt in 1923. It purchased another 26 units of Saunders' stores in 1931. This was four years before Kroger opened its "Kroger Master Store," an early version of the supermarket concept.

INFLUENCE OF CLARENCE SAUNDERS

Saunders' Piggly Wiggly stores, credited with being the forerunner of today's supermarkets, spread from Memphis throughout the nation prior to his financial collapse in 1923. There were over 1200 stores at that time. A unique floor plan, which Saunders had patented, was the feature of what he called his self-serving stores. Customers entered through a turnstile, then took a planned circuitous route through the counter areas in much the same manner as today's food market shopper. Wood railings separated sections. Customers brought their wooden baskets of groceries to the final stop, which Saunders called the

Fig. 22. Clarence Saunders, the colorful founder of the Piggly Wiggly food market chain and other grocery ventures. (Courtesy of Memphis Room, MPL)

"paying station." His concept gained wide appeal in Memphis and elsewhere with the general public of half a century ago.

In the mid-1920s, after Saunders had been voted out of control of the Piggly Wiggly Corporation, he started another chain called "Clarence Saunders, Sole Owner of My Name" stores. This venture failed in the early Depression years before it achieved much success. But Saunders was not done yet with the retail grocery business. In the late 1930s he began experimenting with a system of automating the sale of food. His idea was a mechanical grocery without counter clerks. The customer would use a key to open the different doors to take items from a chute. He christened his first Keedoozle store in 1939. Problems with the system resulted in unusually high operating expenses and after about 10 years of experimenting, Saunders gave up this particular venture. At the time of his death in 1953 when he was 72 Saunders' plans for another type of automated food market were on the drawing board.

Saunders, with his great flair for the dramatic and his innovative retailing concepts, had a profound influence on the merchandising of retail food in Memphis. His gimmicks and his store designs were a distinct challenge to the established practices of selling groceries at the retail level. His aggressive marketing techniques helped create a stronger competitive environment for the major retail chain organizations operating in the city. In terms of land use, Saunders was aware of the importance of good locations for his Piggly Wigglys, and for his later retail ventures, "Sole Owner of My Name" stores and the Keedoozles. His gimmicks worked usually because he had good locations.

Whenever competitors to Saunders made a move, they no doubt did it looking over their shoulders to see what Saunders was doing. He was a controversial figure in many ways. He carried on his various political crusades, many against Crump, with massive, hardhitting advertisements in the daily newspapers that resembled in format his intriguing grocery ads. Saunders was a masterful innovator in the grocery business who made life interesting and entertaining for Memphians for 35 years while helping change the commercial landscape.

12

Ravages of the Great Depression

The final year of the 1920s started off on a fairly low key. On 4 March 1929 Herbert Hoover was inaugurated as the nation's 31st president. In his inaugural address, the emphasis was on enforcement of Prohibition, maintenance of world peace, and court reform.

Hoover was concerned about the plight of the American farmer, and one of his first actions was to call a special session of Congress to pass a farm relief bill. Agriculture in the South, as in other regions, was in a crisis situation and had not enjoyed the benefits of the relatively prosperous 1920s. Cotton prices were falling in 1929 and many farmers went bankrupt.[1] Hoover was successful in getting Congress to approve the Agricultural Marketing Act in 1929 to aid farmers in handling the problem of surpluses. One year later the protective Smoot-Hawley Tariff was passed. Most of the South was against high tariffs as they had been traditionally in matters of tariff policy.[2] Cotton was a sick commodity in 1929 and legislation designed to alleviate its problems was both ineffective and too late. The price had fallen from 20.2 cents per pound in 1927 to 16.8 cents in 1929. In 1930 it fell to 9.5 cents and in 1931 to 5.7 cents. Agriculture was on the brink of collapse as the decade of the 1930s approached. And Memphis mirrored this crisis.

"Black Thursday," 24 October 1929, initiated the downward break in the stock market. Stocks were off $5 billion in the severest downturn in Wall Street history. This October day was only the forerunner of what was to come on 29 October when a total collapse occurred in stock prices. The nation's economy was sent reeling downward as financial disaster struck the United States. New York Stock Exchange values had dropped $26 billion practically overnight.

The decade did not fizzle out. It dropped out of sight completely.

DELAYED REACTION

The collapse of the stock market was felt on Main and Madison streets in Memphis as it was around the world. The total psychological impact, however, seemed to be somewhat delayed. It was 1931 before the visible evidence began to show up dramatically among Memphis residents in terms of joblessness and human misery.

The political leadership during early 1930 seemed preoccupied by the population competition with its rivals and the concept of population growth as a measure of the city's progress. Senator McKellar wrote to E. H. Crump with obvious great enthusiasm in May 1930:

> I never was as proud in my life as I was at the result of the census in Memphis. To think that we have got a city of over a quarter of a million is surely a very, very fine thought, and I am absolutely sincere in the statement and would publish it over my signature, that I think you deserve more credit for the growth of Memphis than any one man. You have worked for her interests in season and out of season, in private life and in public life and in every other way and the people of Memphis owe you an everlasting debt. I believe that the result of the census will be the best advertisement our city will have, and we ought to start upon an unusual growth from this time on. If we could get cheap power shot into Memphis for manufacturing purposes, and for lighting purposes, it would be of great help. Indeed, we need that more than anything else right now.[3]

Memphis had achieved a population of 253,143 in 1930. The total for Shelby County was 306,482.

But there was bitter disappointment that Memphis had fallen from fifth to eighth place in population among the principal cities of the South and Southwest. New Orleans, Louisville, Houston, Atlanta, Dallas, Birmingham and San Antonio all had larger populations. In a paid ad in *The Commercial Appeal,* the city was severely criticized for not putting forth an effort to attract "more factories, more smoke stacks and more payrolls in Memphis."[4] The group sponsoring this ad concluded that, based on the advantages Memphis had which its rivals lacked, it should be second to New Orleans, not eighth. "Wake Up Memphis. Let's Go to Work," was the caption of this huge ad.

The employment figures reported in the 1930 Census as shown in Table 5 were disarming. They were accurate at the time of the census count, but, of course, these figure soon changed dramatically in late 1930 and 1931.

Some 28 percent of those employed were in manufacturing, 24 percent were in trade and 23 percent were employed as domestics or other personal services. Blacks accounted for the bulk of the jobs in the latter category. Another 12 percent were employed in transportation jobs. Only two percent held

TABLE 5
STATUS OF EMPLOYMENT OF WHITE AND BLACK WORKERS, 1930

	Population	Number of Gainful Workers	Persons Unemployed	Percent of Labor Force Unemployed
Whites	*156,593*	*66,337*	*1,839*	*2.8%*
Male	75,722	49,222	1,554	3.2
Female	80,871	17,115	285	1.7
Blacks	*96,550*	*52,034*	*1,833*	*3.5%*
Male	44,859	31,693	1,326	4.2
Female	51,691	20,341	507	2.5

SOURCE: Fifteenth Census of the United States, 1930.

jobs in public service. By today's standards, where public employment is a high percentage of total jobs, this 1930 figure of two percent stands out.

In Shelby County in 1930 there were 8,600 farms, the majority operated by tenants. About 287,000 acres were being farmed, so the average size unit was only about 33 acres. Only a few farms were as large as 500 acres. Farming was a marginal operation for most of the tenants. Two-thirds of all of these farms were operated by blacks, while less than ten percent were black-owned.

THE WORST YEARS

Americans everywhere were victims of the Great Depression. Many people in urban centers and rural regions perhaps suffered a bit more than Memphians, but the city by any standard was hard hit. Blacks and whites alike were leveled economically and it required considerable external help from the federal government to keep the city functioning. It was a period of much heroic work by local citizens, and the city's diverse social and economic groups came together in a common cause for the first time ever. Remember, in the 1878 Yellow Fever epidemic the leadership class and the wealthier citizens fled the city in those desperate months. This time there was no reason to flee. Conditions were not too much better anywhere else in the United States.

The Memphis economy plummeted beginning in late 1930, and most citizens faced a severe economic and emotional crisis. The loss of jobs was just one of the problems. Many lost their dignity and self-respect in their struggle for survival. Many had their health shattered, and some paid the supreme price through death, either from natural causes, tuberculosis, malnutrition, or by suicide. The suicide rate in 1931 and 1932 was far above any previous or subsequent year in the city. In 1932 there were 148 murders, also a record for annual homicides in Memphis.

Memphis unemployment exceeded 17,000 in mid-1932. Many others were listed as employed, but were either working at subsistence wages or living hand-to-mouth doing odd jobs. The true picture of joblessness was more or less disguised by the inexact manner used to calculate unemployment. Estimates were based only on the layoffs which took place at identifiable business and industrial firms. Residents here took no satisfaction in the fact that Atlanta had over 60,000 jobless, and New Orleans and Birmingham, 59,000 each. No one was gloating over any other city's economic misery in the early 1930s.

Nationally, unemployment, which in 1929 was only 1.5 million workers, had reached 13 million when Roosevelt took office in 1933. Relief figures were astronomical. Seventeen million Americans were on relief in 1934. In the 1935-36 period this figure had increased to 25 million, or one in every five citizens. Food, clothing, and fuel were being distributed to jobless families throughout the nation and the annual cost was some two billion dollars.

Memphis responded the best way it could, considering its limited financial resources. City employees were asked by the mayor and the other commissioners to donate one day's salary per month to be used to help the unfortunate. The Mayor's Committee on Unemployment and Relief underwrote the "Buy-an-Apple Campaign" to give needy men jobs. Some 80 men were stationed at various street corners selling apples for five cents each. The program collapsed in 1931 because most sellers were unable to make a profit, although selling apples became the trademark of hard times in larger cities. New York City, for example, had 4,000 apple sellers in its program.

The City of Memphis also organized the Mayor's Employment Committee to find jobs for both men and women. The jobs were not choice, but they provided a little income. A call was put out in October 1931 for 1,000 people to pick cotton for a wage of 40 to 50 cents per 100 pounds gathered. The committee also maintained a wood yard on South Willett Street. Another program was the sale of work tickets; a customer who bought a $1.00 work ticket was entitled to 10 hours of unskilled labor to perform odd jobs around his premises. The Committee furnished wood and fuel as well as food to 3,000 families a month in 1932. It also acted as a clearing house for donations of food and clothing from businesses and individuals.

Nothing better illustrates the hard times of the early Depression years than the contents of the following memorandum published in 1932 by the Mayor's Employment Committee and signed by the director, John Ross:

> We are in urgent need of shoes of all sizes, likewise clothing of all sizes, cooking stoves and other articles of furniture. At the present time we have over two thousand back orders for shoes. This morning at the Wood Yard, I found eighty-five men who were in urgent need of shoes. For about thirty cents we can put old shoes in a condition suitable for wearing.

Fig. 23. Work for the unemployed in early 1932 at one of the wood yards organized by Mayor Watkins Overton's Employment Committee. (Courtesy of Memphis Room, MPL)

Community Kitchens, Incorporated was a voluntary organization to dispense hot meals to the needy, and was supported by donations of food from merchants. Using churches as centers, this organization served one meal a day. Prior to its closing in mid-1933 because of the lack of donations, its highest weekly volume was 60,000 meals.[5] In its struggle to keep going, it put on Sunday shows at the Orpheum and also formed quilting circles to raise funds.

In 1932 the Unemployed Citizens' League of Memphis was organized as part of the barter movement arising in many cities.[6] This was a cooperative self-help program whereby labor was bartered for food, clothing, and furniture, which were collected and stored in the League's commissary.

The grim days of the early 1930s were captured emotionally in the Tin Pan Alley song popularized by Bing Crosby, "Brother, Can You Spare A Dime?" This doleful song was offset by optimistic songs to try to get people to forget their problems. Rudy Vallee and His Connecticut Yankees recorded "Life Is Just A Bowl of Cherries" in 1931, and Dick Powell, in the film *Gold Diggers of 1933*, featured the song, "We're in the Money." And, of course, there was Shirley Temple singing "On the Good Ship Lollypop" in one of her earliest films, *Bright Eyes*.

Foreclosures were a grim reminder in Memphis of the bad times in the 1930s. *The Commercial Appeal* went into receivership in late 1930, and in early 1931 the principal bondholder foreclosed.[7] The Shrine, Hickman, Porter and

Sterick office buildings experienced foreclosure, as did the Parkview Hotel adjacent to Overton Park. The Claridge Hotel failed to pay its mortgage bond-holders anything from 1933 to 1935. One of Memphis' pioneer residential developers filed for bankruptcy listing liabilities of almost $395,000 and assets of $1,400. These were representative situations. There were many, many more foreclosures and bankruptcies.

Property assessed valuation, which had reached a level of $303.8 million in 1931, fell to a low of $276.6 million in 1935. The tax levy in 1930 was $6.7 million. The amount actually collected was $5.9 million. In 1931 the levy was $6.7 million and collections, $5.3 million. By mid-1933 Memphis had uncollected taxes of $3.6 million. Uncollected taxes became a major problem of city government.

The Memphis school system ran out of funds in the spring of 1932. The Board ordered a retrenchment and salaries were cut 16⅔ percent in 1933. This was a drastic action since Memphis teachers had not had a salary increase since 1928. Not only was this a serious financial blow to the teachers individually, but the cuts shoved Memphis into last position in per capita educational expenditures among the 70 cities in the nation with 100,000 or more people, according to a study released in 1937 by the U.S. Office of Education. The average for the 70 cities was $107.19 per capita. For Memphis, it was $45.30.

The birth rate hit a low point in 1933. For whites, the rate was only 12.6 live births per 1,000 population and for blacks, only 16.0. Just five years earlier in 1928, the rate had been 18.1 for whites and 19.4 for blacks. The rates for both whites and blacks remained low throughout the 1930s. Contrast these low rates with the post-World War II rates of 23.9 in both 1947 and 1949 for whites, and 31.1 in 1949 for blacks.

A huge transient society was the product of the tragic economic conditions. Thousands of people—individuals and families—to alleviate their plight picked up and left their traditional homes seeking job opportunities elsewhere. The early 1930s found thousands of migrants on the nation's highways and in some cases in railroad box cars, drifting from rural areas into the cities, or from city to city in search of work. Memphis in this Depression era migration was the destination for many people from the farms and small towns of Tennessee, Arkansas, Mississippi, and other regional states.[8] The great majority were native-born whites, between the ages of 16 and 35. The percentage of blacks migrating into Memphis in the early 1930s was small.

Memphis, like many major cities, took part in the federally-supported Transient Relief Program. Aid was provided for those destitute individuals drifting into Memphis who were ineligible for any local relief programs. Between 1933 and 1935 when it closed permanently, the transient assistance program in Memphis helped 100,000 persons.[9] Help was limited and of a short duration. It was usually a hot meal and a night or two of lodging. The average length of care was 24 to 48 hours. These destitute migrants were usually advised by program workers to return to their towns or farms, and not linger around in Memphis. This was not cruelty on the part of the agency; it was merely realistic advice, given the circumstances.

Indigent Memphians had their own programs as previously cited. Beginning in 1936, after the worst years were over, they could apply for assistance from the new Memphis Welfare Commission if they were not eligible for any form of Social Security. The latter program was approved by President Roosevelt in August 1935, and it became one of the most significant social welfare measures to come out of the Great Depression.

Just a few days after FDR took office in March 1933, he declared a four-day bank holiday nationwide to give banks an opportunity to try to get their houses in order. State and national banks were permitted to reopen if they could prove their soundness. Memphis banks for the most part were sound and were fairly liquid at the time of the four-day closing. The one change on the local banking scene was the takeover in May 1933 of the Bank of Commerce and Trust Company by a new organization, the National Bank of Commerce. There had been a run on the former bank in early 1933 and its management had obtained a $12.5 million loan from the Reconstruction Finance Corporation to pay off depositors. The new bank's management assumed this obligation and by 1935 it had paid back to the RFC a large portion of the loan and had built up its assets to the point where they were far in excess of liabilities. Final liquidation of the old bank came in 1947.

Public confidence in Memphis banks remained high during the early 1930s. Bry's Department Store captured the mood of the local business community in a large ad captioned, "Chins Up! We Believe in America. We Believe in Our Banks."[10]

Settling In to the 1930s

After 1933 the worst of the shocks seemed over, and the city like the rest of the nation settled into a period of stagnation while a variety of economic recovery measures were put into operation by the federal government. Daily life in Memphis for the ordinary citizen was one of austerity, and so he tightened his belt. In the same way, his city government tightened its fiscal belt to keep solvent.

Fortunately for Memphians retail food prices were below the national average for 19 of the 27 standard food products.[11] Milk nationwide, for example, sold for 11.2 cents a quart. In Memphis, milk of comparable quality sold for 9.0 cents. Round steak was 29.0 cents a pound nationally, and 25.6 cents in Memphis. Food actually cost Memphians less in the early 1930s than it did in 1913, according to a U.S. Department of Labor study.[12]

Britling's Cafeteria and the B & W Cafeteria offered daily specials, as shown below, which were indicative of food prices of those grim days:

B & W Cafeteria (June 1, 1934)	*Britling's Cafeteria* (June 1, 1934)
Breakfast Special	*Breakfast Special*
Two eggs, any style with hot biscuits and butter ...10¢	Pork chops, grits and buttered toast ....12¢
Dinner and Supper	*Dinner and Supper*
Broiled Pork Chops......10¢ Chicken Croquette ......10¢ All Pot Vegetables .... 5¢	Braised Beef, a la Mode with Spaghetti ....14¢ Speckled Whole Trout ....14¢ Congealed Salmon Loaf ...... 7¢ Strawberry Cobbler .... 5¢

Food prices inched up very slowly during the remainder of the 1930s. Between 1940 and 1941 the cost of food increased as much as 33⅓ percent to break the moderate pattern of prices.

Rents were of great concern since the majority of Memphians were tenants, not homeowners. In 1936 landlords started raising rents by as much as five to ten percent on houses and apartments. Rents, however, in 1936 were 30 to 40 percent lower than they had been in 1929 before the crash. Families had also doubled up during the early years of the Depression, so housing costs per capita were quite low. By 1938 rent charges had increased an average of 12 percent from the base period of 1935. Housing costs for the middle and upper middle income families ranged from $35 to $75 a month for cottages and bungalows, and from $40 to $150 a month for apartments depending on location and desirability. Poor families paid rents under $15 a month. Of Memphis' 40,000 rental units, some 45 percent were at rates below $15. The amount of substandard housing (units lacking indoor plumbing, central heating and electricity) was appallingly high. Much of the housing stock was unsafe or unfit for habitation. A survey conducted by Works Progress Administration (WPA) in 1940 found that 77 percent of the black population and 35 percent of the white population were living in substandard housing.[13]

Crime did not take any holiday in the 1930s. Memphis was still called the "Murder Capital of the World" as the rate continued at record levels. Memphis' only consolation was the retirement in 1935 of Dr. Frederick Hoffman, Prudential Insurance Company's statistician who for nearly 30 years had been compiling information showing the murder rate in the principal U.S. cities.

Fig. 24. Scene along Beale Street on an October day in 1939. (Courtesy of the Library of Congress)

Memphis invariably headed Hoffman's list, much to the anguish of the Chamber of Commerce and civic leaders. Auto theft increased dramatically. Arrests for passing bad checks also rose during the Depression. *Collier's Magazine* carried an article in 1935, "Sinners in Dixie," in which the authors claimed "Memphis (and I'm not talking about black Memphis now, but white Memphis) supports a population of about 7,000 professional sinners whose sole business it is to provide everybody with a good time."[14] Professional sinners were those men and women who ran dance halls, gambling houses, prostitution, the numbers rackets, and speakeasies.

Periodically Commissioner Joe "Holy Joe" Boyle, a long time key Crump organization figure, would conduct raids on these operations and roust the participants. Although frequently harrassed, bootleggers in particular would have their cases dismissed or get off with light fines, then get back to business as usual. Policy game operators, feeling the pressure of the police, took up headquarters across the river in Arkansas. The operators pleaded that Memphis should consider the fact that the numbers racket gave employment to some 5,000 Memphians. Occasional tight control of Beale Street saloons and gambling operations helped reduce the knifings and shootings in the most notorious establishments. Boyle disliked blacks, and put them on notice that he would not stand for any troublemakers amongst them. He referred to Memphis as "white man's country," and if blacks did not accept this, they should be prepared to get out of the city.

The 1930s were not totally devoid of civility and substance despite the really harsh economic and social conditions prevailing in Memphis. Many citizens managed somehow or other to maintain their sense of humor and their common decency, as was true throughout the United States. Memphians were asked to cooperate and they did respond to the appeals of civic leaders made periodically over radio stations WREC, WMC, and WHBQ to "eliminate those ruthless foes—hunger, poverty, disease and distress."[15] Most Memphians cooperated fully to fight for the whole city's well-being. The spirit of neighbor helping neighbor in Memphis' long history was certainly at its highest peak in the 1930s.

13

Picking Up the Pieces

"Resurgamus!" or from the Latin: "Let us rise again." This exhortation once served as the caption of an editorial cartoon in *The Commercial Appeal* in 1919 when the city was recovering from the effects of World War I.[1] This rallying cry probably was more applicable to the 1930s as Memphians sought to recover from the deep Depression and to continue the industrial growth efforts started in the 1920s. Memphis also became concerned about the city's social conditions, including the serious slum housing problems which came to a head in the 1930s. And city planning as a positive force for guiding physical growth continued to be a major concern and a subject of controversy insofar as it related to zoning regulations.

Memphis like most of America realized it needed help to recover and rebuild, and it accepted enthusiastically the opportunities for various forms of assistance provided by the federal government during the Roosevelt Administration. Due to the magnitude of the emergency, voices protesting massive federal intervention into local affairs as a matter of political philosophy were largely subdued. Roosevelt swept Shelby County in his 1936 election against Republican Alf Landon by a 30 to 1 margin, demonstrating the popularity of the Roosevelt programs locally.

REBUILDING THE COTTON ECONOMY

Memphis, traditionally so dependent on cotton to support its economy, began its fight back symbolically. On 1 March 1931 Memphis held its first Cotton Carnival, spearheaded by Everett R. Cook and A. Arthur Halle, two prominent business leaders. The Carnival's purpose was to publicize Memphis, and to promote the greater use of cotton nationally and internationally. E. H. Crump's political organization got behind this event to insure its success.

175

Fig. 25. Cotton Row broker in the foreground with a cotton classer at work in the background in 1939. (Courtesy of the Library of Congress)

Cotton prices broke in 1929 and continued to drop drastically to 1933. On 1 June 1932 the price was 4.4 cents a pound which represents an all-time low figure. The cotton farmer needed help and Congress responded with the Commodity Credit Corporation in 1933. Farmers could borrow from this agency pledging warehouse receipts on their cotton stored in government approved warehouses.[2] If the farmer got a better price for his cotton, he sold it and paid off the debt. His alternative was to transfer the cotton outright to the Corporation at the loan price. By 1935 some 700,000 bales were in storage in Memphis under this national program supporting farm prices.

In 1933 Congress also passed the Agricultural Adjustment Act. Its objective was to control production through subsidies to farmers who voluntarily reduced the acreage planted. In Shelby County AAA officials signed up enough farmers to cause a 40 percent acreage reduction in 1934.[3] That year, for example, contracts between the AAA and farmers called for payments of $3 to $18 per acre for land left unplanted.[4] The average payment received by these farmers was about 3½ cents a pound for cotton not planted. That year Shelby County farmers received $239,000 in AAA subsidies. Cotton producers in Tennessee, Arkansas and Mississippi received $16.4 million in subsidy payments.[5] The programs apparently helped cotton prices in 1934, 1935 and 1936, but the next four years, including 1940, saw prices fall back drastically as shown in Appendix B.

The AAA was declared unconstitutional in 1936. Without the voluntary acreage restriction contracts, then, cotton production went wild in 1937 when nearly 19 million bales were produced. Down went prices in 1937 creating panic among cotton growers in the South, and generating serious discussion of compulsory crop controls to remedy the overproduction situation. A new Agricultural Adjustment Act was passed in 1938. Through storage loans and marketing quotas the federal government hoped to maintain a price support system by controlling sales.

Southern cotton producers sought means of obtaining greater markets for the commodity. Speaking at a 1937 Cotton Carnival function, Secretary of State Cordell Hull, a native Tennessean, made an appeal for support of greater foreign trade as an aid to the cotton economy.[6] Other speakers suggested promotional campaigns to get more people to use cotton in clothing and for household purposes. There was also much experimenting with cotton to find new uses. Some excitement was stirred when experiments were being made in 1935 to use cotton as a paving material for airport runways. Two Memphians, Everett R. Cook of Cook & Company and W. H. Jasspon, president of Perkins Oil Company, were promoting a "cotton research institute" to find new uses for cotton and cotton seed. In the late 1930s the cotton industry faced a new threat, the introduction of synthetic fibers to compete with cotton. Action was demanded quickly.

Stemming from this great concern of the cotton interests, a Mississippian,

Oscar Johnston, agreed to head a promotional drive to form an industrywide organization to advance the cotton industry. From these efforts came the National Cotton Council, formed in 1938, to promote the increased use of cotton. Memphis was selected as the Council's headquarters, where it is still active today.

In 1940 the U.S. Department of Agriculture launched its Cotton Stamp Plan to help reduce cotton surpluses. Needy families and individuals were allowed to buy at discounts of 50 percent books of stamps in 25 cent denominations which could be redeemed at participating retail stores for various cotton goods. An estimated 12,000 families in Shelby County were eligible. Most of these people were on WPA.

The years just preceeding World War II were ones of accomplishment for the cotton industry. It did not become a healthy industry, but those involved appeared to gain greater control over their future.

RELIEF PROGRAMS

Mayor Overton in a year-end message in 1933 commented, "Looking back at the achievements of 1933 and the prospects for 1934, we're on our way, aided by the CWA and the PWA, Memphis is really swinging along to recover."[7] Overton was referring to the work relief programs which were implemented in 1933. E. H. Crump had been elected to the U.S. House of Representatives in 1931. Needless to say, he won by a landslide. Crump got 90 percent of the votes. Along with Senator McKellar, who was then almost a 20-year legislative veteran in Washington, Crump exerted tremendous influence on Washington agencies to obtain projects and programs for Memphis. The city was fortunate to have been represented by two extremely influential politicians during these crisis years.

The earliest project was probably the Reconstruction Finance Corporation's work relief program implemented in the winter of 1933. Some 14,000 men were signed on as common laborers for several road and highway construction projects in Shelby County. Others were assigned to clean out creek beds in the city. The RFC paid these men $1.25 a day, and provided them with a maximum work week of four days. This agency also had a vegetable garden seed program. All Memphians were encouraged to plant vegetable gardens to provide part of their own food.

The WPA was the best known federal relief program. It was designed to provide jobs for the able-bodied unemployed. Many of the jobs were pick and shovel labor, but the WPA also provided jobs for writers, artists, and other unemployed persons with special skills in projects related to their talents. At one point in the mid-1930s there were 8,000 men and women holding WPA jobs in Memphis. Many public improvements in the city were built with WPA manpower. WPA projects included improvements at the Memphis Municipal Airport, projects at Overton and Riverside parks, Crump Stadium, sewer and

Fig. 26. View of slum housing which bordered downtown until replaced by Lauderdale Courts public housing project in 1937. The burning of soft coal created a blanket of air pollution over the city. (Courtesy of Memphis Room, MPL)

drainage systems projects, work on the Nonconnah Creek levee, and malaria control projects. Monthly wages ranged from $19 to $75, which were lower than those paid for equivalent work in private enterprise. The Public Works Administration, the PWA, provided funds to build a variety of public works projects, thereby creating additional jobs for the unemployed in the building trades. John Gaston Hospital, several schools, the electric distribution system, dorms at the University of Tennessee Medical School, and improvements to Riverside Drive were some of the achievements. With major assistance from the Corps of Engineers, the construction of Riverside Drive corrected a century old cave-in problem on the riverfront and also contributed an attractive scenic route for motorists into downtown Memphis.

The PWA entered public housing in the 1930s, and it is responsible for the construction of Dixie Homes and Lauderdale Courts, Memphis' first two housing projects. The federal government concluded that private builders were incapable of providing housing on any large scale, so it decided to fill this void. As early as April 1934 funds were approved for projects in Memphis and many other large cities with slum clearance areas. The two Memphis projects were completed in 1938 at a combined cost of $6.6 million in federal funds. The Memphis Housing Authority leased these projects from the PWA and operated the 1,124 public housing units. Dixie Homes and Lauderdale Courts were built on cleared bayou slum areas near downtown Memphis. Some 300 shacks occupied by 1,500 people were replaced with these new units housing over 3,600 people.

Mayor Overton announced that these two projects were just the start of slum clearance in the city.[8] Prior to the start of World War II three more projects were completed in other notorious slum areas. Well-known architect Max A. Furbringer and civic leader Ethel R. Jasspon were two strong citizen advocates for getting slum clearance started in order to provide better housing for low income groups. Both prodded the social consciousness of Memphians for many years to achieve this result. Joseph A. Fowler became the foremost promoter and administrator of public housing in Memphis in 1938, when he became Executive Director of the Memphis Housing Authority.

Congressman Walter Chandler, who had replaced E. H. Crump in Congress when he decided against a third term in 1935, fought for a farm subsistence project on part of Park Field, the abandoned World War I air training field. This project was to help families supplement their other incomes from nearby jobs by providing land to raise vegetables and feed poultry and cattle. The War Department was not enthusiastic about the program, and the most it did was to grant a five-year revocable permit to the administrators of this special subsistence program. In 1937 model farms were set up for demonstration purposes.[9]

HOMEOWNERS' RELIEF

Many homeowners faced the prospect of foreclosure by mortgage holders during the Depression. President Roosevelt signed a relief bill for homeowners, and asked lenders to hold up on foreclosure until the machinery was organized to refinance mortgages. The Home Owners' Loan Corporation (HOLC) was created in 1933 by the Federal Home Loan Bank Board to help those unable to meet mortgage payments. The HOLC could lend 80 percent of the appraised value or $14,000, whichever was smaller, on houses up to $20,000 in value. An average middle class home in this period cost between $6,500 and $7,000. This agency gave the homeowner a lower interest rate and longer amortization period.

The HOLC opened an office in Memphis in July 1933, and claimed that in its first two years of operation it saved over 3500 homes in West Tennessee from foreclosure. During the rest of the 1930s the HOLC had an operation in Memphis. Most of its loans proved to be sound, and the record of repossessions was minimal.

The Federal Housing Administration provided for by the National Housing Act of 1934, established the first loan insurance program. This landmark legislation made it possible for people of ordinary financial means to buy a house, and to pay for it on an amortization schedule extending over many years. In Shelby County the FHA program was well-received. From June 1935 to April 1941, the local FHA had insured over 4100 loans; and FHA-insured loans represented about 90 percent of all new home loans made during that period. The FHA also insured modernization and repair loans. Memphis banks made almost 8000 loans under this program. A very influential housing leader during that period was the Tennessee director for the FHA, B. W. Horner. He was called "Mr. FHA" locally, and contributed substantially to the improved housing economy of the latter 1930s. Memphis became known as the nation's first major FHA city.

Rejuvenating the Private Homebuilding Industry

The early Depression years were difficult ones for the homebuilders and the general real estate profession. Despite an optimistic headline in a local newspaper early in 1931, "Real Estate Men See Better Year in 1931," the market did not get better then, or for the next several years. For 1933, 1934, and 1935 an average of 67 housing units per year were built. Innovative realtors tried unique sales approaches to interest customers. Night selling using floodlights to attract interest was tried. Developer-realtor Dave Dermon built what he called a "talking home" at Trezevant and Vollintine. Here the prospect was given a complete demonstration of how the house was built and how it could be financed. Mr. Dermon attracted traffic. Some 15,000 came to see his display.

To stimulate interest some builders experimented with low cost private housing. In 1936 developer Philip Belz built a complex of 24-three room apartments which rented for $15 a month. This gained him considerable recognition at the time. Wallace E. Johnson, practically at the start of his long homebuilding career in Memphis, built what was then called in 1938 Tennessee's first "less than $3000" subdivision. The project was called Fordhurst, and was located near the Ford Plant on Riverside. Another veteran builder, John A. Goodwin, also was building there.

B. W. Horner of the FHA and J. Frazier Smith, a Memphis architect, originated a program to create better designs in building homes and to provide closer control of construction. Some 100 floor plans and exterior designs were developed for homes in the $2500 to $6000 price range. If a prospect were interested, local architects would provide their services at reduced fees. Memphis was the first city to originate such a program to get better quality homes at reasonable prices.

From 1931 to 1940 some 7500 housing units were constructed. Just over 4600 were private units; the rest were public housing units.[10] A sign of the times was the change in the ratio of owner-occupied to renter-occupied housing between 1930 and 1940. In 1930, for example, 37 percent of the housing units were owned by their occupants. Ten years later it was only 30 percent.

One of the major projects in an otherwise unspectacular housing era was the construction of Kimbrough Towers, a nine-story high rise apartment at Union and Kimbrough. Developer John Kimbrough announced that his structure was the "largest concrete apartment east of the Rockies." This building opened just before World War II, with rents from $40 to $75 a month. It was definitely a luxury building, since typical apartment rental rates in better complexes were from $27.50 to $57.50.

Substandard Housing—A Major Liability

Memphis was a slum-ridden city in the 1930s. The WPA survey conducted in 1940 reported that about 50,000 housing units were substandard. The Memphis Housing Authority reported to the public that half of the city's inhabitants were living in substandard housing. As reported earlier, 77 percent of the blacks lived in substandard housing and 35 percent of the whites. The WPA report, in commenting on the black housing problem, added:

> . . . Negro families have had to be contented with inheriting old and nearly worn out houses left by the white population as it expanded and moved further out into the suburbs. . . . These same houses were built in a period when modern plumbing and lighting requirements were luxuries rather than positive regulations.

and the report continued:

> The old expression of a bath once a week, on Saturday night is a grim reality for many families. An amazing total of 26,199 negro families and 2,159 white families do not have any of what is considered normal bathing facilities; in fact, only 10.6% of the negro families in sub-standard homes, and just 25.8% of the white families, are equipped with a private bath. With them cleanliness may be next to Godliness but it also is next to impossible.[11]

The distribution of substandard housing throughout Memphis is shown in Figure 27. Considerable slum housing and blight ringed downtown Memphis. Other areas in desperate need of rehabilitation were the Orange Mound area, Binghampton, South Memphis near the river, North Memphis, and the Chelsea Avenue area.

Many prominent citizens with deep social consciences complained to public officials that slum houses were not only an eyesore, but they also were havens of human misery. Their pleas worked. The Chamber of Commerce's Better Housing Committee conducted campaigns in cooperation with the FHA office to repair and modernize the city's housing. The Memphis Real Estate Board also had a committee to work with the FHA and the city to clean up blighted areas. The major force, however, was the Memphis Housing Authority, which had geared up for a major slum clearance and better housing effort on the eve of World War II. The latter event put a real crimp in the program. The MHA would have to wait until after the war to attack the slum housing problem. World War II reset all federal government priorities.

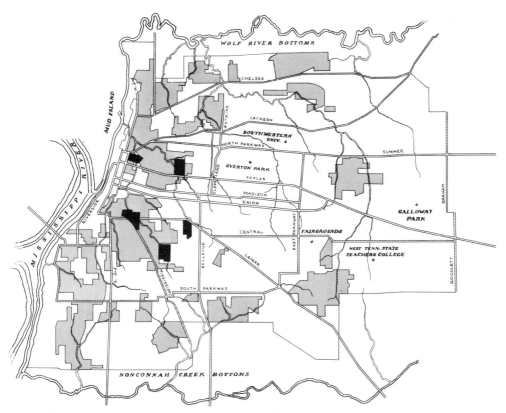

Fig. 27. On the basis of a survey made jointly by the Memphis Housing Authority and the WPA in 1940, the grey areas indicate neighborhoods where the majority of the dwellings were considered substandard. The black areas indicate the location of the five public housing projects built before World War II.

CITY PLANNING CONTINUES

As early as 1931 concern was being expressed about the chaotic land use pattern in the county areas beyond the city limits. State law permitted Memphis to control land use outside, but within 5 miles, of the corporate limits of the city. The result was the approval in 1933 of a comprehensive zoning plan covering this outer suburban territory. This action was really quite an advanced step, and approval came at about the time the Great Depression hit bottom. Even more remarkable was the agitation for countywide zoning, and not just the 5-mile zone.

At the beginning of the 1930s the eastern limits of the city extended about 6 miles from the Mississippi River, and the northern and southern boundaries were about 3 miles from downtown Memphis. In 1930 about 133,500 people lived west of Bellevue to the river, and 119,600 east of this north-south street. Frayser, Raleigh, Bartlett, Germantown, Collierville, and Whitehaven were tiny peripheral communities detached by several miles of open area from the edge of urban Memphis.

Downtown Memphis was reasonably well intact commercially, and was not challenged to any extent by any larger scale retail and office building developments. Industry continued to locate along the railroad tracks. The city did downzone some 23 areas to try to stem blight. Downzoning meant that many areas previously zoned for commercial use were rezoned to residential districts. Similarly, some industrial land was rezoned to a commercial designation.

Air pollution became a major concern of the city in the 1930s, and it led to the establishment of a smoke abatement program aimed at the railroads and owners of buildings with coal furnaces. Downtown Memphis often had a dark blanket of pollution hanging over it prior to the conversion from coal-burning to gas-burning heating systems in the late '30s.

Memphis continued its consulting relationship with planner Harland Bartholomew, who prodded the city commissioners to develop policies which would prevent excessive population decentralization. He feared an acceleration in the number of blighted districts throughout the Memphis urban area. When Walter Chandler became Mayor in early 1940, Bartholomew urged him to promote housing rehabilitation programs in the city's other neighborhoods to help offset decentralization.[12] Stabilizing older areas, he claimed, would also enhance property values. In his 1938 Plan Bartholomew recommended the creation of neighborhood improvement associations to help preserve neighborhoods. And concerning the city's black population the authors of the Bartholomew Plan had this to say:

> It would be advantageous to the city if the bulk of the negro population could be confined to definite districts that have already been established. With a limited increase in negro population expected in the future, improvement of health and sanitary conditions within these districts will largely eliminate further shifting of the negro population.[13]

The city paid Bartholomew $25,000 for the plan in 1938, but refused to act on its recommendations. The plan literally sat on the shelf in the Mayor's office until a decision was made in 1942 to delay action until after the war. Several reasons were given for the reluctance to implement the planning suggestions of Bartholomew. One principal reason apparently was public reaction against the plan's suggestion to further downgrade zoning, particularly from commercial to residential. Owners of commercial property then, like today, were extremely sensitive to downzoning attempts. The city's own planning staff director, obviously disturbed about the public's reaction to the zoning recommendations, suggested to Mayor Overton in 1939 that Memphis invite the National Conference on Planning to hold its 1940 convention in the city. He felt this would help inform Memphians of the fundamentals and desirability of planning.[14]

Although denied by the Crump organization, the break in political relations between Mr. Crump and Mayor Overton and his ally, Commissioner Ralph Picard, was partially responsible. Also, the fact that there was only limited building activity in the late 1930s reduced the urgency the Crump leaders felt to approve the new Bartholomew Plan.

Undoubtedly, planning in the 1930s did represent some progress despite reluctance to accept Bartholomew's recommendations. Some intrusions of business and industries into residential areas were prevented. But the city and county budgeted very little for the day-to-day work of its city planning commission. The total budget in 1937 was only $4,090. The citizens were fortunate that the staff employees were able and dedicated, and performed effectively despite niggardly budgets.

IMPROVING TRANSPORTATION SYSTEMS

A barometer of business conditions was the annual passenger figures of the Memphis Street Railway Company. The 1929 volume was 55 million passengers. Rock bottom was hit in 1931 when only 41.3 million passengers rode the streetcars. Gradually volume returned and by 1940 ridership was back to 54.5 million. The Company had gone into receivership in 1933. In 1934 it was thrown into bankruptcy, but in 1935 a reorganized company appeared to continue providing the service.

Automobiles, which declined in registrations in the early 1930s, started appearing in greater numbers. By 1939 some 63,000 cars were registered. Memphis started rethinking its street, highway, and bridge planning. One bold proposal made in 1934 by long time chairman of the Shelby County Commission, E. W. Hale, was to build an "Outer Parkway" system some six to nine miles beyond Memphis' existing Parkway system. This plan included some 12 forested parks along the route. The State Highway Department actually drew a proposed route.

Memphis had been building eastward in the 1920s. Convenient routes leading north of the Wolf River were lacking; so the completion of the Wolf River Bridge at Thomas provided access to Frayser and Millington.

There was also increasing agitation for a new bridge across the Mississippi.[15] Downtown merchants, realtors and some investors were convinced that the poor access to the commercial heart of the city was choking off business. The Harahan Bridge just was not adequate. Among the suggestions was a new bridge to be built just north of the central business district crossing Mud Island. Some 36 years later when the Hernando DeSoto Bridge opened the north side of downtown Memphis finally got better access to Arkansas.

Street traffic was heavy and the accident rate was increasing. The most dangerous intersection was Poplar and Cleveland in 1933 but it soon lost its position to Union and Cleveland.[16] The congestion was viewed as an indicator of business recovery. The *Memphis Press Scimitar* in late 1935 wrote: "Memphis like other fast growing cities has and we hope will continue to have difficulty in keeping up with itself."[17]

Investors thought Union Avenue had high potential as a quality retail street. A 1934 *Commercial Appeal* headline announced: "Fifty Leading Property Owners Will Gather at the Peabody to Push Plan for Fifth Avenue of the South."[18] An organization was formed to develop the street commercially from Front Street to the East Parkway. Customers would be transported along the street by buses. Times had changed on Union Avenue. Just seven years earlier the residents were battling the Spencer-Sturla funeral home because it was a commercial intrusion in their neighborhood. Despite the new proposal in 1934, only modest conversion to a retail street occurred. It was nevertheless a bold idea considering it was made in one of the worst Depression years.

Union Avenue was extended beyond the East Parkway in the late 1930s and joined Poplar Avenue just east of the Aulon Viaduct, when the latter was built across the railroad tracks. Despite strong citizen protests that the street would become a speedway and property values decline, Central Avenue was widened to provide another major east-west street. This was a WPA project.

When Firestone Tire & Rubber Company came to Memphis in 1937 it gave a major boost to the local economy in terms of jobs and payrolls. It also stimulated the development of North Memphis into a greater industrial area to compete with the veteran South Memphis Land Company on the south side of the city. Philip Belz, one of the pioneer land developers in North Memphis, bought a few acres from the owners of the old North Memphis Driving Park property, and developed one of the first neighborhood retail shopping centers. Belz became an active developer of industrial and residential subdivisions in North Memphis, and was a major force in the early growth of this section of the city.

Meanwhile, the South Memphis Land Company continued to face hard times that caused some anguish among its principals and investors, including B. Lee Mallory, Jr., Senator McKellar, and E. H. Crump. The company had paid only one dividend through 1936, and the price of its stock had fallen to almost nothing. Senator McKellar in correspondence with Crump mentioned that the South Memphis Land Company's stock was selling at two cents on the dollar.[19] This veteran land development company not only had a huge debt burden, but also a large tax delinquency hanging over it. In partial settlement of the back taxes it owed the city, the company deeded to Memphis the 171-acre Pine Hill Golf Course. Senator McKellar wanted the city to build a major east-west street through South Memphis Land's holdings to stimulate development interest. But not until after World War II did this huge tract become a prime area for residential subdivisions.

FLOOD PROTECTION AND MR. CRUMP

For Memphis one of the major public accomplishments of the 1930s was the Flood Control Bill of 1937, signed by President Roosevelt just six months after the great flood in February 1937. Congress approved $9 million for flood control works along the Wolf River and the Nonconnah Creek, which would reduce the hazards of flooding and enormous damage in the low lying areas of the city. The actual cost was $13 million.

The earlier levee system saved the city during the 1937 flood, which gave Memphis a scare it did not forget. The Mississippi crested at 48.7 feet in Memphis as measured on the Weather Bureau's gauge on 10 February 1937. There was some overflow in North Memphis and in South Memphis along the Nonconnah Creek, where there were scenes of great drama. During the height of the flood while leading the efforts of hundreds of workers on the levee to hold back the water, Crump telegraphed this dramatic message to Senator McKellar in Washington:

> I MUST STICK IT OUT HERE ON NONCONNAH LEVEE WE HOPE TO HOLD IT STOP PLEASE KEEP THIS IN MIND LEVEES PUMPING STATIONS AND SEAWALLS SHOULD BE BUILT AROUND MEMPHIS TO PREVENT A RECURRENCE OF FLOOD WATERS FROM THE MISSISSIPPI NONCONNAH AND WOLF RIVERS STOP LEVEES ARE BUILT ALL OVER THE UNITED STATES ON RIVERS TO PROTECT TOWNS AND FARMS WHY NOT LOUISVILLE MEMPHIS AND OTHER CITIES BEST WISHES=[20]

Crump's appearance on the levee in his high-top boots impressed the black refugees at the Fairgrounds' flood relief center. One of the old songs of the blacks heard at the center had these catchy lines showing their awe of Mr. Crump:

> Oh the river's up and cotton's down,
> Mister Ed Crump, he runs this town.[21]

When the U.S. Corps of Engineers finished the floodworks, the city gained protection from flood waters up to 55 feet. The projects gave employment to hundreds of workers at a time when jobs were still badly needed.

CRUMP CONTINUES BATTLING THE PRIVATE UTILITIES

In the early 1930s Memphis was not in the utility business except for the water system that it had purchased in 1903. Electricity, gas, street car service, and telephone companies were privately owned and operated. This was the case in most American cities at that time. Water supply systems were the exception.

It was obvious that Mr. Crump had been waiting for the right moment to champion the cause of municipal ownership of the Memphis Power & Light Company. He had had a running feud with the electric power and gas interests since 1915 when he blamed them for his ouster from the Mayor's Office. He got his chance in the 1930s, setting off a dramatic confrontation between Mr. Crump and the New York-based and controlled private utility companies. In

Fig. 28. Unemployed workers being signed up as emergency flood relief workers during the 1937 disaster. (Courtesy of the National Archives)

1933, led by the then city attorney, Walter Chandler, Memphis went after Southern Bell and Memphis Power & Light Company for rate reductions. The latter agreed to lower light bills about 12 percent. The battle cry of the Crump organization was: "The power companies are getting a strangle-hold on the State."[22] Crump also complained bitterly about the railroads and their rate discrimination in favor of Eastern cities. He was constantly attacking the railroads for their unwillingness to spend more funds for grade separations, and their failure to participate in community fund-raising drives.[23] Crump called them "poor citizens" and threatened them with the possibility of not renewing their franchises to operate in Memphis. Crump also started after the Memphis Street Railway Company in the early 1940s, and constantly badgered company officials about the fares being charged.

The emergence of the Tennessee Valley Authority in 1933 started the formal process of lowering the cost of electric power. Memphis political leaders had long been interested in getting lower utility rates both for citizens and for industrial development purposes. The TVA opened up a great opportunity and the Crump organization exploited it fully. Memphians in 1934 voted 17 to 1 for a bond issue raising funds to build a distribution system bringing TVA power into Memphis. Despite this early enthusiasm the first TVA power did not arrive in Memphis until mid-1938. The city had not been able to reach an agreement with the Memphis Power & Light Company to buy its system, so Memphis decided to build a competing system.

Crump had pushed for cheaper utility rates for nearly 25 years. He was determined to achieve his goal in the late 1930s. He relished telling Memphians that he was fighting to free the city from the "Wall Street gang" that controlled the utilities. Victory was achieved in June 1939 when the Memphis Power & Light Company agreed to sell. The State authorized Memphis to issue $11,750,000 in bonds to buy the electric facilities, and $5,250,000 to buy the gas system. The Memphis Street Railway Company, owned by Memphis Power & Light, and the generating plant of the utility, were excluded from the sale.

Once Crump applied pressure to the Memphis Power & Light Company it was just a matter of time before he would win over the utility, and buy the company at his price. This private utility was charging fairly high rates. In a Federal Trade Commission rate study in 1936 Memphis utility customers were found to be paying higher monthly rates than those in 28 other cities with populations over 100,000. To counteract the bad publicity emerging from its rate structure, Memphis Power & Light lowered rates in 1936. The city charged the utility with concocting a rate reduction scheme to prevent Memphians from enjoying cheap TVA power.[24]

Memphis Power & Light Company had joined 18 other private power companies in attacking the constitutionality of the TVA Act and in calling the TVA a radical socialistic experiment. In the case *Ashwander, et al.* v. *Tennessee Valley Authority,* decided in 1936, the U.S. Supreme Court upheld TVA's right to sell its surplus power. With that case settled, Crump and the City of Memphis moved forward in the purchase negotiations.

The Company wanted $21,000,000. Memphis first offered $18,127,000. The city was then starting to build a competing system to receive the TVA power. The city warned the utility that it was going to take into consideration every penny it spent on this system if negotiations dragged out. Crump accused the company of stalling for time, hoping that the U.S. Supreme Court might rule adversely against the TVA before an agreement. Crump fired off a blast: "Diogenes with his lamp was out to find an honest man. I am sure he would have passed up the Power Trust monopoly."[25] In December 1938 the city offered $17,385,000 for the combined electric and gas properties. Meanwhile Memphis Power & Light lowered its electric rates to match those being charged by the city's rival system, which was just getting started.

The negotiations led to a political split between Crump and Mayor Watkins Overton. Apparently Overton on his own agreed to a price with the utility company without clearing it with Crump. The Mayor was publicly embarrassed by Crump who accused him of negotiating a very poor trade. The feud began in October 1938 and ultimately led to Overton's decision to not seek reelection in 1939. The long drawn out negotiations and the war of words in the press ended on 27 June 1939, with Crump the hero of the long battle. When the new city-owned Memphis Light, Gas and Water utility told its 68,000 electric customers, 50,000 gas customers and 53,000 water customers in 1940 that it had saved them $2.4 million during the first year of public ownership, the citizens were well pleased with the Crump political organization. And, of course, Crump had scored a victory over an old and bitter enemy, the electric utility.

CREATING MORE JOBS

Crump's interest in cheap power was not only his desire to settle an old political score, but also an interest in attracting new industry to Memphis. Crump was actively interested in industrial development for Memphis, and worked very hard behind the scenes to bring it to Memphis. He once came down hard on Senator McKellar for not paying close enough attention to the matter of jobs and payrolls in Memphis. Crump told McKellar: "Please remember, the best business is the best politics."[26] Crump telegraphed McKellar the following message in 1937 to make a point:

> HOPE YOU WILL GO SLOW ON BREAKING UP THE RE-
> GIONAL HOLC IN THE STERICK BUILDING FIVE HUN-
> DRED TWENTY FIVE CLERKS PAYROLL SEVEN HUNDRED
> TWENTY THOUSAND DOLLARS MEAN A LOT TO MEMPHIS
> THAT IS ALL THAT MEMPHIANS ARE INTERESTED
> IN AND FURTHER PLEASE LET ME ASK YOU THIS IF YOU
> ABOLISH THE REGINAL OFFICE THAT SERVES SIX STATES
> WONT THE ONE STATE OFFICE BE MOVED TO NASHVILLE
> AND GRACIOUS KNOWS NASHVILLE HAS ENOUGH NOW.
> UNDERSTAND SEVENTY PERCENT OF THE EMPLOYES ARE
> TENNESSEANS ABOUT HALF MEMPHIANS I THINK YOU
> ARE MAKING A HORRIBLE MISTAKE IN FACT MANY OF
> YOUR FRIENDS FEEL THE SAME WAY WE ARE NOW FIGUR-
> ING ON A CAMPAIGN TO ADVERTISE MEMPHIS FOR MORE
> FACTORIES AND DISTRIBUTORS AND RIGHT IN THE FACE
> OF THIS TO BUST UP AN OFFICE THAT EMPLOYS OVER
> FIVE HUNDRED PEOPLE WHO SPEND THEIR MONEY IN
> MEMPHIS WILL LOOK MIGHTY BAD TO THE CITIZENS AND
> TAXPAYERS OF THIS COMMUNITY SENATOR PLEASE VIEW
> THIS FROM A BUSINESS STANDPOINT FOR THE GOOD OF
> MEMPHIS=[27]

Crump was obviously distressed about the employment situation. The labor force had grown since the early 1930s, but unemployment remained high.

The special federal job census, released in early 1938, indicated that 17,800 Memphians, or one out of every five, were without jobs.[28] Peak unemployment at the depths of the Depression in the early 1930s had been 17,100, or about one out of every four.

Manufacturing was a weak sector, and the Chamber of Commerce, Crump, and prominent businessmen all worked to improve the number of jobs and the value of output. Memphis had had 16,700 manufacturing workers in 1929, but only 13,900 in 1939. Crump again addressed himself to this issue. He came out strongly for lower tax assessments, stating: "We must fight now for lower assessments, lower taxes. Low taxes attract manufacturing. Manufactures give employment and build cities." Crump also pleaded for more national advertising of Memphis' advantages to attract business. Among his suggestions for new industries were all types of textiles. He pointed out that Memphis should be a great cattle raising center and that the city is a natural distributing point.

Although manufacturing jobs had fallen, the city did get some significant new industries. HumKo Company was founded by S. L. Kopald and Herbert Humphreys in 1930, and located on North Thomas near the old North Memphis Driving Park. This company started out producing shortening, then branched out with a variety of edible oil products. In 1952 it became an operating division of Kraftco Corporation. Continental Can Company moved to Memphis in 1933 because the city was the biggest market for cans in the South. Armour & Company built a fertilizer plant in the Mount Pisgah section in 1935, and that same year bought the Memphis Packing Company. Armour said it expected to make the city the meat packing center of the South.

With the arrival of Firestone, the Chamber of Commerce spoke of 1937 as being the most important industrial year of the 1930s. With 100 employees at the start of 1937, it ended the first year with 1000. Firestone, which considered Memphis the commercial hub of the South, replaced the Murray Wood Products Company, then owned by Fisher Body Corporation, which had closed because of the change from wood to steel body frames. Firestone occupied the old Murray plant in North Memphis and sold its first tires to the Memphis plant of the Ford Motor Company. Firestone used Mid-South cotton for tire fabric. Its raw rubber was transported from New Orleans by barge.

The 18th Amendment was repealed 5 December 1933. The first year following repeal Memphis-based Tennessee Brewing Company produced some 4,650,000 gallons of its Goldcrest beer. The company was back in the beer business after a long hiatus, and it began a heavy marketing campaign to capture the Mid-South market. A typical ad read:

> Goldcrest is the all-season beer, good in summer, winter, autumn, spring, anytime, anywhere. And remember, when you drink a bottle of Goldcrest you are drinking a toast to Southern prosperity.[31]

Anderson-Tully Company, a box manufacturer, was also a beneficiary of the repeal. It added several hundred workers to build wooden beer cases for Tennessee Brewing's Goldcrest bottles.

The Belz Upholstered Furniture Company, organized by Philip and Sam Belz, was another homegrown industry born in Memphis in the Depression years. There were other Memphians also starting new businesses.

Working Conditions

Wages varied substantially depending on the industry and the job skills of specific workers. Ford raised its minimum wage from $4.00 a day in 1932 to $5.00 in 1934, and to $6.00 in May 1935 when it was turning out 200 cars and trucks per day. Before the Depression Ford had been paying $7.00 per day. These wages were based on an 8-hour day.

In another factory, the Memphis Furniture Manufacturing Company, in 1937 the pay was from $.13 to $.25 an hour for white workers, and from $.09 to $.20 for black workers. At the Tri-State Dress Manufacturing Company, where 150 women were employed as garment workers, some were being paid as little as $5.00 to $8.00 a week for 54 hours of labor. The higher paid workers made only about $12.00 a week.

Union scale of wages in the building trades in Memphis in 1935 was $1.25 an hour for plasterers, plumbers, and steam fitters. Sign painters got $1.125 an hour; tile layers, $1.00; sheet metal workers, $.90; carpenters, $.875; and building laborers, $.50. The highest union scale went to stonemasons and bricklayers. They got $1.375 an hour.

Common laborers were paid $.20 to $.25 an hour for an 8-hour day. Shelby County paid its laborers $1.50 a day for a 9-hour day.

Unskilled blacks and whites were at a bare subsistence wage level, particularly those employed to pick cotton. Clark Porteous, veteran Memphis newsman, wrote a feature article in the *Memphis Press Scimitar* in 1938 about those unfortunate people who signed on to pick "white gold."[32] Some 15,000 blacks were loaded up each morning well before dawn to pick cotton in Arkansas. Competing white truck drivers would conduct a heated bidding for workers to get on their trucks. "70 cents a hundred!" "60 cents a hundred!" When the trucks were loaded, they would pull out for Arkansas where they would arrive at the fields about dawn. The work day was from dawn until dusk for about 60 cents a day. Plantation commissaries got part of the pay back through the sale of food and beverages. By today's standards this was a pathetic scene repeated day after day during the cotton harvesting season.

Ford's 8-hour day, and Plough's 5-day week were considered very progressive at the time.

Labor strife started in a major way in 1937. At the Memphis Furniture Manufacturing Company some 450 workers, half of them blacks, walked out striking for an increase in wages and a 50-hour week. After a 10-day strike, these workers accepted the company's offer of a five percent wage increase.

Fig. 29. Early morning recruitment of black workers on West Virginia Avenue near the present intersection of Crump Blvd. and I-55 to hoe cotton on eastern Arkansas farms. (Courtesy of the Library of Congress)

Efforts of the workers to organize a union to affiliate with either the AFL or the CIO failed, and they remained unorganized. That same year the CIO-International Ladies Garment Workers called a strike at the Tri-State Dress Manufacturing Company. Violence broke out between women strikers and nonstrikers, and the Memphis police put up a blockade around the plant to quell the riot. Mayor Overton got involved, declaring that the city had no sympathy for any firm not paying its workers a living wage. The strike was settled after three days, and the CIO claimed its first victory in Memphis. The dress company agreed to a closed union shop, a 40-hour week and payment of at least $12 a week for female workers of average ability.

When the United Auto Workers Union attempted to organize the Ford Assembly Plant and the Fisher Aircraft Plant in 1937, representatives of this CIO affiliate were received with hostility by plant management and by the City of Memphis leadership. They were called agitators and Communists. Mayor Overton warned the organizers that "No foreign labor agitators will be tolerated in Memphis."[33] Memphis banned the organizers. Some of the organizers were beaten by unknown assailants. Others were escorted unceremoniously out of the city by Ford workers.

The CIO-UAW's attempt to organize Ford workers in Memphis was just a few months after the famous "battle of the overpass" at Ford's River Rouge Plant in Michigan when Walter Reuther and his key aides were physically assaulted by Ford security forces. Although both General Motors and Chrysler were unionized in 1937 Henry Ford stated he would never submit to any union.[34] Ford was finally organized in June 1941, and the company granted the union shop for all workers in its plants around the country.

Crump feared the CIO. Its efforts to unionize factory workers and other laboring people were considered damaging to Crump's plans for industrial development in Memphis.[35] Crump had always had good rapport with the American Federation of Labor, and the bold intrusion of the CIO organizers on the scene in Memphis in 1937 threatened the Crump-AFL alliance. Memphis had been a trade union city for nearly half a century, and the AFL was firmly entrenched here. The CIO came on the scene at a time when many American factory workers sought organizational status. The fact that some of the CIO's critics called them Communist sympathizers and left-wing agitators created concern in the conservative South, and Crump made the most of it.

Ultimately, the CIO succeeded in organizing many of the workers in Memphis although that did not occur on a large scale until the early years of World War II. The CIO became the bargaining agent at Firestone in 1942, and this was a major victory for the union. The CIO also gained control at the Buckeye Cotton Oil Company, the U.S. Veterans Hospital, Ford, and several other major employment centers.

The ironic twist to Crump's fight against the CIO was when Mayor Walter Chandler, part of the Crump organization, warmly welcomed the Tennessee CIO delegates to a convention held in Memphis in mid-1942.[36] By that time Ford, Goodyear, Westinghouse, and other major national holdouts had been successfully unionized by the CIO, and the fight against this major industrial union was over. By 1946 the CIO was the predominant labor organization in Memphis with some 30,000 members. Crump, nevertheless, turned his attention to the CIO Political Action Committee in 1946, branding it "Communistic."

Factory workers were not the only wage earners who wanted a union umbrella. Sharecroppers in the Mid-South were very receptive to the organizational efforts in 1937 of the Southern Tenant Farmers Union, an interracial movement of tenant farmers.[37] Northeast Arkansas was the main target, where sharecroppers considered themselves economic slaves. Wages paid to farm workers in the cotton fields were as low as 40 cents per 100 pounds of cotton picked. The Southern Tenant Farmers Union was born in Memphis. At its 1937 convention here, among other reforms, the Union demanded $1.00 per 100 pounds as the minimum wage. Shortly after this meeting it became part of the CIO-affiliated United Cannery, Agricultural, Packing and Allied Workers of America. The creation of the Farm Security Administration by Congress, which sponsored a loan program to assist tenant farmers in buying their holdings, was through the efforts of this union.

In 1955 the AFL and the CIO merged and out of it came the AFL-CIO, a union of some 15 million workers.

A major piece of federal legislation passed in 1938 was the Fair Labor Standards Act—the wage and hour bill. The new law applied to all employees engaged in interstate commerce. Minimum wages for the first year were 25 cents an hour. Thereafter, it was to move up to 40 cents. The law also prohibited child labor under 16 years of age. Memphis workers of course benefited from this new law.

GROWTH OF TRANSPORTATION INDUSTRY

The bright spot of the 1930s was the improvement of river traffic on the Mississippi moving through Memphis. The following tonnage figures illustrate this growth rate:

TABLE 6

WATER-BORNE COMMERCE OF MEMPHIS HARBOR

Year	Tonnage
1920	692,000
1925	838,000
1930	1,591,000
1935	1,538,000
1940	1,841,000

SOURCE: U.S. Army, *Annual Report of the Chief of Engineers,* Part 2, various years.

The Memphis Harbor Commission was created in 1929 to promote the city's port interests, replacing another agency which had been in existence since 1919. During the 1930s, this new citizen's board was the overseer of a major riverfront improvement effort covering a 10-mile area. The old wasteland of garbage and trash thrown over the bluff in previous decades was eliminated, and replaced by the improved Riverside Drive. The Commission also worked with the U.S. Corps of Engineers as that group deepened and widened the Wolf

River Channel. As the riverfront was being improved, railroads complained about the unfair rate advantage water transportation had over them. They claimed that the Federal Barge Line was given a toll-free route on the Mississippi River constructed and maintained by the federal government. The Line also paid no taxes because it was a federal agency.

Air service was on the rise as railroads declined. Chicago & Southern Air Lines in the late 1930s had three flights a day on its route between Chicago and New Orleans. Its Lockheed Electras seated 12 passengers. Eastern Airlines had one daily flight between Memphis and Tampa, with stops at Birmingham, Montgomery, and Tallahassee. American Airlines had three flights daily into Memphis on its route from New York to Los Angeles. Flight time from Memphis to the West Coast was 13 hours on brand new Douglas DC–4's carrying 42 passengers.

The motor freight business had been growing steadily since 1925. By the end of the 1930s some 750 trucks were moving in and out of the city daily.[38] There were 100 motor freight carriers operating here. Ads carried the claim, "Fast overnight service within a 300-mile radius."

Rail passenger service declined somewhat. There were 78 trains daily in and out in 1938. In the early 1920s Memphis had 90 daily passenger trains. The popular trains of the 1930s were the Illinois Central's Panama Limited (operating between Chicago and New Orleans) and Chickasaw (between Memphis and St. Louis); the Yazoo and Mississippi Valley's Planter (Memphis and New Orleans); the Missouri Pacific's Delta Eagle (Memphis and Tallulah, Louisiana); the Rock Island's Choctaw Rocket (Memphis to Amarillo and on to Los Angeles); and the L & N's Azalean and Pan American (Memphis to Cincinnati). The big rage were the "streamliners"—sleek, modernistic, diesel-powered locomotives pulling equally stylish passenger and baggage cars. Fast service and maximum comfort were offered the traveling public.

As an adjunct to its transportation facilities, Memphis at the end of the 1930s had 700,000 square feet of dry storage warehouse space and 1,500,000 square feet of dry or cold storage space. Warehouses had a capacity of one million bales of cotton. The Federal Compress and Warehouse Company's facilities could handle 500,000 bales. Warehousing was a major business activity in Memphis which served very well the storage requirements of the cotton producers during the critical Depression years of surpluses and low prices.

DOWNTOWN BUSINESS

Real estate values declined drastically in 1930, 1931, and 1932, finally stabilizing in 1933. Changes in property ownership were primarily the result of foreclosures. Store vacancies were prevalent in the early '30s even in that zone on Main Street referred to as the "100 percent district" which extended from the south side of Jefferson to the north side of McCall. Locations there were considered the best in the city for retail operations. By late 1936 business had improved and few vacancies existed in the so-called 100 percent district.[39]

Bry's Department Store, an aggressive merchandiser, modernized its store in 1936, and added air conditioning. To stimulate business it annually promoted its big sales event called, "Bry's Daring Sale." This event was started first in 1933, and continued through the decade. Bry's added 700 clerks to its normal staff of 600 during the sale. The company also promoted Bry's Juvenile Hour, a radio program on WMC originating from the store. Management claimed that by 1937 some 3000 children had appeared on this talent program.

The year 1936 was considered a turning point not only for retailing but also for commercial office building. In some 14 buildings surveyed annually, the vacancy rate for office space was 31½ percent in 1934. In mid-1936 it had fallen to 22 percent, and then to 18 percent in 1938. Few investors, however, were making much profit, although in the latter 1930s membership increased in the Memphis Real Estate Board indicating that the real estate market was improving. By 1939 the Board had 48 member firms, 78 salesman members and 29 associate members.

Movies were very popular with Memphians, but this did not necessarily guarantee solvency for some of the theaters. The Orpheum struggled to survive by violating the Sunday closing ban in effect in Memphis. The famous "Sandwich Show" on a Sunday in 1934 was an attempt to get around the law. The operator sold sandwiches and refreshments to the audience, and threw in the movie "free." Some 3200 persons came. The theater's gross income was $1200, and its court fine, $25.

The sordid aspects of the entertainment scene were embodied in the endurance dance marathon contests, popular all across the country. One such event in early 1933 led to the elimination of this cruel spectacle in Memphis. Called the International Walkathon Marathon, it lasted three months. Dancers, to the delight of the audience, were required at various intervals to "run a derby" and "stay in a chain gang," thus eliminating competitors by exhaustion. The end of dance marathons came when the promoter "fixed" the contest and also cheated the winners out of the announced purse. Mayor Overton ran the event out of town.

More respectable dancing took place at the Claridge Hotel where Jan Garber, "the Idol of the Air Lanes," and Art Kassel, with "Kassels in the Air," appeared with their touring dance bands; or at the Peabody's Moroccan Roof where it was Herman Waldman and his orchestra featuring Evelyn Ochs, the "Glamorous Girl of Song" for a $1.00 cover charge; or Seymour Simons and his orchestra. Of course, the city's largest dance floor, the Casino which opened at the Fairgrounds in 1930, was not part of the downtown recreation scene.

Traffic congestion became a problem. Registered vehicles in Shelby County increased to just over 62,000 in 1940. To try to alleviate the tight parking problem in the downtown area, 1900 parking meters were installed just prior to World War II. Main Street parking cost five cents for one-half hour. Parking in front of banks was one cent for 15 minutes. Parking on most other streets was five cents for either one hour or two hours.

Fig. 30. Main Street in the mid-1930s. (Courtesy of Memphis Room, MPL)

Fig. 31. Negotiations at a Beale Street secondhand clothing store in 1939. (Courtesy of the Library of Congress)

Downtown Memphis appeared to be well on its way to recovering in the latter 1930s. It had been in a desperate state in 1931 and 1932, and reflected the general condition of the overall Memphis economy. Perhaps the best indication of recovery was the introduction of the parking meters.

THE CITY'S FINANCES

The decade began with rising tax delinquencies, and with major assessment inequalities among different types of property. Owners of more expensive homes were assessed at lower assessed-to-market value percentages than owners of either moderate or inexpensive homes. Many premium commercial properties were underassessed. The city simply was not getting all of the revenue it was legally entitled to receive in the early 1930s. The Depression did not cause all of the major tax delinquencies, however; many were carryovers from the 1920s or even earlier periods.

The drive began about 1933 to try to collect back taxes. Mayor Overton asked the Memphis Real Estate Board's president to instruct members to have any of their clients owing taxes to pay up, and to tell them that it was urgent that the city's credit be perserved.[40] The city was trying to collect about $3 million in delinquent taxes; and in a special gesture it announced that if any back taxes dating from 1921 to 1931 were paid, the delinquent taxpayers would not be charged any costs, commissions or penalties. Pressure was put on the assistant city attorney to push the tax suits, but he pleaded with Mayor Overton for more manpower. He said that under present conditions, trying to collect taxes was "like trying to sweep the ocean back with a broom."[41] In 1936 long-time close aid to E. H. Crump, Joe Boyle who was Commissioner of Finance and Institutions, spearheaded a tax collection drive. Five years later the city had collected only $1 million of the back taxes.[42] Collecting delinquent taxes was very tough going.

Among the principal tax delinquents were the South Memphis Land Company, the Lyric Theatre, the properties held in the estate of Robert R. Church, Sr. that were being managed by Robert R. Church, Jr., and the property of attorney and civic leader, Tom Collier. Neither the South Memphis Land Company nor the Lyric owners had paid any taxes in years. Bob Church, Jr., had not paid any taxes since 1920. The city finally claimed all of Church's property, including the family home on South Lauderdale for back taxes.[43] Property values had declined substantially in the Beale Street area in the 1920s and 1930s, and the annual income from the Church properties had diminished considerably.[44]

The all-time classic tax delinquency case in Memphis involved the colorful and controversial Thomas B. Collier. The "Tom Collier Tax Case" stretched out for 31 years. Collier fought off the city and the state in and out of the courts for so many years that when asked one time what his occupation was, he replied, attorney and tax litigant. The Collier property was delinquent from 1905 to

1936; and the city had a claim on Tom Collier for $300,000 in back taxes, plus interest and penalties which pushed the total indebtedness to over $750,000.

The Collier property was a large, undeveloped tract in the East Parkway-Central Avenue area. On part of the site today is the campus of Christian Brothers College. The total holdings, valued at one time at about $4 million, encompassed 280 acres. When Collier was in the Tennessee legislature in 1903 his bill to incorporate his property as the town of Alicia was rejected by the Senate. Shortly thereafter the long running battle began. Collier, to aggravate the city, tried to reclaim that part of the East Parkway bordering his property, holding that the city violated the original provisions of his land dedication by permitting trucks to use the Parkway for a detour. He also filed a suit against the city claiming the development of the Fairgrounds caused water to drain off on his property.

The scrappy landowner, known for his red ties and his jousting with the Crump organization, was once asked, according to veteran newspaperman Eldon Roark, Jr., "Why don't you pay the tax bills, sell the property, and live like a millionaire—enjoy yourself?" Collier responded, "Enjoy myself? Why, I'm having the time of my life!" He finally settled with the city in 1936. The city got 200 of his 280 acres, most of which was on the south side of Union Avenue. Collier died in 1944, and his obituary in *The Commercial Appeal* had the following headline:

> Death summons Tom Collier From Courts and Politics—Famed Tax Litigant and Opponent of Crump Administration Dies Unexpectedly on Street—Colorful Career Had Covered 66 Exciting and Stormy Years.[45]

Collier, who for years jogged on the streets of Memphis barefooted and who needled Crump and his key lieutenants unmercifully at public meetings, qualifies as one of Memphis' all-time personalities. He was also as gracious as he was tenacious. When Walter Chandler was reappointed City Attorney in 1931, Collier sent him a box of roses with this message: "Solicitations to Captain Chandler from one who is persecuted through you, but not peeved at you. Tom Collier"

Tight budgets were a feature of the city's financial austerity campaign of the 1930s. Tax delinquency forced restraint. Watkins Overton was mayor, but it was really Mr. Crump who was the chief financial watchdog on matters pertaining to municipal finances. Crump was exceedingly tight with money. He even spent time looking at expense accounts of city employees. One example illustrates Crump's attention to detail. The city planning director in the 1930s received a salary of $200 a month plus gas for his car. Part of the director's duties were to map the county area, so it required a lot of driving. Crump saw a monthly gasoline bill for $17 and sent a curt message to Mayor Overton expressing his concern.

This niggardliness with the public's money resulted in a surplus of $1.5

million in 1940. The bonded indebtedness in 1940 was $46.4 million. Some $25.3 million was for the Light, Gas and Water Division debt, which was being retired expeditiously by the revenues from that public agency. Memphis Power & Light Company was convinced that the wily political leader's real interest was the profits generated by this private company. Crump, they claimed, looked upon the acquisition as a source of additional revenue for the city.

RECOVERY

Memphis spent a decade in adversity along with the rest of America. Hardships came with frequency and from all direction in the early years of the 1930s, and were unrelenting in their severity. The city retrogressed economically during this period. But in the latter 1930s, through a fairly effective system of social planning and discipline, Memphis did reclaim some of its lost ground. Municipal government with substantial federal financial help did a good job in identifying problems and attacking them. Mr. Crump was very effective in dealing with Washington and getting about the maximum of assistance when he requested it. He also remained a pragmatist in the use of power; he took on several adversaries, including the private utility company and the CIO, to show his strength. He probably felt deeply that he was protecting the citizens of Memphis. He wanted cheap power and he wanted a peaceful labor situation going into negotiations with any new industries that might have been considering a relocation to Memphis.

One of the city's many achievements was getting strong civic support for improved housing and slum eradication. The groundwork was laid in the late 1930s for an urban renewal and housing program that would become significant in the 1950s and 1960s.

The Memphis economy was not particularly strong at the end of the 1930s, but it was stable. No major changes had occurred in its underlying economic base to raise incomes along the broad front of the population. Memphis still had a large unskilled labor force incapable of commanding much income for its productivity. Somehow or other, despite the economic structural problems, Memphis seemed more mature on the eve of World War II, and it had greater self-confidence in its ability to respond to new opportunities.

14

World War II and Recovery

The decade of the 1940s started off for Memphians in a bizarre fashion at 12:15 A.M. on a Central Station platform beside the Illinois Central's Panama Limited. Here, surrounded by a huge band of his followers that included the high command of the Shelby County Organization, E. H. Crump took the oath of office as Mayor of Memphis.[1] Promptly upon completion of the swearing-in Crump handed City Attorney Will Gerber an envelope which contained a letter of resignation to be delivered the following day to the City Commission. The midnight ceremony was indeed a strange sight. Many of the political loyalists were in New Year's Eve formal attire. All were in a festive mood to honor Crump and to see him off on his trip to the Sugar Bowl game in New Orleans later that day.

Crump had been elected Mayor with no opposition. Almost 32,000 votes were cast for him in the November 1939 election. Prior to this election Crump told the electorate that he was strictly a stand-in for U.S. Congressman Walter Chandler,[2] who did not want to resign his House seat until after a vote was taken on an important bill before Congress. So Crump ran for Chandler. Crump made no campaign speeches and he offered no platform. His organization, however, got out the vote.

Acceding to Crump's wishes the City Commission on 2 January 1940 selected Walter Chandler the city's mayor. Once again, to no one's surprise, Mr. Crump had demonstrated to the citizens his awesome political power and his total command of government in Memphis and Shelby County. Crump decided how local government should be run and who should run it.

PRE-PEARL HARBOR DAYS

The decade started off in a climate of hope that economic conditions were

Fig. 32. Boss Ed Crump, waving, and his principal organization leaders pose while attending the 1940 Democratic Party Convention in Chicago. In front to the immediate left of Crump is Senator Kenneth McKellar. In front center is the dapper Governor Prentice Cooper. To the right of Crump in the rear is Mayor Walter Chandler. (Courtesy of City of Memphis Archives)

improving. Civic boosters did not seem as concerned about the 1940 Census figures for Memphis as they had at the beginning of preceeding decades. There was less of a feeling of intercity growth competition, and far less dismay when, as shown below, Memphis was in sixth position among its rivals in the South and Southwest.

TABLE 7
1940 CENSUS OF POPULATION FOR SELECTED CITIES

City	Population
New Orleans	494,537
Houston	384,514
Louisville	319,077
Atlanta	302,288
Dallas	294,734
MEMPHIS	292,942
Birmingham	267,583
San Antonio	253,854

Memphis had not annexed any contiguous surburban areas in the 1930s to help boost its 1940 population figure. Planning consultant Harland Bartholomew may have succeeded in convincing the city in his 1938 Plan that it had more than enough open land within the existing boundaries on which to grow. The next annexation to occur was in 1944.

Unemployment was still high in 1940. Just over 14 percent of the labor force was either on the WPA rolls or seeking work. Of those employed, one of every four was working in the wholesale and retail trade sector. One out of five was in manufacturing; and one out of five was in the personal services category. Only 3.1 percent were employed in government jobs.

Business conditions improved noticeably in 1941, and the Chamber of Commerce enthusiastically pronounced the year the best business year in history.[3] The city ran full page advertisements in *The New York Times* and *The Chicago Tribune* promoting Memphis as a location for wartime and postwar industries. Its leaders were optimistic about the city's future economy, and considered the stagnation of the 1930s past history. Memphis responded to improve conditions in the cotton market. As Appendix B demonstrates, cotton sales in Memphis were high in 1941, and the general cotton market was on the threshold of better times.

The war in Europe in 1940 and 1941 was causing great concern in the United States. France had fallen to the Germans, and so had the Netherlands, Belgium, Luxembourg, Denmark and Norway in 1940. The Battle of Britain was in full swing in September 1940 as the Luftwaffe pounded England, with the survival of that nation at stake. The Japanese were moving toward French

Indochina; and the United States was warning them against aggression. Then in 1941 the Germans invaded Greece, Yugoslavia and Russia. The war area was expanding rapidly.

Memphis like the rest of the nation began to feel the effects of the war. Congress passed the Selective Service Act in 1940 and 16 million Americans registered, including 49,000 from Shelby County. The war threats stemming from Europe added to Japanese aggression, raised concern about inflation and possible shortages of basic commodities. By 1941 some industrial production in Memphis was defense related. The Chickasaw Ordnance Works began operations on a site between Millington and Shelby-Meeman State Park. The plant, operated by DuPont, originally produced explosives for the British. Later its production was for American munition requirements.

Many Memphians realized that we were unofficially at war in 1941; but it took the attack on Pearl Harbor on 7 December 1941 to make it official, and to make America's entry direct and forthright.

MEMPHIS AFTER PEARL HARBOR

The reaction of the nation and all Memphians was probably best summed up in public statements on Pearl Harbor by Mr. Crump and Mayor Walter Chandler on 7 December:

> *Mr. Crump:* "It's now war to the finish and all Memphians and people throughout Shelby County and the State of Tennessee will rally to the cause."
>
> *Mayor Chandler:* "This means hari-kari for Japan, the firing squad for Hitler and ultimate victory for the democracies. Memphians will do their duty to the limit as they have done in every great struggle. The City Commission already has an excellent defense program worked out. It will be put into effect immediately."[4]

A few days later *The Commercial Appeal* headlined an article, "Hearts Pound As Young, Old Flock to Colors While City Girds Its Loins for Battle."[5] The Recruiting Office at the Post Office was swamped with volunteers, and personnel there went on a 24-hour basis to sign up a large number of enlistees. Twelve Selective Service boards were set up in Shelby County, and during the early years of the war they handled 160,000 registrations. Some 40,000 of these registrants actually entered the armed services.

The war was a great cause for Memphians. The public came forth to support war loan drives, scrap metal drives, the Victory Book Campaign to provide books for servicemen, volunteer work in local hospitals, staffing the Cotton Carnival Servicemen's Hall on North Main or the USO Club in the Tennessee Club Building, and countless other volunteer causes. The Office of Civilian Defense, a federal agency, offered courses in air raid warden training and in first aid, and some 25,000 Memphians completed these courses in 1942. Great cooperation was given throughout Shelby County in the practice blackout held on 9 June 1942. *The Commercial Appeal* on that morning warned its readers: "Don't forget to blackout your lights tonight at 9:00 o'clock—It might save lives in the future in case of air raids." The public did without protest!

Rationing began throughout the United States on 27 December 1941 as a war measure. Auto tires were the first item to be rationed. The first ration books issued in 1942 provided coupons for sugar. Shortly thereafter coffee and gasoline were rationed. Rationing on a point system started in 1943 for a variety of food products. The federal agency in charge was the Office of Price Administration (OPA), which was responsible for fixing prices and controlling rents. Price ceilings were set on all commodities except farm products. But even with strict wartime controls, by V-J day consumer prices in the United States had risen 31 percent despite strong efforts to prevent inflation.

The war created jobs in Memphis, including jobs for several thousand women who had not worked before. Most of DuPont's employees at the Chickasaw Ordnance Plant were women. The Memphis Street Railway Company hired women drivers for buses and operators for streetcars. The various government installations employed women heavily.

Major military and naval installations helped pump huge payrolls into the Memphis economy during the war. Among the largest installations were the Quartermaster Supply Depot on Airways; the Air Force Depot on Jackson; and the Naval Air Technical Training Center, Naval Air Station and Naval Hospital—all at Millington. The Kennedy General Hospital, located at Park and Getwell, opened in 1943, and by 1945 it had a bed capacity for nearly 4600 patients. The Second Army Headquarters was in Memphis from 1940 to 1946. The Fourth Ferrying Group, engaged in global ferrying operations, was stationed at the Memphis Airport.

Firestone stopped producing private automobile tires and went into the manufacturing of rubber life rafts and tires for army vehicles. Ford shut down its automobile assembly line, and from 1941 through mid-1943 turned to war work producing airplane engines. Fisher Aircraft Division of General Motors built wings and fuselages for bombers and Continental Can Company manufactured shell cases. Plough, Incorporated also entered war related work, producing pharmaceutical products under government contract. Kimberly-Clark came to Memphis in 1941 to manufacture cellu-cotton products, and Quaker Oats came in 1943 to produce furfural alcohol needed for synthetic rubber.

War production was a major part of the Memphis economy, and it helped the city reach its goal of becoming a manufacturing city that had so long eluded it throughout its history. But industrial war production placed heavy burdens on the city to provide housing for the several thousand war workers who migrated to Memphis from 1942 through 1945.

HOUSING SHORTAGE

The Chamber of Commerce published an industrial promotion brochure in March 1941 which carried the following comments on housing conditions in Memphis:

> There is no housing shortage in Memphis and building is helping with the growth of the City. Memphis is well-housed. Memphis is singularly free from crowded and adverse tenement conditions. With an area of 50.68 square miles, the average density of population is 8.51 per acre, a most favorable ratio.[6]

The Chamber was obviously trying to put the city's best foot forward, and distorted the real housing facts. In 1941 there was a critical housing shortage in Memphis, and much of the existing inventory was in the substandard category. Defense workers moving into Memphis quickly absorbed any surplus housing units, and by early 1942 there were virtually no houses or apartments for those not engaged in war work. The situation got worse as an estimated 30,000 to 40,000 people flocked into Memphis between the time of Pearl Harbor and mid-1943.

Several agencies were organized for the sole purpose of trying to find housing. The Chamber of Commerce formed the Rent Bureau. Mayor Chandler appointed the Citizens Housing Committee to try to find solutions. There was also the Memphis War Housing Center and the Homes Registration Bureau. Later in 1944 the Mayor established the Emergency Housing Committee, and named Joseph A. Fowler, Executive Director of the Memphis Housing Authority, as Chairman.

Mayor Chandler labeled the housing shortage the city's number one problem. He asked citizens with extra space to make sacrifices to provide housing for war workers, military personnel and other newcomers to the city. Many converted attics to apartments in older homes. Many tiny cottages were converted to duplexes. Even abandoned gasoline stations were converted to housing. Fire Chief Connie O'Sullivan expressed great concern about fires in these crowded conditions. Many renters were evicted during the war years by landlords. There was practically no housing available for blacks.[7]

New housing production came to a halt in 1942. The War Production Board froze all new home construction except that classified as prime defense housing.[8] Rehabilitation of housing was permitted by the WPB, and local builders were encouraged to fix up older houses to meet the demand. Building permits in 1942 were down to only $4.3 million in valuation versus $15 million in 1941.

The federal government feared that housing shortages in heavy defense and military-oriented cities were leading to private real estate market speculation; so in April 1942, through the OPA, a rent freeze was imposed.[9] The OPA also watched very closely those property sales in which the new buyer attempted to evict the building's tenants. Purchasers had to put one-third down on the price and the tenants given 90 days notice before the new owner could ask the existing occupants to move. All rents were ordered rolled back to the levels of 1 March 1942. Through the OPA's Memphis office in the Sterick Building a staff of investigators and attorneys checked to see that all landlords complied with the rent control order.

The City Planning Commission's director continued to keep alive the matter of redevelopment planning to rehabilitate housing and to eradicate the city's slums.[10] It was his suggestion that Memphis should prepare redevelopment plans so that when the war ended private capital could take a direct interest in this program.

PUBLIC TRANSPORTATION

Gasoline rationing reduced the use of private cars, and increased ridership on the Memphis Street Railway Company's streetcars and buses. The passengers carried annually increased from 60 million in 1941 to 127.7 million in 1946. To serve the heavy demand, new coaches and buses were added and new routes established. Industries staggered their work hours to help alleviate the congestion.

During 1944 the Street Railway Company's 50-year franchise expired, and Mr. Crump decided that this was the time to try to buy this utility. Crump had apparently had his eye on taking over the company as far back as 1938 when the city was negotiating to buy the Memphis Power & Light Company. The Crump organization kept emphasizing publicly that the Street Railway Company was part of the "old Wall Street crowd," and that there was secret speculation in the company's stock.[11] The city did not buy the company, and ended up granting another 20 years on the franchise beginning in 1945.

INDUSTRIAL PROMOTION

Memphis business leaders were not in any state of euphoria over the potential for lasting results from the war-created industrial economy. They knew that at war's end the city faced problems on the closing of the defense-related facilities. This possibility became a concern, and some consideration was given to planning for postwar diversification. The Chamber of Commerce and the Cotton Exchange promoted the idea of making Memphis a textile center. A study was prepared which claimed that cotton mill operators could operate more profitably in Memphis because of the city's proximity to an estimated 37 percent of the U.S. market.[12] It pointed out the transportation cost savings, the city's large labor supply and low taxes available to textile manufacturers. The local concerns about postwar industry were not premature. Soon thereafter Memphis had to face reality.

V-J Day

"War Over, Tokyo Says Terms Accepted" stated the 14 August 1945 headline of *The Commercial Appeal*. The atomic bomb was dropped on Hiroshima on 6 August 1945. Four days later the Japanese announced they were ready to surrender. The final instrument of surrender was formally signed on the battleship *Missouri* on 2 September 1945. Commissioner Joe Boyle lifted the city's antinoise ordinance for the wild celebration. And the city celebrated!

Memphians had lived through another crisis period. Some 40,000 from Shelby County had been in uniform by war's end. Of this number, 662 died or were missing in action when the final tally was made in mid-1946. Civilians who had remained at home had played an important role, and although they had not made the ultimate sacrifice or been injured in combat or other service-related actions, these citizens had made many sacrifices.

Memphis began planning for the next phase in its economic history. Mr. Crump, still very active and still very much in control politically, provided the initial leadership.

Memphis Faces Postwar Recovery

The sudden termination of the war brought some potentially serious economic problems for the United States and for Memphis, which had been rather deeply involved with defense production industries as well as with military and naval installations. Wartime plants closed almost instantly in September 1945. This shutdown released thousands of civilian war workers to enter the job market once again. But this time there was added competition from a horde of returning war veterans. President Truman told the nation that it faced a period of great prosperity, but that there might be problems during the transition period. Shortages of products might cause inflation and while private industry rejuvenated itself during the transition, there might be unemployment. Fortunately, the worse fears of federal government planners and many economists were not warranted. The transition period did not last very long.

Memphis was no different from the rest of the nation in the transition year of 1946. The United States Employment Service office in Memphis in February 1946 had 7,000 job applications and only a few hundred job requests from employers. Staff members of the Employment Service canvassed the entire city to find jobs for the unemployed. Many veterans chose to enroll in college or in vocational training programs under the G.I. Bill of Rights which relieved some of the pressure. Without the G.I. Bill of Rights the number seeking jobs would have probably doubled during 1946 in Memphis.

The strain of the transition lasted just about one year in Memphis. By April 1947 in Shelby County and West Memphis, Arkansas, the total employed labor force was 178,000. Only 9,500 people were unemployed and seeking work. The unemployment rate before World War II was 14 percent in 1940. In 1947 it was only 5 percent. And as shown in Table 8 the size of the employed labor force had grown considerably in this 7-year period.

TABLE 8
EMPLOYED CIVILIANS IN THE MEMPHIS METROPOLITAN DISTRICT

Workers	1940	1947	Change
Male	90,196	117,366	+27,170
Female	42,993	60,729	+17,736
Total	133,189	178,095	+44,906

SOURCE: Bureau of the Census, Current Population Reports, "Labor Force Characteristics of the Memphis, Tennessee, Metropolitan District", April 1947.

Memphis had a good start in industrial employment and its leaders were optimistic that the city was on the move. Always behind the scenes in manipulating the promotional efforts was Mr. Crump. He constantly pushed for publicity and for programs which he felt would help the city. Immediately after V-J Day he was pressuring Senator McKellar to arrange for the Army-Navy football game to be played in Memphis in 1947. In his letter to McKellar, see Figure 33, he also mentioned that he wanted a World's Fair for Memphis in 1950, and that perhaps McKellar should look into obtaining federal financial assistance. Memphis was unsuccessful in attracting the Army-Navy game or in getting funds to stage a World's Fair, despite Crump's agitation for this kind of promotional effect.

Although Crump felt the Army-Navy game and a World's Fair would be helpful, he was negative toward horseracing in Memphis as a recreational attraction. Crump was an avid racing fan, and seldom missed the Kentucky Derby or the major stakes races in Hot Springs, Arkansas, but he did not think racing should be permitted in Memphis. He could not see a race track contributing anything to a commercial city like Memphis.[13]

Crump continued to play his role as the city and county's unofficial but principal city planner. Through his support a major bond election was held in March 1947. The citizens endorsed a $25 million bond program covering some 24 different public improvements by a 93 percent favorable vote. Mr. Crump's favorite pastime seemed to be riding around Memphis and the county area noting where improvements were needed. A year before his death in 1954, Crump at the age of 79 was still making lists of major improvements he felt the city and county should consider. At the time he was quoted as saying:

E.H.CRUMP & CO.

INVESTMENT BANKERS

REAL ESTATE LOANS-MORTGAGE BONDS
INSURANCE-REAL ESTATE

MEMPHIS, TENN.

3
TO
25
YEAR
EASY PAYMENT
REAL ESTATE
LOANS

Sept. 26, 1945

Senator Kenneth McKellar,
Senate Office Building,
Washington, D.C.

Dear Senator:-

Memphis must not sleep on any of its opportunities to keep in the limelight during these next few years of sharp competition among American cities to capture a maximum of the postwar expansion which is just beyond the horizon for those who are willing to reach out and get it.

Among other efforts, it seems to us the time is ripe to go after an Army-Navy football game for Memphis in 1947. Of course, we will need your help and are counting strong upon it. Once the ball is started to rolling, I am sure that you may rely upon the assistance of many of your colleagues, not only those composing the Tennessee delegation, but also those Senators and Congressmen representing adjoining states.

There is no reason that I know of why this great annual football classic should not come South for a change, particularly since the Democratic party is sitting firmly in the saddle in Washington.

I am sure you will need no suggestion from me as to how to proceed. The main thing, as I see it, is for us to take time by the forelock and get going before some other Southern city beats us to the draw. I would appreciate your reaction to the idea of obtaining this wonderful advertising for our city and state.

Am also advocating a World's Fair for Memphis for 1950. Dallas, Richmond, Nashville, Atlanta, New Orleans and St. Louis have had World's Fairs. Also New York, Chicago, Philadelphia, Buffalo, San Francisco and Seattle. I understand the government contributed a neat sum to all of these enterprises and, of course, the states likewise contributed. This idea for the moment is more or less in an embryonic state, but it is something well worth thinking about even this far in advance, and I hope you will give me your ideas about it.

Best wishes,

Your friend,

EHC:H

Copy to Senator Tom Stewart
Congressman Clifford Davis.

You know, of course, Army-Navy plays in New York, Philadelphia, and Baltimore. A few years ago they went out West - to Chicago. We would like for them to come to Memphis for their Southern game - our stadium will be enlarged for it.
E.H.C.

The South's Largest Direct Writing Insurance Agency

Fig. 33. Mr. Crump requests the aid of Senator McKellar in attracting the 1947 Army-Navy football game to Memphis. (Courtesy of Memphis Room, McKellar Papers, MPL)

I am in love with this beautiful city. It gets better and better all the time. Let's not be short-sighted. Figure the city as a whole for all the people. We cannot afford to stand still. We dare not content ourselves with what measure of growth we have had. Let's all say we are full of new beginnings and the city will move on . . . .[14]

Among Crump's long standing crusades was his running battle with the railroads concerning grade crossings and overpasses. One such impediment that rankled him was the Union Belt Line overpass right over the intersection of Central and East Parkway. Crump, a letter-to-the-editor writer of long standing in Memphis, took his case to the public:

If Memphis is to be a tremendous city and it will be there should be more subways here and there. That bottleneck overpass almost in the heart of Memphis . . . should be and will be done away with. That contraption is not only unsightly, but dangerous where so many automobiles meet there.[15]

The overpass eventually came down in 1951, and the tracks were rerouted after considerable wrangling between Crump and the railroad.

Crump had bulldog tenacity once he got an idea. But he did not always win. One suggestion which failed was his agitation to get huge lighted pylons installed at the entrances to the Memphis-Arkansas Bridge. He prodded Senator McKellar to get approval from the federal government, and he prodded federal officials directly. Crump felt that if Louisville had impressively lighted pylons, Memphis should, too. His correspondence on this one issue was extensive.

This type of pressure to gain physical improvements was typical of Crump. He seemed to have his finger in every pie in Memphis during this postwar period of city improvements. But Crump was also heavily involved in economic development planning and he probably deserves most of the credit for the city's excellent recovery following World War II.

His greatest economic contribution was one which blossomed after his death in 1954. This was the project which closed the Tennessee Chute of the Mississippi River, separating the Memphis riverfront from Presidents Island, and led to the development of this huge island into a major industrial district. Crump had precipitated study of the idea when he discussed with civic leaders in mid-1945 the lack of industrial sites on the riverfront. Shortly thereafter Major General Max Tyler suggested closing the chute and building a connecting link from the shoreline to Presidents Island. From that point on, Crump, aided by many civic and governmental leaders, pushed through this giant project to develop Presidents Island and McKellar Lake. At the time of Crump's death the industrial development of Presidents Island had just barely started, so he did not get to see the final results of his push for industrial sites.

The city renewed its annexation program in 1947 by annexing almost 47 square miles of area, including Presidents Island. In 1950 it took in another 18 square miles. These two additions brought into the city about 75,000 people.

This physical growth by annexation created some serious city planning problems. The city's planning department was largely without a technical staff and incapable of providing proper zoning, street planning, and transit planning for these new sections of the city. In the early 1950s the assistant city planning engineer appealed without effect to Mayor Overton, who had returned to city government, to provide staff so this work could be undertaken. The lack of an effective city planning staff was a persistent problem in the post-World War II period, and the city lost the attention it had given planning in the 1920s and early 1930s when the Bartholomew Plan still generally guided its physical growth.

POSTWAR HOUSING

Immediately after V-J Day, when some 30,000 war veterans began to return to Memphis, the city became aware that the housing problem had reached the level of a calamity. Some 19,000 of these veterans were married and looking for housing.

Mayor Walter Chandler referred to housing as the city's number one problem. Almost one year later the Citizens Housing Committee, discouraged by the short term outlook, labeled the housing problem as the darkest picture in the city's history. Some 200 barracks-type housing units were dismantled in Florida and brought to Memphis in 1946 for a project called Pendleton Place near Park Avenue and Pendleton, and over 3,900 veterans applied for this housing.[16]

Another concern was the potential impact on rents when the rent controls, administered by OPA, expired on 30 June 1946. Landlords said they would be raising rents from 10 to 20 percent, and this sent a chill throughout Memphis. Rent controls were reapplied one year later when Congress passed a new control act.

The greatest shortage was in single family units in price ranges most Memphians could afford. There was concern whether local builders could provide houses within the price range of most prospects. The problem was to find a way to get housing built for people who could not pay $8,000 for a house, or $70 a month for a rental unit.

Added to the shortage of standard housing was the festering problem of the city's slums. Joseph A. Fowler, Executive Director of the Memphis Housing Authority, pointed out that six square miles of the city's area were wretched slums.[17] The City and the MHA appealed to private builders to find ways to build inexpensive housing. The latter group cooperated by starting some 8,500 housing units in 1946 and 1947. By mid 1952 the shortage, except for blacks, was largely eliminated. In the Memphis area some 40,700 residential units had been completed, nearly 25,500 of them in the city.

Housing for blacks continued to be a serious problem. In 1950 Fowler

TABLE 9
Birth Rates in Shelby County, Selected Years

Year	White Population	White Births	White Birth Rate [1]	Black Population	Black Births	Black Birth Rate [1]	Combined White/Black Birth Rate [1]
Depression Years							
1930	180,200	3,467	19.2	128,300	2,075	16.2	18.0
1935	192,200	2,590	13.5	140,700	2,541	18.1	15.4
1940	203,600	3,130	15.4	155,900	2,850	18.5	16.7
War Years							
1942	220,600	4,365	19.8	157,500	3,338	21.2	20.3
1943	230,100	4,554	19.8	159,600	3,331	20.9	20.3
1944	239,500	4,375	18.3	161,500	3,424	21.2	19.4
1945	248,500	4,595	18.5	163,600	3,437	21.0	19.5
Immediate Postwar Years							
1946	258,800	5,329	20.6	165,300	3,947	23.9	21.9
1947	269,200	6,431	23.9	168,600	4,564	27.2	25.1
1948	281,500	6,197	22.1	171,300	4,999	29.1	24.8
1949	291,500	6,960	23.9	175,100	5,451	31.1	26.2
1950	303,000	7,166	23.7	180,000	5,973	32.9	27.2

SOURCE: Memphis and Shelby County Health Department.
1. Live births per 1,000 population in Shelby County.

estimated that, if housing could be built to rent for less than $40 a month, the demand by blacks would average 5,000 units a year.[18] MHA's Fowler estimated that blacks then occupied 35,000 of the city's 50,000 slum units. The local FHA director also saw a good market among blacks for new single family units selling below $5,000.

The multitude of public works projects, plus the thousands of residential units under construction after 1946, created a huge demand for construction workers. Some 7,300 were employed in the early spring of 1947. Another 2,000 got construction jobs over the next several years as Memphis tried to catch up with the postwar demand for housing.

POSTWAR POPULATION

When the war ended, Shelby County had an estimated 412,400 residents. Five years later, the county had almost 483,000. Part of the increase was due to an increasing birth rate for both the white and black populations. The majority, however, was due to net in-migration into the Memphis area.

The birth rates changed drastically from the low rates prevailing in the 1930s. As shown in Table 9, the birth rate started to accelerate following the war, increasing more rapidly for blacks than for whites.

END OF THE TRANSITION

Memphis made the transition from a wartime to a peacetime economy without too many strains. The approximate cut-off point for the postwar recovery was probably the early 1950s. Unemployment remained at five percent of the labor force despite continual enlargement of the numbers of persons in the labor force. Median incomes in Memphis, as reported for 1949 in the 1950 U.S. Census, were $2,264 for whites and $986 for blacks. The comparable median figures for the entire United States were $2,053 for whites and $961 for blacks. Memphis figures for both whites and blacks were also comparable with the median figures for Atlanta, Birmingham, and New Orleans.

Mr. Crump was very much in control of the destiny of Memphis. He proved it over and over again during the transition years. Crump had a falling-out with President Truman because of his support of civil rights legislation. Along with Senator McKellar, Crump opposed Truman's nomination in 1948. In the presidential election that year Shelby County gave Strom Thurmond, the States Rights Party candidate, 40 percent of its vote; Truman, 37 percent; and Thomas E. Dewey, the Republican candidate, 22 percent. Meanwhile, the statewide results were Truman, 49 percent; Dewey, 37 percent; and Thurmond, only 13 percent. Crump feared that President Truman's committee on civil rights would have police powers over cities and counties in Tennessee and in other Southern states.[19]

Crump was influential in the developmental progress Memphis was making in the late 1940s. He continued to exercise his influence in Memphis right

Fig. 34. The theme of the 1951 Cotton Carnival was "King Cotton Fights for Freedom." The King, pictured above, was 28-year-old Edward W. (Ned) Cook. His Queen was 20-year-old Eleanor Eugenia Turner. (Courtesy of the Mississippi Valley Collection, John Brister Library, Memphis State University)

up until his death of a heart ailment at the age of 80 on 16 October 1954. In *The New York Times* obituary, Crump was referred to as "one of the nation's last old time, big city political bosses."[20] Crump left his imprint on Memphis in a multitude of ways. The history of the Memphis economy from 1909 to 1954 certainly was influenced mightily by Crump. And, of course, in politics Crump completely dominated that segment of life. His "last hurrah" in his long and colorful life was Memphis' postwar recovery period.

15

Dynamic Urban-Suburban Land Form Changes

In 1938, Memphis was told by its planning consultant, Harland Bartholomew, that its ultimate population would probably be about 344,000, reached sometime between 1960 and 1970.[1] In the Depression years Memphis had an incorporated area of 48.5 square miles. Bartholomew and his staff were confident that there was adequate undeveloped space within the city's boundaries to be capable of absorbing all but about 12,000 of the anticipated 60,000 increase in population. Birth rates had fallen nationally, as in Memphis, and population experts were forecasting general population slowdowns for the future. Bartholomew acted on these trends in preparing his forecast. At that very unspectacular period in Memphis' economic growth, the best estimate was that the greatest increase of population in the city would be "out East." In 1938, "out East" meant a mile or two east of East Parkway in the vicinity of Highland Avenue.

There is no reason to fault the planners of those Depression days for their shortsighted forecasts. Very few Americans in the 1930s were particularly optimistic about growth in the near and intermediate future. Bartholomew and his staff in their wildest dreams could not possibly anticipate the extensive physical growth of Memphis following World War II. They did not quite have the imagination to foresee that "out East" would be a loosely defined geographic area extending miles to the east of Highland Avenue. Their crystal ball was not clear enough to indicate postwar land absorption for residential subdivisions, shopping centers, and industrial facilities to the north of the city beyond the Wolf River and to the south below the Nonconnah Creek, in areas traditionally remote from Memphis.

Strange then was the forecast in 1947 of Memphis real estate professionals who boldly stated that Memphis would have a population of 1,000,000 by 1995 or 2000. But when Bartholomew's staff came back in the mid-1950s to prepare another plan, these consultants estimated that by 1980 the city would have 800,000 residents and the surrounding county area another 150,000.[2] This time Bartholomew's staff was more on target with their estimates. Memphis was advised that it must annex the growing suburbs of Frayser to the north of the city and Whitehaven to the south, or else be strangled by sprawling, unplanned urbanizations where planning standards might not be high if permitted to grow large without controls.

These suburban areas, and other undeveloped land within the city, were the locations of numerous residential subdivisions developed to serve a huge market of middle and upper middle class people looking for new homes. Aided by FHA and VA financing, thousands of families and individuals qualified for home loans which required only modest down payments and which permitted amortization over periods of 20 to 30 years. It is extremely doubtful that the suburbs of most American cities would have expanded so rapidly in the late 1940s and in the 1950s had there been no FHA or VA financing.

The suburbanization movement started almost immediately on the return of World War II veterans. The first major signs of large, new subdivisions were seen in 1947. Peripheral areas were cleared to make way for housing developers. The fringe areas being developed in a more or less leapfrog manner were primarily within the present-day Memphis expressway system. After 1960, as shown in Table 10, new subdivisions were developed in zones beyond today's expressway system.

TABLE 10
POST-WORLD WAR II POPULATION GROWTH

	1950	1960	1970
Memphis Incorporated Area	*396,000*	*497,500*	*620,800*
a. Within Expressway System	396,000	468,700	449,500
b. Remainder of City	—	28,800	171,300
Other Shelby County	86,400	129,500	97,900
Total Shelby County	482,400	627,000	718,700

SOURCE: Mississippi-Arkansas-Tennessee Council of Governments (MATCOG), and the U.S. Bureau of the Census.

The motor vehicle aided and abetted the sprawl away from the prewar central city area. In 1938 motor vehicle registration figures indicated that there were about 60,000 cars and trucks. In 1950 in Shelby County registrations exceeded 137,000. And by 1976, they exceeded 456,000. The automobile, inexpensive land on the fringe of the city, and government insured housing loans changed land use patterns not only for residential, but also for business and industrial usage. These powerful forces putting pressure on postwar land use should have brought to the public's attention planner Harland Bartholomew's admonitions in the 1920s and 1930s that if Memphis were to remain physically efficient it must grow in an orderly fashion. Unfortunately for Memphis the city's longtime planning director Lawrence Cockrill died in 1948 and his death left a serious paralysis in planning until about 1955 when planning consultant Harland Bartholomew and his firm completed their third city plan for Memphis.

Between 1948 and 1955 hundreds of subdivisions came before the city's Planning Commission, and most requests were approved. There was little time or resources available for technical staff review. Some observers claimed the Planning Commission operated under this policy: "If the citizens don't object, allow it; if they object, turn down the applicant." In 1951, Mayor Overton answered his critics, who had been charging that the city had no plan, by stating that he saw no need for hiring an expensive city planner. He believed that existing city agencies were doing an adequate job.[3] Meanwhile, the nonpartisan Civic Research Committee, a group of community-minded leaders interested in better government, had been studying other cities in an effort to come up with recommendations for better planning for Memphis. Other groups were also expressing great concern over planning, or the lack of it.

Both the Homebuilders Association and the Memphis Real Estate Board passed a joint resolution recommending that the city quickly secure a comprehensive long-range plan prepared by a competent city planning consultant. They pointed out that the city had been operating for years without a plan. The *Memphis Press Scimitar* carried an editorial in 1953 with the title, "Give Memphis Real City Planning."[4] It warned Memphis that if it did not spend thousands now for real city planning, it would lose millions in the future. A cross section of complaints included massive spot zoning, inadequate north and south traffic arteries, and a proliferation of utility districts in areas north of the Wolf River and south of the Nonconnah Creek.

Watkins Overton resigned as mayor in February 1953 after a continual feud with the other city commissioners and the general Crump organization. His successor, longtime public servant Frank Tobey, became mayor. Soon after he took office, the City Commission signed a contract with the Bartholomew organization for the preparation of a comprehensive plan. Tobey told the public that Memphis needed a long-range capital improvement plan, expressways, and a payroll tax.[5] Tobey was particularly interested in developing an expressway system.

Mayor Tobey died unexpectedly in September 1955. City planning, or lack of it, became a major campaign issue in the heated mayoral race of late 1955 that pitted businessman Edmund Orgill against former mayor Watkins Overton. Orgill had been chairman of the Civic Research Committee when it took up the cause of city planning, and he argued that Memphis had had no effective comprehensive planning from the administration of Rowlett Paine in the 1920s until Mayor Tobey's tenure beginning in 1953.[6] Candidate Orgill, the subsequent victor in this race, promised that if elected he would eliminate secrecy in the future planning of Memphis. He also promised to appoint a representative Planning Commission, including persons from labor, business, and civic or service clubs, to counteract previous domination by real estate interests. After Orgill's election, the city and county created the joint Memphis and Shelby County Planning Commission. A new zoning ordinance had been enacted into law in May 1955, the first major revision in zoning since 1931.

Unfortunately the suggestion that the city and county hire a professional-quality city planning director failed to gain approval. The city apparently did not want to pay a professional planner at a salary level above the scale for other employees. Influential city and county officials were also lukewarm to the suggestion of hiring an outsider. The result was that the city and county's planning staff was directed by nonprofessionally trained city planners for the next seven years, until Jerrold Moore was hired in 1962. Moore came to Memphis from Wichita where he was a planning technician. He had a Master's degree in city planning from Georgia Tech, which caused his critics to say he was too much of an intellectual for the job.

Immediately after adoption of the Bartholomew Plan in 1955, the incumbent Planning Commission pledged that it did not intend to engage in capricious rezonings just to benefit a particular landowner. However, by the 1960s rezoning application approvals were numerous, causing great alarm by the professional planners. They talked about "an unfortunate zoning game, played for high stakes."[7] The planning staff pleaded for a change in the law to make it tougher to rezone. Confrontations took place between development interests and city planning directors with the latter forced to yield to the liberal land development philosophies prevailing politically in Memphis and Shelby County in the 1960s and early 1970s. The planning staff's recommendations were rejected more than 50 percent of the time.

One of the major technical staff recommendations during the 1960s was the "multiple centers" proposal for handling suburban residential and commercial growth in a more orderly fashion. The idea was to create a series of designated subareas where office buildings and retail facilities would be concentrated in an orderly physical fashion to take advantage of coordinated transportation and public service systems and to serve their surrounding residential communities. Decision-makers failed to follow through on this planning recommendation, which would have helped stem the tide of strip commercial development along many of the suburban thoroughfares.

In the late 1960s, the Planning Commission's staff completed its "Community Facilities Study," a ten-volume series of reports outlining the city and county needs through 1990. Out of this technical work came the city's first long-range capital improvements plan. The first five-year plan covered the period 1968–1973, and concerned such improvements as sewers, police and fire facilities, parks, and schools. This work was a major breakthrough in the history of city planning staff accomplishments, and it provided the basis for future long-range planning. Unfortunately, through technical staff shortages and preoccupation with zoning applications, there was little follow-through on long-range planning as of the early 1970s.

In an effort to eliminate the pitfalls previously experienced in the administration of city planning, the Memphis and Shelby County Planning Commission was dissolved officially in December 1976. This 21-year-old joint city-county commission had become ineffective as a positive force in guiding the land use of Memphis and the surrounding county area. It had been assigned responsibility for overseeing planning and for administering zoning, but at times it was helpless to do either well. Its technical staff was short-handed and overburdened with day-to-day matters, and their recommendations were often capriciously overturned by the City Council or County Court. Finally, even those bodies recognized that an overhaul was essential and agreed to make some changes. In its place the city and county created the Land Use Control Board, an advisory agency of citizen members, to handle those matters relating to zoning and subdivision development. A new staff agency, the Office of Planning and Development, was organized at the same time to engage in planning studies related to matters of land use, public facilities, housing, and transportation. This group was placed directly under the chief administrative officers of the city and county.

ANNEXATION MOVEMENT

At the end of World War II Memphis had an incorporated area of 50.9 square miles. In 1978, some 33 years later, the city's incorporated area had been increased to 280 square miles. In this time the city's percentage share of the total Shelby County land area was enlarged from 7 percent to 36 percent. The urban sprawl of the postwar years was partially responsible for some 70,000 acres of productive farm land going out of existence. Much of this contiguous farm land went to developers of residential subdivisions, shopping centers, industrial sites, and office parks. Part of it went for schools, parks, churches, and hospitals.

Some of the suburban sprawl either encroached directly on the flood plains of the Wolf River and Nonconnah Creek, or came very close, creating new potential flooding problems in areas previously uninhabited or only lightly inhabited.

The city grew by a series of annexations (See fig. 35). Several stand out historically because of the events which led to the city's decision to approve. The annexation of Presidents Island, from the standpoint of economic development and flood control, and the annexations of Frayser (1958) and Whitehaven

MEMPHIS CITY LIMITS
ORIGINAL CITY-1979

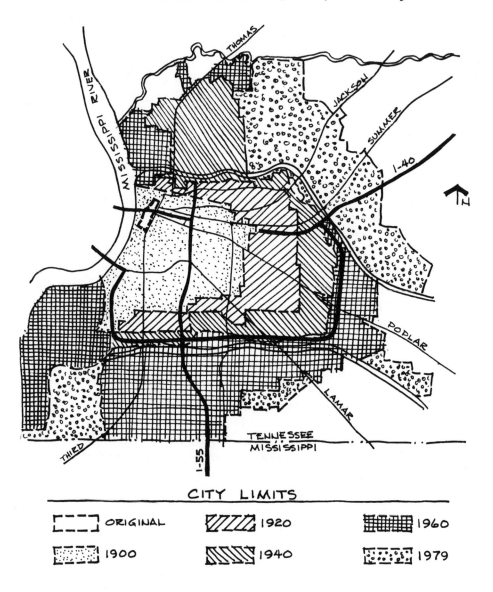

Fig. 35. Through annexations over its 160-year history, Memphis' physical area expanded from the miniscule original town site laid out by Surveyor William Lawrence to 280 square miles in the latter 1970s. Source: Memphis and Shelby County Office of Planning and Development.

(1969), from the standpoint of urban cohesiveness and control, were particularly significant.

At various times in Memphis' economic history Presidents Island had played a minor role. Occasionally parts of it were farmed. And it had served as a haven for various social undesirables whether they were prisoners at the Shelby County work farm or bootleggers or promoters of cockfights. The fact that the Island was isolated from the Memphis riverbank, and also that much of it was subject to periodic flooding, made it practically useless for any productive activity in the prewar period.

Congress incorporated the Memphis Harbor Project in the 1946 Flood Control Bill. This called for a dam to be built at the head of the Tennessee Chute, which would shut off the direct flow of the Mississippi River between the shore and Presidents Island. The old Tennessee Chute, which until 1904 was the main channel of the Mississippi, became the sheltered deep-water harbor designated McKellar Lake and Presidents Island became protected land suitable for industrial development. This enormous public works project created over 900 acres for processing plants and terminal storage facilities. Construction started in 1948, and the first industries occupied sites in the early 1950s. The dedication in 1952 was one of the historic events in the long economic history of Memphis. Thousands of people turned out for the dedication ceremonies.

The development of Presidents Island, McKellar Lake, and the flood control improvements represented years of dedication by Mr. Crump; Senator McKellar; Jack Carley, an editorial writer for *The Commercial Appeal* and member of the Memphis Harbor Commission; Frank Pidgeon, Chairman of the Memphis and Shelby County Port Commission; and the U.S. Corps of Engineers. The latter group carried out the complex planning and construction of the project.

During its first ten years, some 50 industries located on Presidents Island. As of 1978, it had reached 163 industries. With this successful project, at least part of Mr. Crump's wish for more industrial sites in Memphis had been fulfilled. And formerly useless land had been improved, creating jobs and capital investments, while contributing more than $2 million annually in property taxes.

The annexations of Frayser and Whitehaven probably prevented Memphis from being encircled by a series of separate suburban communities over which the city would have had limited or no control. Frayser, the residential community just north of the Wolf River, was annexed on 1 January 1958. Some 20,000 people residing in a 15.4 square mile area became Memphians after a long ordeal. This particular annexation was anything but cut-and-dried. Memphis was reluctant to take on the burdens of municipal services which Frayser desperately needed when a citizens group from that community appealed for help in 1954. Mayor Frank Tobey told the Frayser citizens that Memphis could not bear the burden of providing a sewer system, garbage collection, and police protection because it was already involved in expensive capital improvement projects to take care of its own rapid growth.[8]

Frayser residents had debated the issue of incorporation versus annexation to Memphis since 1949. Nothing had been resolved, and by 1954 those seeking annexation had became more numerous and more vocal. In 1956 several thousand signed a petition which was forwarded to Mayor Edmund Orgill of Memphis. Orgill was receptive, and so was Henry Loeb, then a member of the City Commission. The target date was set for 1 January 1958. One veteran observer claims the cost to Memphis of the Frayser annexation delayed the annexation of Whitehaven more than ten years.[9] Frayser contributed $9 million to the city between 1958 and mid-1964, while Memphis spent $19 million in Frayser on a variety of services.

Mayor Orgill, who had assumed office in 1956, was also an active proponent of annexing Whitehaven, the emerging unincorporated area of many housing subdivisions lying south of the Nonconnah Creek and extending to the Mississippi state line. Orgill wrote the following memorandum to the City Commissioners in 1959:

> It is my feeling that the annexation of Whitehaven and the Whitehaven area generally will not be anything like as expensive as the annexation of Frayser.
>
> It is my belief that sewers are more adequate as well as the streets.
>
> The Whitehaven area contains a lot of property on the west side adjacent to Fuller Park and to the Frank C. Pidgeon Industrial Park Development which is a "natural" for Negro housing. It is relatively close to the industries located in South Memphis.
>
> I think that an intensive and complete study should be begun in this project with the hope that it might be accomplished by January 1, 1961, or January 1, 1962.[10]

The issue of annexation to Memphis had been discussed informally in Whitehaven in 1953. Many local residents at the time were still upset about the city of Memphis' reneging on its promise to furnish water to Whitehaven in 1947. Memphis Light, Gas and Water accepted a deposit of $52,000 from a group of Whitehaven developers for water service. But City Commission, led by Mayor James J. Pleasants, Jr., refused to allow MLGW to proceed unless the deposit was doubled.[11] The Commissioners justified their action by claiming that Whitehaven was too far removed and too lightly populated to justify the expenditure. Many observers suspected that E. H. Crump gave the order to stop construction of the water line to Whitehaven because he did not want Memphis to grow south of the Nonconnah Creek. Crump was often accused of "forcing" urban development of Memphis to the east, and harassing developments to the north and south by holding back on north-south streets and bridges.[12]

In the 1950s Whitehaven had about 15,000 residents. Developers were active in subdivisions, and Whitehaven had developed its own water system, although rates were higher than those in Memphis. Not much retail development occurred until the 1960s. After 1960, Whitehaven became a fairly large commercial center serving a local population which had then grown to 32,000. Its water district was then serving 11,300 customers. It was obvious that Whitehaven was becoming a giant, sprawling on the southern border of Memphis. The city grew quite concerned about the lack of planning in its unincorporated neighbor, and this was one of the reasons it pushed successfully for annexation in 1969. So, ten years after Mayor Orgill's suggestion that Whitehaven be annexed, it was accomplished. The city gained almost 40,000 new residents.

Memphis had been active in annexing contiguous residential areas to the east, northeast, and southeast from 1950 onward. By 1960, it had largely annexed all of the area within the expressway loop. In 1963, it annexed the Memphis International Airport area. In 1965, it was the Fox Meadows area; and then the Raleigh area beginning first in 1972 with 8,335 acres around the established community, and again in 1974, when two more areas were annexed adding nearly 7,600 additional acres to the city.

But not all the towns bordering Memphis have been annexed. The neighboring incorporated cities of Bartlett and Germantown were very small communities as recently as 1960. The former only had 500 residents then; and the latter, about 1,100. Bartlett was incorporated in 1866. Germantown was incorporated in 1854, lost its charter, and then was incorporated again in 1880. Since 1960, both communities have grown significantly in population size, and both have contributed to this growth by annexation programs of their own. As of 1978, Bartlett had an estimated 14,000 residents and Germantown, 17,100.

Bartlett and Germantown both are nearly surrounded on three sides by Memphis. Agreements have been worked out between Memphis and these contiguous communities pertaining to future annexation policies in order to cooperate and avoid any conflicts.

Millington, Collierville, Arlington, and Lakeland are the other separate incorporated communities of Shelby County. They are all part of the Memphis metropolitan area. Similarly, the neighboring unincorporated community of Southaven in Mississippi, just south of the Tennessee state line, and the city of West Memphis in Arkansas are both part of the urban land development picture and the economic base. Land use decisions of these outlying communities have a direct impact on the land form of the Memphis urban area. This was one of the major reasons why the Mississippi-Arkansas-Tennessee Council of Governments was formed in 1967. The need for coordination among various county and city governments in the Memphis regional area had become a major concern. MATCOG works to achieve this cooperative regional planning to bring about better land use allocations in a six-county area.

TRAFFIC PROBLEMS

The stresses and strains of growth in the 1950s and 1960s were reflected in traffic congestion on many Memphis streets, and the lack of easy access from the older to the newer parts of the city. Traffic circulation was poor, and the daily flow of people and goods was inhibited by narrow streets, jogs, and other discontinuities that reduced traffic efficiency.

The privately-owned and operated Memphis Street Railway Company was failing fast in the mid-1950s as annual passenger volumes continued to decline. The city and the Railway Company launched the "Memphis Transit Plan— 1956" to try to increase the system's efficiency and its return on investment. New routes and new fare structures failed to halt the decline in ridership as the public chose the private automobile more and more to transport itself around the city. Bus passenger volume continued dropping rapidly.

In December 1960 the city of Memphis bought the nearly bankrupt transit company for about $2.3 million and went into the bus business. The change of ownership, however, did not halt the deep slide of transit patronage through the 1960s. Transit officials blamed the decline on the inroads suburban shopping centers had made on retail business in downtown Memphis. Similar to most other American cities which had had strong public transit systems prior to World War II, Memphis' system yielded to the private automobile in the postwar years.

Bartholomew's 1924 plan contained recommendations that 20 east-west traffic arteries be built and 14 north-south routes. Following World War II, as Memphis was in the early stages of postwar urban sprawl, it became apparent that Memphis traffic circulation was a serious problem. For example, the free flow of automotive traffic north and south was excessively cumbersome because of the lack of an adequate number of streets or because of obsolete existing streets. Bartholomew had suggested some 14 north-south streets; but only Riverside Drive, Third Street, and the Airways-East Parkway-Hollywood routes had been built. And none of these three arteries traversed the entire city north and south. To compound the problem, two of these three were located in the far western end of the city.[13]

Access to Frayser and other residential areas north of the Wolf River and to Whitehaven south of the Nonconnah Creek were reached by the Federal highways routed through Memphis. Critics blamed City Hall politics on the poor street access problem. Leadership in the 1920s and 1930s had favored the eastern sections of Memphis by authorizing construction of many of the streets suggested in the Bartholomew plan. The Crump organization gave preferential treatment to the subdivision developers "out East." Mr. Crump's advocacy of another bridge across the Mississippi resulted in the construction of the Memphis and Arkansas Bridge. When this $14.5 million project was completed in December 1949, it helped eliminate automobile bottlenecks on both sides of the river. The Harahan Bridge, built prior to America's entry in World War I, was incapable of handling post-World War II traffic.

It was apparent to Memphians in the latter 1940s that an extensive public works program was needed to correct many other traffic deficiencies throughout the city and suburbs. In 1948, the city took the first step and hired a traffic consultant to develop a street improvement plan. It was not a comprehensive review of total problem areas. The consultant's responsibilities were confined to suggestions for alleviating congestion on the principal streets through channelization, signal improvements, and traffic routing. One major task was to improve circulation in downtown Memphis.

The responsibility for providing suggestions for improving areawide traffic circulation was assigned to the city's Traffic Advisory Committee. As a result of this committee's work over a period of several years, it was the consensus that Memphis needed expressways. The suggestion caught hold in Memphis. The Tennessee State Highway Department and Shelby County leaders were also interested in a comprehensive expressway system. Again, the Bartholomew firm was called upon for planning assistance. At the time Bartholomew's staff was already at work on its third city plan for Memphis. The opportunity to develop an expressway plan fit perfectly into work this firm was already doing on its plan for city streets.

The Federal Highway Act of 1956 established the authorization and funding for this system. In getting the approvals for Memphis, and the work started, much of the credit has been given to Will Fowler, the veteran city engineer.

The Bureau of Public Roads approved the Bartholomew firm's recommendations for interstate routes in 1956.[14] The first three miles were under construction in 1958. By 1963, some 18 miles had been completed, including Interstate 240 along the city's southern perimeter, and that section of Interstate 55 extending from the Mississippi-Tennessee state boundary to the Memphis and Arkansas Bridge. The northern leg of Interstate 240, which follows a route near the Wolf River, was originally scheduled for completion in 1975. Delays forced postponement of this section until 1979.

The opening of the Hernando DeSoto Bridge in 1973, the first bridge to be located on the north side of downtown Memphis, created better access to and from downtown Memphis to Arkansas. The discontinuity of Interstate 40 through midtown Memphis, however, has lessened this bridge's effectiveness in moving regional and metropolitan traffic efficiently through the heart of the urban area. Several major delays prevented an early completion of the total expressway system as it was originally planned. Perhaps the greatest obstacle has been the failure to resolve the question of the Overton Park route.

OVERTON PARK EXPRESSWAY CONTROVERSY

Among the greatest controversies in the long history of Memphis has been the plan to extend Interstate 40 through city-owned Overton Park. As of 1979, all that remained to complete I-40 across the state of Tennessee was a 3.6 mile link which included 4,200 feet across this historic public park. Interstate traffic coming from the east on I-40 was forced to exit 1.6 miles east of the park, and traffic from the west was required to exit 1.2 miles short of the park's western boundary. Local streets were carrying this interrupted flow of expressway traffic.

The Bartholomew expressway plan recommended an east-west, midtown route extending across the northern section of the park. The route was overlayed on the existing bus lane thoroughfare crossing the park. The much wider expressway route required the destruction of a considerable portion of a heavily forested section of the park. The route also separated the city's Zoo and its parking area from the bulk of the park area. The route selected required that 26 acres of the 342-acre park be yielded for the expressway. As it traversed the 4,200 feet through the park, the width of this expressway varied from 250 to 450 feet.

Protests reached an early crescendo at the original public hearings held in October 1958. "Save Overton Park" was the slogan adopted by the several thousand opponents active throughout the city in the latter 1950s when the issue reached the point of confrontation. The opponents argued vehemently that the expressway would destroy an irreplaceable community asset. They further argued that there were alternative routes which should be considered. A strong plea was made for a circumferential expressway north of the city.

But the opponents had not coordinated their efforts, and between 1958 and 1964 formal protests were sporadic. When design work by the state of Tennessee highway planners began in 1964, however, the aggressive citizens group that called its organization, Citizens to Preserve Overton Park, were solidly united. The initial membership was upper middle class whites, the majority of whom either lived or worked near Overton Park. Some of the group's leadership came from the Southwestern at Memphis faculty. The CPOP group adopted the position that any encroachment of Overton Park was unacceptable.

The battle lines were quickly drawn. Favoring the park route were the Memphis Chamber of Commerce; the new City Council that took office in 1968; the Downtown Association, a business group; Future Memphis, Incorporated, a civic-business planning group; the state of Tennessee; the Shelby County Court; the AFL–CIO Labor Council; the NAACP; the Mid-South Medical Center Council; the Memphis Junior Chamber of Commerce; the Memphis Branch of the American Society of Civil Engineers; the Memphis Society of Professional Engineers; and many other organizations.

These groups were in favor for a variety of reasons. The downtown interests felt that the route would be helpful to the economy of the business district by improving access from the eastern sections of the city. Other groups believed the route would greatly relieve traffic congestion on local streets and also improve public safety. Dire predictions were being made that midtown traffic conditions would become intolerable if no relief were found for the constantly increasing burden on the city's major arterials.

In addition to the CPOP, the lead group in the fight against the Overton Park route, the Sierra Club, the Audubon Society, the Council for a Greener Memphis, the Hein Park Civic Association, the Mid-Memphis Improvement Association, and the Southwestern at Memphis Student Government Association all contributed to stop Interstate 40.

The Citizens to Preserve Overton Park sought support for its cause from the national headquarters of the Sierra Club. Legal assistance and advice was provided by Sierra Club attorneys during the long struggle in the Federal courts and before governmental agencies. The National Audubon Society has also helped publicize the cause of these Memphis ecologists in their battle to stop Interstate 40 from crossing Overton Park. In the January 1970 issue of *Audubon,* published by the National Audubon Society, Overton Park was designated "Case #7" in a special section entitled "Death Row." This issue was published just after representatives of the CPOP went into the U.S. District Court in Memphis seeking an injunction against U.S. Secretary of Transportation John Volpe and a Tennessee State Highway Department official to stop construction.

In 1970, the U.S. Sixth Circuit Court of Appeals in Cincinnati upheld Memphis Federal Judge Bailey Brown who had ruled that the expressway opponents did not have a sufficient case to go to trial.[15] He argued that under the Preservation of Park Lands Act, passed by Congress in the mid-1960s, taking of publicly-owned park land was prevented if a feasible and prudent alternative route could be found. The Sixth Circuit Court's decision gave the go-ahead to start construction.[16] But in December 1970 the U.S. Supreme Court remanded the case back to the District Court in Memphis for a full review of the decision approving the Overton Park route made by the then U.S. Secretary of Transportation John Volpe.[17]

Meanwhile, much to the benefit of the CPOP, Congress passed the National Environmental Policy Act of 1970. This new law stated that no park land could be taken unless public hearings were held, environmental impact statements prepared, and no feasible or prudent alternative routes were available. Secretary Volpe was instructed by the U.S. District Court to abide by this new act. To the great surprise of State highway planners, Volpe ordered a new round of hearings to review matters related to design and location.[18]

In 1973, Volpe gave approval to the Overton Park route provided it were tunneled. From that point on, the Overton Park case became one of confrontation between the State of Tennessee Highway Commission and the U.S. Department of Transportation over the type and design of tunneling which would be acceptable to the Federal department. The state considered total tunneling to be prohibitive in construction costs and in subsequent maintenance costs. But the state's proposals for partial tunneling and sunken plaza designs were rejected by Federal authorities.

The future of the plan to cross Overton Park was still in limbo at the end of the 1970s. The titanic struggle was then in its 24th year.

REGIONAL TRANSPORTATION PLANNING

Areawide transportation planning became accepted as a permanent function of public agencies with interests in efficient urban land use. In 1969, the Metropolitan Urban Area Transportation Study (MUATS) project was implemented. Since then, street and highway improvements in the metropolitan area have been guided by a master plan developed through the cooperative efforts of the Memphis and Shelby County Office of Planning and Development, the Tennessee Department of Transportation, the Mississippi State Highway Department, and the DeSoto County, Mississippi, Planning Commission with Federal financial assistance.[19]

The MUATS plan has been updated several times to take into consideration growth trends in its 850 square-mile planning area containing roughly 4,000 miles of streets and roads. Its planning staff has been conducting studies aimed toward solutions to a number of important traffic circulation problems, including the critical East Memphis corridor extending to the Germantown area.

The planning program also has the responsibility for coordinating street and highway plans with the plans of the Memphis Area Transit Authority (MATA), which operates the bus service; the Memphis-Shelby County Airport Authority, which oversees activities at the Memphis International Airport and two other airports; the Memphis-Shelby County Port Commission; the seven trunk line railroads serving Memphis; and with the Mississippi-Arkansas-Tennessee Council of Governments (MATCOG).

Continual interest has been shown in studying the feasibility of a downtown Memphis riverfront expressway to help alleviate traffic bottlenecks, and also to assist in the revitalization efforts of the downtown area.[20] Commuter rail transit systems to help move people quickly throughout the Memphis area have also been discussed generally, but no detailed cost-benefit type studies have been prepared exploring any specific proposal.

Restoration of a partial streetcar network between the downtown and major activity centers such as Overton Square, the Fairgrounds, and the Medical Center have been suggested. Another idea has been to use the Southern Railroad's track, which moves in an east-west direction through the heart of the urbanized Memphis area.

The Memphis Area Transit Authority, successor to the old Memphis Street Railway Company and the Memphis Transit System, was given a new lease on life in the mid-1970s. Ridership had fallen to a desperately low annual volume of 16.5 million in 1973. Its survival was very much in doubt at that time. New management and new equipment, combined with a major public relations campaign, were implemented in the latter 1970s in an effort to provide the general public with a transportation alternative to the automobile. In 1976 the city contracted with a private transit management firm to operate the system for the Authority. By 1978 ridership had crept up to 17.6 million.

CHANGING LAND VALUES

The opening of suburban areas for development changed property values. The expressway system probably had the most dramatic and most immediate impact on land values. Undeveloped land doubled and tripled in price in broad areas influenced by the Interstate system.

Industrially zoned land with good access experienced great price changes in the latter 1960s. In some cases prices went from just a few hundred dollars an acre before the expressway construction to as much as $10,000 an acre. Industrial locations in the Brooks Road area south of Interstate 240 were considered choice sites, and prices reflected this market interest.

Population pressure in outlying residentially zoned areas caused a doubling and tripling of acreage prices in the five-year period from 1968 through 1973 before the bust in the Memphis real estate market in 1974 and 1975. Developed residential lots had phenomenal upward price movements during these active years in Raleigh, Bartlett, Parkway Village, Fox Meadows, Balmoral, Germantown, and Whitehaven. Owners of rural acreage more than willingly sold their holdings to builders, or to speculators who were convinced that Memphis' growth, as they saw it, would make them wealthy in just a short time. Speculation was rampant in the early 1970s, and in many instances prior to the real estate collapse, the prices paid were unrealistic and unsupportable from any measure of economic feasibility.

THE CHANGING LANDSCAPE

Memphians casting backward glances at their remembrances of the city's urban land form before World War II might conclude that its miniscule size in those days probably contributed to its lack of dynamism as an economy (See fig. 36). Too often in today's world urban significance and economic power have been equated with physical size and population. Many fail to realize that physically compact cities with high population densities per square mile of corporate area functioned well for decades in the United States and in Europe.

The public's aspirations changed in the postwar period of general affluence. Many sought their piece of the American good life in the suburbs and outer fringes of the older central city. The majority of the working population had the economic means to make the physical transition, and they exercised it

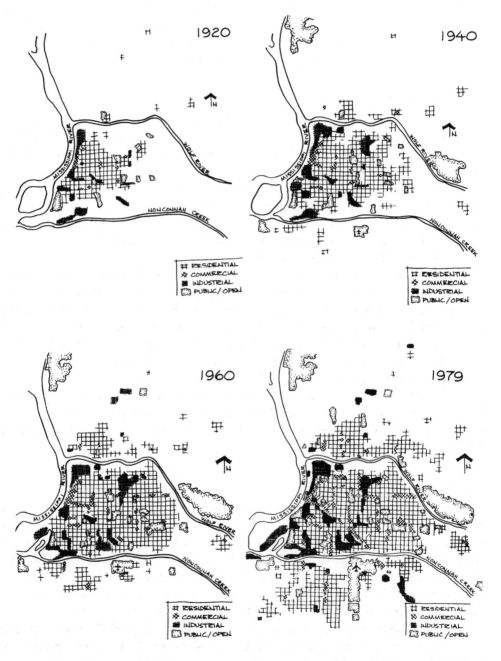

LAND USE PATTERN
MEMPHIS, TENNESSEE 1920-1979

Fig. 36. The Memphis urban area expanded eastward before World War II, confining its boundaries between the Wolf River on the north and the Nonconnah Creek on the south. Following the war, suburbanization carried land development far beyond these two physical barriers.

rather enthusiastically for the three and one-half decades following V-J Day. Memphians were no exception.

The phenomenon of suburban growth changed Memphis in many ways. It created new economic opportunities. But, it also added a new set of physical and social problems to ones still pending in the older central city. The political and business leadership were challenged to oversee and guide this growth to insure that new growth was an asset, not a liability. Within the fluid boundaries of the postwar metropolitan area the interaction of individual and business locational decisions produced millions of dollars of new private investment. Suburban growth also began to place heavy financial burdens on the general public to support public works and services to meet the demands of the city's changing constituencies. Most assumed that the public costs were far exceeded by the benefits.

These developments contributed a new and more complex chapter to the economic and urban land use history. The urban land form had changed dramatically. City planning guidance was desperately needed to achieve a semblance of orderliness and to protect the public's investment in its older public works and utility systems while the city was building new facilities to accommodate the new growth outward from the pre-World War II municipal boundaries. And although formal and coordinated planning was at best mediocre within local government during the growth decades of the 1950s and 1960s, the resulting urban form and its effectiveness in serving the daily needs of the citizens was remarkably good, all things considered.

16

Memphis Builds and Builds

Real estate development became big business once again following World War II. But this time it dwarfed in comparison all previous eras of construction. Those in the land economics profession, which includes developers, lenders, architects, contractors, city planning technicians, and such professional trade organizations as the Memphis Board of Realtors and the Homebuilders Association of Memphis, all played key roles in creating a new city and a new metropolitan area. The resurgence of activity brought jobs, income, and substantial property valuation increments. It provided substantial support to the area's economic development efforts.

Previously undeveloped suburban and rural fringe acreage was converted into housing subdivisions, retail centers, office buildings and office parks, new industrial plants and warehouses, schools, churches, public facilities including streets and utility systems, and every other conceivable type of land use. During the Depression years and World War II, only limited new construction had taken place. Unemployment and marginal family incomes and business profits were not conducive to real estate development in the 1930s. The war period was one of shortages of both materials and manpower.

After Memphis shook off the aftereffects of World War II in 1946 and 1947, this pent-up demand for housing and most other types of real estate broke loose. Many people who could afford a down payment on a house, and had a job to help carry the monthly mortgage payment, raced to the suburbs to make their selections. A new type of entrepreneur sprang up to provide housing in quantity, called a "developer." Before the war, because homes were constructed in smaller quantities and were often custom-built, these individuals were called housebuilders, or builders and carpenters. The new postwar breed

237

bought land in quantity, cleared it, put in the utilities and streets, and constructed dozens and dozens of houses at one time in numerous projects in the Memphis area. Housing deprivation for many was a thing of the past.

Housing developers had very little difficulty selling most of what they built. Backed by the FHA and VA financing programs, buyer and seller reached easy accord. Developers of shopping centers of the larger type, and of other larger scaled commercial projects, lagged behind during the early postwar years. Later they came on very strong to serve the demand in growing metropolitan areas. Population growth stimulated this activity.

The Memphis area was growing in population aided primarily by the phenomenal baby boom in the 1950s and 1960s. Birth rates had been modest during the Depression, one of the reasons why Memphis planners were so conservative in their long-range population forecasts made in the 1930s. But all of this changed in the postwar period. The average annual birth rate in the 1950s was close to 29.0 live births for every 1,000 residents of Shelby County. This included both the white and the black populations. The latter had substantially higher rates than the whites, but both races were prolific. As shown in Figure 37, the high rates of the 1950s and 1960s were extreme compared with the rates of the 1970s. This contrast has been rather startling. In 1978, for example, the birth rate for whites was only 12.5 and for blacks, 23.2. The 1978 rate for whites was less than half of the all-time high for whites of 27.0 in 1955. For blacks the 1978 rate was very modest compared with their record high rate of 37.0 achieved in 1956.

Some 140,000 babies were born in Shelby County in the fecund decade of the 1950s. Another 154,000 new births occurred in the 1960s, despite some fall off in the birth rate for both whites and blacks. These impressive figures helped give impetus to the local area economy as reflected by the strong emergence of the construction industry and new businesses of all types.

Population growth in the Memphis area from 1946 to 1978 has been generated largely by this internal Shelby County birth rate. Without a productive local citizenry, Memphis' population growth of the past 32 years would have been sparse. In-migration of newcomers slowed to a trickle. The absence of large-scale postwar economic development affected the migration levels. Turn of the century migration brought wholesale numbers of rural whites and blacks to Memphis seeking opportunity. These waves of newcomers helped swell the size of the city in this earlier period. But this migration came to a halt after the 1920s.

The declining birth rates for both whites and blacks have had an impact on both the real estate economy and on the general commercial economy of Memphis since the mid-1960s. Certainly, the full consequences of these declining rates seemed little understood by many civic leaders and planners during the late 1960s and early 1970s.

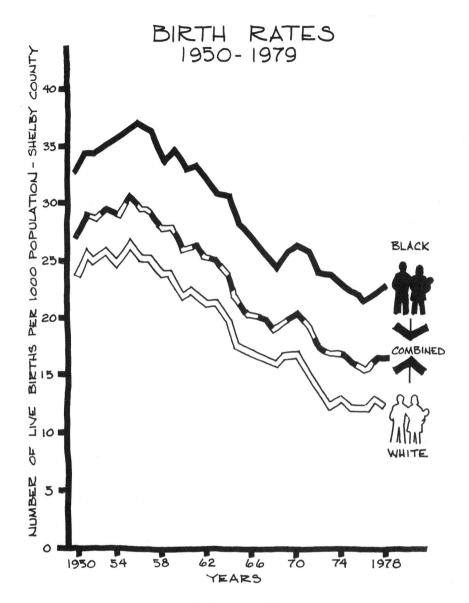

Fig. 37. The huge birth rates of both the white and black populations in the 1950s and 1960s were in marked contrast to the low rates of the Great Depression years. By the 1970s, however, birth rates for both races declined dramatically. Source: Memphis and Shelby County Health Department.

THE HOUSING MARKET TO 1970

The housing stock of Memphis was very old in 1946 before the housing boom started. A heavy portion of it was built before 1910, and a high percentage was substandard. Blacks occupied much of the latter.

The immediate postwar boom did not include much replacement of older, obsolete housing. Its thrust was new single family homes, duplexes and apartment units in newly developing parts of the metropolitan area. A big year was 1947, because it represented the first burst of activity in almost 17 years. Permits that year for Memphis and the rest of Shelby County totaled over 5,600 units. The high mark prior to the late 1960s and early 1970s was in 1950 when permits had peaked at 9,200 units. The average annual volume of new housing units for the next 15 years was about 7,300 a year. A heavy capital investment was being made in housing.

The following statistics from the decennial U.S. Census of Housing show the trend in the size of the housing stock in Memphis and for all of Shelby County from 1940 to 1970.

Census Year	City of Memphis	Total Shelby County
1940	83,246 units	99,413 units
1950	116,340 units	138,759 units
1960	151,972 units	184,868 units
1970	197,967 units	222,649 units

In these 30 years the net addition to the total housing supply for Shelby County, including Memphis, was over 123,000 units.

The first wave of subdivisions for the upper middle class market was in a large quadrant north of Poplar and east of Highland. Dozens of subdivisions were built eastward beyond the city limits to locations just beyond Mendenhall and White Station roads.[1] About 25 percent of the housing built in the early 1950s in the Memphis area was in this general vicinity. Major developers were Clark & Fay, Incorporated; Jacobson & Lovitt; Chandler & Chandler; H. Dlugach & Company; and Ben Dlugach. Three-bedroom homes sold for an average price of $12,500. Building lots sold for a variety of prices depending on the social status of the neighborhood. Half-acre lots on fashionable Shady Grove Road east of Perkins sold for $1,750. Considerably smaller lots fronting on Galloway Golf Course in the Red Acres Subdivision sold for $1,500. Other lots sold for prices under $1,000.

In the 1950s a large area south of Park and east of Getwell was under intensive residential development. The largest of all of the subdivisions being developed was the 1600-lot Country Club Estates. Housing prices in this quadrant of East Memphis ranged from $10,500 to $14,000. Typical advertisements announced such appealing purchase terms as "$1.00 down payment and 30-year loan maturities to veterans;" or "100% GI loans to veterans and FHA terms to non-veterans."

Whitehaven was also a popular area for new subdivisions. Selling prices varied according to the size of the home and its location. The John B. Goodwin Company, the largest developer organization operating in Whitehaven, was offering homes in the 1950s in its Graceland Subdivision for prices ranging from $14,750 to $16,450. More popularly priced houses elsewhere in Whitehaven sold in the $9,500 range. Besides Goodwin other developers active in that growing suburban market were Wallace E. Johnson, Carrington Jones, Morris Mills, Lacey Mosby, Frank Robinson, Louis Weeks, Jr., Welch Construction Company, and others.

Across the river in West Memphis, Arkansas, hundreds of homes were built in the 1950s. That city's great boom year was 1955 as developers found a ready market for their homes.

The momentum of the 1950s extended into the 1960s, and the housing market was strong except for 1966 and again in 1969 when mortgage funds dried up to inhibit sales. Despite these temporary setbacks, a 21 percent increase in housing units was achieved during the 1960s. The areas of greatest activity were the new subdivisions located beyond the boundaries of the Interstate 240 expressway loop. Heavy development was occurring in the Oakhaven and Parkway Village areas in southeast Memphis and the Raleigh and Frayser areas on the other side of the Wolf River. And Whitehaven continued in the 1960s to be a popular area for new housing, including many apartment projects.

Overbuilding was never a real concern in Memphis prior to the 1970s, but still there were temporary concerns earlier that supply might exceed demand to cause a housing downturn. In 1963 and 1964 some local analysts warned that overbuilding was a possibility with apartments. In 1963, for example, permits were issued for constructing 3,500 apartment units, but only 900 single family or duplex units. These concerned analysts at that time could not have visualized that roughly ten years later permits would be issued for 30,000 apartment units in the three-year period, 1971 to 1973. This latter condition broke the local housing market, and gave Memphis a housing depression of enormous magnitude.

During the 1960s about 51 percent of the housing units constructed were single family homes. The other 49 percent were apartment and duplex units. This distribution was a significant change from the pattern of the 1950s when only 20 percent of the new units built were apartments and duplexes. In the early 1960s the most popular price range for a three-bedroom, one and a half bath house was $15,000 to about $17,200. Although the Memphis FHA-insuring office was kept active processing home loan applications, mortgage bankers and savings and loan associations were active issuing conventional loans, too.

High rise apartments formed a specialized part of the housing market. Prior to World War II, Memphis had Kimbrough Towers on Union Avenue, the converted Parkview Apartment Hotel next to Overton Park on Poplar Avenue, and the Gilmore on Madison at McLean. By the early 1970s the city had just over 2,700 nonsubsidized high rise rental units. Most of these units were built in the 1960s and represented only a fraction of the total number of apartments constructed. Consumer preference had been for the garden-type and town-house rental units.

THE HOUSING MARKET AFTER 1970

The active housing market of the 1960s whet the appetite of homebuilders and apartment developers for even greater activity in the early 1970s. There had been occasional warnings by veteran local developers that there was the distinct possibility of overbuilding and that the market demand was near the saturation point. The serious lack of market communication among local builders, and the entry of out-of-state development companies into the Memphis area, brought forth Memphis' most serious real estate crisis in its modern history. The city had never experienced a "feast or famine" real estate cycle prior to the early 1970s. Supply and demand for the most part had been in close tandem. There had not been too many serious miscalculations in the residential market. Thus, the Memphis real estate community was almost totally unprepared for the impending calamity of 1974 and 1975.

Figure 38 illustrates dramatically the surge in residential construction beginning in 1971 and extending through 1973. Single family housing starts moved upward rapidly. But the sharpest upward turn was in apartment construction. In this sector the years 1971 through 1973 defied all trend lines. Some 30,324 permits were issued for this 3-year period. This was an average of about 10,100 apartment units a year. This high volume was a marked contrast to the annual average of 3,800 units a year for the previous six years, 1965 to 1970.

The lack of professional market analysis plus an incredible spirit of optimism brought on the total collapse of new apartment construction. The overly generous and unwise policies of the old Memphis and Shelby County Planning Commission through the 1960s and early 1970s permitted an inordinate amount of suburban acreage to be zoned for high density apartment and condominium projects.[2] Market feasibility was equated with zoning.

The Memphis office of the FHA issued a warning about overbuilding, but that did not dissuade many from proceeding with their plans. And not all participants in the local real estate industry agreed with these conclusions of the FHA. Local lenders, and developers armed with loan commitments from a variety of institutional sources, rationalized away the problem of overbuilding. Some kept leaning on the argument that Memphis still had an extensive pent-up demand which had been carried over from the mid-1960s. They really had only the sketchiest type of market research to back up their opinions. They also argued that investors in Memphis apartment projects could withstand higher vacancies because of the city's lower land costs and property taxes.

At the time national lenders had ample supplies of mortgage funds, and they were anxious to put them to work. In the early 1970s many cities were overbuilt, and lenders had problems placing loans during this period of satura-

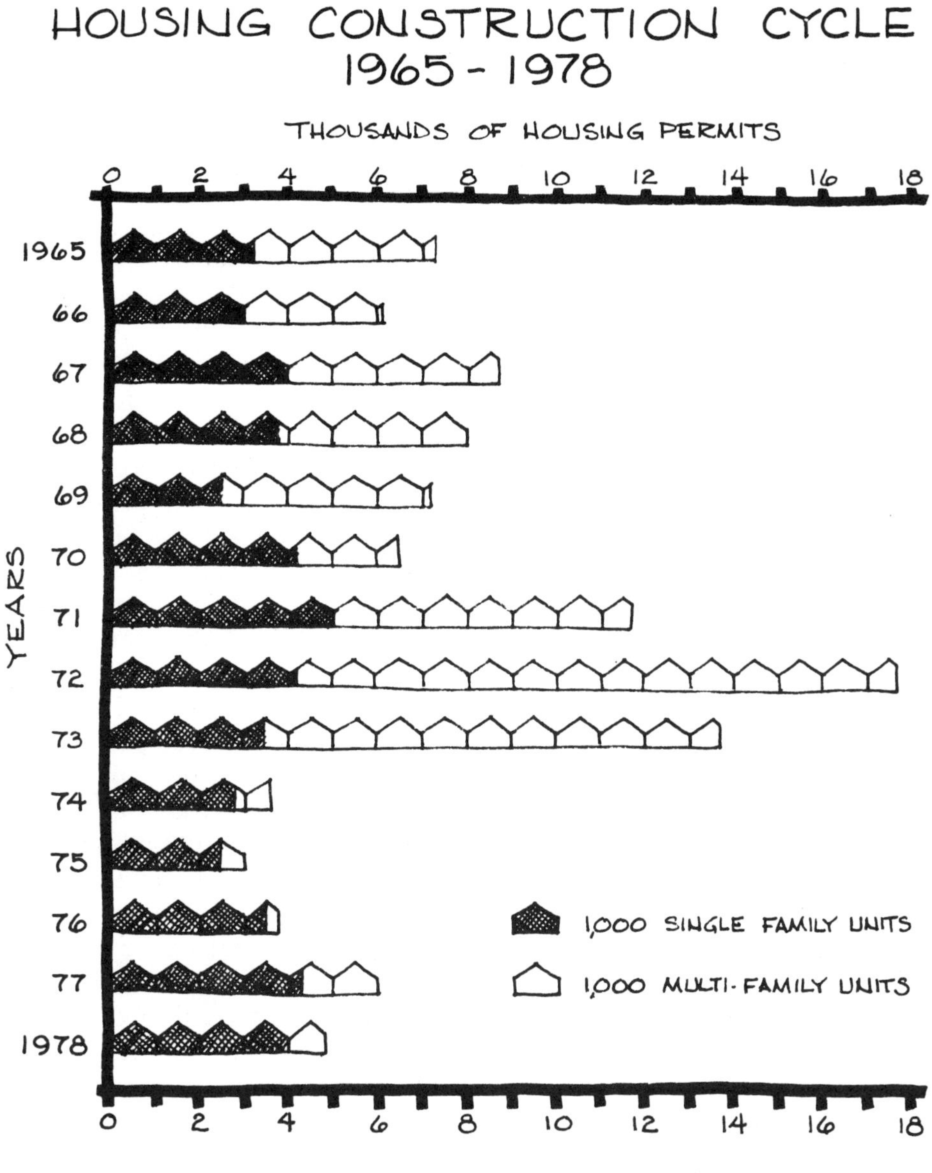

HOUSING CONSTRUCTION CYCLE
1965 - 1978

THOUSANDS OF HOUSING PERMITS

Fig. 38. The "feast or famine" character of the Memphis area housing market in the latter 1960s and early 1970s is shown in this chart. Serious overestimation of the demand for housing led to dramatic oversupplies with the resultant collapse of the real estate economy in 1974 and 1975. Source: Bureau of Business and Economic Research, Memphis State University.

tion. Major life insurance companies, real estate investment trusts (REITs), limited partnerships, savings and loan associations, and banks needed desperately to get these millions of dollars into active loans. The word got out that Memphis was a "hot" market. Few of these eager lenders did any feasibility analysis of individual projects or looked critically at general housing market conditions in the Memphis area. The true supply/demand figures were hidden from these undiscerning eyes.

Ultimately the construction dam broke in Memphis. In late 1974 huge vacancies became apparent even to the most unsophisticated. Panic-stricken apartment owners ran newspaper ads offering the incentives of one to three months' free rent, free moving, choice of premiums such as television sets and washers and dryers to find tenants for their hundreds and hundreds of brand new vacant units. Renters got "bargain basement" leases.

Many projects went into foreclosure. Lenders found themselves reluctant owners of projects often in an uncompleted state. Cries went up through Memphis: "What happened?" It was a totally routed marketplace, and it was the greatest real estate collapse Memphis had ever experienced. With this glut, accompanied by negative reactions of investors, new construction was largely postponed for the remainder of the 1970s. While many Memphis-based and out-of-town apartment developers went under financially, there were a few significant exceptions. Avron and Robert Fogelman, the largest apartment owners and operators in the city, successfully weathered the storm. So did the Boyle and the Belz interests. These investors were far more sensitive to market realities.

Condominiums were introduced in Memphis in the early 1970s. This sector of the housing market was a late arrival compared with the pattern in most major cities. For Memphis the specific market timing could not have been worse. The first large supply of units was placed on the market only about one year prior to the general real estate market bust. Adverse national publicity stemming from Florida condominium complexes hurt the image of this new American concept of residential living, and this had an effect on consumer acceptance in Memphis. And there was the very real problem of construction quality in many of the local projects being placed on the market. Many projects were built originally to serve as apartments, then later their developers tried to sell them as condominiums. These factors impeded early success and forced developers and their lenders to offer units at bargain prices to salvage some portion of their investments. During this early phase of the entry of condominiums into the Memphis housing market some 7,500 units were built. In 1973, 1974 and 1975 sales were poor. Beginning in 1976 this initial inventory started to be absorbed, and consumer acceptance began to emerge. In 1977 and 1978 the active resale market for these first generation units was excellent, proving that Memphians will buy condominium units at market rate prices.

The single family housing market was also in a state of euphoria in the years immediately preceding 1974. In the decade of the 1960s market absorption of new housing was roughly 3,500 units a year, but from 1970 through 1973 an average of about 4,200 units went on the market.

Here, too, there was overbuilding, and this sector of the real estate market partially collapsed in 1974. The combination of overbuilding and tight money brought numerous Memphis homebuilders face-to-face with bankruptcy. Tight money and rising interest rates shut off many potential new home buyers. The excess inventory of completed homes could not be moved at the former pace of the easy years in the 1950s and 1960s. Savings and loan associations and private mortgage lending firms in Memphis like similar institutions throughout the nation saw their home mortgage funds disappear. Savers withdrew their funds from savings and loans to take advantage of higher yielding government securities and corporate bonds.

Interest rates on home mortgages rose from 7½ percent on conventional loans to 9 percent on high ratio loan-to-value mortgages. Rates varied depending on the amount of down payment made by the borrower. In August 1974, the FHA and VA interest rate ceiling was raised to 9½ percent from 9 percent.

The full impact of the nation's business recession which began in late 1973 came later in Memphis than in most other major cities. Long after economists had officially declared that the United States was in a full blown recession, Memphis real estate practitioners seemed to refuse to acknowledge this fact locally. Construction continued on well into 1974 here before reality caught up with the local market, and the wheels ground to a halt. So it was 1975 in Memphis that housing starts for single family homes fell in response to market conditions. New home sales averaged about 2,600 a year in 1975 and 1976 before returning once again to the normal 3,500 homes a year average rate in 1977.

There was a failure to recognize that the combination of a real slowdown in the birth rate and the modest rate of industrial development in the late 1960s and early 1970s resulted in a lack of underlying economic support for housing above the normal absorption rates of most postwar years. When annual construction rates for single family and apartment units exceeded the norms of both for several years standing, it was only a question of time before supplies would far outpace demand, and severe adjustments would become necessary.

DECENTRALIZATION OF RETAILING

Downtown Memphis was still dominant in retailing following World War II. In 1948 its dollar sales were 28 percent of total retail sales in the metropolitan area. It was still strong in the mid-1950s, but the first real competitive challenges were being felt. From that point forward, downtown business volume descended rapidly, and by the 1970s retail business there was just 5 percent of metropolitan sales. No longer was retailing one of the principal anchors of the downtown economic base. Retailing power had gone to the suburbs where population densities and buying power were concentrated, and where land was available both for retail facilities of all types and for ample free parking. The pattern of change is shown in Table 11.

TABLE 11

THE SHIFTING LOCATION OF MEMPHIS AREA
RETAIL SALES SINCE WORLD WAR II
Percentage Distribution

Year	CBD[1] (Downtown Memphis)	Remainder of City	Remainder of Standard Metro Stat. Area[2]	Total Area Retail Sales in Millions
1948	28%	67%	5%	$ 485.4
1954	21	74	5	610.7
1958	15	75	10	740.5
1963	12	72	16	895.1
1967	9	75	16	1180.7
1972	5	78	17	1917.5

SOURCE: U.S. Department of Commerce, Bureau of the Census, *Census of Business,* 1948, 1954, 1959, 1963, 1967 and 1972.
1. "Central Business District" is that area bounded on the north by Poplar Avenue, on the east by Third Street, on the south by Calhoun Avenue and on the west by the Mississippi River.
2. In the federal censuses conducted in 1948, 1954 and 1958 by the Bureau of the Census, the defined SMSA included only Shelby County. In the 1963 and 1967 censuses, Crittenden County, Arkansas was added. In the 1972 Census two more counties were added: Tipton County, Tennessee and DeSoto County, Mississippi.

A ring pattern of commercial retail centers developed in the 1950s just beyond the Parkway system. In the mid-1960s substantial retailing appeared beyond the Interstate expressway system. The veteran department stores and many of the specialty stores placed units in the suburbs first as a defensive measure, then later as a full-blown economic commitment to these newly emerging market areas. From the mid-1950s through the 1970s several layers of retail facilities of all types ringed the city as it expanded outward for many miles. Shopping centers of different physical magnitudes were developed by opportunistic investors who foresaw the need and proceeded to fill it. Interspersed were free-standing retail outlets of all types including service stations, car washes, fast food restaurant outlets, and auto dealerships. Banks, savings and loan associations, and movie theaters also faced reality and moved with the fluid suburban market.

The traditional downtown in Memphis was compact. Most stores were within short walking distances of each other, as were the restaurants, the movie theaters, and the financial institutions. Suburban developments were of a different physical configuration. Shopping centers were built in nodes, often several miles apart. And a large portion of new Memphis retail and commercial businesses aligned themselves in lineal, or strip, fashion along well-traveled arterial streets. Some retail streets stretched out for miles as zoning policies were implemented which almost as a routine matter designated the major streets as "commercial." Instead of just grocery stores in the neighborhoods, as was the case before World War II, now the full line of retail establishments came to the people. The retail philosophy became "customer convenience."

During the early 1950s, Lowenstein's, Goldsmith's, Gerber's, and Bry's department stores were major downtown retail forces. These veteran retailers seemed to react indifferently at first to suburban growth. They considered their Main Street locations as flagship stores where merchandise in-depth would continue to be stocked despite suburban competition for some types of consumer soft and hard goods. Among these four large department stores they had 835,000 square feet of selling space, and they had reputations as merchandisers known throughout the Mid-South region. They were seemingly impenetrable by suburban competition except for Sears which had been operating at its North Watkins site since 1927.

Lowenstein's built a modest sized store of 30,000 square feet in 1949 at the city's first major shopping center, Poplar Plaza, on the then eastern fringe of Memphis. The location decision was made just in advance of the heavy subdivision development period east of Highland Avenue. In 1954 Lowenstein's and Franklin Simon stores were enlarged to accommodate this growing market. Poplar Plaza developed by John Goodwin and L. Hall Jones was more or less an experiment but its early acceptance prompted a substantial expansion after the fifth year and it became for a time the city's largest suburban shopping center.

In 1956 developer John Goodwin built Whitehaven Plaza and Lowenstein's became an anchor tenant in this suburban center in rapidly growing Whitehaven.

Bry's, an aggressive Main Street department store for over 50 years, was sold in 1956 to the parent company of Lowenstein's. By the late 1950s it was feeling the competitive pressure from the new suburban discount centers. In an attempt to compete Bry's went into a self-service type operation. This concept was too little too late and the store went out of business. On Bry's old site Lowenstein's built its new downtown department store headquarters and the Lowenstein Towers apartment complex in 1967. Lowenstein's vacated its old Main and Monroe store where it had been operating since 1924. In going ahead with its new downtown store, Lowenstein's management felt that the newly expanded Civic Center would be a real asset in helping to turn downtown Memphis around from its declining retail role in the area.

Gerber's slogan had been: "As Memphis grows, Gerber's grows." It opened its first suburban store in 1961 at Laurelwood, its second store at Southland Mall in Whitehaven in 1966, and its third store in Germantown Village Square in the early 1970s. Gerber's was sold to DAC Stores, Incorporated in 1973. The new owners closed the venerable Main Street store in 1974 to concentrate on the suburban market. In 1975, facing bankruptcy, the new owner sold the former Gerber suburban stores to the M.M. Cohn Company, a Little Rock-based retailer.

Goldsmith's also made its first suburban move in the early 1960s when it opened its Oak Court store at Poplar and Perkins. Jack Goldsmith, company president at the time, said it was "the best location in Memphis present and future."[3] Across the street at the new Laurelwood Center its promoters were predicting that it would be in the geographic center of Memphis by 1966.[4] The next suburban stores of Goldsmith's were in 1966 at the Southland Mall and in 1971 at Raleigh Springs Mall. Goldsmith's management stated that it was responding to the rapidly growing suburban areas of Memphis in its locational decisions.

By 1978 this major retailer had some 800,000 square feet of selling space and 200,000 square feet of warehouse space in the city. Federated Department Stores, Incorporated, bought Goldsmith's in 1959 and has proceeded to make it the dominant retail merchandiser in the metropolitan area. The company plans additional suburban stores in growth sectors of the city. Like Lowenstein's, it still maintains a major store on Main Street in downtown Memphis.

Sears started its branching in the mid-1950s. It built stores at the Laurelwood Center, Southland Mall, and Raleigh Springs Mall to stay in close proximity to growing suburban areas and the huge volume of retail purchasing power among their residents.

Veteran Memphis clothing stores like Oak Hall, Julius Lewis, and Woolf Brothers closed their downtown stores and staked their future in the growing suburbs. They were joined by other firms in the 1960s and 1970s transferring operations from the downtown. Many of these businesses had been fixtures on Main Street since the nineteenth century. Even the cafeterias closed due to declining business from shoppers, hotel guests and from office workers. Britling's closed in 1971 after a 50-year history downtown to concentrate its attention on suburban shopping centers.

Discount department stores, and junior department stores specializing primarily in clothing, entered the suburban competition in the late 1950s and the 1960s. Many failed to survive the intense retail competition and disappeared. National chains like K-Mart, Kent's, Woolco, Zayre's, the Treasury, and J. B. Hunter came to Memphis and established stores in both the mid-city and suburban market areas.

The suburban shopping centers became a new type of specialized real estate venture for developers. Their potential as investments was recognized by local developers such as John B. Goodwin, L. Hall Jones, Philip and Jack Belz, Kemmons Wilson, the Boyle Investment Company, Wilkinson & Snowden, Dan Turley, and others. The successful Raleigh Springs Mall is a venture of the DeBartolo Corporation of Youngstown, Ohio; and the Southland Mall, of the Meyerhoff Corporation of Baltimore. The larger centers draw their customers not only from the Memphis urban area, but also from the tri-state area.

Not all of the centers have enjoyed outstanding financial success. Some of the specialty shopping centers built in the 1970s have failed to achieve projected volumes due to premature development, extensive competition, and manage-

Fig. 39. The 1970s was marked by the spread of strip commercial land use along many of the heavily traveled thoroughfares in suburban Memphis. The above is Mt. Moriah Road, south of the Interstate 240 interchange. (Courtesy of Thomas A. Wofford)

ment problems. For example, the black-operated and partially black-owned Metro Shopping Plaza of 18 stores at E. H. Crump and Danny Thomas Boulevards has struggled to survive. The Small Business Administration, a federal agency, provided the major bulk of the funds for this center which opened in 1970. At the outset 11 of the stores were black-owned operations, four were jointly black and white, and the other three were white-owned and black-operated. One of the reasons for the struggle was the lack of black consumer support. Ben Hooks, current executive director of the NAACP, was owner of a fried chicken establishment which folded. Hooks, in analyzing the problem, stated: "I've seen my longhaired brothers, with their hands up in a black power salute, shuffle right on by to Colonel Sanders."[5]

The phenomenon of the fast food restaurant business struck Memphis and most of America like a tornado in the decade of the 1970s saturating most of the major urban and suburban arterials. Memphians were delighted to know that the drudgery of home cooking could be eliminated if they so chose now that eating was made so simple and convenient. Hamburger fast food operations assumed the lead in the race for the appetites of Memphians, closely followed by fried chicken establishments. The sedate older streets and the new suburban boulevards were brightened by a panoply of eye-catching colorful plastic signs beckoning the public to "tastelessly" designed buildings housing the hamburgers, fried chicken, tacos, pizza, seafood, donuts, and ice cream.

The race to stay in step with the fluid population was not confined just to retailers and food franchises. Financial institutions long entrenched in their imposing buildings downtown also responded to this growth in suburbia. Banks and savings and loan institutions established branch locations throughout the metropolitan area. And in the 1970s a new technological innovation was introduced—automatic banking tellers. "Convenience" became the principal criterion in locating new branches. In earlier days customers had to go downtown to do business. But in the 1960s and 1970s financial institutions brought their services to the neighborhoods.

The enormous branching which has occurred for a selected number of Memphis institutions over the 25 years between 1953–1978 is illustrated as follows:

Number of Branches

Institution	1953	1978
Banks		
First Tennessee	6	34
National Bank of Commerce	3	21
Union Planters	9	31
Tri-State (black-owned)	0	2
Savings & Loan Associations		
Leader Federal	0	11
Home Federal	0	5
First Federal	0	1

From a dozen or so locations right after World War II, financial institutions in the latter 1970s were doing business at more than 150 locations. Public library branching into the suburbs was a similar postwar phenomenon. In 1951 the library system consisted of one branch. In the 1970s there were 20 branches.

These institutions saw opportunities in the suburbs. Commerce again followed residential development. Banks recognized the potential for new accounts in the suburbs and for business and consumer loans. Savings and loans reacted to the family savings potential and to the opportunities to provide home mortgage funds. Convenience for customers and high traffic visibility have been the key locational considerations.

The last of the elegant motion picture theaters built in the 1920s to close was Loew's Palace Theatre. The last film shown there was in 1977. Just a year earlier, the Malco (Orpheum) Theatre closed as a movie house. Loew's State closed in 1970 after business had dwindled to below a break-even point financially, and the structure was demolished in the Beale Street I urban renewal project. Warner's had closed in 1968, and was torn down to make way for Commerce Square, the plaza and 32-story National Bank of Commerce Tower. With the passing of these theaters, Memphis' "White Way" of the previous fifty years was gone forever. Both the competition from television and from new, conveniently located suburban movie theaters were fatal.

In the 1950s and 1960s, Memphis' business district dramatically changed from the region's dominant retail and entertainment center to just one of many competing centers within the Memphis trade area. Goldsmith's and Lowenstein's, two of the area's principal department stores, continued to operate downtown stores. But instead of these stores being the flagship stores, they have been reduced in status to just ordinary links in the metropolitan operations of these organizations. Beginning in the mid-1960s downtown stores began to rely heavily on two types of consumer markets to survive: the 40,000 daytime office employees on a Monday to Friday basis, and the city's black population residing within the inner city neighborhoods or nearby in the North Memphis and South Memphis sections of the city.

The geographic position of the downtown became its liability. It is anchored at the extreme western end of the urbanized area. Almost 100 percent of the urban population lies east of it. To the immediate west is the Mississippi River and the extensive, uninhabited flood plains across the river in Arkansas. The downtown in the 1960s and 1970s found itself some 5 to 15 miles removed from the major portion of the metropolitan area's population. The old, compact urban Memphis of pre-World War II days, when it was reasonably well-served by public transportation, vanished with the changing tide. Downtown Memphis became more and more geographically isolated from the consumer as the bulk of these people moved further north, east, and south of the downtown business district.

The quantity of suburban retail space which is economically supportable is a function of the area's population growth, and the spending potential of these residents. In the competitive rush to gain these retail dollars the Memphis suburban zones have been recipients of an enormous number of retail facilities. Unfortunately, many of these shopping areas have been built without careful attention being paid to their economic feasibility. Overbuilding has been a problem and it is likely to continue to be a problem as more centers are built to compete in a relatively slow growth metropolitan economy.

CBD-SUBURBAN OFFICE DEVELOPMENT

Retailers advanced aggressively into the suburbs once it became apparent that the center of consumer purchasing power had shifted. Developers and investors in commercial office buildings were slower in identifying their market

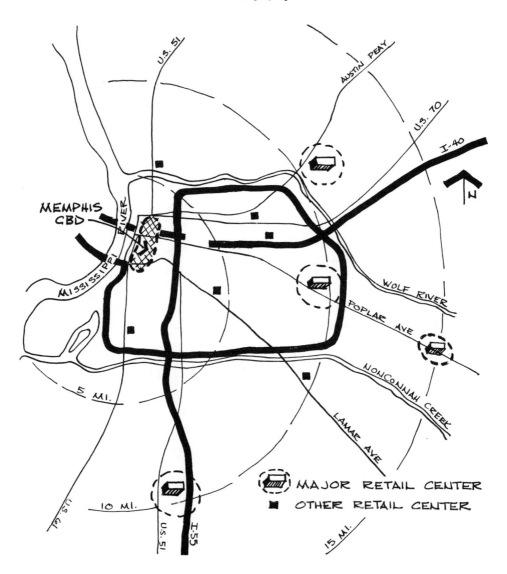

CENTERS OF RETAILING
1979

Fig. 40. During the 1960s and 1970s new centers of retailing were developed in the expanding residential suburbs.

opportunities beyond downtown Memphis. Not until the latter half of the 1960s did the opportunities become clearcut. Suburban office complexes were being constructed in many other cities from 5 to 10 years earlier than in Memphis, but the movement here lagged until large portions of the expressway system were completed.

The wholesale flight of tenants from downtown Memphis started about 1968. Those tenants who did not have a compelling business reason to be downtown picked up and left when their leases expired. They were attracted by the convenience of many outlying projects, and they liked the less congested atmosphere.

From 1968 to 1973, suburban office building enjoyed outstanding leasing success. Much of it was at the expense of older downtown buildings or brand new buildings just entering the competitive market for tenants. In 1968 some 1,100 of the city's 1,500 nonmedical professionals had offices downtown. By mid-1973, only 725 of the city's 1,800 professionals were located downtown. The market share of the nonmedical professionals in downtown Memphis had declined from 72 percent to 58 percent.

Tenant raiding largely ceased after 1973, and downtown Memphis stabilized at a substantially reduced level of leased office space. Vacancy rates soared in buildings previously well-tenanted. The brand new NBC Tower had just entered the market with its 32-story building, and 346,000 square feet of office space. The timing was anything but favorable for new downtown commercial space.

Mid-city, East Memphis, and the Memphis International Airport areas were the newly emerging office building centers. The bulk of the new construction was in these subareas. Leasing experience continued high until late 1973 when available new space far outpaced demand. Overbuilding, combined with the 1973–75 business recession, caused these new outlying office building developments to falter badly. Construction largely ceased with the exception of some smaller projects. Furthermore, rental rates being charged in many instances were too low to permit any satisfactory return on investment.

Similar to the single-family, condominium, and apartment markets, commercial office buildings entered a depressed economic period, and their developers were also asking themselves "Why did it happen?" Again, the answers were related to the matter of poor market communication and over-generous lending institutions who loaned funds on the basis of a developer's reputation and not on economic feasibility grounds. Suburban office building growth was heavily at the expense of the downtown market. Few new businesses and industries were entering Memphis to create a strong demand for office space. Thus, when all of the possible tenants from downtown office buildings were lured to the new outlying buildings, market demand for space tailed off dramatically.

The postwar growth of office-based jobs is shown in Table 12. As indicated, the increase in jobs has averaged just over 5 percent a year. This is a growth rate in keeping with the moderate growth rate of the metropolitan area in population and in business activity. Necessarily, this modest annual increase is a controlling factor in the market for additional office space. But developers failed to consider the pace of growth in the area economy and built too much office space between 1972 and 1974. Since the growth rate has not been fast enough to fill these buildings in a reasonable lease-up period high vacancy rates have appeared.

The ornate Sterick Building was completed in 1929. This was an inauspicious time to be leasing a huge amount of office floor space, and a stroke of very bad luck for its Texas-based developers. This was the last office building of any size to be built in the downtown for the next 26 years. The Great Depression of the 1930s took a heavy toll in bankruptcies. There was only limited, temporary demand during World War II, and in the early postwar years there was a surplus of space in the existing buildings to absorb new demand. The 12-story Tenoke Building opened in 1956, but this was a relatively small addition to downtown office space and hardly an indicator of a pressing demand for space.

Seven years later, in 1963 and 1964, several Memphis financial institutions built headquarters office buildings which provided additional space over and above their own requirements. The 25-story First National Bank, with its 590,000 square feet of floor area, was the largest of these new buildings.

The 38-story 100 North Main Building, the city's tallest building at 450 feet, opened in 1966 to enter the competition for office tenants. Heavy leasing interest was shown in this building by attorneys. The fact that the Civic Center with its various courts was contiguous turned out to be the principal market appeal. Other new high rise buildings and the older, but still serviceable, buildings were several blocks removed from the Civic Center area. Lawyers desiring close proximity to the courts were attracted to the 100 North Main Building because of its location. The other buildings lacked this advantage.

The last major building to open in the downtown was in 1973, when the National Bank of Commerce tower at Commerce Square was dedicated. Its opening occurred at a time when the downtown had been largely vacated by tenants who saw advantages in being located elsewhere in the metropolitan area.

The *Memphis Press-Scimitar* briefly observed in early 1958: "Modern office buildings are being fashioned up and down the 'Golden Strip' of Union and Madison, where brick and stone houses had become 'hand-me-down' offices."[6] This was the start of the exodus from downtown. Movement was gradual at first. The pace increased considerably, however, in the latter 1960s. Many office tenants began to see advantages in being in office buildings near their homes, or near the new expressway interchanges, or near the Medical Center, or near the rapidly expanding Memphis International Airport.

Downtown traffic congestion became an increasing burden. The combined factors of time and distance for the daily journey to the office were considerations of higher paid executives in choosing more convenient locations. And some companies seeking corporate identification physically were attracted to suburban office parks where they could gain a better public image.

TABLE 12
Principal Commercial Office-Based Employment in Shelby County

Type of Activity	1947	1959	1965	1970	1975	1976	Average Annual Percentage Growth Rate 1947–1976
Financial, Insurance & Real Estate Organizations	5,700	9,000	12,950	14,650	17,500	17,400	3.9%
Business Services Firms	1,600	2,500	3,850	6,600	10,050	10,900	6.8
Non-Profit Membership Organizations	600	2,350	3,150	4,500	4,650	4,850	7.5
Professional Services (Nonmedical)	600	1,250	1,300	1,600	2,200	2,100	4.4
Total Nonmedical	8,500	15,100	21,250	27,350	34,400	35,250	5.0
Selected Medical Services Based in Commercial Office Facilities	800	2,000	2,800	4,050	4,300	4,700	6.3
Total All Office Employment	9,300	17,100	24,050	31,400	38,700	39,950	5.2

Source: Compiled from U.S. Department of Commerce, *County Business Patterns* (various years).

Fig. 41. The 32-story Clark Tower and the 22-story White Station Tower, located on heavily traveled Poplar Avenue in East Memphis, helped establish a new commercial center some 8 miles east of downtown Memphis. (Courtesy of Jim Hilliard)

A radical break with tradition occurred in Memphis when veteran real estate developer William B. Clark, Sr., built the 22-story White Station Tower in 1966 in East Memphis. When Clark announced his second tower in 1968, the 32-story Clark Tower building, he based his decision on his expectation of a growing demand for first-class office space in East Memphis. He anticipated that his new 550,000 square foot Tower would accommodate 4,000 people in the various offices and attract some 10,000 visitors daily.[6]

The three emerging competitive subareas—Midtown, East Memphis, and the Memphis International Airport area—designed their specific office space leasing campaigns to appeal to the special locational interests of different tenant groups.

Owners of new Midtown buildings made their appeal to the medical profession wanting to be near the Medical Center and to executives residing in Midtown neighborhoods. Executives living in East Memphis and Germantown became prime tenant prospects for complexes like White Station Tower, Clark Tower, Boyle Investment Company's Ridgeway Center, or Farnsworth-Crow's Lynnfield Office Park. These projects offered modern space within a few minutes drive of many upper middle class neighborhoods.

Access to the Memphis International Airport and to the Interstate 240 and 55 expressway routes were the positive locational advantages stressed by the Vantage Company's Executive Park and State Farm's Nonconnah Corporate Center.

Instant profitability was by no means guaranteed in the case of these new suburban office buildings. During their early years leasing activity was often a prolonged process. High vacancy rates persisted in some of the complexes for several years until demand caught up with supply. Investors in many of these projects, even when high occupancy rates were achieved, faced a market of modest or low rental rates that made it difficult to realize adequate rates of return on their investments.

Market conditions in the suburbs improved markedly in the latter 1970s, and suburban investors felt more secure with the economic feasibility of their buildings. Market rental rates were expected to rise when existing buildings achieved zero vacancy. Because of the costs of construction and exceedingly high interest rates, it was very unlikely that the suburban office market would be overbuilt again.

Downtown Memphis office buildings failed to enjoy any of the successes of the new suburban projects. Without any major change in the economic development rates of the metropolitan area, downtown office space probably will remain relatively static. Some downtown investors hoped that the Mid-America Mall and other downtown improvements would help them recapture some suburban-based tenants, but so far their hopes have remained unfulfilled.

THE CHANGING HOTEL-MOTEL SCENE

When Memphis entrepreneur Kemmons Wilson opened his first Holiday Inn at 4947 Summer Avenue in September 1952 he was well ahead of his competition in foreseeing the changing market forces in the lodging industry. Wilson pointed out at the time, "I got into this business because it, to me, is the greatest untouched business in the country."[7] Now in the motel business, Wilson had expanded his activities beyond his major homebuilding business and his building supply business.

Wilson's first motel had 120 rooms and a restaurant. He followed up on his first success with motels on other major arteries carrying the automobile-oriented traveling public. His plan was to encircle the city with his motels.

Memphis homebuilder Wallace E. Johnson joined Wilson in 1953, and they laid their plans to build a national chain of motels, all with relatively the same physical and operational characteristics. Their concept revolutionized the lodging business, and it brought heavy pressure on the traditional, downtown-oriented hotel industry.

In the 1950s, despite Kemmons Wilson's new lodging complexes, the suburban growth of motels was modest in Memphis. A few small projects were built in downtown Memphis, but there were no projects rivaling in size the major front line hotels that had been built in the 1920s. But major changes occurred in the 1960s. More intensive motel construction took place away from the downtown area. The Hotel Chisca, built in 1912, yielded to the competition by adding its own motel complex adjacent to the older building. The largest downtown complex built in the 1960s was the 248-room Albert Pick. Now renamed the Sheraton Convention Center Hotel, it opened for business in 1969, then struggled to survive during the next few years under several managements.

The market timing of downtown hotel construction in the 1960s was incredibly poor. The venerable Gayoso Hotel had closed in 1962 to permit Goldsmith's Department Store to expand into its vacated space. The Gayoso was an obsolete hotel, so its demise was no surprise. But, on the other hand, any astute analyst of the downtown Memphis hotel scene should have noticed the increasing monthly and annual vacancy rates beginning in the mid-1950s. The widely acclaimed Peabody had been losing business for a decade and had been allowed to deteriorate physically and operationally. If the Peabody with its wide reputation could not make it competitively, then what other major downtown hotel could, faced with the rising inventory of suburban motel rooms with their convenient access and parking areas adjacent to their rooms.

The Peabody had been sold to a Tulsa, Oklahoma, group in 1953 for $7.5 million.[8] Twelve years later Equitable Life, holder of the first mortgage, foreclosed. Business had been bad for the Peabody and the operators did not make the mortgage payments. In dramatic fashion at high noon on 15 December 1965 on the Shelby County Courthouse steps the hotel was sold at auction to wealthy Memphian Robert B. Snowden (whose family had built it in 1925) for $2.3 million, one-third of the sale price of 1953 when the Snowdens had sold the hotel to the Alsonett Corporation.[9] Snowden immediately leased the hotel to the Sheraton Hotel Corporation, which began a restoration program in an attempt to lure guests back. Snowden spoke enthusiastically about a real promotional effort to attract convention business.

The Peabody despite the heroics of its new owners was not able to reverse the tide. After struggling another ten years, it went into bankruptcy in March 1975. This time at the auction block on the Shelby County Courthouse steps the property brought only $540,000. The proud old hotel closed on 1 April 1975. As of 1979 it had not reopened.

The death knell had previously rung on the Chisca, Claridge, King Cotton, and William Len hotels. In the 1970s even the new hotels desperately fought to survive financially. The Downtowner failed, and management was assumed by the Ramada Inns organization. The Albert Pick experienced high vacancy rates in spite of its location near the brand new Cook Convention Center. The Sheraton Corporation assumed management of this property in 1976.

Although it is frequently identified as a downtown Memphis hotel, the 550-room Holiday Inn-Rivermont is located on Riverside Drive about two miles south of the Civic Center. The initial complex was built by developer Harry Bloomfield in the early 1960s as headquarters for a private club. Holiday Inns bought the property for use as a hotel in 1966. This particular facility has enjoyed good convention business, and it appears to be reasonably successful.

Construction of suburban hotels and motels flourished in the mid-1970s. The two major ventures were the 400-room Hyatt Regency at the Ridgeway Center near Poplar and Interstate 240 in East Memphis, and the Nonconnah Hilton, a 300-room hotel near the Memphis International Airport. The Airport area has become the hotel-motel center on the basis of guest room count. East Memphis, near the Interstate 240 expressway system, is also a significant center of new guest rooms.

The hotels and motels built outside the downtown area represent a huge investment of capital. Only limited postwar investment has been made in downtown facilities. This locational shift has compounded that area's economic base problems. Thus, as the city's leaders contemplate the future of downtown Memphis, they are hoping for a revival of investor interest based on stepped up convention and other tourist-visitor activity there.

PRIVATE AND PUBLIC INSTITUTIONAL CONSTRUCTION

Private investment has done much to change the urban land use pattern, and has contributed heavily to the economy in terms of jobs and capital investment. Equally important to postwar growth has been the huge investment in facilities of private nonprofit agencies and institutions and governmental units. Several of the developments of these nonprofit and public agencies are singled out for review.

Medical Health Care Facilities. A major component of postwar construction has been the building of numerous hospitals and other health care-related facilities. The Medical Center complex, which lies just east of downtown Memphis, is one of the largest such developments found in any major urban area of the nation. The inception of the Memphis Medical Center was probably in 1897 when the old Memphis General Hospital was built on the site of St. Peter's Cemetery on Madison near Dunlap. The original Baptist Hospital was well into the planning stages when the University of Tennessee relocated in Memphis in 1911 and merged with the Memphis College of Physicians and Surgeons. And in 1912 when the 150-bed Baptist Hospital received its first patients, its administrators granted the University clinical privileges for medical student teaching purposes. These early facilities formed the core of the Medical Center which continued to evolve over the years.

City-owned John Gaston Hospital replaced the then antiquated Memphis General Hospital in 1936. Modest growth occurred until the early 1950s when a wave of new medical facilities came into being. Heavy pressure was placed on the limited supply of contiguous land. The University of Tennessee started buying private sites nearby, but it faced increasing difficulty negotiating additional purchases. Urban renewal was just starting at this time in Memphis, and the Memphis Housing Authority—the city's renewal arm—offered its help in acquiring land for expansion of Medical Center facilities. During the next two decades MHA carved out its extensive clearance program to provide this room for growth.

The Medical Center has over 7,000 beds, employs over 15,000 persons, and has an annual payroll of well over $100 million. Baptist Hospital, a 1,915-bed complex located on six acres, is the largest private hospital in the United States. Nearby Methodist Hospital, a 1,100-bed facility, is the nation's fourth largest private hospital.

The University of Tennessee's Center for Health Sciences, with one of the nation's major medical schools, is located there, and utilizes the city's John Gaston Hospital as a teaching facility. The University of Tennessee has built eight major buildings in the Medical Center on land made available in the city's urban renewal program. The University of Tennessee's Dental School and the Southern College of Optometry, also located there, have added substantial new facilities.

Still, despite the outward physical spread of the Center on newly cleared land, there was growing concern among the privately and publicly owned hospitals and clinics that they were drifting without a comprehensive master plan for future development. In 1968 a plan was prepared by the Mid-South Medical Center Council, a group representing the various interest groups in the Center. But this planning effort did not resolve the myriad physical and operational problems facing this huge institutional network. Problems of access and circulation, and more important concerns relating to matters of patient care, medical teaching programs of the University of Tennessee, excess bed capacity in the private hospitals, and duplicate daily operational support services were causing strains. Effective comprehensive planning of this major community asset continues today as an on-going matter.

General hospitals have been as consumer-oriented as the homebuilders, the apartment and condominium developers, and the retailers and office building investors. To provide the most effective service and to remain financially solvent, privately-supported hospitals in the 1970s followed the population to suburbia. Methodist South opened in Whitehaven in 1973; St. Joseph East on Park Avenue east of Interstate 240 in East Memphis in 1975; Methodist North on Austin Peay Highway just northeast of Raleigh in 1978; and Baptist East on Walnut Grove east of Interstate 240 in East Memphis in 1979.

Some 1,300 beds were added in the suburbs in the 1970s in response to consumer demand for suburban-based health care facilities. Hospital administrators had taken their cue from the marketing strategies of Goldsmith's, Lowenstein's, and Sears.

College and University Development. Huge physical expansions have been experienced by all of the area's institutions of higher education since 1945. Memphis State University, founded in 1909 as the West Tennessee State Normal School, remained a small and relatively insignificant school in facilities and enrollment until it started a surge of growth in the 1950s and 1960s. Enrollment in 1940 was 950, and in 1950, only 2,400. In the 1970s, it reached a full-time and part-time enrollment of about 23,000.

As of the late 1970s Memphis State University's physical plant, including land, had a replacement value of $150 million. The 100 buildings contained a total of 3 million square feet of floor area. The main campus covered 150 acres.

The South Campus at Park and Getwell is a 146-acre site formerly occupied by the World War II era Kennedy Veterans Hospital. This complex, now used for athletic facilities and married student housing, was deeded by the Federal government to the city of Memphis, which then deeded the property to Memphis State.

Credit for the tremendous physical development program of MSU belongs to former president Dr. Cecil C. Humphreys, who guided the school from 1960 to 1972.

Southwestern at Memphis, Christian Brothers College, and the merged LeMoyne-Owen College all added new buildings and expanded enrollments following World War II. Shelby State Community College—a two-year institution—opened in 1972 with 1,100 students. By 1978 it had built a multimillion dollar campus on the eastern fringe of downtown Memphis at Union and Manassas and had attained an enrollment of about 5,000. The State Technical Institute at Memphis opened its campus in 1968 with 348 students. By 1978 enrollment there had reached 5,650.

Other area schools which contributed to the enormous investment in educational facilities were Harding Academy and Graduate School of Bible and Religion and the Memphis Academy of Arts. In 1959 this latter institution moved into its modernistic new building adjacent to the Brooks Memorial Art Gallery in Overton Park. Northwest Mississippi Junior College in 1974 bought the 52-acre Alodex Corporation property in Southaven, Mississippi, for a branch campus serving the rapidly growing population in that portion of the Memphis metropolitan area lying in DeSoto County, Mississippi.

The new campus of the Southern College of Optometry, including the 12-story main building, was started on Madison and Bellevue in Midtown Memphis in the late 1960s. The University of Tennessee Center for Health Sciences has contributed several new structures, including the Winfield Dunn Dental Clinic Building, the Basic Medical Sciences General Education Building, and the Wassell Randolph Student Alumni Center. All of these buildings are located in the Memphis Medical Center.

Siena College closed permanently in 1971 after being at its Poplar Avenue campus for 18 years. The 32-acre campus adjacent to Goldsmith's Oak Court store is zoned residential. Developers eyeing its retail potential have fought unsuccessfully for rezoning to commercial use.

Recreational-Entertainment Complexes. The Mid-South Coliseum, an 11,187-seat indoor arena, was dedicated in late 1964. And in September 1965 the Liberty Bowl Memorial Stadium was dedicated. They were built adjacent to one another at the Mid-South Fairgrounds. These sports facilities were quickly followed by Overton Square in 1970, a privately financed adult leisure area, and Libertyland, a theme amusement park that opened on 4 July 1976.

The Coliseum serves as the home floor for the Memphis State University Tigers basketball team, and as the site of wrestling, high school basketball, popular concerts and ice shows. From 1970 until 1975, before the demise of professional basketball in Memphis, the Coliseum was the successive home of the old Memphis Pros, TAMS, and Sounds during their brief history. From 1964 to 1969 the Central Hockey League had a team playing there. The Coliseum, jointly owned by the city (60 percent of the original contribution) and the county (40 percent), has been profitable since the early 1970s. The surplus over operating expenses has been put toward paying back the original cost.

The 50,180-seat Stadium, built at the incredibly low cost of $3.7 million, has been the home field of Memphis State's football team since 1965, and the site of the annual Liberty Bowl postseason football classic, held each December since 1965. During the short life of the World Football League in 1974 and part of the 1975 the Memphis entry, the Grizzlies, played there. Professional soccer became a Stadium tenant in 1978. The Stadium, owned by the city, remains just below an annual break-even point, and has not been in a position to transfer any surplus funds to the city treasury to repay its initial investment.

Both of these sports facilities, while contributing to the area's overall recreational attractions, also bring substantial benefits to the Memphis economy through the visitors they draw.

On 4 July 1976, Libertyland, a theme amusement park, was formally dedicated at its Fairgrounds site. This entertainment complex, operated by the Mid-South Fair organization, was funded by general obligation bonds of some $8.3 million sold by the city of Memphis and Shelby County. This attraction was designed to draw visitors from the regional areas as well as Memphians. Additional investments have been made in Libertyland to expand its facilities.

An enormously successful privately financed and operated venture has been Overton Square. The innovative developers in the late 1960s saw an opportunity to renovate an obsolete mixed residential and retail area near the intersection of Madison and Cooper in Midtown Memphis, and create an adult-oriented commercial attraction consisting of restaurants and bars, retail specialty shops, and other businesses. The developers, headed by Ben Woodson, believed their concept built around leisure-type activities would work in Memphis. There was a need and they felt Overton Square would fill it.

T.G.I. Friday's which opened in 1970 was the start of this Midtown project. Several new businesses were added quickly. A few failed but were replaced by new operators. The developers stuck with the project experimenting to find the combination with maximum consumer appeal.

Overton Square is one of the few successful ventures of this type. Gaslight Square in St. Louis, the Underground in Atlanta, and Market Square in Hous-

Fig. 42. The Mid-South Fairgrounds is the site of the 50,180-seat Liberty Bowl Memorial Stadium; the 11,187-seat Coliseum; and the theme amusement park, Libertyland. (Courtesy of Memphis State University Photo Services)

ton, for example, started out profitably with huge patronage, then faded because of poor management or crime in the vicinity. In contrast, Overton Square has continually improved its marketing position.

Civic Center Project. The favorable approval of the Civic Center Plan by the old City Commission in December 1959 launched one of the greatest postwar city betterment projects. By its acceptance of the suggested plan prepared by the Memphis League of Architects, the Commission gave impetus to developing badly needed governmental office and courtroom space, and to revitalizing a major portion of the downtown central business district. There were high hopes that this was the catalyst to turn around the declining economy of the downtown area and to lead the way for new private investment.

The Memphis League of Architects, representing the Memphis Chapter of the American Institute of Architects, received a $30,000 contract from the city to prepare a plan. The citizens group appointed by the City Commission to spearhead the drive for a new civic center was called the Civic Center Advisory Committee. Robert E. Galloway was chairman and Everett R. Cook, vice chairman of this committee.

The consulting team issued its report in the fall of 1959. These architects offered a number of suggestions concerning not only project design, but also the impact the new Civic Center could have on revitalizing the Main Street retail core. The Civic Center, they claimed, would serve as a stabilizing physical and economic force at the northern end of the downtown. With their proposed plan the new government facilities would also tie in with the Municipal Auditorium. The architects were convinced that if the plan were implemented the project would be a source of great community pride. To maximize its potential they urged that particular attention be paid to exploiting the panoramic view of the Mississippi River.

The consulting team offered some additional suggestions to stimulate maximum local and tourist interest in the Civic Center and in the general downtown retail district. One which warranted some consideration was the proposal to build a 350-foot pylon-like tower with an observation deck near the top. They suggested the name, the DeSoto Memorial Tower. The structure would serve as the city's trademark being visible for miles around. Unfortunately Memphis for the second time declined to approve a symbolic theme structure on the river bluff. At the turn of the century a huge pyramid structure had been proposed and rejected. The city could possibly have received the same type of publicity which later came to St. Louis in the 1960s when the impressive Gateway Arch was opened in that Mississippi River city. During its first year, this St. Louis attraction drew some two million visitors. In 1975, for the third time in Memphis' history, another proposal was made for a distinctive downtown "theme" landmark. This time the suggestion was that a 30-storied gold and glass-mirrored pyramid be built in the Front Street area. Again, no civic enthusiasm for this type of attraction.

A civic center was one of the major subjects considered by planning consultant Harland Bartholomew in his 1955 plan for the city. In that study, the Bartholomew staff had recommended that the proposed center's boundaries be Poplar, Lauderdale, Adams, and Third streets. It was the suggestion of the Memphis League of Architects' design team in its 1959 study that the center be moved further west to be closer to the river.

In Memphis there had been common agreement for many years that new buildings were needed to house governmental administrative agencies and the courts. The city and county agencies shared the Shelby County Courthouse, and they were jammed together. The Courthouse when it opened in 1910 served the needs of a combined city-county population of only 191,439. In 1960 the population had increased to 627,019. The State of Tennessee's offices were scattered around the city. Federal courts were bursting at the seams at Front and Madison, while other Federal agencies were located all over downtown Memphis. All levels of government operating from quarters in Memphis required new buildings to consolidate agencies and to provide better service.

The final report of the study team contained a recommendation to close Main Street to traffic between Adams and Exchange, and also to close Washington between Front and Third. The team suggested a pedestrian mall, but very loud protests came from Main Street businessmen, the city's Traffic Advisory Committee, and the Fire Department. These groups did not want Main Street closed and won their case before the City Commission. The idea of pedestrian malls was considered a deterrent to the free flow of downtown traffic. Interestingly enough, 16 years later the city dedicated its Mid-America Mall which closed Main Street to vehicular traffic between Exchange and McCall, some 10 city blocks. There was also concern about the lack of parking in the Civic Center area. A major source of aggravation was the decision of the Federal government not to provide any parking facilities for its employees and visitors to the Federal Building.

The first building completed was the Shelby County Administration Building which was dedicated in January 1960. Several of the existing buildings were remodeled and enlarged. An addition was put on the Police Building in 1961. The 11-story Federal Building opened in 1963. Memphis City Hall was erected in 1966, the Tennessee State Office Building in 1967, the Memphis Branch of the Federal Reserve Bank of St. Louis in 1971, and the Everett R. Cook Convention Center and Exhibition Hall in 1974. The latter complex cost $31 million.

The use of the powers of urban renewal as administered by the Memphis Housing Authority was considered a vehicle to develop the civic center that had been discussed for years. Six buildings were located on land cleared in the Court Avenue I Urban Renewal Project area. Some 141 substandard structures were cleared in this 36-acre project area to make way for the new facilities.

The Shelby County Criminal Justice Center was under construction in the late 1970s. This complex costing about $40 million is located on a site bounded by Poplar, Third, Washington, and Fourth. It was not one of the structures proposed in the 1959 Civic Center plan.

Management of the Memphis Light, Gas and Water system decided against a Civic Center location. Its $6.4 million headquarters was built at Main and Beale streets at the south end of the Main Street retail district. Its site was selected in the Beale Street I Urban Renewal Project area.

Three other public agencies decided that better service could be rendered to citizens from locations in the Memphis Midtown area. In 1962, the Board of Education for the Memphis City Schools and the Memphis Park Commission built a joint headquarters administration building at 2599 Avery, near the Mid-South Fairgrounds. The Main Branch of the Memphis-Shelby County

Fig 43. Heart of the Memphis Civic Center in the latter 1970s. Mud Island, site of Volunteer Park, is at top of the photo. (Courtesy of Saul Brown)

Public Library and Information Center moved from its historic Front Street location to McLean and Peabody in 1954.

Airport Development. A huge community success story is the growth of the Memphis International Airport. This self-supporting operation, providing multiple transportation services for the Memphis and Mid-South regional area, has been one of the backbones of economic life of recent decades. Not only has it served the passenger market effectively and the air cargo and general aviation markets, but it has also been a catalyst for substantial business and industrial activity on land contiguous to or near the Airport site. National airport experts consider the Memphis facilities among the most modern and progressive in the United States. The Airport has become a showcase facility for Memphis and it is considered a vital link in the city's drive for increased economic development.

From the humble beginnings of 1929 on 200 acres of farmland, that original site of the old Municipal Airport has long since been swallowed up by the contemporary 3330-acre Airport complex. The early planners who may have considered the 200-acre site a bold step would have been shocked if they could have foreseen the future a half century later with its advances in aviation technology and the market acceptance of air travel by the Memphis and regional community.

Memphis' modern era in the development of the Airport's facilities probably began in the early 1960s when optimistic civic leaders and planners decided that the city must get ready for the growing air transportation market. And despite some open negativism on the part of a few political leaders and business interests, they gambled that expansion of the Memphis Airport would be justified in the marketplace. The year 1963 was the start of the rapid physical expansion of facilities. With United Nations Ambassador Adlai Stevenson as the principal dedication speaker at the June 1963 ceremony, Memphis opened its new Terminal Building and its 8400-foot north-south jet runway, and entered a new expansion period.

This functional airport is also architecturally unique. The Terminal Building's hyperbolic parabolic roof was selected because it was considered economical and functional as well as visually distinctive.[10] The facilities create an excellent impression of Memphis in the minds of business and tourist visitors to the city.

Subsequent growth following the 1963 dedication exceeded the most optimistic projections of the airport planners and within a short period, expansion was again considered essential if Memphis were to be ready to accommodate greater passenger volumes of the 1970s and beyond. By 1978, for example, the number of passenger loading positions had increased to 54. Memphis had set the pace among the cities it had long considered competitive, including St. Louis, Atlanta, and New Orleans. It had managed to have the facilities available when needed by the public and by the commercial airlines.

Dramatic evidence of the Memphis International Airport's growth is best illustrated in the increases in the annual enplaned passenger volumes. In 1950 the number of passengers was only 177,225. The figures increased to 417,989 in 1960 and to 1,401,317 in 1970. In 1978, the annual total was 2,367,715. How these figures would have startled Mayor Watkins Overton and that small group of Chamber of Commerce leaders who pushed Memphis into commercial aviation!

In 1969 the city's responsibility for the ownership and management of the

Fig. 44. Terminal Building of the Memphis International Airport. (Courtesy of Roy P. Harrover and Associates, Architects)

Airport was transferred to the newly formed Memphis-Shelby County Airport Authority. This body also was given control of the two general aviation reliever airports, General De Witt Spain Downtown Airport and the Charles W. Baker Airport in the north central part of Shelby County.

The public's investment in property, plant and equipment in MIA as of 1978 was $100 million.[11] The Airport has been a profitable entity, however, and operates without the benefit of local tax funds. Fees and charges levied on the air carriers and others using the aviation facilities provide the bulk of the annual income. In addition, a variety of other profit centers are utilized to raise revenues, including the leasing of land in International Park, the Airport's industrial area, for use as office and industrial-warehouse sites.

Shelby Farms

No less significant in the degree of influence on land use and urban development has been the final resolution of the Shelby Farms controversy. The decision to keep public control of surplus county property at the Shelby County Penal Farm was reached only after years of public debate and indecision.

At issue was some 4,400 acres of undeveloped, rural acreage that had been part of the County's Penal Farm holdings for years. The land lay on the eastern perimeter of Memphis with relatively convenient access provided to parts of the tract from Interstate 40 and Interstate 240.

Until the final years of the discussion over its reuse, little mention had been made of possibly developing the large site into public recreational land. In 1957 and 1958 the County had unsuccessfully promoted a 2,600-acre parcel for a major industrial park. Over subsequent years several full and partial studies were made in an effort to find a workable development solution. Not until Garrett Eckbo and Associates, an urban design and environmental planning firm, completed their $150,000 master plan for Shelby Farms in 1975 was a final determination made that this publicly-owned property would be the site of a huge regional park and recreation area.

In 1966 it seemed inevitable that real estate developers would be given authorization to purchase all or portions of this surplus county land. The report of the Memphis and Shelby County Planning Commission had recommended that the Penal Farm site be developed as a planned residential community. At that time several major national corporations were interested in developing prototype model communities to test new technologies in engineering and construction. General Electric, Westinghouse, Gulf & Western, and Exxon all showed interest in possible development of a planned community. Several railroads also had discussions with county officials. But no action was taken by any of the parties.

In 1970 the city and county hired the Bartholomew firm to restudy the Penal Farm site. These consultants concluded, "The 5,000 acres of Shelby Farms . . . present an opportunity probably unprecedented in the history of American city building."[12] In this proposed planned community, a project expected to take 20 years, they visualized a new town with some 40,000 to 65,000 residents. Housing would be provided in all price ranges. The town center would be developed with a variety of commercial and recreational facilities to serve the surrounding residences.

One of the significant statements, made in the report's "Summary," gave this prognosis for Shelby Farms: "Over the next 20 years, it has the potential of absorbing a significant portion of the residential and industrial development of Shelby County and the MATCOG area." This forecast certainly did not go unnoticed by metropolitan area real estate developers.

Several groups expressed an interest in buying part of the site. One serious proposal came from a consortium which included the Rouse Company, developer of the new town, Columbia, Maryland; and two Memphis groups, the Boyle Investment Company and the First Tennessee National Corporation. This proposal made in 1973 set off a reaction in Memphis among civic leaders, environmentalists, and local real estate developers. The pressure exerted by these forces helped kill the idea of selling off Penal Farm land to private developers.

Proponents of continued public ownership of the surplus Penal Farm land had won a victory, they said, for future generations of Memphians and others. They felt that the value of Shelby Farms as a public asset would increase substantially in the future. But some critics of these public ownership advocates claimed that if the land were developed into a regional park, it was too far removed geographically from citizens in the older, central parts of Memphis. They claimed it would benefit only the affluent.

To counter these charges, Shelby County created an advisory group called Shelby Farms Planning Board. Prominent civic leader and environmentalist Lucius Burch, Jr., became chairman. It was this board which hired the Eckbo planning firm to prepare the master plan for the regional park and recreational complex on the Penal Farm property. Philanthropist and civic leader Abe Plough, who had been a longtime supporter of this type of public cause, contributed $50,000 to the study. To honor his many contributions the county's agency involved with Shelby Farms was renamed the Plough Development Area Advisory Board.

Eckbo's plan for Shelby Farms included proposals for a 3,500-acre pastoral park, with a golf course, equestrian center, arboretum, a skeet shooting range, a wildlife area, camping facilities, picnic areas, and fishing lakes.[13] To be developed over many years, one rough guess was that the ultimate development cost might be $120 million.

Since large financial resources were required to build the major elements recommended by the Eckbo Plan, projects undertaken in the short term will be carefully selected because of budget constraints. The initial development was a minimal cost picnic and general recreation area which opened in 1977. The next two elements proposed for construction were an arboretum and an equestrian center.

The full impact on metropolitan area land use will be felt in the future. The Penal Farm property is in the center of several developing residential communities, and its reuse affects private development decisions and strategies in the entire eastern sector of the county.

City's Renaissance

The postwar building boom of countless private and public improvements contributed millions in investment. Certainly the new facilities in Memphis did not outrival similar types of development in other cities during the same period. The unique feature of Memphis' growth in physical facilities is that this city probably overcame more deficiencies than most other cities. In 3 decades Memphis came to excel in new public facilities. It built a major state university, a huge regional medical center, a civic center, a metropolitan airport, and a huge industrial district and flood control works on a previously useless island and channel of the Mississippi River.

All of these improvements provided strong underlying economic support for the metropolitan area during the construction period. They contribute assets supporting future economic growth in the city.

17

Rebuilding and Renovation

Renewal and revitalization became a priority goal of Memphis following World War II. In the late 1930s, there was widespread concern among public and civic leaders over slum conditions in the city. Providing better housing and cleaning up urban decay were deep social and economic concerns evolving out of the Depression period, and considerable momentum was achieved in those years immediately preceeding Pearl Harbor. The war years, however, obscured concern over the plight of thousands of blacks and poor whites living in the city's slums. If anything, during the war years the existence of any type of housing was considered an asset to house the thousands of war workers and military personnel who migrated into Memphis.

The last public housing project to be opened prior to Pearl Harbor was the 842-unit LeMoyne Gardens, a project exclusively for blacks. These final prewar units brought the total of public housing units to 3,337, all built between 1938 and 1941. So, prior to the war only a small dent had been made in the city's 7.5 square miles of slums. Other major cities were also active in slum clearance for public housing during the same years, then had to cease operations during the war.

Some critics of public housing hurled charges that the concept was socialistic or communistic. The Memphis Housing Authority answered its critics by saying: "If public housing is socialistic or communistic, then it is only fair to evaluate our slums as symbolic of free enterprise. Fair-minded, informed citizens will testify that neither the one or the other is true."[1]

Following V-J Day, the Memphis Housing Authority, under the leadership of Executive Director Joseph A. Fowler, resumed its campaign to step up slum clearance and redevelopment activity. Fowler and the Board members of the

MHA promoted residential construction by private enterprise. They encouraged the building of market rate housing in all price ranges, and they were particularly interested in getting builders to construct low-cost, budget housing for lower income groups. Although the MHA operated the public housing program, its leadership was very supportive of the interests of the private real estate community.

The MHA prefaced its *1946–1947 Annual Report* with this statement of what it felt were the city's assets and liabilities:

> We of Memphis, Tennessee, pride ourselves in our time honored slogan, "The City of Good Abode." . . . We think in terms of people. Truly, they are our greatest assets. Their homes, their happiness and their welfare make them better and more useful citizens...
>
> Our liabilities are the approximately 13,000 houses in Memphis that definitely should not be characterized as standard. Many of these houses are without running water or toilet facilities. They are a menace to the health and safety and morale of the city. They are found in great numbers in a twilight area hugging close-in to the business district and forming a belt that well could force some of the city's businesses into suburban areas. Evidence of this shifting of commercial interest already is seen, and a wisely guided redevelopment program to replace slums with modern commercial, industrial and housing developments seems to be the answer.

For many of the city's blacks, housing was a particularly desperate matter. Conditions for them had gotten worse during the war years. Better housing for blacks became one of the priority programs singled out by the Citizens Housing Committee, the public group of civic leaders who were monitoring the progress of postwar housing development. The Committee advocated that 5,000 low-rent housing units for blacks be built immediately.

But there were delays. Construction of public housing did not resume again until 1953. That year a new 450-unit project opened, followed in 1954 by another project of 572 units. A logical question is: "Why was there this 12-year gap in public housing construction considering the magnitude of the substandard housing problem at that time?" The answer appears multifaceted. It is known that influential private real estate interests feared the possible competition of public housing. It is also known that Mr. Crump had grown more and more concerned about Federal government intervention in Memphis local matters. Federal funds financed public housing, although the MHA, a local agency, administered the program.

Despite the impressive rate of private subdivision development beginning in 1947, the deterioration of older housing continued to mount. Subdivision developers were building most of their projects in the suburbs of the late 1940s and early 1950s. The 1950 Federal *Census of Housing* reported that 38 percent of the city's housing units had no private bath or were dilapidated; and that 19 percent of these units had no running water or were dilapidated. Slum housing was not just a problem for Memphis. A comparison of conditions in competitive cities for 1950 indicated the following:

City*	No Private Bath or Dilapidated	No Running Water or Dilapidated
Nashville	48%	27%
Birmingham	38	16
MEMPHIS	38	19
Atlanta	33	17
Louisville	30	10
New Orleans	25	17
Houston	18	9

SOURCE: *U.S. Census of Housing,* 1950.
*Excludes suburban areas beyond corporate limits.

These deplorable conditions in many of the nation's cities prompted Congress to pass the Housing Act of 1949. Title I of this legislation authorized slum clearance for urban redevelopment. Under provisions of this program, the Federal government contributed two-thirds of the cost of buying, clearing, and reselling slum land. The MHA was given the assignment of urban renewal administration, and its staff in 1949 started surveys. But nothing happened for the next seven years. The first official urban renewal project was launched in 1956 when planning began on the Railroad Avenue project, a 42-acre tract just southeast of the downtown section of the city.

Memphis chose to undertake private renewal in its efforts to rid the city of slums. In 1953, Mayor Frank Tobey, with strong support from the Homebuilders Association of Memphis, organized the Mayor's Urban Rehabilitation Advisory Committee. W. D. Jemison, Jr., a Memphis homebuilder, was elected chairman. The main thrust was to incorporate into Memphis "the Baltimore Plan" of housing improvement. This plan was a block-by-block rehabilitation system. Good housing was to be conserved, and substandard housing was to be rehabilitated or demolished under this program.

The Commercial Appeal editorialized: "Powerful forces have been mobilized for an attack on Memphis slums where blighted lives and neglected buildings soil the goodness of our city."[2] Mr. Crump liked the Baltimore Plan idea, and passed the word on to the Mayor's Committee to proceed. Crump was a one-man inspector of the city's physical appearance. Early in 1954 he said after one of his frequent automobile rides around the city: "I'm the best reporter of bad conditions in Memphis, and there should be a lot more riding of the city, checking up on affairs. I note dilapidated houses that need repair, or tearing down. I make notes of bad streets, piles of trash and other bad conditions, and I report them."[3]

The city organized the Department of Housing Inspection in 1954 and gave it an initial budget of $57,000 to start its inspection of dwelling units on a block-by-block basis. It selected the Greenlaw area just north of the downtown for a pilot study. In this first project area the inspectors found 14 dwellings receiving light from oil lamps. This was 1954, not 1854!

The Chamber of Commerce organized in 1956 its Memphis Operation Home Improvement Committee. This group planned an all-out publicity campaign to stimulate homeowners to repair and remodel their homes. A speakers bureau, newspaper and radio ads, and a proclamation by the mayor were used to create maximum interest.

By 1957, under the city's housing improvement program, some 7,000 structures had been rehabilitated. That year Mayor Orgill appointed a special committee to promote "do-it-yourself" projects by homeowners. The FHA made available long-term loans on homes not sufficiently deteriorated at that point to be designated slums.

The two public housing projects which opened in 1953 and 1954 added another 1022 units to the city's housing stock. All seven public housing projects built since 1938 had helped clear only a combined total of 240 acres of blight. By 1955, the number of substandard housing units was increasing, and rehabilitation could not keep pace. Conditions were deteriorating. Something had to be done quickly.

Mr. Crump died in October 1954, and any prohibitions he may have enforced against Federal intervention into urban renewal projects in Memphis no longer existed. Memphis in 1955 turned to the Federal government for funds to help finance slum clearance programs. The MHA staff prepared the required "Workable Program" document which outlined what Memphis had already accomplished and what improvements were needed. Once accepted by the Federal government, the MHA was authorized to proceed with urban renewal planning and implementation.

The 42-acre Railroad Avenue project began in 1957, and it was the start of a 20-year program of urban renewal in Memphis. The first acreage in that initial project became available for reuse in 1959 and was sold to the Board of Education. That same year some 11.5 acres in the Jackson Avenue renewal project were sold to St. Jude Hospital.

Originally, the Federal program was based on replacing slum housing with new housing and supportive types of facilities. Later, more diversified types of renewal treatment were permitted, and cities were not compelled to replace slum housing with new housing. Memphis during the Orgill administration became strongly committed to urban renewal. Between 1956 and 1960, the city's leaders saw urban renewal as the key to a new governmental center downtown and a medical center on project land. The leadership, however, did not turn its back on replacement housing. Several major housing projects subsequently were built on urban renewal land. A total of 1,500 housing units were constructed.

CONTRIBUTION OF PUBLIC HOUSING

Memphis first became involved with public housing in the latter 1930s when Lauderdale Courts and Dixie Homes received their first residents. The inventory of units owned or leased by the MHA in 1978—some forty years later—was 7,246 units. There were 5,938 conventional units owned outright by the MHA. Another 481 units were being leased from private investors. In addition, 827 high rise apartment units for the elderly had been built and were being operated by the MHA. Public housing provided shelter to some 28,000 individuals.

Public housing units were desegregated in 1965 in compliance with the Civil Rights Act of 1964. By the late 1970s, the majority of the housing was occupied by blacks. Almost 100 percent of the conventional units were occupied by blacks, and some 60 to 70 percent of the high rise units for the elderly housed black residents.

Shelby County organized its public housing authority in 1970, saying that it might have to build as many as 2,000 units in the ensuing five-year period. As of 1977, it had only 175 units, and nearly half of these were vacant.[4] The lack of good transportation and proximity to shopping areas were blamed for the lack of demand.

Location of public housing projects and of other government assisted housing projects has been a problem faced by most cities. Memphis has been no exception. Substantial resistance has come from largely all-white neighborhoods when these projects have been proposed for their areas. The common complaint is that these public or publicly-assisted complexes will cause depreciation in property values. When faced with strong citizen pressure, city councils in many cities have rejected proposals of local housing authorities or the U.S. Department of Housing and Urban Development (HUD).

URBAN RENEWAL

The span of the urban renewal program in Memphis was exactly 20 years. The first project was started in 1957, and in 1977 the Memphis Housing Authority turned over its control of the remaining project acreage to the city's Community Development Division. The latter agency was created under the authority of the Housing and Community Development Act of 1974. Congress replaced the traditional urban renewal concept of clearance with a new program concept concentrating on a neighborhood rehabilitation approach to urban improvement.

During those two decades, the MHA largely changed the physical character of the 11 federally-approved urban renewal project areas. (See fig. 45) It took over the designated 560 acres; cleared off some 3,000 structures; redesigned and constructed new streets, utility systems, and other major physical improvements; and sold off most of the land to developers or public agencies or private tax-exempt institutions. At final disposition, MHA turned over just 18 acres of

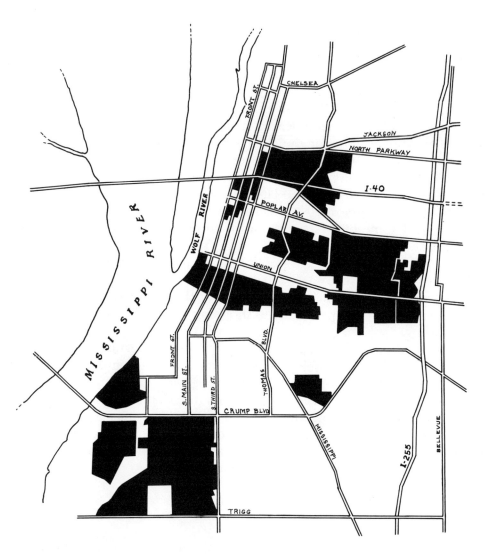

Fig. 45. The areas in black, covering some 560 acres, represent the locations of the 11 urban renewal projects undertaken by the Memphis Housing Authority from 1957 to 1977. Source: Memphis Housing Authority.

unsold property. Some additional acreage was under contract, but not yet developed.

The net contribution in physical assets was improvements valued at $207.6 million. A large portion of the blighted inner city area ringing downtown Memphis had been vastly improved physically. The gross cost before deducting for income received from the sale of land was $131 million. Some $60 million was realized from land sales, so that the net cost was $71 million. The Federal government's share of this cost was $47.3 million, and the city's share, $23.7 million. But Memphis was given credit by the Federal government for public improvements the city would have had to build anyway. So the city's effective cost for urban renewal was approximately $10 million.

Through urban renewal Memphis gained the Civic Center, a prestigious Medical Center, other new private hospital facilities, new commercial office buildings and other commercial facilities, new private and public housing, park areas, and improved streets and traffic circulation. The projects eradicated blighted areas which had become a heavy social and fiscal burden on the city. The taxes contributed from renewal areas exceeded the taxes contributed from these areas before renewal. This is rather remarkable considering that much of the renewal land was sold to tax-exempt entities. Decisions to build the 38-story 100 North Main office building, Lowenstein's Department Store and accompanying apartment tower, and some of the new financial institution headquarters buildings were influenced by the Civic Center project and by the enthusiasm in the late 1950s and early 1960s for rejuvenating the general downtown economy.

Critics abounded, however. Not all Memphians were pleased with the urban renewal program. Some property owners complained that the MHA had too much power with its right of eminent domain and condemnation. Particularly upset were landowners in the Medical Center project area. They did not like the idea of the MHA acquiring property for the use of Baptist Hospital, a private, tax-exempt organization.[5] Some prominent realtors labelled the MHA's discretionary powers a threat to the private ownership of property.[6] City Council members grew uneasy about the slow pace of progress on some of the projects and the fact that results were often hard to see.[7]

To offset some of the frictions, Mayor William Ingram in 1966 organized the Memphis-Shelby County Citizens Advisory Committee for Community Improvement. This 38-member committee was responsible for keeping the public informed about the progress of urban renewal and for offering suggestions to public officials on what should be done.[8] This liaison group was particularly interested in getting action in the Beale Street renewal project. Market analysts recommended to the city that a Beale Street commercial district would help fight off the increasing encroachment of the suburban shopping centers on downtown Memphis business.

Beale Street renewal was a concern to civic leaders not only in the early days of urban renewal in Memphis, but also throughout the 1970s. The Beale Street I project, an area of 115 acres lying generally between the river bluff on the west and Danny Thomas Boulevard on the east, did not receive Federal approval until 1969 despite the city's approval five years earlier. Federal red tape hampered the start of this project. By the time it was approved downtown Memphis had absorbed some devastating economic blows. Even before the sanitation workers' strike and the assassination of Dr. Martin Luther King, Jr., in the spring of 1968, the central city had been largely deserted by the white middle and upper middle class shoppers. The King murder was one final lethal blow to the dying commercial downtown district. After King's death there was a noticeable decline in property values, as an analysis prepared in connection with the MHA's appraisals of Beale Street properties showed. The MHA staff found that the Beale Street project was the only one of all the urban renewal projects where values had declined from the time of the first appraisals to the final appraisals of project properties. The King murder occurred in between the two separate rounds of property appraisal in the Beale Street project area.

In the 151-acre Beale Street I project area, the Memphis Housing Authority demolished 300 substandard buildings. Included in the massive clearance were Loew's State Theatre on South Main and the 80-year-old Randolph Building, a historic downtown office structure on the corner of Main and Beale. The Orpheum Theatre was spared as were a few other adjacent South Main Street commercial buildings. Extensive clearance took place between Second Street and Danny Thomas Boulevard. About the only structures left standing were a thin strip of old commercial buildings fronting on both sides of Beale Street between Second and Fourth streets. When clearance was finished in the early 1970s and the MHA announced the project site ready for reuse, the area resembled a bombed-out Berlin of 1945. A tremendous open gap had been created from the previous high density slum area surrounding Beale Street. The *Memphis Press-Scimitar* remarked: "Urban renewal destroyed Beale Street, and with it, a part of Memphis."[9]

Beale Street, U.S.A., a private development group, was given development rights by the MHA in 1973. Failing to gain financing, this group yielded its rights in 1974. Development responsibility was then inherited by the Beale Street National Historic Foundation, a 33-member group of citizens, created in 1974. Using some $2.1 million in Federal funds, the Foundation bought the Beale Street Blue Light project area from the MHA.

The proposal of the MHA to build a multilevel pedestrian shopping and recreational mall failed to receive approval from the National Advisory Council on Historic Preservation. This Federal agency rejected the plan totally, stating that the proposal was merely a theme shopping center with no real emphasis on maintaining historical authenticity of the Beale Street commercial area. The MHA staff wanted the proposed Beale Street Mall to connect with the city's new Mid-America Mall to tie together the pedestrian traffic of both.

The Beale Street Foundation, failing to get the project off dead center, turned it over to the city's downtown revitalization agency, the Center City Commission, in 1977. This latter agency assumed responsibility for managing the Beale Street project.

The city's new plan was to work with private developers to restore Beale Street. The city agreed to lease the existing buildings to a private development group who, in turn, would rehabilitate and then sublease the improved buildings for the various commercial components of the Blue Light District. The anticipated result was a major commercial-entertainment attraction appealing

Fig. 46. Aerial view of Beale Street in the latter 1970s after completion of the Beale Street I Urban Renewal Project. (Courtesy of Memphis Room, MPL)

to Memphians and to out-of-town visitors. In August 1978, the Center City Commission selected two private developer firms to undertake this project. Thus, with adequate funding, construction was scheduled to start in 1979.

The Memphis Housing Authority, despite its lack of success in getting action on the Blue Light District project in the Beale Street I renewal area, did successfully dispose of the bulk of the land in this particular renewal project. The headquarters of the Memphis Light, Gas and Water Division and the main branch of the Tri-State Bank were built on urban renewal property. The Mohammed Ali movie theater and the Dr. R. Q. Venson Center for the Elderly, a 215-unit high rise, were also built on Beale Street project land.

MHA's marketing program was more successful in the 51-acre Beale Street II project which was located just east of Danny Thomas Boulevard. There 174 substandard buildings were torn down.

The precise cost/benefits of Memphis' entry into urban renewal are difficult to quantify. The original goals established by the Federal government for urban renewal seemed to have been largely satisfied. These goals were: (1) reducing blight, (2) improving low income housing by making sites available for subsidized units, (3) upgrading low income neighborhoods, and (4) strengthening the city's economic base by encouraging investment. Public agencies and private nonprofit institutions have been the direct beneficiaries. But, in a greater sense, the community at large benefited, although there were social costs to many private citizens who were displaced by urban renewal, or who lost control of their property. Relocation was a frightening experience for many of the long-term residents of the areas chosen for clearance. But the MHA's relocation policies were aimed toward providing these displaced persons with better housing and placing them in stable neighborhoods.

Urban renewal was a complex program for American cities during its 25-year existence. Memphis seemed to have fared well in comparison to most larger cities. The reuses here have made an important economic and physical contribution to the city. And, unlike many cities, Memphis successfully marketed most of its renewal property for appropriate public and private reuses.

COMMUNITY DEVELOPMENT GRANT PROGRAM

"Preservation instead of the bulldozer and no more of the tear-'em-down approach" became the objective of the federally-funded Community Development Block Grant program which replaced urban renewal. Memphis phased out urban renewal beginning in 1975. Rehabilitation and environmental improvement responsibilities in Memphis' neighborhood areas became the assignment of the Division of Housing and Community Development under the leadership of Gwen R. Awsumb, a former member of the Memphis City Council and prominent civic leader.

In 1975, Memphis received $30 million for neighborhood revitalization to be spent over a three-year period. The city's grant for fiscal years 1979 through 1981 was $46 million. The Federal government in awarding these block grants gave recipients rather broad leeway in how these funds were to be used. Memphis, through the assistance of a 39-member Action Program Advisory Committee, has selected a number of priority neighborhoods to be improved. The main efforts have been directed toward rehabilitating housing and improving streets, curbs, recreational, and other neighborhood facilities. Loan assistance has also been provided to homeowners.

During the first three years, the Memphis Community Development program was responsible for bringing 1,600 dwellings up to housing code standards. Several of the priority neighborhoods in North Memphis were those poorly planned subdivisions of the 1900 era when land speculators sold their lots to any and all with no feeling of responsibility for access, street layouts, or public health and sanitation problems.

This agency also committed $2 million in community development funds for the Beale Street Historic District project. This sum was in addition to the $2 million grant from the Federal Economic Development Administration in early 1979.

ADDITIONAL GOVERNMENT-ASSISTED HOUSING

Memphis has taken advantage of several federally-supported housing programs designed to help low income and elderly citizens. When George Romney served as Secretary of the U.S. Department of Housing and Urban Development (HUD) in the first term of the Nixon Administration, he was an enthusiastic advocate of industrialized or modular housing as a remedy to the rising costs of conventional residential construction. His experimental pilot program announced in 1969 was called "Operation Breakthrough." Cities throughout the nation were invited to compete for one of the limited awards of demonstration projects. Memphis made a very strong community effort in this competition, and it was selected by HUD for an "Operation Breakthrough" project.

The site selected for this prototype housing experiment was a 15-acre parcel in the Court Avenue III urban renewal project area. Five housing complexes were built. MHA built its Paul Borda Tower for the elderly. Private developers built the other high rise and the three low rise rental complexes. Two of these privately-owned and operated projects were reserved exclusively for student housing. Completing this successful experiment were two HUD-supported projects for low-income families.

In addition to the block grants program in the Housing and Community Development Act of 1974, which provided Memphis and other cities with funds for local community development, Congress also created the Section 8 housing subsidy program for lower income persons. Those eligible were to pay a minimum of 15 percent to a maximum of 25 percent of their monthly income toward the fair market rental rate charged by the private owner of multifamily residential units. Operating under the provisions of Section 8, both private and private nonprofit development groups have qualified, including owners of the high rise Memphis Towers, Wesley Camilla Towers, and St. Peter Manor. These three high rise apartments added over 1,000 housing units to the city's inventory in the latter 1970s.

PRIVATE REVITALIZATION

A growing movement of the latter 1970s was the revitalization of older neighborhoods in the midtown section of Memphis. Led by active neighborhood associations, substantial efforts were being made in refurbishing older homes, as well as improving physical and social conditions within the general community areas.

Memphis was somewhat behind other major southern cities in getting neighborhood revival operative. Atlanta, New Orleans, and Charleston, for example, had been active a decade earlier. Despite the lag, Memphis made the commitment in the 1970s to save many of its older neighborhoods while there was still time. Active work began about 1973. There were apparent signs of a back-to-the-city movement, particularly on the part of younger couples who found the midtown section attractive and its older housing appealing. Equally, longtime residents were enthusiastic about preserving their neighborhoods and have been major participants in the preparation of goals and plans for these subareas. Among the most active associations were the Central Gardens area, Annesdale Park, Annesdale-Snowden, Rozelle-Annesdale, Cooper-Young, Glenview-Edgewood Manor, Vollintine-Evergreen, and Mid-Memphis Improvement Association.

The Central Gardens area, through its 600-member organization, raised $10,000 to hire a consulting firm to prepare its neighborhood improvement plan for the future utilization of property in its central city community. The City of Memphis accepted this plan as the guideline for the control of land use in the Central Gardens area.

Through the dedicated work of the citizens of Annesdale Park, this historic residential neighborhood was accepted for inclusion in the National Register of Historic Places. A concerted effort had been made by its residents to halt any further transition away from the single-family home character of this midtown neighborhood of 125 residential structures.

Memphis banks and savings and loan institutions, aided by loan guarantee programs and support from the Federal National Mortgage Association's ("Fanny Mae") Affirmative Urban Lending Program in providing for low down payments and 30-year repayment terms, have made it possible for many buyers to finance older neighborhood housing. The home improvement and neighborhood revitalization programs have made a contribution in the saving of older housing that certainly would have ultimately sunk into the substandard category if left untouched.

PRESERVATION OF LANDMARK BUILDINGS AND DISTRICTS

The 1970s marked the turn-around in the long-term, pervasive deterioration or abandonment of structures which had historic and architectural significance. A sudden surge of interest arose in Memphis to act quickly lest the few remaining landmark buildings and historic residential or commercial districts be obliterated for parking lots or other commercial reuse. A change in the ways of viewing these landmarks also occurred. Instead of just looking at buildings or districts for historical preservation purposes, many were being viewed for their reuse as productive, income producing facilities. Investors and preservationists found ways to work together in several Memphis projects.

The preservationist movement came late to Memphis. As a result, many structures of historical interest had already been demolished in the wake of urban renewal and other land clearance purposes. But the agitation for preservation carried on by small groups of interested citizens finally caught the public's interest in the early 1970s, and more concerted efforts were being made to protect valuable historically and architecturally significant structures from destruction after that point.

One of the first successful efforts at restoration was the work of the nonprofit Victorian Village, which restored some 14 historic homes and other structures in the Adams-Jefferson Street area just east of the heart of downtown Memphis. This group, which was organized in 1972, has restored such well-known buildings as the Fontaine House, the Lee House, the Mallory-Neely House, the Lowenstein Club, and St. Mary's Cathedral. All of these buildings are representative of middle to late nineteenth century architectural styles, and have been included in the National Register of Historic Places.

Memphis Heritage, another private preservation group, was organized in the late 1970s. Its goal was to save landmark structures and older historic districts.

The city's public involvement began officially in 1975, when the City Council created the Memphis Landmarks Commission. This advisory agency was instructed to "designate, protect, enhance and perpetuate" historic buildings and districts in the city. The initial interest of the Landmarks Commission was directed to the downtown area and contiguous older districts. Its work became very much a part of the total Memphis effort to revitalize the downtown and to create new citizen and visitor interest in its attractions. The Commission successfully gained approval from the city for its designated Cotton Row Historic District. This is a 9-acre area incorporating that part of Front Street and immediate environs which played such a dominant role in the nineteenth and early twentieth century commercial life of the city. The Commission recommended preservation of the historic cotton mercantile houses, and applications filed to have Cotton Row included in the National Register of Historic Places were approved in 1979.

The Landmarks Commission also singled out for preservation an area adjacent to Cotton Row called the Gayoso-Peabody District. This particular area centers around South Main and Gayoso streets and includes within its defined boundaries the Peabody Hotel and the old Gayoso Hotel structure now occupied by Goldsmith's Department Store on South Main Street. The Commission was also intent on preserving the old commercial and residential district just north of the Cook Convention Center, among other areas.

The Peabody Hotel and the Orpheum Theatre—both built in the mid-1920s—were placed on the National Register of Historic Places in 1977. The acceptance by the National Park Service for inclusion in the Register provides opportunities for the owners to qualify for certain Federal financial assistance. The National Historic Preservation Act of 1966 authorized the inclusion of properties of local and state significance as well as national importance. Added benefits of being accepted for the National Register were the special tax benefits provided by the Tax Reform Act of 1976. The act permits favorable tax treatment for rehabilitation of historic structures by granting developer groups rapid depreciation write-off privileges for the costs of rehabilitation.

Federal tax incentives were implemented to stimulate the rehabilitation and reuse of many structures which have an income producing potential. This legislation was viewed very favorably by preservationists as the key to stimulating more private investment in restoring landmark buildings.

One of the city's major downtown private development efforts has been the Beale Street Landing project sponsored by the nonprofit Memphis Development Foundation. This group was organized in 1975 by Union Planters Bank to promote new investment on a portion of Memphis' historic riverfront area. The Foundation's purpose was to act as a catalyst to attract private investment in a two-block district of old, abandoned cotton warehouses. The planned complex of restaurants, shops, other entertainment facilities, and apartments were to be housed in these converted warehouse structures. The Foundation's initial success was its sale in 1978 of the warehouse complex to a private investor group.

The Orpheum Theatre was purchased by the Foundation, as well as some 6.4 acres of Beale Street I urban renewal project land located between the Orpheum Theatre and the Beale Street Landing complex. Plans called for the Theatre to be restored and put into use as a performing arts and entertainment center.

Other private interests in the latter 1970s began converting several older warehouses and loft space into apartments and condominiums. The total effort was small, but there were indications that there might be a snowballing effect in the 1980s. Tentative plans were being made for the conversion of several older high rise office buildings into residential projects. There was the expectation that a "back-to-downtown" residential movement would come in the 1980s, and that there would be increasing citizen interest in not only recycled older structures, but also in new housing complexes. The Mississippi riverfront area was considered to have the greatest future potential for downtown privately developed housing. And it was being evaluated on economic feasibility grounds by an increasing number of private developers.

REVITALIZATION OF DOWNTOWN COMMERCE

The entire decade of the 1970s was spent trying to find the solutions to reviving downtown business activity. The creation of the Center City Commission by the

City Council in 1977 and the launching of a coordinated planning approach by private and public agencies gave excellent signs that downtown Memphis had a promising future. Prior to this new approach, each passing year through the 1950s, 1960s, and early 1970s found downtown Memphis in worse shape physically and economically, despite the huge investment that had been made in the Civic Center at the north end of the central business district.

Signs of economic and physical decline were apparent to downtown businesses and property owners as early as 1951. Traffic strangulation and suburban competition were already creating pressures on downtown business. At the formation meeting of the Downtown Association of Memphis in 1951, Frank Ragsdale, chairman of the city's Traffic Advisory Committee told the 100 business representatives the following:

> The time is here when there is hardly room for the customer in downtown Memphis. How can people not be expected to go elsewhere to shop. Downtown Memphis is becoming akin to a dead-end street, or you might say traffic is like a four-inch pipe pouring water in, and a one-inch pipe carrying it away.[10]

In 1955 a traffic study found that 131,000 cars were entering downtown Memphis daily, but that there were only 20,000 parking spaces for those conducting business in the downtown. The problem would have been even more acute had any large percentage of the 50,000 persons working downtown stopped using bus service. Almost 75 percent of downtown workers were using the bus system as late as 1956. Of course, it was soon after 1956 when more and more commuters stopped using bus service altogether and opted for their private automobiles.

There was some action downtown to try to alleviate the major problems. Some parking garages were built in the mid-1950s. Major retailers expanded their stores, and several of the principal hotels modernized trying to remain competitive.

A temporary complacency may have settled in as a result of these commercial improvements. Merchants and investors were impressed with the report that the central business district was contributing 25 percent of the real estate tax revenues from an area which represented only one percent of the Memphis area's physical size. Unfortunately, the exodus of business was well underway as these statistics were being announced, and downtown property assessments were soon to reflect this transition. Assessments declined steadily after 1955.

By 1959, a sense of panic had set in for many retailers. The Downtown Association sought financial help for an economic survey and for planning studies seeking solutions to parking and ingress and egress of traffic in the downtown. The Association pledged $10,000 for the cost of an economic survey if the city or county would pay an estimated $30,000 for physical planning studies. The City Commission turned down the businessmen for a direct appropriation, arguing that the Planning Commission had competent and experienced personnel to conduct such a study.[11] The Memphis League of Architects offered the city its services to act as technical advisor to a study and plan for the downtown business district. The League was in the process of completing the plan for the Civic Center and had a team ready to act. Thomas F. Faires, the professional group's president, told the city, "the age of complacency among our citizens and the penny-wise and pound-foolish policy our city government has long pursued will have to go."[12]

No action resulted from this strong interest in a comprehensive downtown plan. The Memphis League of Architects withdrew its offer when the City Commission refused to act. Some city officials and civic leaders did take reconnaissance trips to Toledo and Kalamazoo to look at their new downtown retail malls, but nothing formal developed in Memphis on the mall idea at this point.

The Downtown Association continued seeking solutions to traffic and parking problems within the downtown. It also became an active supporter of the east-west leg of Interstate 40, the route through Overton Park. Throughout the 1960s, it pushed for downtown rehabilitation. In 1968, another major push was made by the Association for a comprehensive development plan. Mayor Henry Loeb pledged his support to downtown revitalization efforts, but he told the Association not to expect any large amount of city funds.[13]

As Table 11 demonstrates, the downtown retail district continued to slip. Retail sales had fallen to $87.7 million in 1967 from $107.7 million in 1958. And 1967 sales represented only seven percent of total metropolitan area sales. Back in 1948, downtown Memphis had captured 28 percent of total area sales.

The first professionally prepared studies of downtown Memphis were authorized in 1971. A Washington, D. C.-based city planning and architectural firm, Marcou, O'Leary and Associates, started feasibility studies. In a final report issued in 1974, these consultants made a series of recommendations for retail and office building projects, public facilities including Volunteer Park on Mud Island, housing in the downtown core area, and parking.[14] One dramatic proposal of these consultants was the "Promenade Gateway," a galleria concept including shops, commercial office space, and a hotel. The proposed complex would be built in the area of Court Avenue and extend from the Mid-America Mall to near the Mississippi riverfront.

Other groups were also pushing for downtown and areawide improvements. Future Memphis, an organization of some 100 business and civic leaders organized in 1961, was active during the 1970s. In its "Blueprint for Memphis" issued in 1973, it called for a revitalized central business district, adequate hotels to serve the new Cook Convention Center, development of the riverfront for residential and recreational purposes, and the completion of Interstate 40. Future Memphis also suggested the implementation of appropriate zoning measures to aid downtown investment.

Some 15 years after the idea of a downtown mall had been suggested by the Memphis League of Architects, the city took bids for a 4,000-foot mall to extend

Fig. 47. Main Street in Downtown Memphis was transformed into the Mid-America Mall, an all-pedestrian thoroughfare. *Above,* looking south from Court Square (Courtesy of Mid-America Mall Office). *Below,* looking north from Madison; compare with Fig. 30, p. 198 (Courtesy of E. Alan McGee Photography, Inc., Atlanta, GA).

on Main Street from McCall on the south to Exchange on the north side of the downtown business district. The budgeted expenditure was $6.7 million. In 1976, the project area was designated the Mid-America Mall, and the name, Main Street, was dropped from this 4,000-foot pedestrian area.

At the time of its initial approval, the leadership of the Memphis Area Chamber of Commerce claimed that the Mall was "an absolute necessity in terms of redeveloping downtown Memphis."[15] The Mall was completed in 1977, and active promotion began to create local area and visitor interest in the Mall. Results, measured in increased business activity and dollar sales volume, were slow coming. Goldsmith's and Lowenstein's, however, have decided to keep their downtown department stores. Some small new retail outlets and restaurants have opened along the Mall, but there has also been an offsetting exodus of longtime retail businesses. As of mid-1979 there was no convincing evidence that the Mall had helped brighten the downtown retail economy.

Volunteer Park, another project included in the planned facilities to re-build interest in the downtown, was under construction in the late 1970s. When completed in 1981, this will be a public recreational attraction on Mud Island. For over half a century, Memphis had faced the perplexing question of what to do with Mud Island, lying opposite the downtown waterfront. Numerous suggestions had been made over the years, most involving some recrea-tional usage, although there were also proposals for industrial use. Finally, after years of indecision and neglect, the city accepted the proposal to build Volun-teer Park, the name given to that part of Mud Island south of the Hernando DeSoto Bridge. The principal attractions when the Park opens will be a large river museum dedicated to the theme of the Mississippi River, a 4,000-seat amphitheatre and a general park area. Visitors will be transported to the Park by a monorail system.

When the Hotel Peabody closed, most Memphians and many long-time visitors to the city were shocked. The first of April 1975 was probably the day when morale was lowest for those who were working to revitalize the downtown. But it should not have been any surprise when the landmark hotel closed. Business had been poor for many years. Hopes had been raised when the Belz family, a major real estate development and investment force in Memphis, bought the hotel. For the next four years, the new owners and downtown financial institutions and city agencies sought a way to find a feasible solution to restoring and reopening the Peabody. There was a concensus that Memphis needed the Peabody, as well as a new Convention Center hotel, if it were to compete for convention visitors and tourists in the downtown area.

The future of the Hotel Peabody seemed to be resolved in January 1979 when the Federal Economic Development Administration tentatively agreed to guarantee a $9 million loan to be provided the hotel's owners by a consortium of Memphis financial institutions. Early in 1979 the Convention Center hotel ques-tion was still unresolved.

A major change in downtown development strategy was made in 1977 that gave strong encouragement to Memphians interested in strengthening downtown investment. The City Council established the Center City Commission, an 11-member group, to promote downtown development and to help generate projects by private investor groups. This new Commission replaced the 26-year-old Downtown Association. An advisory group, called the Community Resource Coalition, was created in 1977 to recommend priorities and funding for proposed downtown projects.

A financial arm of downtown development called the Center City Revenue Finance Corporation was established by state law in 1978, as an adjunct group to the Center City Commission. It acts as a catalyst in obtaining funding for qualified projects and has the authority to make low interest loans and to grant freezes on property taxes in selected projects. This agency, for example, granted a 10-year property tax freeze on the Hotel Peabody property. This means that despite the improvements expected to be made by the Belz interests to the hotel, the property taxes will not be increased during the moratorium period.

In the decade of the 1970s, despite indecision and delays at critical moments and despite doubts expressed by many observers that the downtown had any future other than as a center of government, there were some signs that the long decline which had begun in the 1950s had stopped and that perhaps for the first time in a quarter of a century there was hope for the future. New concepts in land use reinforced with considerable renovation on the riverfront were creating some degree of new investment interest. More and more Memphians and particularly vested downtown interest groups of long standing were beginning to realize that if the downtown was to play any role in the private economy it must be structured to fit the locational realities of urban and suburban life in the late twentieth century and not the late nineteenth and early twentieth centuries. More of the business power structure were coming to realize that any attempts to emulate the historic commercial status of downtown Memphis were destined to fail. They realized that the area's greatest chance for success lies in concentrating on the attainable: in solidifying the governmental complex and capitalizing on the recreation-entertainment potential of downtown.

REBUILDING RESULTS

By any measure Memphis was a badly decayed city physically when World War II ended. Little renovation of obsolete structures and neighborhoods had been undertaken during the Depression years of the 1930s except for the several public housing projects built on former slum land. And most construction ceased during the war years of the 1940s. The city was badly spotted with residential slums. And there was commercial blight even in the heart of downtown Memphis.

Thousands lived in substandard conditions that were personally oppressive and degrading to those citizens directly concerned. But this physical and social blight was also a tremendous drag on the city's economy. The poor were incapable of making much contribution. In addition, the blighted areas where the poor resided were a drain on city finances. The cost of the public services provided far outbalanced the tax revenues derived.

Postwar Memphis expanded rapidly into the suburbs, leaving behind a substantial investment in now badly deteriorated physical facilities. Civic leaders had identified the problems in the Depression years, but the city and county finances could not help much to correct the blight. The war came along before Federal money could help very much.

After World War II, the Federal government recognized that urban decay was a serious national problem. It then proceeded to establish a series of programs for public works, urban renewal, and housing assistance to help cities fight the problems of urban decay.

Memphis was greatly assisted by these programs. Memphis, however, deserves considerable recognition for its role in helping to eliminate blight and to halt deterioration in older areas which had not yet gone into a substandard status. Many of the programs and projects often conflicted with the prevailing social and political attitudes of different blocks of citizens. Compromises, based on these realities, have brought more often than not rather surprising and positive results in the urban land form of older sections of Memphis.

The private rehabilitation efforts of neighborhood organizations, of nonprofit business corporations, and private businesses have taken renovation one step further in Memphis. The 1970s saw urban renewal phased out permanently, and in its place a more universal type of redevelopment substituted. The new emphasis was to save structures from going into a state of deterioration and to find new uses and new life for buildings worth saving.

18

The Modern Entrepreneurs

A new phase of Memphis' economic history unfolded after World War II. The Depression years froze innovation and change in Memphis and the Mid-South. Some new enterprises came on the scene like HumKo, Firestone Tire and Rubber Company, and Armour and Company; but overall new activity was limited. The postwar years brought changes. Old line Memphis-based companies expanded operations. Plough, Incorporated grew rapidly and expanded its pharmaceutical product lines. E. L. Bruce Company, the world's leading producer of hardwood flooring, grew rapidly in the 1950s in response to the nation's housing boom. Conwood Corporation (formerly called the American Snuff Company), and Malone & Hyde, a wholesale grocery concern, took on new business expansions. There were many other similar examples of growth.

Memphis was sought out in the postwar years by many well-known national corporations for branch operations. Some of these firms included Caterpillar Tractor, Continental Can, Du Pont, W. R. Grace, International Harvester, Kellogg, Kimberly-Clark, Ralston Purina, RCA, Schlitz, and Sharp Electronics. Some national firms left the city during this period, including Ford and RCA.

Home-grown industries also contributed to the building of the Memphis area's economic base. A selected list includes Dobbs Houses, Federal Express, Guardsmark, Holiday Inns, and United Inns. Cook Industries, one of the city's most mercurial corporations, originated in 1969 as a result of a merger of Memphis-based Cook and Company and E.L. Bruce. Because of this conglomerate's expansion in the period from 1969 through 1977, it could be considered a postwar Memphis industry.

Many financial institutions, retailers and business services industries were born, or expanded their scope of activities. New business leaders and personalities joined long time industrial and commercial activists like Philip Belz, C. Arthur Bruce, Martin J. Condon, III, Everett R. Cook, Elias J. Goldsmith, Leo Goldsmith, Herbert Humphreys, J. R. Hyde and J. R. Hyde, Jr., S. L. Kopald, Lee Mallory, and Abe Plough.

Memphis again geared up to compete with other major cities.

AGRICULTURE—THE HISTORIC UNDERPINNING

The city's greatest concern has continued to be the heavy dependence of the area's economy on agriculture. Memphis leaders certainly wanted to continue receiving strong economic support from agricultural activity, but they also considered the hazards too great to continue to be so heavily dependent on this economic sector so subject to fluctuation. *The Commercial Appeal* editor C.P.J. Mooney, early in the twentieth century, alerted the Mid-South and Memphis that they were entirely too dependent on cotton. He pleaded for agricultural diversification. Some of the early businessmen's organizations sought to bring more "smokestack" industries to Memphis to diversify the economic base and to obtain greater capital investment in the city.

Memphis did from time to time try to diversify. But it was never successful in getting an effective balance of agriculturally-related industries and nonagriculturally-related industries. The regional agricultural orientation to cotton and to timber attracted to Memphis the type of industry which processed these commodities. There were exceptions both before and after World War II, but they did not counterbalance effectively the contribution to the local economy provided by the region's agricultural resources. From the past to contemporary times, directly or indirectly, Memphians have watched nervously the movement of crop production figures for cotton, soybeans, or rice, and the national and world market prices for these commodities.

Cotton and soybeans dominate the Mid-South regional agricultural economy. The former historically provided for much of the area's wealth. More recently soybeans have become a major Mid-South crop. These commodities face production and marketing challenges annually. Cotton producers are at the mercy of the levels of domestic consumption, and foreign mill consumption. The cotton industry has continued to face the challenge of synthetic fabrics. And the farmer has contended with rising prices of fertilizers, weather, labor and energy. Costs have increased and frequently yields have been disappointing. The most recent problems facing cotton producers have been the questions of cotton dust control and worker protection.

This two-crop dominated economy creates continual uncertainties.

ATTEMPTS AT DIVERSIFICATION

Recent diversification promotional efforts were launched in the 1960s and 1970s through the Memphis Area Chamber of Commerce. Between 1968 and 1972 a huge campaign was launched, backed by a good portion of the $6 million fund contributed by Memphis business leaders, to "sell" Memphis to the outside world.

One of the principal selling points of the business promoters was Memphis' geographic location. Prospective industries were shown the transportational and distributional advantages of a Memphis location. During this period Memphis leaders discovered for themselves the locational advantages of Memphis for certain types of industries and services. These advantages were roughly the same as those offered by Lt. Matthew Maury, Robertson Topp, Robert C. Brinkley, "Lean Jimmy" Jones and others in the 1840s and 1850s when they were promoting a railroad route to the Pacific through, or originating at, Memphis. In contemporary Memphis promoters of economic development were emphasizing its strategic central position in a huge diamond-shaped region flanked on the north by St. Louis and the Midwest, on the east by Atlanta, on the south by New Orleans and the Gulf Coast, and on the west by the Dallas-Fort Worth area.

The comparative advantages of Memphis were being stressed. Its lower tax rates, its quality water supply, and its transportation and distribution conveniences were featured in the presentations to prospective businesses and industries.

Economic consultants hired by a consortium of concerned corporate leaders in the latter 1970s recommended that Memphis seek industries involved in innovative new technologies.[1] Great encouragement had been given Memphis leadership by the phenomenal early success of Memphis-based Federal Express Company. The youthful, aggressive air express package company had been able to capitalize on its base of operations in Memphis.

Memphis business leaders began their interest in a drive to attract industry to Memphis in early 1968. Fund-raising to promote the city had actually begun before the assassination of Martin Luther King, Jr., on 4 April 1968. The shock waves of that momentous event helped to speed up fund-raising efforts and to launch a major program aimed at economic development for the city and improved economic opportunities for minority-owned and operated businesses.

By 1972 the efforts had largely subsided. The program lost its punch and the sense of urgency faded. The Memphis Area Chamber of Commerce, spearheading the development drive, languished. A series of internal leadership and financial problems, plus the loss of community support and confidence, brought the Chamber to almost total collapse in the 1977–78 period. A herculean effort was made in 1978 to restructure the Chamber, and to keep alive just one of its former functions—promotion of industry. One year later the salvage efforts appeared to have been successful.

MEMPHIS AS AN INDUSTRIAL CITY

Covetously, since the latter nineteenth century, some of Memphis' business leaders have eyed manufacturing. Despite the heavy historic reliance on cotton, there was always recognition that Memphis might be well-advised to try to lure manufacturing investment into the city to provide a broader economic foundation. Serious promotions were made from time to time. A certain envy existed for the successes which were being enjoyed in St. Louis, Cincinnati, Louisville, and Birmingham. But as shown in earlier chapters, results here were modest. Promoters of Memphis endured numerous disappointments over the half century prior to Pearl Harbor.

Attracting industry became a priority after World War II. Sporadically, campaigns were launched to bring "smokestacks" to Memphis. Again, results were below expectations, and manufacturing as an economic component of the Memphis economy represented only a modest share. As a percentage of total private industry jobs, manufacturing actually fell from 32 percent in 1947 to 22 percent in 1976. The closing of the Ford Motor Company's plant in 1958 and later the closing of the RCA plant damaged attempts to build a large base of manufacturing jobs.

Still, Memphis was not necessarily doing any worse in attracting manufacturing jobs than its traditional Southern urban rivals. Except for Louisville, most of the Southern cities had not achieved a really significant position as industrial cities. A recent comparison of several cities is shown in Table 13.

TABLE 13
ECONOMIC CONTRIBUTIONS OF MANUFACTURING, 1976
(DOLLAR AMOUNTS IN MILLIONS)

Metropolitan Area	Number of Employees	Value Added by Manufacture	New Capital Expenditure
Southern Cities			
Louisville	108,900	$3,498.7	$139.7
Nashville	78,500	1,538.0	108.7
Birmingham	63,200	1,788.7	254.3
MEMPHIS	61,300	1,778.1	139.4
New Orleans	50,500	1,620.6	126.6
Atlanta	46,000	1,335.5	49.1
Other Regional Cities			
St. Louis	239,700	7,335.8	372.2
Cincinnati	156,300	4,499.8	230.8

SOURCE: U.S. Department of Commerce, *Annual Survey of Manufactures, 1976.*

Memphis had substantially more manufacturing jobs than Atlanta or New Orleans. Atlanta's rapid postwar growth in employment was centered in the huge increase in services jobs, particularly within the category of business services.

The "food and kindred products" manufacturers in Memphis employed the largest number of persons. Among the best known companies have been Armour, Buring Food, HumKo, Kellogg, Ralston Purina, and Schlitz.

The chemical industries; manufacturers of machinery, except electrical; and paper products have also contributed a large amount of employment in Memphis in postwar years. Some of the best known firms in these groups have included Du Pont, W. R. Grace, International Harvester, and Kimberly-Clark. Firestone, manufacturer of tires and other rubber products, has long been one of the city's major employers. In 1979 it employed 3,200 workers.

The growth of the principal manufacturing industry groups since 1947 is shown in Table 14.

Memphis has been able to present an imposing list of *Fortune 500* corporations and other nationally-known industries with plants in the area. Why did these firms happen to choose a Memphis location? One of the key attractions has been Memphis' pivotal position geographically within one of the nation's most productive agricultural regions. Many of these firms had close ties with the region's agricultural products—cotton, soybeans and rice. Some were suppliers of agricultural chemicals and fertilizers. Some produced tractors, cotton pickers and other farm machinery. And others were processors of agricultural commodities.

The transportation network and the distribution facilities in the Memphis area were found to be well-positioned within the Southern tier of states. Memphis was within close reach of a large portion of the mid-continent. The city could serve the growing population centers in the southeastern and southwestern states.

AGRIBUSINESS ECONOMIC BASE

Memphis had long been an agribusiness center before the term was coined in recent decades. The change has been in the complexity and the sophistication of those businesses associated with or dependent on agriculture in the Memphis economy. These businesses also exercise a powerful influence over the city's many financial and services institutions, and over the growth of the distribution activities which play such a dominant role in the local economy.

As a site for branch plants, the agricultural chemical industry found Memphis a hospitable location. The Mississippi Delta and other agricultural regions were close at hand. Transportation service and its cost were considered low to and from Memphis. Cheap TVA electrical power was available in Memphis. And the city's huge artesian water supply continued to be a major locational attraction for industries requiring large amounts of water in their operations.

International Harvester opened its huge plant in 1948. The site selection criteria included the factors of proximity to a productive agricultural region and good rail and water transportation facilities.[2] Memphis was selected as the best location, considering these guidelines, for the production of cotton pickers.

Kellogg, which produces a full line of cereals, came to Memphis in 1959. It cited as reasons for locating in Memphis its desire to cut shipping costs to

TABLE 14
Number of Jobs in Manufacturing in Shelby County

2-Digit SIC Code[1]	Manufacturing Industry Group	1947	1959	1965	1970	1976	Average Annual Percentage Growth Rate 1947–1976
19	Ordnance & Accessories	—	—	226	(D)	—	—
20	Food and Kindred Products	6,635	8,578	7,913	9,907	10,206	1.5%
21	Tobacco Manufacturers	448	(D)	(D)	(D)	(D)	—
22	Textile Mill Products	1,452	992	(D)	(D)	(D)	—
23	Apparel & Related Products	790	1,550	2,208	2,024	1,700	2.7
24	Lumber & Wood Products	6,381	4,717	4,956	4,764	2,923	-2.6
25	Furniture & Fixtures	3,135	2,800	3,067	3,116	3,236	0.1
26	Paper & Allied Products	1,091	3,403	3,518	4,618	4,805	5.2
27	Printing & Publishing	1,359	2,046	2,630	3,038	3,104	2.9
28	Chemicals & Allied Products	3,590	3,340	4,885	6,247	5,453	1.4
29	Petroleum & Coal Products	357	427	453	456	538	1.4
30	Rubber & Plastic Products	5,436	(D)	(D)	(D)	(D)	—
31	Leather & Leather Products	46	(D)	(D)	(D)	(D)	—
32	Stone, Clay & Glass Products	460	684	864	697	944	2.5
33	Primary Metals Industries	—	683	902	1,075	723	—
34	Fabricated Metal Products	871	1,529	1,630	3,209	3,967	5.4
35	Machinery, except Electrical	1,279	3,583	3,459	4,866	5,024	4.8
36	Electric & Electronic Equipment	457	1,173	2,209	5,219	2,069	5.3
37	Transportation Equipment	1,788	729	1,449	1,741	1,653	-0.1
38	Instruments & Related Products	66	—	194	444	574	7.7
39	Misc. Manufacturing	576	1,074	1,464	1,362	1,804	4.0
	Administrative & Auxiliary	—	705	1,146	2,266	(D)	—
	Total	36,949	41,840	48,176	60,526	56,484	1.5

Source: Compiled from U.S. Department of Commerce, *County Business Patterns* (various years).
1. Industry classifications are based on the 1972 edition of the *Standard Industrial Classification (SIC) Manual* issued by the Office of Federal Statistical Policy and Standards, U.S. Department of Commerce.
2. Employment data are for the mid-March pay period of each year.
(D) means withheld to avoid disclosing figures for individual companies.

Southern markets, and the availability of rice from Arkansas and corn from Illinois. Kellogg was also impressed with the population growth in the South.

Ralston Purina opened in 1958 to produce a complete line of chows for the regional livestock and poultry economies. The raw materials used included soybean meal, cottonseed meal, grains and packinghouse by-products, all available regionally.

Many of the city's meat packers originally came to take advantage of what at one time were adequate supplies of livestock within a radius of 100 miles. When these supplies shrank in the 1960s and 1970s, this particular industry found a Memphis location less advantageous.

Cottonseed products continued to be manufactured in Memphis. The city maintained its position as one of the largest producers of cottonseed and oilseed products. Memphis ranked second to Decatur, Illinois, as the leading soybean processing center.

Agribusiness-oriented concerns headquartered in Memphis which grew rapidly in the 1970s include the Buring Food Group, Cook Industries, Conwood Corporation, The Federal Company, and Valmac Industries.

The Nat Buring Packing Company, a long-term Memphis meat packer, was acquired in 1967 by Holiday Inns. The latter sold its food processing group in 1975 to a new corporation called the Buring Food Group, Incorporated. In 1978 this company was merged into Riverside Buring, Incorporated, a unit of Riverside Foods, a Chicago-based concern.

Until its dramatic pluge downward in 1976 and 1977, Cook Industries had grown into the nation's third largest grain conglomerate and was one of the largest cotton merchandisers. This new company was formed in 1969. The old line Memphis cotton and grain merchant firm of Cook and Company, organized by business-civic leader Everett R. Cook in 1919, and the equally veteran firm E. L. Bruce Company, merged to become Cook Industries.

Edward W. "Ned" Cook, son of the founder of Cook and Company, in just a few short years brought this new firm to the heights of the grain trading business. Cook Industries became front page news in Memphis because of its dramatic business successes. Grain sales to the Russians became very controversial and brought national attention to the firm.[3] In 1974 the company's stock sold at an all-time high of 26¼. The company continued to make news and some of it was unfavorable. One of its officers was found guilty of irregularities in grain trading. The company was accused of short weight practices in the sale of its grain from its Louisiana elevators. Nonetheless the company prospered until it had to face up to huge losses as a result of speculative trading in soybean futures. On 14 July 1977 *The Wall Street Journal* headlined its front-page story, "Battered Bettor: How Cook Industries Speculated and Lost Millions on Soybeans." Market miscalculations relating to transactions in soybeans, and soybean oil and meal brought to a halt the meteoric rise. Cook's market strategists guessed wrong on the short and long term prices of these commodities. From a yearly high of 17⅝ a share in January 1977, the price had drifted downward to 12¼ when trading in the stock on the American Stock Exchange was halted on 25 May because of the news that Cook expected a huge loss in that quarter. Trading in the stock resumed on 18 August and at day's end the stock closed at 7½. Ultimately, the stock achieved a low of about $6.00 per share. The aftermath of the staggering loss of $81.1 million in fiscal year 1977 brought forth major personnel and operating changes. In a recovery move Cook Industries sold off its agribusiness assets which were located throughout the nation and withdrew completely from the business of trading in grain and cotton. In 1977 Cook discontinued the operations of E. L. Bruce Company and its venture into real estate development after both proved unprofitable. Cook Industries survived this upheaval and reset its corporate goals. The surviving businesses included Terminix, a pest control service, and Cook, Treadwell & Harry, an insurance business.

Although none were quite so bold as Cook Industries, several other Memphis companies also expanded into the world of agribusiness. Conwood Corporation diversified as a company and expanded into a variety of consumer products. Prior to 1966 it was known as the American Snuff Company, and it concentrated on the manufacture of tobacco products. Another firm, the Federal Company, moved heavily into processing poultry and manufacturing flour and baking supplies, feed and pet food. Until 1968 this company also operated cotton warehouses. In a change of corporate direction it disposed of its warehouse empire to concentrate on the processing and food manufacturing business through a network of plants in 21 states. Valmac Industries, also Memphis-based, had its origin in cotton marketing. Its expansion included heavy commitments in poultry processing. HumKo Products, a company founded in Memphis in 1930, merged with National Dairy Products Corporation in 1957. The latter company became Kraftco Corporation, and changed its name to Kraft, Incorporated in 1976.

THE HARDWOOD ECONOMY

Memphis still retained its title as "the hardwood capital of the world," but its former luster as a shining star in the area economy had dimmed as a result of market setbacks. The hardwood flooring business, personified at one time by the successes of the E. L. Bruce Company, diminished. Hardwood flooring gave way to wall-to-wall carpeting in most new housing following the FHA's approval of carpeting as an item covered in the basic home loan in 1966. In the peak year, 1955, some 1.2 billion feet of hardwood flooring were sold. In 1975 only 96 million feet were sold. The declining sales took their toll in Memphis. After 54 years with a plant in town, E. L. Bruce closed in 1975. Two years later, Cook Industries dropped this subsidiary. Anderson-Tully Company, a leading hardwood lumber producer in Memphis since 1888, closed its operations in the city in 1975.

Furniture, however, continued to be manufactured in Memphis. The largest user of wood products was the Memphis Furniture Manufacturing Company, one of the city's oldest firms.

Tourism—A New Industry

In an amazing stroke of good fortune Memphians rediscovered the Mississippi River in the 1970s and also discovered that it was one of several physical assets in the city that tourists and other visitors would spend their money to see. The river was seen as a catalyst for developing new attractions and facilities which would give nonresidents a reason to visit and to patronize the hotels and motels, restaurants, stores, and entertainment businesses located throughout the city.

The untimely death of world celebrity and entertainer Elvis Presley in August 1977, shocked millions of people who had identified with him and his style of music and showmanship over the two decades of his colorful career. His home Graceland in Memphis immediately became a "must see" attraction for thousands of people who wished to visit the gravesite and to pay their respects to this unusual entertainer. These visitors have contributed substantially to the city's income from the tourism industry. Graceland will probably remain a major tourist destination for years to come and the city's economy will be a beneficiary of this sustained interest.

That portion of the visitor industry that has lagged in the postwar years has been convention business. Memphis had not kept pace with many other of the larger urban areas in attracting convention groups. The opening of the Cook Convention Center in 1973 was expected to reverse Memphis' mediocre performance in competing for national and regional conventions, but for a variety of reasons the turnaround expected did not materialize in the near term. Among the principal reasons for the lag was the lack of modern hotels near the Convention Center to house the delegates. Regardless of the past record, however, Memphis was hopeful that the convention portion of the visitors market would improve substantially in the 1980s.

Memphis-Based Corporations

Memphis had placed heavy reliance on its agribusiness economic base, while worrying that it lacked adequate diversity. Nonetheless, the city has developed a nucleus of strong and innovative corporations that have become successful entities. Some like Plough have been operating in Memphis for decades. Others like Federal Express, Holiday Inns, and several small corporations came on the scene rapidly in the contemporary period. Most of these corporations were organized by aggressive entrepreneurs who responded to new technologies and to previously unserved markets. Some of these firms deserve special recognition because of their direct contributions to the Memphis economy, and for the national and international publicity they have contributed.

Plough, Incorporated continued to grow rapidly following World War II. In the 1930s it was a small company with plants in Memphis and Mexico City, producing St. Joseph Aspirin, Penetro products and Black and White beauty products. In the 1940s, founder Abe Plough started a major acquisition program which included radio stations, including Memphis' WMPS. By 1950 Plough increased its net sales to $16.4 million; and by 1960, to $45.9 million. The year before its merger with the Schering Corporation in 1970, Plough's net sales had increased to $134.3 million and its net income, $15.8 million. The merged entity was named Schering-Plough Corporation with headquarters in New Jersey. Plough, Incorporated became a subsidiary. Its Memphis facilities continued to be one of the city's principal industrial employers.

When Kemmons Wilson cut the ribbon on the first Holiday Inn in 1952 it was a landmark moment in the business history of Memphis. Shortly thereafter, the 39-year-old Wilson teamed up with veteran Memphis homebuilder Wallace E. Johnson to form Holiday Inns of America. In the lodging industry great success nationally and internationally soon come to this innovative Memphis-based organization.

The founders' original idea was to establish a national system of company-owned and licensed motels from coast to coast. Growth was rapid. By 1960 there were 157 Holiday Inns. Nearly 15,000 guest rooms had been built. Because of the company's penetration into the foreign market in the 1960s, the corporate name was changed in 1969 to Holiday Inns, Incorporated. By 1970 the total number of inns had grown to 1,713, and the guest room inventory to 279,000. Holiday Inns had far outpaced any competitive hotel or motel chain organization. The name Holiday Inn was practically synonymous with the term "motel" in much of America at this point in the history of this Memphis-based company.

Along the way Holiday Inns became a conglomerate organization. Management decided on a policy of diversification to broaden its opportunities. Among the new activities added were furniture manufacturing, institutional supplies including furnishings, and transportation. In an exchange of stock of more than $200 million, Holiday Inns acquired an entity which owned Continental Trailways, a major intercity bus transportation company, and Delta Steamship Lines, a New Orleans-based shipping company operating from the Gulf of Mexico to points in South America and the West Coast of Africa. Management felt this tie-in of transportation with its established interests in guest room accommodations would give Holiday Inns a wide competitive edge. But like so many of the large industrial conglomerates formed in the 1960s, many of management's acquisitions often did not prove profitable. At midpoint in the 1970s Holiday Inns disposed of some of these operations, or discontinued them. Management turnover and internal reorganizations became a fact of business life during these years of adjustment.

The intrepid Memphis entrepreneurs Kemmons Wilson and Wallace Johnson during the development period of Holiday Inns found time to team up in a number of large scale commercial real estate ventures unrelated to their

Fig. 48. Founders of The Holiday Inns, Inc., Wallace E. Johnson on left; and Kemmons Wilson, right. (Courtesy of Holiday Inns, Incorporated)

interests in Holiday Inns. The driving energy of these modern business giants was reminiscent of their counterparts a century earlier—Robertson Topp, R. C. Brinkley and Henry A. Montgomery. All were innovators and risk-takers.

The emerging entrepreneurial star of the 1970s was Frederick W. Smith.

Fig. 49. Federal Express Corporation, organized in 1972 by entrepreneur Frederick W. Smith (insert), then 29 years old, became an instant success. Corporate headquarters and principal operations are located at the Memphis International Airport. (Courtesy of Federal Express Corporation)

At the age of 29 he founded Federal Express Corporation in 1972. Smith seized the opportunity to provide a door-to-door, largely overnight, nationwide small package air freight service. The concept's success depended on a skillfully integrated air-ground transportation system. Memphis was developed into the center of what the company identified as a "hub-and-spokes" pattern of operations. The quick rise to success was reflected in the $20 million net income reported in 1978. Congressional approval of legislation deregulating the air cargo industry in 1977 permitted Federal Express to fly larger aircraft. Without that approval this aggressive company faced an uncertain future.

The company experienced a very successful public sale of its stock in early 1978 and later that year it reached another milestone when its stock started trading on the New York Stock Exchange. The success of this company gave Memphis industrial promoters encouragement that the city could serve as a base for other new technology industries.

Great success was achieved by Malone & Hyde in the 1970s. The expansion of operations of this wholesale and retail food firm was directed by J. R. Hyde, III, grandson of the cofounder, who was 29 when he became chairman in 1972. Annual sales increased from $422.1 million in 1970 to nearly $1.4 billion in 1978. This company, founded in 1907 by Joseph R. Hyde and Taylor Malone, started with a capital investment of $5,000.

Orgill Brothers & Company, a pioneer concern in Memphis dating back to 1847, continued to expand in its 14-state market area. This Memphis-based wholesale hardware firm remained a privately-owned company despite its huge growth following World War II.

Businessman and civic leader Frank M. Norfleet, chief executive officer of Parts Industries Corporation, a holding company, lead his automotive replacement parts organization into a major expansion era in the 1960s and 1970s. Its principal subsidiary was Parts, Incorporated. Operations were principally in the South.

Dr. William B. Cockroft, then a practicing dentist in Memphis, was 54 years old when he founded United Enterprises in 1956. The corporate name, United Inns, emerged in 1961. The company's growth escalated when it became the major licensee of Holiday Inns. Later it added furniture manufacturing and a car wash operation called Mr. Pride Car Wash. Net income in 1978 was nearly $8.6 million, the company's best year to that date.

Guardsmark, a nationwide security and protection service firm was founded by Ira A. Lipman in 1963. Lipman was 22 at the time. William B. Tanner in the 1970s built his Memphis-based company into the world's largest service organization for broadcasters, dealing in radio and TV commercials and station programs. Dunavant Enterprises, headed by William B. Dunavant, Jr., encompassed W. B. Dunavant and Company, a major national and international cotton broker, and other enterprises including the luxurious Memphis Racquet Club.

Dobbs Houses were the creation of James K. Dobbs, Sr., with his business partner Horace H. Hull. These two were well-known Mid-South auto dealers, and had been in business together since 1921. They laid claim to the title "World's Largest Ford Dealer" right before World War II. The new venture, Dobbs Houses, formally organized in 1946, became a successful restaurant and airline catering firm. At one time in the company's early life it was in the oil drilling business in the Southwest. In 1966 Beech-Nut and Dobbs Houses merged; the latter became a division of Beech-Nut Life Savers, Incorporated. Later E. R. Squibb and Sons acquired Beech-Nut. Dobbs Houses became this new entity's food-service subsidiary with corporate headquarters in Memphis.

Welcome Wagon International, founded in Memphis in 1928 by Thomas W. Briggs, became part of Gillette Company in 1971. Headquarters of this unique hospitality-oriented commercial firm remained in Memphis. Since Brigg's death in 1964 the organization has been headed by women executives including Rosanne Beringer, Eleanor O'Neill, and Barbara Marshall.

J. Don Richards founded a small company in 1934 to produce surgical and orthopedic products. Following World War II, this company grew to be the world's largest manufacturer of permanent implants for the human body. Wm. H. Rorer, Incorporated, a major pharmaceutical corporation headquartered in Pennsylvania, acquired the Richards Manufacturing Company in 1968. At about the same time Richards began operations in Europe and on the West Coast, in addition to its Memphis production facilities.

A major Memphis industry is publishing. The Memphis Publishing Company, a component of the Scripps-Howard network, was organized in the 1930s succeeding the former *Press-Scimitar* and *Commercial Appeal* companies. In 1978 it employed 1,200 people. *The Commercial Appeal* in 1978 had a circulation of about 205,000 for the daily edition and 282,000 for the Sunday edition. Just after World War II, the circulation figure for the daily edition was 168,000, and about 217,000 for the Sunday edition. *The Memphis Press-Scimitar,* published daily except Sunday, did not fare so well. Its 1978 circulation of about 110,000 was 16,000 less copies than in 1947.[4]

Among other Memphis-based corporations organized since World War II were Burk-Hall Company, engaged in the manufacture and sale of paint, which acquired the nineteenth century-organized True-Tagg Paint Company in 1973. Care Inns, incorporated in 1967, operated a chain of nursing homes in the South. Hillhaven Corporation, organized in 1965 as Medicenters of America, had primary interests in convalescent and health care facilities. Memphis is also the piano manufacturing center of the South. Aeolian Corporation, the world's largest exclusive manufacturer of pianos, entered Memphis in 1951. Its other plant is in Rochester, N.Y. James H. Patton founded the forerunner of National Bedding and Furniture Industries in 1910. It too expanded greatly in the postwar period from its manufacturing base on Presidents Island. The new Federal Compress and Warehouse Company, founded in 1968, was acquired by Roger Malkin and Associates of New York and became a dominant bonded storage company throughout the South and West by developing new warehouses or acquiring existing properties. Other locally-based corporations included Piper Industries (diversified manufacturing), Servico, Incorporated, (motels), and Union Service Industries (cotton compresses and warehouses, and equipment leasing), formerly the Union Compress and Warehouse Company.

Branch Operations of National Corporations

Memphis was selected as a site for branch manufacturing plants by a number of industries not classified as agribusiness concerns. Kimberly-Clark, a major manufacturer of consumer-oriented paper products, came to Memphis in 1946. Its decision was influenced by the existing transportation facilities linking Memphis to major population centers in the South and Southwest. The company was also impressed with the availability of pure artesian groundwater. It was followed in 1949 by Hunter Fan and Ventilating Company, a division of

Ohio-based Robbins and Myers, Incorporated. It has continued to expand its Memphis facilities.

The announcement in 1969 that the Jos. Schlitz Brewing Company was coming to Memphis gave a great lift to the city's leaders. The Greater Memphis Program had been launched full scale after the Martin Luther King, Jr., assassination. The city wanted action. It wanted new investment and jobs. The 22 April 1969 edition of *The Commercial Appeal* carried the banner headline, "$60 Million Schlitz Brewery Will Be Built in Shelby."

The company's president spoke favorably of Memphis' industrial climate and the anticipated growth in the marketing area. Schlitz was also impressed with the quality of the local water supply. The Memphis plant with a yearly capacity of 4.4 million barrels opened officially in May 1972. At approximately the same time Schlitz was building a carbon copy of the Memphis plant in Winston-Salem, North Carolina. Schlitz seemed on the move as a leading national marketer of beer.

Severe competition among the major national brewers, plus internal corporate management problems of this Milwaukee-headquartered company which came to a climax soon after production started at its Memphis plant hurt production goals. During the 1970s, as this company struggled in the competitive brewing business, the Memphis brewery failed to reach full production capability.

Caterpillar Tractor launched its Memphis operations in 1976. Its location here solved the problem of what to do with the huge RCA plant that had been vacant since that company abandoned Memphis at the end of 1971. The plant had 28 acres of covered floor area in addition to extensive appended land. Memphis leaders had been very encouraged that General Motors would become a major manufacturer locally when it bought the RCA property in 1973. GM had planned to build specialty vehicles and trucks, but poor market conditions in 1974 led the company to call off its plans to operate in Memphis. Again, this was a huge disappointment to Memphians. When Caterpillar entered the scene to operate a parts distribution center, the worrisome problem of the old RCA plant had been resolved. Caterpillar chose Memphis because of the city's transportation network.

In 1978 when Sharp Electronics Corporation announced it had selected Memphis for its second U.S.-based manufacturing plant, the city received this news enthusiastically. A relatively long drought in the entry of large-scaled manufacturing plants into the Memphis area had been broken. The Japanese-owned Sharp plant expected to start production of a line of consumer products in late 1979.

SOME LOSSES

Memphis also lost some of its principal industries in contemporary times. Chicago and Southern Air Lines moved its headquarters operation to Memphis just prior to World War II, and then moved to Atlanta in 1952 when it merged with Delta Air Lines. Most of its 800 employees and its large payroll were transferred to Atlanta.

Ford Motor Company closed its assembly plant in June 1958. This ended Ford's manufacturing tenure in Memphis that had begun on Union Avenue prior to World War I. The 1958 closing affected 950 workers. The company claimed that its Riverside Boulevard plant was too small, and that it could not justify building new facilities in Memphis since it had adequate production capacity in its more modern plants in Atlanta, Dallas, and Louisville.[5] Mayor Orgill tried to influence Ford to keep operating some phases of its operations in Memphis, but the company declined.

The closing of the RCA plant on 31 December 1970 was a great shock economically and psychologically. There had been much exhilaration when the RCA board of directors formally approved construction of a $20 million TV receiver manufacturing plant in Memphis in early 1966. The *Memphis Press-Scimitar* carried the huge headline, "RCA Board Makes It Official."[6] Company officials estimated the peak employment would be as many as 8,000.[7] The plant, built on Raines Road near Outland, employed about 3,000 at its peak point of production.

The brief operating history of just over four years was not entirely smooth.[8] RCA supervisors brought to Memphis to operate the plant criticized the production skills of the local labor force. They complained in the early years about worker attitudes, job discipline, and absenteeism. Local workers reacted in some instances to what they described as management's lack of sensitivity. Early confusion was to be expected. Most of the RCA assembly workers had no previous industrial experience. And RCA's supervisors had come to Memphis from plants where workers had a long history of industrial plant experience.

The reasons given by RCA for closing its Memphis plant, according to analysts, were the true ones.[9] Competition from Japanese and other Far Eastern TV manufacturers was fierce, and it was difficult for domestic producers to meet the price competition. Also, the American consumer was buying color sets. The Memphis plant was heavily involved in the production of black and white sets.

The exodus of RCA left some local psychological scars that lingered on well into the 1970s. Some feared that RCA's abandoning Memphis would hurt the city's chances to attract other types of assembly operations. The decision of Sharp Electronics to open a large plant in Memphis helped overcome this apprehension.

ROLE OF FINANCIAL INSTITUTIONS

The degree of profitability of the city's banks, savings and loans, and other principal financial institutions has largely been a direct reflection of the trends in the Memphis region's economic growth. In the day-to-day commercial life of the area, these institutions provide a variety of essential business services. To varying degrees they furnish the capital funds supporting the expansion plans of businesses and industries, and the funds utilized in the real estate market. Directly and indirectly they play a vital role in the economic development of the city.

Prior to the 1970s Memphis-based banks competed and grew as institutions without any major crises. The three largest banks, the First Tennessee Bank, Union Planters Bank, and the National Bank of Commerce, along with a number of other banks competed hard for new local and regional business. In most instances the business power structure of Memphis was represented on these boards of directors. In this contemporary business era the city's influential business families continued their historic control of banking policies.

The 1970s, however, brought traumatic changes in traditional Memphis banking. Growth continued, but it continued in a rocky manner, particularly during the mid-part of the decade. The relative business stagnation in the Memphis region because of the lack of any substantial influx of new industry and capital investment was reflected in total bank deposits and loans. Since Memphis' major banks were performance-minded, this forced the adoption of new programs and policies.

Intense competition developed among the top three veteran city banks for business. Boards of directors and stockholders wanted improved earnings. The challenge to grow was made all the more difficult with the proliferation of other banks, many of which were newcomers into the Memphis community. Banks went after each other's customers in a competitive game resembling musical chairs. Since growth was hard to attain on the basis of generally slow community or regional economic growth, banks expanded into the complex world of large scale real estate lending. Heavy financing went into apartment and condominium developments, office buildings, shopping centers, and other real estate ventures in Memphis and elsewhere. Union Planters Bank, the city's number two bank in deposits, led the way in the early 1970s in real estate activities.

The institution of the bank holding company entered the scene in the latter 1960s. The First Tennessee Bank was acquired in 1969 by the First Tennessee National Corporation which had been incorporated just a year earlier. This holding company then began an intensive acquisition program of banks located throughout Tennessee in the 1970s. Union Planters Bank was acquired by the Union Planters Corporation in 1971. The latter's acquisition program was much more limited than its leading competitor. Memphis' number three bank in size, National Bank of Commerce, was acquired in 1971 by the United Tennessee Bancshares Corporation, which had been organized in 1966.

Why the vehicle of the holding company? They were created to give banks greater mobility in operations. By expanding their geographic market area, banks could attract much more business and broaden their financial base.

Despite the changes, Memphis area banks did not experience any dramatic growth changes. On 30 June 1977 the combined 30 banks in the Memphis Standard Metropolitan Statistical Area (SMSA) had deposits of $3.0 billion.[10] For those banks locally in Shelby County, total deposits were almost $2.8 billion. Four years earlier in 1973, the combined Memphis SMSA deposits were $2.7 billion.[11]

Market shares of deposits were as follows in 1977: First Tennessee Bank, 36 percent; Union Planters, 24 percent; National Bank of Commerce, 15 percent; and all of the other banks combined, just 25 percent. In 1973, before Union Planters had to face its greatest crisis in its then 104-year history, it had 35 percent of the Memphis SMSA deposits. It was neck-and-neck competitively with the First Tennessee Bank which then had 37 percent of the area deposits.

During the 1974–1975 period all of Memphis' banks experienced some strain. Tight money nationally and within Tennessee, the state's usury law, and the intensive interbank competition for business hurt these financial institutions. The venerable Union Planters, however, had a series of additional problems stemming from management problems and a record of poor loans. These shocks almost brought the ultimate downfall of this well-known bank.

Union Planters suffered heavy real estate losses. The 1974 recession in real estate nationally and locally was an inopportune event for the bank. But many of the loans were questionable on grounds of economic feasibility. Union Planters also had severe internal management problems. There were illegal actions and charges of bank fraud. Quick action was necessary to salvage the bank. The problems were complex, and it took months to uncover the extent of the wrong-doing and the accounting for the true financial condition of the bank. The Union Planters' board hired William M. Matthews, a successful Atlanta bank executive, to undertake the drastic actions necessary to turn the bank around. Matthews arrived in 1974. That year the bank reported a loss of $16.8 million. In 1975, it was a loss of $2.7 million, and in 1976, a deficit of $0.8 million. In 1977 Union Planters reported its first profit since 1973. Matthews had performed a miracle in saving this venerable Memphis bank.

Among competitive Southern cities Memphis ranked sixth in total deposits in mid-1977. Table 15 compares the standings of these various SMSAs.

Among the area's savings and loan associations, Leader Federal under the aggressive leadership of chairman of the board and president, Edgar H. Bailey, dominated the scene in the 1970s. At the end of 1978, it had assets of $899.1 million and a first mortgage loan portfolio of $785.3 million. The $723.1 million in savings accounts was double the figure in the early 1970s. Before Bailey assumed control in 1972, Roy M. Marr, his predecessor, had taken charge of an institution with only $4 million in assets in 1944 and built these resources to over $300 million. Among Memphis financial institutions Leader Federal was the postwar star performer.

Home Federal, the second largest savings and loan, was less than one-fifth the size of Leader Federal. The city had four other associations.

TABLE 15
TOTAL BANK DEPOSITS IN SELECTED SOUTHERN CITIES
(30 JUNE 1977)

City (SMSA)	Deposits
Atlanta	6,303,788,000
New Orleans	4,268,432,000
Nashville	3,609,235,000
Louisville	3,425,858,000
Birmingham	3,042,567,000
MEMPHIS	3,022,859,000

SOURCE: Federal Deposit Insurance Corporation, *Summary of Deposits in All Commercial and Mutual Savings Banks, June 30, 1977.*

Memphis had the home offices of four life insurance companies. Lincoln American Life and National Trust Life were white-owned companies. Universal Life and Union Protective Life were black-owned.

The oldest was Universal Life which was founded by Dr. J. E. Walker in 1923. Since 1952, the wealthy black business and civic leader, A. Maceo Walker, son of the founder, has led this company. Assets increased from $13.7 million in 1955 to $52.4 million in 1977. Life insurance in force in 1977 was $414 million.

In 1933 Union Protective Life, another black-owned life insurance company, was organized by H. David Whalum. With just over $4 million in assets and $18.9 million of insurance in force in 1977, it has remained a very small institution.

National Trust Life began in 1930 as the National Burial Insurance Company. The present name was adopted in 1964. Assets in 1977 were $103.3 million. Life insurance in force was $801 million. Chairman of National Trust was Alvin Wunderlich, Jr.

Lincoln American Life, which had merged with Columbia Mutual Life in 1965, grew rapidly in the 1970s. Between 1971 and 1977 it doubled its life insurance in force to over $1.1 billion. Assets in 1977 were $88 million. This company which began in 1959 merged with the former Consumers National Corporation in 1973. Headquarters of Lincoln American has been the former Columbia Mutual Tower (renamed Lincoln American Tower). Current president is Harvey G. Smuckler.

BOND DADDY CAPITAL OF THE WORLD

Memphis, to its chagrin, gained the ignominious title of "bond daddy capital" in the early 1970s. "Bond daddies" were those colorful, high living super salesmen of municipal bonds. Their individual and collective flamboyance was often exceeded only by the enormity of their high pressured approach to selling millions of dollars worth of municipal securities for which they received handsome commissions.[12]

The wrath of the Securities and Exchange Commission came down hard on these Memphis-based wheeler-dealers in 1973. Civil suits were brought against three local firms on the grounds of misrepresentation and fraud. Many unsophisticated investors, particularly small town bankers around the Mid-South and wealthy persons seeking tax-free income, were the principal purchasers of these poor quality bonds. Memphis survived the "bond daddies," but it did throw a cloud over the securities business for a period of time.

LOOKING BACK THIRTY-FIVE YEARS

The city's economy expanded in the post-World War II period and it changed somewhat structurally. The city gained a number of new firms large and small to replace those which had faded due to competition or changes in business and industrial technology. Despite the entry of some manufacturing enterprises, no real inroads were made in achieving greater industrial diversification. By and large Memphis still maintained a heavy dependence on the region's agricultural resources. The term "agribusiness" became a key one in the economic lexicon of the business power structure—and rightfully so. The business promoters had recognized that agriculture still held the key to the city's economic wealth, and that it was Memphis' annuity if all attempts to find new nonagriculturally-oriented industries failed. This awakening to the fact that Memphis could probably capitalize even more on the richly endowed agricultural resources of the Lower Mississippi Valley was one of the encouraging events of the decade of the 1970s.

The nonindustrial business sector has expanded modestly and helped add some variety to the economy. The bright spot here has been the number of home grown businesses that were born and nurtured in Memphis. It has helped make the point that if Memphians could continue to develop more new technology businesses locally then the urgency to attract national and international companies here would not be as critical a matter as it has been over the past century.

19

The Contemporary Memphis Economy

Mr. Crump always awaited anxiously the decennial Census of Population figures for Memphis. It was his barometer of how well the city was progressing. He forced annexation on occasion to keep the city one of the leaders among Southern cities. Bigness was equated with greatness.

But in the contemporary period, from the end of World War II to the latter 1970s, business and civic leaders concerned themselves less and less with just the raw population figures as a principal economic indicator. They were more concerned with the productivity of the population, and the potentials to attract industry paying higher wages and salaries and investing heavy amounts of capital locally.

The Memphis metropolitan area ranked 41st in size in 1976 among the nation's metro areas. It had improved its relative position one notch since 1970 when it dropped to 42nd. Thus, it had regained its 1960 ranking.

Maintaining its position was at least psychologically important to Memphians. Buiness leaders knew that this holding pattern did not strengthen to any degree the community's economic base; but many felt it would help them in promoting the city to outside industrial prospects. A slip in the standing had an implication that a city may have been dying as a sound economy. Recruitment would have been that much harder. And locally, a decline may have had negative implications. It is likely that some locally invested capital may have been permanently transferred out of the city.

Memphis in its development promotion drive beginning in the late 1960s stressed that the city was not one of the giant metropolises with all of their attendant problems. Memphis emphasized to industrial prospects that the city was just the right size. Stress was placed on the theme that it was a manageable, medium-sized metropolitan area with control over its destiny; and that the small town atmosphere of friendliness was intact. Promoters in the late 1960s during the Memphis Area Chamber of Commerce's *Greater Memphis Program* frequently used the phrase "better, not bigger."

THE TRANSFORMATION

No one could doubt Memphis' great change physically since 1945. The city had spread out, and much of it was brand new. Even parts of the older, central city had been changed and rejuvenated. A Memphian returning after a long absence had to be impressed with this transformation.

Economically, the city and its metropolitan area had also changed. But this change had not been quite so dramatic or self-fulfilling as measured against broad community expectations. The good signs were that employment had grown paralleling population growth. There were numerous new industrial plants and commercial businesses. Older firms modernized and expanded. A greater percentage of blacks were working in semiskilled occupations, in service industries, and in the professions. Some progress had been made in enlarging the opportunities of women for upward mobility. The results may not have been satisfactory, but some restrictions had been removed in job latitude.

As startling as many of these social and economic changes may have been to traditionalists within the Memphis business community, there still was no substantial progress toward increasing the collective (community and individual or family income) financial strength necessary to be considered a healthy, vibrant metropolitan economy. The Memphis area had not been able to perform as well as many other of the nation's metropolitan areas. The problems faced by Memphis were no secret to the city's leaders. Local business profits and family and individual annual incomes for both white and black citizens reflected some of the problems in the economic structure of Memphis and the Mid-South.

Memphis in the postwar years had not been able to find solutions to a number of vexing questions. Some of these areas of frustration related to the type of natural resources found in the Mid-South region surrounding the city. In most instances there was little the city's industrial promoters could do about any absences of developed resources. Some nagging questions relating to the adequacy of the area's labor pool were being asked in an effort to find solutions. Concern was being expressed about the lack of internally-saved investment capital within Memphis. There were even questions being raised concerning matters of geographic location, despite the fact that location had long been considered one of the city's principal assets. For example, certain consumer products manufacturers have avoided operations in the Memphis region because the surrounding Mid-South region was considered much too thin in population to be economically served.

EMPLOYMENT TRENDS

The number of jobs had tripled since World War II despite some basic economic structural problems and lack of a sustained and carefully conceived industrial promotion program. Many of the job additions over the years were in unskilled categories and in low wage or salary positions. And much of Memphis area employment had been in government and private institutions, or in lower paying categories in service industries and retail and wholesale trade. The greatest gains were in government jobs, including public school teachers; city, county, and state employees; and federal employees.

In this contemporary period manufacturing jobs still represented just a modest portion of total Memphis area employment. The annual growth rate since just after World War II through 1976 had been at the unspectacular rate of 1.5 percent. In contrast, within the private sector, service industries grew at an annual rate of nearly 5 percent. The latter area included various personal, business, and health services occupations. In terms of the increasing economic role being played by service-type industries, Memphis was patterning the national trend. Table 16 lists the major group of private industry jobs, and the changing levels of employment from 1947 to 1976.

Public and nonprofit private institutions continued in the 1960s and 1970s to be the largest single employers in Memphis. The Naval Air Station at Millington in Shelby County was a dominant employer. The City of Memphis and its school system also was a major employer. These government bodies combined accounted for one of every 10 working people. The three major hospital institutions—Baptist, Methodist and St. Joseph—employed over 3 percent of the labor force.

The area's principal private employers, exclusive of hospitals, were Holiday Inns; Sears Roebuck; Plough; Firestone Tire and Rubber; and South Central Bell. Memphis still did not achieve major manufacturing status; but at the end of the 1970s it did have 18 manufacturing firms with more than 600 employees each.

EMPLOYMENT STABILITY

Annual joblessness rates have been modest throughout most of the postwar years. In 1947, it was 5 percent, but throughout the 1950s and 1960s the rate remained under 5 percent. In the period from 1970 through 1974, the annual average was 3.8 percent. It jumped to 7.3 percent in 1975 during this recession period before declining slightly to range between 5.5 and 6.5 percent in 1977 and 1978.

During the height of the 1973–1975 national business recession Memphis remained at least two percentage points below the nation's overall unemployment rate. The city benefitted from the stabilizing influence of jobs provided by the large governmental and private institutional employment base. Layoffs did not occur on any mass basis during any of the recessionary periods following World War II.

Some of Memphis' private sectors were hard hit during the 1973–75 recession, and layoffs were high for a period. But overall, Memphis area unemployment was less severe than in the nation's more industrial metropolitan areas. Still, Memphis found out during this period that it was not immune from

TABLE 16

NUMBER OF JOBS IN MAJOR PRIVATE INDUSTRIAL GROUPS
IN SHELBY COUNTY

Industry Group[1]	1947	1959	1965	1970	1976	Average Annual Percentage Growth Rate 1947–1976
Agricultural Services, Forestry, Fisheries	129	271	395	544	597	5.4%
Mining	660	280	286	400	178	−11.7
Contract Construction	7,272	10,494	13,404	13,244	15,261	2.6
Manufacturing	36,949	41,840	48,176	60,526	56,484	1.5
Transportation and Other Public Utilities	8,094	10,540	12,253	15,386	16,843	2.6
Wholesale Trade	15,083	19,404	21,694	26,218	29,529	2.4
Retail Trade	25,769	30,702	34,420	42,841	54,907	2.6
Finance, Insurance and Real Estate	5,703	8,987	12,951	14,661	17,392	3.9
Services	15,118	24,429	32,386	46,739	60,850	4.9
Total	115,312	147,452	176,447	221,767	253,059	2.7

SOURCE: U.S. Department of Commerce. *County Business Patterns* (various years).
1. Excludes government employees; railroad employees, and self-employed persons. Employment data are for the mid-March pay period each year.

national recessions. The 1973–75 period was a sobering one for many businesses and individuals in Memphis. It was a period of very limited economic growth.

The heavy reliance of the Memphis economy on service industries—both government and private—results in a wage and salary structure which is more modest than those prevailing in the more industrially diversified metropolitan areas.

INDUSTRIAL SUPPORT SYSTEMS

Memphis boosters had long stressed to industrial prospects the availability of quality industrial sites, storage facilities, transportation facilities, and utilities. Most of the major firms that located in the Memphis area since 1945 cited one or more of these components as an important reason why they selected Memphis.

The city and its private developers had been extremely progressive in keeping the inventory of industrial sites ahead of the continuous demand beginning in the early 1950s and through the 1970s. The development of Presidents Island in the immediate postwar years created some 960 acres uniquely attractive to heavy and medium types of industry. At the end of the 1970s only a few acres had not been occupied. The Memphis and Shelby County Port Commission continued to plan for additional port-oriented industrial districts, including a 4,000-acre site called the Frank C. Pidgeon Industrial Park. Forward planning by port officials was not neglected. The city's major industrial development firms were equally aggressive. The Belz interests undertook the construction of the land and water improvements in its 425-acre Rivergate Industrial Port bordering McKellar Lake opposite Presidents Island.

The Airport Authority developed its 500-acre International Park on Airport-owned land adjacent to the Memphis International Airport facility. Veteran developers, Russell S. Wilkinson and Robert G. Snowden, beginning in 1960, started the Airport Industrial Park in southeast Memphis. The developers and their investment partners continued planning expansions of the Park area on the basis of their success in selling sites to a variety of concerns needing manufacturing plants or warehouses.

The Boyle Investment Company, Bell & Norfleet, the Southwide Development Company, Holiday Inns, and the major railroads all helped develop an increasing supply of industrial sites. Few, if any, industrial prospects turned down a location in Memphis because of any shortage of quality sites. Memphis had not been laggard here.

Geographic location had long been one of Memphis' key advantages in its appeals to industrial prospects. The Mississippi River at the city's doorstep was a major outlet for Memphis until the 1880s. Then railroads began to dominate local and regional freight and passenger traffic. The river languished for several decades before making a slow but steady comeback in the 1920s and 1930s.

World War II helped step up river commerce, and bring it to the attention of industry and agricultural interests once again.

Air passenger service increased dramatically in the 1960s and 1970s. Airport planners correctly anticipated this expansion when they greatly enlarged the physical facilities at the Memphis International Airport. In the 1970s Memphis was sought out by several major commercial airlines as a hub for their traffic systems. Federal Express, based at the Airport, also found Memphis an acceptable center for its air freight operations.

Memphis had grown rapidly in the 1930s as a motor freight terminal. After World War II, it continued to expand as a base of the motor freight industry in the South.

Rail service maintained its historic position in the freight business. Of course, passenger service died in Memphis as it did nationwide in the 1950s and early 1960s. Amtrak provided limited service between Chicago and New Orleans through Memphis.

The rising stars were the Mississippi River and air service. The river was rediscovered as a great economic asset to the community. Back in the late 1930s a *Memphis Press-Scimitar* editorial contained these observations:

> We must never forget that our biggest commercial asset is the Mississippi River. It brings more merchandise to us. It brings us new factories, new business and new citizens. It insures and enriches our growth.[1]

The full significance of these observations seemed to be appreciated by Memphis business leaders 40 years later. Industrial promoters brought to the attention of prospects the economic benefits of river transportation.

Tonnage figures for agricultural and industrial commodities through the Port of Memphis increased significantly in the postwar years as shown as follows:

Year	Tonnage
1950	2,938,258
1960	6,336,252
1970	10,017,785
1977	11,890,000

During this contemporary period Memphis and St. Louis engaged in a tough competitive race to become the leading inland waterways port. Leadership was determined by the volume of annual tonnage handled in each of these ports. In 1972 St. Louis changed the geographic boundaries of its port jurisdiction, and took the lead in the competition for tonnage handled. By including tonnage handled in a broad area of 70 miles on both the Missouri and Illinois sides of the Mississippi, St. Louis increased its tonnage from 11.2 million in 1971 to 22.0 million in 1972. Memphis port officials cried foul. They felt this was an unfair tactic if St. Louis' only purpose was to pull far ahead of Memphis in annual tonnage reported. Memphis felt it had substantially better and more functional port facilities and that these facilities were located in a compact area within the city limits. In the late 1970s planning was underway by the city of West Memphis, Arkansas, to develop additional metropolitan area port facilities across the river from the city.

Despite great optimism about the future use of the Mississippi as an avenue of commerce, there were some uncertainties. Periodic low water disrupted commerce. Occasionally tows and barges went aground hitting snags during low water. During the 1970s there was also growing concern that Congress would enact a tax on river fuel which could affect future traffic. A user tax on water-borne transportation was being supported by rail and motor trucking interests who had long complained about the unfair competition from a rival mode of transportation which paid no taxes.

Cheap power was another incentive extended to prospects by Memphis economic developers. The city-owned utility, the Memphis Light, Gas and Water Division, bought TVA electrical power for resale to its customers. Rates charged were typically lower than rates in most non-TVA served metropolitan areas. Rates were also moderate for natural gas which MLGW purchased from Texas Gas Transmission Corporation for resale to Memphis and Shelby County-based industrial, commercial, and residential customers. Memphis had one of the lowest rates for natural gas of any major city.

Great concern was being expressed in Memphis at the close of the 1970s over the issue of future gas rates. The Texas-based private supplier, responding to new authority granted by Congress under the Natural Gas Policy Act of 1978, announced a substantial increase in rates. Questions were being asked whether the rising costs of energy would impede Memphis' industrial growth just at the time of the community-wide consensus that the city needed much more industry and quickly. One-half of the natural gas sold by the MLGW was going to existing local industries. While only one-fourth of the electrical power sold went to industries. Much depended on whether other competitive cities would face a similar crisis on energy rates.

BLACK BUSINESS

After checking off the names of Robert R. Church, Sr., A. Maceo Walker, and a few other Memphis blacks past and present, one is hard pressed to come up with additional names of blacks who have built large, successful enterprises. Many blacks have successfully operated small firms or establishments within Memphis' black community, but few made much impression in the white community even in contemporary decades of greater economic mobility for blacks.

Memphis leaders were proud to point to the successes of the Universal Life Insurance Company and the Tri-State Bank of Memphis as businesses created and built by blacks. But these two financial entities were largely the creations of black entrepreneur A. Maceo Walker aided by a handful of able black executives holding high positions in these two organizations. Since Reconstruction days the Memphis black community has always had numerous small retail and service-type businesses catering exclusively to the black trade. Typically they were businesses characterized as easy entry; that is, limited capital and limited experience were required to start up operations.

In the contemporary period black entrepreneurship was still at a minimal level. There were very few black-owned businesses with any degree of capitalization or of any size measured by annual sales volume and jobs provided. Even after blacks had achieved victories in the civil rights movement in the late 1950s and early 1960s, not much change occurred. The encouragement given blacks by the Memphis Area Chamber of Commerce in the aftermath of the King assassination was not sustained and results were largely unnoticed a decade later.

Some 1,400 black-owned businesses were listed in a 1971 publication, *Black Business Directory of Memphis*. The breakdown of these enterprises is interesting. Some 53 percent were personal and business services type operations. Another 40 percent were small wholesale and retail businesses. Table 17 lists the principal types of businesses.

TABLE 17
SELECTED BLACK BUSINESSES IN MEMPHIS
1971

Type	Number	Type	Number
Beauty shops	273	Night clubs	45
Barbers	184	Contractors	38
Restaurants	149	Cleaners	31
Sundries	93	Fast food-to-go	27
Service stations	78	Auto repairs	23
Grocers	77	Shoe repairs	23

SOURCE: Memphis Area Chamber of Commerce, *Black Business Directory of Memphis*, January 1971.

An examination of this list reveals that these types of businesses were largely the same in the 1970s as those operated by blacks since early in the 20th century. The majority were very small neighborhood oriented businesses. And many were in the city's black ghetto areas. In this 1971 list there were only 17 physicians, 12 attorneys, 3 accountants, and 2 architects among a black population estimated then at about 250,000. In business volume, the contribution of black-owned businesses to total community sales has been miniscule.

There were a few noteworthy successes. Perhaps the greatest postwar strides among Memphis black-owned businesses were accomplished by the Tri-State Bank. In 1978, some 32 years after it opened its doors for business, assets had reached $28.3 million. Deposits were $25.7 million. Its impressive headquarters building at Main and Beale was completed and occupied in 1975, and there were two branches as well. In charge of bank operations was the well-known civil rights leader in Memphis during the 1950s and 1960s Jesse H. Turner, Sr., executive vice president. Turner was also a member of the Shelby County Quarterly Court and its successor, the Board of Commissioners.

The *Tri-State Defender,* founded in 1951, with John H. Sengstake as publisher, had a circulation of about 8,300 copies. Another black-owned newspaper the *Mid-South Express,* started publishing in 1975. The well-known black businessman and civic leader, Art Gilliam, was owner and general manager of radio station WLOK.

One of the few attempts to establish a black-owned and operated manufacturing operation ended in disaster. The Federal Office of Economic Opportunity gave a $1 million grant to the Chamber of Commerce-sponsored "Greater Memphis Urban Development Corporation" in 1971 to help fund black-owned businesses. The first grant—some $164,000—went to a firm called the Memphis Tubing Company, organized to manufacture automobile tailpipes. When the firm lost its contract with the Chrysler Corporation in 1975, it went bankrupt.

The black-owned Metro Shopping Plaza, which opened in 1969 at E. H. Crump and Danny Thomas Boulevard, struggled to show a profit. Black patronage fell far short of expectations and vacancy rates were higher than anticipated, hurting profitability.

Stax Records, Incorporated, a soul and rhythm and blues recording firm, was organized in 1959 by Jim Stewart, a white. Al Bell, a black, who had been executive vice president became sole owner in 1972. At the time of its bankruptcy in 1976 the recording company had 150 employees. The firm was besieged with legal and financial problems when ordered closed by federal bankruptcy court. Union Planters Bank was a $10 million creditor to Stax at the time of collapse.

THE LABOR MOVEMENT

In the closing years of the 1930s the organized labor movement was gaining momentum. At the start of World War II, Memphis had some 25,000 union members. Nearly 40 years later in early 1979 union membership exceeded 60,000.

Organized labor publicly demonstrated its intentions of gaining greater acceptance in Memphis when the AFL, CIO and the Brotherhood of Railway Trainmen marched some 18,000 strong in the 1947 Labor Day parade. One labor leader told a cheering crowd of union members:

> The time has come in Shelby County when people have to make up their minds to be on one side or the other. We must chase out that particular brand of politician who thinks he can continue through life carrying water on both shoulders. One thing I know, and that is a man either is with union people or against them . . . there is no middle road.[2]

Union gains were often hard won victories in Memphis. The early postwar years were successful organizing years in the larger industrial firms; but progress was slow in the white collar job areas. The conservative white community was apprehensive of the union movement and resisted when possible. Labor leaders after V-J Day felt somewhat more secure in Memphis as it began its postwar drive for new members. The CIO, in particular, made strides. It claimed 30,000 members in a city not known to be pro-union.

The CIO Council, composed of various CIO local unions, took a strong anticommunist stand. It kicked out Local 19 of the Food, Tobacco and Agricultural Workers Union charging it with harboring communist sympathies. Soon after the Council's action, this suspect union adopted the new name, Distributive, Processing and Office Workers Union of America, Local 19, and became a prime target of Senator James Eastland's Senate Internal Security Committee.[3] This Senate group in 1951 was investigating subversive activities throughout the United States and came to Memphis specifically to question the union's leadership. This strong stand against Communism by the CIO must have pleased Mr. Crump. He had thrown up every possible barrier in the way of the CIO organizers in the immediate prewar years, calling them Communist agitators.

Organized labor resumed its drive for members in 1946. The first target was an effort to organize retail clerks, butchers, and bakers employed in retail grocery stores. *The Commercial Appeal* of 11 June 1946 carried the headlines: "Unions Open 'Strongarm' Drive to Organize Groceries Here" and "Deliveries of Meat and Bread Cut Off and Pickets Placed in Front of Stores After Demand of Contract is Turned Down." Four AFL unions bonded together in this action.

Walter Reuther, president of the United Auto Workers, came to Memphis in 1947 to help organize the International Harvester Plant. The union won recognition in April 1948 after an overwhelming vote for UAW representation. Memphis employees were receiving less per hour than workers in International Harvester plants located elsewhere. So in 1950 the UAW went on strike for 4 months seeking coverage under the national contract of the UAW and International Harvester. The UAW struck again twice in the 1950s and again in the 1970s. These were UAW strikes against all of International Harvester's operations.

Beginning in January 1950 violence erupted to upset the delicate balance in labor relations which existed between conservative Memphis industrial managements and aggressive labor organizers. Some 324 workers at the American Snuff Company walked out on January 13th. These striking employees were members of the United Steelworkers (CIO). The majority were women, and the principal issue was wages. The steelworkers wanted a minimum of 90 cents an hour. American Snuff's minimum at that time was 79 cents. The strike dragged on for 185 days, finally ending on 16 July 1950. During the long ordeal, many incidences of violence, including bombings, broke out. At various times attempts to settle the strike were made by the Chamber of Commerce, Mayor Watkins Overton and City Commissioner Joe Boyle, as well as the Federal Mediation and Conciliation Service.[4] Finally, on 16 July the Steelworkers removed their pickets from in front of the plant at Front and Keel streets and the strike was over. The workers got a 5-cent-an-hour increase, and the checkoff of union dues.

The 1947 Tennessee Legislature outlawed the right of organized labor to require the implementation of the closed shop in industries where it had gained bargaining rights. Under the new Tennessee law workers in these industries had the choice of belonging to the union or not. In adopting right-to-work laws Tennessee joined 18 other states, mostly located in the conservative South and Southwest areas.

Nationally the AFL and the CIO merged in 1955 and adopted the combined name, AFL-CIO. The Memphis AFL-CIO Labor Council was granted a charter in 1957. This was the same year that the Teamsters were expelled by the AFL-CIO. The United Auto Workers were affiliated with the AFL-CIO until 1968.

In Memphis the AFL-CIO Labor Council became the umbrella organization for 115 local union organizations. Collectively the Council represented some 45,000 union members. The largest single unit was the 10,000-member Memphis Building and Construction Trades Council.

The Teamsters, independent of the AFL-CIO, had three locals in Memphis. The combined membership was about 11,000. The largest of the Teamster's unions, Local 667, represented employees of major truck lines. Most of the city's beer truck drivers, and production and maintenance workers at the Schlitz plant were members of Local 1196.

The UAW had 4,000 members among the employees of International Harvester, Caterpillar Tractor and Ford Motor Company's Tractor and Implement Operations.

A dramatic change in the direction of the labor union movement began in 1964. That year the American Federation of State, County and Municipal Employees chartered Local 1733 in Memphis. Public employees were late arrivals in the history of organized labor in the United States. In the 1950s, there were only a few, scattered unions. But in the 1960s there was increasing momentum. In what has been referred to as "the quiet revolution" the unionization of public employees throughout the United States accelerated at a rapid pace in the 1970s. Organized labor's greatest recruiting ground was in the ranks of public employees.

In Memphis among public employees, sanitation workers were the first to organize. Two years later the Memphis Education Association was recognized by the Memphis Board of Education as the bargaining agent for members. In 1969 Local 2032 of the American Federation of Teachers (AFL-CIO) was organized, but the Board of Education refused to recognize this second organization of public school employees. This latter union's membership was only a fraction of the MEA's.

In 1971 some 700 Memphis firemen joined the International Association of Fire Fighters (AFL-CIO) Local 1784. This union grew rapidly, and at the time of its eventful strike in early July 1978 membership had doubled. The next group to organize were the police. The Memphis Police Association emerged in 1973 as an unaffiliated union. At the time of the police walkout in August 1978 the MPA had 1,200 members.

In the city's long and colorful history it had faced many adversities. But ranking high among the most calamitous of all of these tragic events was the sanitation workers strike in 1968. The focus of the nation often was on Memphis during the early months of that year as the sanitation workers' strike received direct attention from leaders of the civil rights movement. World attention turned to Memphis in the immediate aftermath of the assassination of Martin Luther King, Jr. The publicity Memphis received was bad. The most lasting ill effects, directly and indirectly, were psychological ones. The Memphis economy as well as social relationships between whites and blacks were damaged. Although there was no way to quantify the harm done, most seemed to agree that the city had been seriously hurt.

The strike began on 12 February 1968. Some 1,300 workers, members of the AFSCME Local 1733, struck. Most of the workers were blacks. Mayor Henry Loeb, then in the second month of his second term as mayor, declared the strike illegal. He issued the ultimatum "Return to work or be fired." Loeb went on to say: "This new administration is not going to be pushed around right off the bat in office. If it does it's in for a mighty tough four years."[5] Loeb refused to yield. The strike dragged on for nine weeks amid great confusion and bitterness in the city.

Shortly after the strike ended, national labor leader Walter Reuther, who had been in Memphis during the course of the strike, was highly critical of Loeb's hard line stand and accused the Mayor of having an eighteenth-century attitude on hourly wages.[6] About one-half of the sanitation workers received $1.70 per hour; and the other half, $1.80 per hour at the start of the strike. The federal minimum wage at that time was $1.60 per hour. The pay scale in Memphis was higher than the rate in effect in Nashville, Birmingham, New Orleans or Little Rock, but lower than that in effect in St. Louis or Dallas. Atlanta's rate was $1.80 per hour.

Martin Luther King, Jr., made his first visit to Memphis on 18 March 1968. He returned again on 28 March, and for the third visit on 3 April 1968. The next day, 4 April, King was assassinated in Memphis. King, in supporting the sanitation workers' demand for union recognition, called the protest "a strike for the dignity of labor."

Some 12 days later, on 16 April, the strike was settled. The AFSCME was

Fig. 50. Henry Loeb, Mayor of Memphis 1960–1963 and 1968–1972. (Courtesy of City of Memphis Archives)

given recognition by the city. Sanitation workers received a 10-cent-an-hour raise starting 1 May 1968, and were promised another 5-cent raise four months later.

The next target of the AFSCME was St. Joseph Hospital. The union started picketing the hospital on 5 October 1969, claiming it represented 1,000 employees. St. Joseph officials, including Sister M. Rita, the hospital's administrator, refused to recognize the AFSCME as the bargaining agent. After 12 weeks, the strike was called off by the union. Most Rev. Joseph A. Durick, Bishop of Nashville and spiritual head of the Tennessee Catholic population,

Fig. 51. Scene at Main and Beale during the 1968 sanitation workers strike depicts the intense drama of that event. (Courtesy of AFSCME)

asked the strikers to accept a moratorium. The hospital hired back all but those it considered to be the most militant.

Jesse Epps, AFSCME leader during the 1960s, was ousted in 1970 as executive director, charged with misappropriating union funds. Union leadership was assumed during the 1970s by Rev. James E. Smith, one-time Tennessee field secretary for the Congress of Racial Equality. Membership continued to grow rapidly as more city and school employees joined this union.

The 7-day strike in January 1975 by 2,400 members of the International Brotherhood of Electrical Workers (AFL-CIO) Local 1288 employed by the city-owned Memphis Light, Gas and Water Division was another labor dispute in the public sector.

In a contract dispute with the City of Memphis, the Memphis Fire Fighters Local 1784 went on strike on 1 July 1978; 90 percent of the rank and file union members walked out. Thus began another series of calamitous events that had so long plagued Memphis. The strike lasted three days and it was the prelude to a summer and early fall of civic turmoil as the firemen were followed in striking by the police and public school teachers.

The Memphis Police Association, with almost unanimous support from its members, went on strike on 10 August and stayed out until 18 August. The Fire Fighters Union returned to the picket lines between 14 August and 18 August. The Memphis Education Association went on strike on 10 October and stayed out for 12 days. But whereas 90 percent of the members of the police and fire

Fig. 52. One of the mass marches held by the Memphis sanitation workers during the 1968 strike for union recognition and higher wages. (Courtesy of AFSCME)

fighters unions struck, only about 60 percent of the MEA members supported the teachers' strike.

The principal strike issues with the police and firemen involved salaries. Both unions wanted more than the city was offering. The police also wanted a 1-year contract. The city's offer was a 2-year agreement with both the police and firemen. At the settlement both unions accepted the city's original offers on the basis of a guarantee by the city that a three-member advisory board would be created to study future differences and to help resolve them. The teachers sought both salary increases and improvements in working conditions. In the settlement of this particular strike, the teachers won some nonfinancial, professional benefits.

The tradition that public employees should not be permitted to strike, particularly those responsible for the protection of the community's health and safety, collapsed in the United States in the 1970s. Memphis was not the only city where this tradition had been broken. Yet in few other cities were there the dramatic confrontations between union leadership and the city and the school board; dusk to dawn curfews; mass physical destruction by incendiaries; incarceration of certain local union officials for contempt of court orders; or a city patrolled by imported Tennessee National Guardsmen that took place in Memphis in 1978.

When the dust of the 1978 strikes had settled, there was concern that the unfavorable publicity Memphis had received in the national media as a result of both the police and fire fighters' strikes would discourage new industry from moving into Memphis.[7] When Sharp Electronics Corporation announced its decision in late 1978 to locate a plant in Memphis, business and political leaders gave a huge sigh of relief.

Mayor Wyeth Chandler and the majority of the City Council, obviously upset by the strikes, fought back. They succeeded in placing on the ballot at the November 1978 general election a proposition to amend the City Charter. To deter future strikes the proposed change would penalize strikers by stripping them of their seniority and other benefits. And if these striking workers were hired back, they would start all over again at the bottom. Memphians voted 78,381 for the amendment and 44,333 against it. The majority of citizens apparently were distressed too by what Mayor Chandler referred to as "these black days of August."

Work stoppages in recent years, as shown in Table 18, indicate that the years of the greatest losses of working days were 1970, 1974 and 1976. Strikes in the construction trades unions caused the abnormal losses in 1970 and 1974. In 1976, the bulk of the lost days were attributed to the Memphis Firestone Plant. Nationwide, the United Rubber Workers of America conducted a 131-day strike that year against the "Big Four Tiremakers," including Firestone.

TABLE 18
WORK STOPPAGES IN THE MEMPHIS AREA

Year	Number of Stoppages	Workers Involved	Man Days Idle During the Year
1969	38	10,000	176,400
1970	25	12,600	435,400
1971	26	7,900	80,600
1972	25	18,700	169,100
1973	27	14,400	144,000
1974	35	13,500	345,100
1975	22	4,300	60,800
1976	27	17,900	473,900

SOURCE: U.S. Department of Labor, Bureau of Labor Statistics, *Analysis of Work Stoppages*, various years.

Memphis' record of work stoppages compared favorably with those in Atlanta, Birmingham, Nashville and New Orleans during the recent period, 1969–1976. Far fewer stoppages occurred in Memphis than in Houston and Louisville. Overall, labor-management relations in Memphis were considered reasonably harmonious.

Almost one of every five nonfarm workers belonged to a labor union in the Memphis area in the latter 1970s. The Tennessee statewide ratio was approximately the same. Union officials in Memphis were estimating that their potential membership was some 80,000 to 90,000 in Shelby County, or some 20,000 to 30,000 above 1979 union membership levels.

Labor unions appeared to have reached a level of community-wide acceptance by the 1970s. Memphis in earlier decades was not entirely hospitable to unions because the conservative background of the city's leadership, businessmen, and many ordinary working people was a strong barrier to labor organizers. But as more and more workers sought means to adjust to inflation, they became convinced that union membership might help them keep their wage scales up.

During the 1970s more and more blacks joined unions in Memphis. And many white collar workers appeared to be considering union membership. The trend was toward an increase in the percentage of union members in the total labor force.

CHANGES IN FAMILY AND PER CAPITA INCOME

The true measure of the general economic health of Memphis is the change in the level of family income and per capita income over a reasonable period of time. The postwar period was one of improved income levels if considered generally.

Some individuals and families, particularly whites, made some gains. While blacks were somewhat better off financially than in the Depression years, a large percentage were still below the proverty level in the 1970s. In a comparison of the Memphis metropolitan area with selected competitive cities over a 16-year period, 1959 to 1975, income measured on a per capita basis in Memphis remained below these other cities, as shown in Table 19.

Memphis' median family income, reported in the 1970 U.S. Census, was $8646. This meant that one-half of all families had incomes above this midpoint figure, and one-half below this figure. This $8646 figure for Memphis was 15 percent below the nationwide figure of $10,196.

Comparing Memphis with selected other cities, reveals that it had a higher median family income than Louisville ($8359), Nashville ($7433), New Orleans ($7033), or Birmingham ($6939). Only Atlanta ($8769) and Houston ($8686) were higher. Although Memphis' income structure continued to stay below the nationwide level in the postwar years, the city was not on the bottom rung among Southern cities.

The black population in particular remained largely confined to the marginal income and poverty categories. The median income figure for blacks was approximately one-half of the median figure for whites.

PROGRESS OVER THREE DECADES

Memphis has not experienced great changes in its economic structure since V-J Day. The major industrial components of the 1940s were still intact 30 years

TABLE 19

TRENDS IN PER CAPITA INCOME IN MEMPHIS AND
SELECTED OTHER METROPOLITAN AREAS

CITY (SMSA)	Per Capita Income			Ranking Among 261 U.S. SMSA's	
	1959	1969	1975	1959	1975
Houston	$2395	$3755	$6795	57	21
Atlanta	2205	3857	6117	105	71
Louisville	2168	3741	5895	114	103
New Orleans	2110	3504	5703	129	124
Birmingham	1856	3270	5636	187	133
Nashville	1851	3412	5638	189	131
MEMPHIS	1802	3206	5456	200	163
Total United States	$2167	$3733	$5903		

SOURCE: U.S. Department of Commerce, "County and Metropolitan Area Personal Income," *Survey of Current Business,* April 1977, pp. 28–30.

later with few exceptions. The same types of industries were operating there, although some had grown larger and some had shifted product lines.

More entrepreneurs surfaced to stimulate Memphis-based corporate activities. Unions had made greater inroads among private industry workers. And they added the public sector to their recruitment targets.

The community's black citizens remained largely an undeveloped economic resource. The general lack of broad scale labor skills was a depressant on their wage and salary levels.

The transportation facilities—long considered a principal community asset—were enlarged and improved. The city recognized the promotional importance of these assets and put additional financial resources behind their development.

Memphis wanted economic development badly in order to move forward. It worked for three decades trying to find the key.

20

Still Building and Searching

Beginning about 1950 Memphis began a political and social transition which changed in different ways the lives of all of its citizens. A complex and often bewildering social revolution was just in its embryonic stages. Soon powerful legal and moral forces, backed by federal law and authority, compounded the concerns of civic decision-makers then wrestling with matters of attracting new business to Memphis and managing postwar physical land use.

Municipal public administration, molded and guided by Mr. Crump since 1910, appeared incapable of managing problems of growth. An antiquated municipal form of government—a carryover from quieter days of Memphis life—struggled to stay abreast of change. The issue of what legal form of municipal government should guide the city became another major public battleground in these years of rapid change.

For the past thirty years, Memphis—a city which loved its traditions and which had perpetuated them from one generation to another in the white community—has struggled trying to reach an accommodation with the complex new conditions of American urban society.

POLITICAL CHANGES

The early years of the 1950s were still dominated politically by Crump's Shelby County organization. Handpicked candidates of the machine won easily in the municipal elections. The Crump forces seldom were embarrassed by the vote cast.

The defeat of Senator McKellar by Albert Gore in the 1952 Democratic primary was considered a blow to the Crump organization. McKellar had already served 36 years in the United States Senate, and was seeking his seventh term. Yet McKellar was then 83 years old; and Gore, his opponent, was only 44. McKellar's age was a handicap in the race with the popular and liberal Gore.

One significant change politically in Tennessee was the elimination of the poll tax requirement for voting. The State Constitution was changed in 1953, making it easier for blacks to vote from that point forward.

Watkins Overton, who had been mayor earlier from 1928 to 1940, went back into office again in early 1949 at the request of the Crump organization. Early in 1953 Overton resigned in a dispute with other members of the City Commission. Longtime Crump aide and city official, Frank T. Tobey, became mayor and served until his death in September 1955.

Tobey was a popular mayor. Perhaps his greatest single accomplishment was convincing President Eisenhower at a White House meeting in July 1955 to cancel the controversial Dixon-Yates contract which had become a huge political football nationally. Dixon-Yates, a private combine of power interests, had a contract to build a steam electric generating plant, privately-owned and operated, in West Memphis, Arkansas. This utility had planned to sell power to the United States Government feeding into the TVA system. In turn, Memphis would receive its power through TVA. Memphis had plans to build its own generating plant. It felt that it was not in the city's best interests to be buying its power from the Dixon-Yates plant. Tobey gave President Eisenhower assurances that Memphis would build its own plant and the city kept its word. In 1959 the $120 million Thomas H. Allen Electric Generating Station was completed.

The 1955 mayoral election brought forth a new political face, Edmund Orgill. His opponent was the political veteran, Watkins Overton. The election was heralded as the citizens' first free choice of mayor in over three decades. Interestingly, both Orgill and Overton were descendants of pioneer Memphis families.

Orgill, a popular businessman and civic leader, won handily, 52,177 to 33,061. What was interesting was that Orgill was supporting the city manager-council form of government for Memphis, while Overton supported retention of the commission form. The latter form was also the recommendation of remnants of the Crump organization leadership who were trying to hold on after their leader's death in October 1954.

Orgill served only one term. He decided not to run in the 1959 election because of illness. Henry Loeb III entered that race, and was elected by an overwhelming majority over his two opponents. Loeb, a prominent businessman, had just finished serving four years as a city commissioner, in charge of the Public Works Department. And prior to that public service, he had been a member of the Memphis Park Commission. Loeb resigned in October 1963, before his term ran out to take over the family business.

Still, despite growing support within the civic and business community for the elimination of the five-member city commission form of government, no change had been made. The mayor's position carried no more authority than the other four elected commissioners. Memphis had a weak-mayor form of government. But those mayors with strong personalities did command the public's attention. Loeb was one of these types of individuals.

The next elected mayor, William B. Ingram, Jr., took office in 1964. He defeated his closest challenger, Democratic Party leader, William Farris, by just over 7,800 votes. Ingram, who had been a controversial municipal judge received strong voter support from labor unions and the black community.

During Ingram's term, the group called Program of Progress (POP) supporting the strong mayor-city council form of government succeeded in getting this issue on the ballot in November 1966. The new form was actively supported by well-known civic leaders. Henry Loeb in a paid political ad stated he was concerned about the rising cost of municipal government since 1950. He argued that Houston, St. Louis, and New Orleans had outstripped Memphis in attracting new industry, and that they had done so without burdening their taxpayers. The politically conservative Loeb called the 56-year-old Memphis City Commission "a five-headed, headless monster."[1] Loeb's personal endorsement of the mayor-city council form of government carried great weight in the white community.

The vote on this city charter amendment was 57,895 for the change, and 39,554 against. The controversial Mayor Ingram made a last minute attempt to defeat the charter amendment. Ingram did not think a city council of 13 members represented progress. In an open letter in the 17 October 1966 issue of the *Memphis Press-Scimitar* Ingram made this strong denunciation of the proposed change:

> I am in favor of progress and the right kind of changes when necessary. However, I do not believe in change for the sake of change. In my humble judgment POP government does not represent progress by going back to ward-heeling type of politics with the POP-type of government which bankrupted the city in 1883.

Ingram fought a losing battle on this issue. One year later he was defeated in his bid for the new "strong" mayor's office by Henry Loeb, 78,470 to 66,628. Loeb was back in office for the second time.

The election held in 1967 was one of the most important city elections in the 148-year history of Memphis. A mayor with executive powers was elected, and 13 councilmen were elected to four-year terms. The latter assumed legislative powers. Six councilmen were elected at-large and seven elected from districts. This first Mayor-Council group assumed office on 1 January 1968. Mayor Loeb in his speech that day after the swearing in ceremonies stated to the gathering:

> There is a new spirit in the community, a new sense of awareness and a

new sense of purpose . . . I am indeed grateful for the opportunity to serve and hopefully, to be part of directing Memphis toward a proper and rewarding place in the scheme of life as the leading city in the Mid-South. I am grateful for the opportunity to make Memphis once again a place of good and humble abode—to help make Memphis once more a city of which we can be proud.[2]

Thus came to an end the era of commission government. Memphis was the last major city to discard this system of rule which was born in the American municipal reform era at the beginning of the twentieth century. For most of the Crump period of control in Memphis, his organization worked through the vehicle of the commission to run the city his way.

In 1974 by referendum the citizens of Shelby County approved the Re-structure Act of 1974. The old 3-member County Commission was abolished and in its place was substituted the office of County Mayor, with full executive and administrative powers. The traditional name for the County's legislative body, the Shelby County Quarterly Court, was dropped in 1978. Henceforth, this 11-member body was to be known as the Shelby County Board of Commissioners. Former County Sheriff Roy Nixon became the County's first mayor in 1976. He served one term and was succeeded in 1978 by another former County Sheriff, William Morris.

Consolidation of the city and county governments came into the discussion stages more frequently in the 1970s than ever before. Many political leaders were professing the merits of consolidation. Efficiency of services and cost savings were singled out as reasons why consolidation should be expedited. Many services had been combined already, including the assessment functions, libraries, hospitals, health departments, ports and harbors and many others.

A postwar accomplishment had certainly been the improvements in municipal public administration. The prospects for further changes in the future were bright. Despite some agonizing delays in the 1950s and 1960s even the strongest advocates of local governmental reform had to admit that Memphis had come a long way in modernizing local government.

INTEGRATION AND THE RISING VOICE OF THE BLACK COMMUNITY

During much of the Crump era the blacks residing in Memphis were treated paternalistically. Political leaders gave some consideration to physical and social conditions in the black community, but these were of a caretaker variety and based largely on the reward system.

Following World War II blacks in Memphis started their drive for greater recognition very slowly. Dr. J. E. Walker, the black founder and head of the Universal Life Insurance Company, offered himself as a candidate for the Memphis Board of Education in the 1951 municipal elections. Walker turned out to be the only candidate—black or white—to oppose the slate of candidates offered by the Crump machine.

Walker, the first black candidate for public office in half a century in Memphis, campaigned hard in the black neighborhoods. He pulled a vote of 7,483. The four white candidates for the Board of Education seats all received more than 21,000 votes each. Philosophically, Walker commented after the election, "had we not offered as a candidate, one vote would have elected the entire machine ticket."[3]

Less than 20,000 blacks were registered to vote in 1951. Intensive voter registration drives in the early 1950s increased the registration figure to about 46,000 in 1956. One of every four voters was a black by 1956. Many blacks were beginning to develop a political awareness.

The U.S. Supreme Court in the momentous 1954 decision in *Brown v. the Board of Education of Topeka* declared that the separate-but-equal doctrine had no place in the field of public education. Shock waves flowed throughout the nation. In the South white political leaders and many white citizens were bewildered and resentful. They feared that traditional community alignments and customs were going to change, and that amicable relations between the races would give way to suspicion and hatred. A form of pandemonium broke loose. Business leaders who had been guiding economic development in the South worried that race conflict would impede progress.

Some 96 members of Congress from the South, including Congressman Clifford H. Davis who represented the Memphis area, signed a statement called the Dixie Manifesto in March 1956 denouncing the Supreme Court's decision. Southerners in general wanted the Court's decision reversed and as quickly as possible.

In Memphis there was apprehension, but there was a prevailing attitude that sooner or later the integration of the schools was inevitable. There was a hope that it could be delayed as long as possible. A group of conservative civic leaders, including remnants of the Crump political organization, formed an organization called Citizens for Progress in 1956. In addition to being against racial integration, they were strongly in support of the retention of the commission form of government. The organization's slogan was: "Keep Memphis Down in Dixie." The group resisted change.

The Memphis chapter of the NAACP led the fight for racial equality. As early as the mid-1950s the young Reverend Benjamin L. Hooks, an NAACP activist, urged his fellow blacks to "rock more boats and create more storms in the fight for equal citizenship."[4] In 1955 civil rights attorney H. T. Lockard petitioned to open the city's parks, golf courses, and swimming pools. The NAACP filed a suit against the Memphis Street Railway Company in 1956 to desegregate the buses. Another NAACP leader, Jesse H. Turner, in 1957 appealed to the Memphis Public Library Board to permit blacks to use the Main Library at Peabody and McLean.

The first major successes enjoyed by the blacks were in 1960. That was the year of the black college student sit-ins at downtown lunch counters and at the Brooks Art Gallery, the Cossitt Library, and other public places. During the year Memphis buses and all of the facilities of the Memphis Public Library were desegregated. This was the start of the collapse of all barriers to blacks in public facilities during the following four years. Movie theaters, restaurants and other businesses desegregated quietly at the same time.

Memphis started desegregating its public schools in October 1961. That first year 13 black students were admitted. The following year the black enrollment in previously all-white schools was 53. The entrance of the blacks was orderly and without fanfare in Memphis in contrast to the experience of disorders and violence in many other cities. The process of complete integration of the public schools was speeded up by order of the U.S. Sixth Circuit Court of Appeals in 1964. It ordered the Memphis Board of Education to desegregate all junior high schools by the start of the 1965–66 term and all high schools by the 1966–67 term.

Desegregating the schools did not slow down the rapid enrollment increases of the late 1960s. On the contrary, they increased annually until the 1971–72 school year. The fall 1965 enrollment was about 122,000. It peaked in 1971 at a level of 145,500. But at this point enrollment started dropping even before the implementation of court ordered busing in January 1973. By the fall term in 1973 enrollment had fallen to 119,415. The "white flight" of the public schools had made serious inroads by then. Only 32 percent of the enrollment in the 1973–74 term was white. By 1978 enrollment was down to 113,000, and the white share had shrunk to 26.5 percent.

Busing had become another crisis for Memphis. It was held responsible for the huge "white flight" from the public schools and for the concerns of civic leaders that the educational system might deteriorate to the point of affecting seriously the long range economic development potential of the city. The public school issue became one of the major crises in the long history of the city. The long range implications worried Memphis leaders of the 1970s.

BLACK POLITICAL LEADERSHIP

The first major push for public office by Memphis blacks was in the 1959 municipal elections. A voter registration drive increased the number of qualified black voters to 50,164. The blacks organized what they called the Negro Volunteer Ticket and placed five candidates on the ballot.

The strongest bids were made in the races for Commissioner of Public Works and for Judge of the Juvenile Court. In the former race, black Russell B. Sugarmon, Jr., lost to William Farris, 58,951 to 35,237. In the other race, Elizabeth McCain, the incumbent judge, defeated Ben Hooks, 53,654 to 32,068. Both Sugarmon and Hooks pulled a good vote and surprised the white community with their showing.

Emerging from the NAACP activist group came the first elected black officeholders since the nineteenth century. Civil rights attorney H. T. Lockard won an upset victory in 1964 and became the first black to serve in Shelby

County government since Reconstruction days. Another leader, A. W. Willis, Jr., was elected a state representative in 1964, and became the first black elected to the Tennessee Legislature since 1886.

When the new 13-member City Council took office in January 1968 it included blacks Fred Davis, an insurance executive; the Reverend James L. Netters, a Baptist minister; and J. O. Patterson, Jr., an attorney. Patterson had been elected to the State Senate in 1967; so he held these two offices simultaneously. Later, John Ford, another black, also held a City Council seat and State Senate seat at the same time.

Other well-known black leaders elected to important local offices included Walter L. Bailey; Washington R. Butler, Jr.; W. Otis Higgs, Jr.; Odell Horton; Minerva Johnican; Maxine A. Smith; Dr. Vasco A. Smith; and Jesse H. Turner.

In 1974 State Senator Harold Ford in a stunning upset defeated three-term incumbent Congressman Dan Kuykendall, 67,715 to 67,141. The Eighth Congressional District of Tennessee, which covered much of the Memphis urban area, was represented for the first time by a black. Ford won reelections in 1976 and 1978.

The major attempt to elect a black to the Mayor's Office in 1975 failed. Mayor Wyeth Chandler, the incumbent, defeated Otis Higgs in a runoff election, 112,515 to 81,460. Leading black political leaders, however, continued to set their sights on the Mayor's Office as a major objective.

A number of other blacks frequently made headlines because of their leadership in both civil rights and other major black causes during the 1960s and 1970s. Among the group were activist Cornelia Crenshaw; labor leader Jesse Epps; clergyman, attorney, businessman and NAACP leader Ben Hooks; Reverend Samuel B. Kyles of Operation PUSH; Reverend James M. Lawson, Jr.; Bishop J. O. Patterson, Sr., present leader of the Memphis-based Church of God in Christ; and attorney Russell B. Sugarmon, Jr.

The blacks in a relatively short number of years had established their voice by means of the ballot box. As a result of placing many of their race in public offices, they gained a more effective forum to influence policies and programs. The blacks had moved up considerably in the political decision-making echelons of the community and destroyed the old traditions of white paternalism toward blacks in political, educational, and some economic matters. While blacks had gained political power, as of the 1970s they had not made serious inroads into gaining economic power. The slow-growth Memphis economy of the 1960s and 1970s made the latter a most difficult task. Forces, many of which were far beyond the control of the city, inhibited greater upward economic mobility.

PLANNING FOR ECONOMIC GROWTH

At various times in the postwar years many Memphis white leaders adopted the Mr. Micawber approach to the future: "Something will turn up." They felt that

Fig. 53. Otis Higgs, the first black to run for the Mayor's Office debates incumbent Mayor Wyeth Chandler during the 1975 mayorality race. (Courtesy of Samuel Brackstone)

national companies would discover the great transportation facilities in Memphis, including the Mississippi River, and also the lower power rates prevailing here. A consistent and aggressive approach to growth planning was lacking. But it would be a mistake to expect forthright planning in those pre-April 1968 days when the city's leadership was so preoccupied with the local civil rights movement. Memphians had been tied up with this broad and powerful issue for over a decade. Also, there was an element in the white community that feared growth would change Memphis and destroy what they felt was a truly unique urban lifestyle. The power of this group was subtle.

Conservative fiscal politics were the cornerstone of local governrnent. The foremost proponent of keeping municipal expenditures and taxes in line was Mayor Henry Loeb. His critics accused him of being a penny pincher and of being too conservative. His followers endorsed his austere policies and his attitude toward holding down the property tax rate. Self-assertive, 6-foot 5-inch tall businessman Henry Loeb was very popular with large segments of the white community because of his tough approach to managing the affairs of the city. Proudly, he announced that nobody owned a piece of him, and that he was open and honest. Blacks in general disliked Loeb.

Lip service was paid to economic development. Industrial promotion campaigns were endorsed. Loeb was for encouraging industry so long as no subsidization was required to attract new ventures to the city, or to keep existing businesses from leaving. This was the prevailing climate before the shock of the 4 April 1968 assassination of Martin Luther King, Jr., and the burst of economic development protomotional activity which followed in the immediate aftermath. Some basic economic studies were prepared, but prior to the King assassination they were not action-oriented documents.[5]

The issue of *Time* magazine immediately following King's death referred to

Memphis as a decaying Mississippi River town located "in a Southern back-water."[6] This type of reference was a powerful jolt to Memphians. They did not like much of the post-assassination national analyses that Memphis was a city of racial conflict, violence, curfews, and decay.

Judge W. Preston Battle at the time of the sentencing of James Earl Ray to a 99-year prison term told the courtroom:

> Memphis has been wrongfully and irrationally blamed for the murder of Martin Luther King, Jr. Neither the defendant nor the victim lived in Memphis. Their orbits merely intersected there.[7]

From the turmoil emerged the Greater Memphis Program, a plan and an organization selected as one way to build a strong community through a concerted effort to attract new businesses and industries. New investment, new jobs and payrolls, many felt, could help both whites and blacks in Memphis. Some fund raising had preceeded King's death. The real work, however, came after that event. The major business leaders united for this cause.

The spearheading agency was the Memphis Area Chamber of Commerce. It hired David W. Cooley, a successful chamber of commerce executive in Jacksonville, Florida, to become chief executive officer at a salary of $35,000. Cooley assumed the job in August 1968. His approach was to conduct economic research to pinpoint the type of industry that would find it advantageous to locate in Memphis. Slogans such as "Mid America's Big New City" and "Action City" were part of restructuring the national image of Memphis.

The most prominent business leaders and corporations got behind the program called by some "the Grand Design for Memphis." For a time there was a community-wide exhilaration that great days lay ahead in the near future. A national economic consultant brought to Memphis by the Chamber of Commerce told its membership that the Memphis area economy was potentially at a "take-off point."[8] He pointed out that Memphis' greatest asset was manpower. That asset, he claimed, was even more important than the city's location.[9] Catch phrases such as "Multicenter," "Megatown," and "Pacemaker City" were used to describe its potential.

Cooley proved to be a very frank and perceptive spokesman for the challenges faced by Memphis. He told an audience at Memphis State University in 1970:

> The greatest barrier to a better Memphis is ignorance. . . . What are some of our problems of urban growth? . . . a deteriorating central city . . . bad housing for a large percentage of our population . . . lack of skills training . . . poor worker mobility . . . in-migration of poverty level people . . . undereducated and underemployed people in large numbers . . . token acceptance of blacks in decision-making positions.[10]

A great deal of money was spent in the early years of the Greater Memphis Program. Research studies, promotions, task force missions, and assorted de-

Fig. 54. Influential business and civic leaders attending a Greater Memphis Program meeting. Front center is A. Maceo Walker. In the center are Abe Plough, left; Kemmons Wilson, center; and Frank M. Norfleet, right. In the rear center is B. Lee Mallory III, 1979 president of the Memphis Area Chamber of Commerce. (Courtesy of Saul Brown)

velopment programs quickly consumed the original capital contributions of $6 million.

When interest waned, the Chamber in 1973 launched its "Believe in Memphis" campaign. Nationally-known clergyman and "positive thinker" Norman Vincent Peale told an audience of 1,000 at the kick-off:

> Believe in Memphis; believe in yourself; believe in God; believe in your country; believe in people; believe in the future . . . If you believe in Memphis and talk it up and work it up, a greater Memphis will flow back to you.[11]

Cooley resigned at the end of January 1973 to take a substantially higher paying job with the Dallas Chamber of Commerce. With Cooley's departure went a dynamic executive figure who seemed able to make Memphians take a hard look at themselves and their city.

At the end of 1973 the Memphis Chamber of Commerce experienced a $320,000 deficit. The following year the deficit was about $635,000. Membership started declining rapidly. The national business recession was then in full swing in 1974, and Memphians were feeling its impact. This was an untimely event for the chamber's program. Internal problems within the chamber's membership, including disagreements about program objectives, brought it to the brink of collapse in mid-1977. The optimistic business leadership of Memphis in the late 1960s had vanished, replaced by bickering and disillusionment.

What did the Greater Memphis Program accomplish? Unfortunately, the results were substantially below expectations in terms of new business investment, jobs, or general community revitalization. It was difficult to quantify results. The Program did bring together for one glorious moment business interest groups for a serious community problem. Once again as it so often had happened in Memphis' history, it took a tragic event to stir the business elite into action for the economic and social betterment of the city, and not just their own personal interests.

The Memphis Area Chamber of Commerce, the organization traditionally entrusted with the role of economic development, once more became the pivotal force for promoting new investment and jobs in the late 1970s when the business community decided to give it one more try. Stripped down to only one function—the promotion of industry—the chamber's leadership in early 1978 set a goal of 75,000 new jobs in the Memphis area by 1983. The chamber's president, mortgage banker James E. McGehee, Jr., succinctly stated the streamlined organization's motto: "A City Worth Fighting For!"

THE QUEST FOR LEADERSHIP

Following Crump's death in 1954 Memphians began to think more and more about the question of leadership. While Crump was running the city, discussions of leadership were purely academic. But his departure left an enormous vacuum. Crump left no successor to carry on his special brand of paternalism.

In the latter 1950s and into the 1960s and 1970s a few leaders emerged from the white community to enter politics at City Hall and at the Courthouse. Some were well-known businessmen. But these individuals produced no real forward direction for Memphis either in their rhetoric or in executive or legislative actions. None emerged with a "great vision" for Memphis to captivate either the white or the black communities. Their leadership was described as "the caretaker variety." Often they were reactive leaders; that is, they waited for problems to emerge, then took some form of action. They were largely frugal with public funds and this stewardship of tax funds became a massive preoccupation with many of them.

The visionary aspects of community planning were left by political leaders to others, including the Chamber of Commerce and the 100-member civic group, Future Memphis, Incorporated. This group since its inception in 1961 had included most of the top industrialists, bankers, attorneys, architects and educators. The group patterned itself after the successful civic leadership organization in Dallas. These Memphians referred to Future Memphis, Incorporated as a community building group which was not only concerned with economic growth and city planning, but also with matters of social concern and education. In the latter two areas, for example, Future Memphis, Incorporated, in its 1973 report, *Blueprint for Memphis* listed as priority items the following:

> *Equal employment opportunity with emphasis on economic growth through which a high employment rate will result with an adequate level of wages. Educational institutions should concentrate on supplying talent needs of industry and business.
> *Elimination of personal, social and institutional racism and chauvinism with the goal of achieving together a community of excellence and a life style of dignity regardless of race, sex or creed.[12]

Future Memphis appeared to have identified most of the major community problems and put priority ratings on them. But for obscure reasons this organization of highly influential business and professional leaders maintained a much lower than expected community profile. And this Memphis group, unlike its counterparts in Dallas and Atlanta, had a lower than anticipated batting average in getting its recommendations implemented through the local political process.

In the 1970s more Memphians than ever before were involved in discussing the future of their city and its surrounding region. This was a very hopeful sign that many concerned citizens were taking a realistic look at their city for the first time. Seminars sponsored by Southwestern at Memphis' Urban Policy Institute were designed around challenging topics of public administration, economic development and the urban land form. These periodic conclaves brought into one room representatives from a wide range of interest groups to probe for solutions and to reach a consensus on action required.

As the decade of the 1970s closed, more community concern than ever was being expressed about the diffused and largely ineffective status of leadership. Plans were launched to formalize the process of developing effective leaders. In 1978 Leadership Memphis was organized to serve as a training school for future civic leaders. In early 1979 the initial class of 42 persons representing different professions, income levels, race, and sex began their training. Memphis was following the lead of Atlanta and Nashville in trying to structure "leadership" in the community.

At least as the 1980s approach there were reasons to be optimistic that Memphis might achieve what it had lacked over the previous 160 years of its existence—leaders with broader perspectives as a result of being trained for their roles in the public arena.

MOVING FORWARD WHILE PRESERVING TRADITIONS

Beginning in the 1950s adjustments in social and economic relations occurred in both the white and black communities to upset historic balances. Memphis had always been a proud city, and one rich in tradition. Those in control of the economic and social power wanted their traditions preserved regardless of what might occur in the development of the economy, in the urban land pattern, or from advances in civil rights gained by black citizens. This accounts for much of the anguish experienced by many in both the white and black communities today.

Memphis in two centuries had been through many frantic moments. These events undoubtedly had much to do with molding the character of its people and institutions. The crises are best remembered because of their dramatic nature. The greatest of these—the Civil War and its aftermath, the Yellow Fever Epidemic of 1878, the Great Depression of the 1930s, and the recent civil rights movement—brought anxiety to Memphians of all walks of life. For a period of time many wondered how the city could survive the enormity of the problems and the turmoil. Pessimism followed in the wake of each of these historical events, and for a while the city lost direction and purpose.

Contemporary Memphis, so caught up in a multitude of urgent civic crises, has found it a luxury to use much of its time for contemplating the future. If it had the time, it might be amazed to find that it has been continually adjusting to the external changes from beyond the city and region, and to internal changes within the city and region. Because of much deep soul searching and concern by an increasing number of citizens over their city, it is possible that Memphis might be able to find ways to more adequately meet the needs of its citizens in the future than in the past. One place to start, for example, is with school systems. In terms of the city's economic future the level of labor productivity, job growth, and "take-home" income will be greatly affected by the quality of the products emerging from the educational system. Despite periods of discouragement in the race to attract new business and industry to the city, Memphis must continue to strive to train a labor force with many of the skills being demanded by national and international businesses.

What Memphis needs is a streak of luck in attracting new industries and new technology to the city. Greater injections of investment capital, higher paying jobs and more of them, would diffuse much of the pressure which has debilitated Memphis for so long.

Historically, Memphis has been the victim of bad luck in its promotional efforts to attract new investment and jobs for the city. Other cities which expended far less effort often were the recipients of new industries. In many instances, these cities were surrounded by far greater natural resources than Memphis, or they were located in more populated sections of the United States than the Mid-South.

Fig. 55. View of contemporary downtown Memphis and the Mississippi River looking Northwest. The De Soto Bridge, which opened in 1973, connects Memphis to Eastern Arkansas. (Courtesy of the Memphis District, U.S. Corps of Engineers)

Perhaps Memphis can do more to make its own luck in the future. Preparing for growth through a better managed city and through a responsive educational system are ways of increasing the odds in Memphis' favor. This is the way to "Believe in Memphis."

The traditions need not be sacrificed. All they need are some realistic adjustments as Memphis moves toward its third century.

**Appendices
Notes
Index**

APPENDIX A

Mayors of Memphis, 1865-1980

A. *Immediate Post Civil War Period*

	Mayor
1865–1866	John Park
1866–1868	William O. Lofland
1868–1870	John W. Leftwich
1870–1874	John Johnson
1874–1876	John Loague
1876–1879 (31 January 1879)	John R. Flippin

B. *Taxing District Period (1879–1893)*

	President
1879 (February)–1881	David T. Porter
1881–1883	John Overton, Jr.
1883–1891	David P. Hadden
1891–1893	William D. Bethel

C. *1893–1910*

	Mayor
1893–1898	Walter L. Clapp
1898–1906	John J. Williams
1906–1910	James H. Malone

D. *Commission Government Period (1910–1967)*

	Mayor
1910–1915	E. H. Crump
1915–1916	George C. Love
1916–1917	Thomas C. Ashcroft
1917–1918	Harry H. Litty
1918–1919	Frank L. Monteverde
1920–1928	Rowlett Paine
1928–1940	Watkins Overton
1940 (1–2 January 1940)	E. H. Crump
1940–1946 (2 January–31 August 1946)	Walter C. Chandler
1946 (1–17 September 1946)	Joseph P. Boyle (acting Mayor)
1946–1947 (17 September 1946– 15 April 1947)	Sylvanus W. Polk, Sr.
1947–1949	James J. Pleasants, Jr.
1949–1953 (15 January 1949– 28 February 1953)	Watkins Overton
1953–1955 (1 March 1953– 11 September 1955)	Frank T. Tobey

1955 (20 September 1955–
 31 December 1955)   Walter C. Chandler
1956–1960   Edmund Orgill
1960–1963 (1 January 1960–
 11 October 1963)   Henry Loeb III
1963 (11 October 1963–
 12 November 1963)   Claude Armour (acting Mayor)
1963–1968   William B. Ingram, Jr.

E. *Mayor-City Council Period*
 1968–1972   Henry Locb III
 1972–1980   Wyeth Chandler

SOURCE: Compiled with the assistance of the History Department, Memphis/Shelby County Public Library and Information Center.

APPENDIX B

National and Local Cotton Market, 1865–1977

Crop Year	U.S. Crop Harvested[1]	Receipts/Sales in Memphis[2]	Percent Memphis Sales of Total U.S. Crop	Seasonal Average Price Per Pound[3]
1. Civil War Period to 1900				
1865–66	2,097	112	5%	31.6¢
1866–67	2,520	218	9	24.9
1867–68	2,366	253	11	29.0
1868–69	3,012	248	8	24.0
1869–70	4,352	291	7	17.0
1870–71	2,974	511	17	20.5
1871–72	3,933	380	10	18.2
1872–73	4,168	415	10	17.0
1873–74	3,836	249	6	15.0
1874–75	4,631	322	7	13.0
1875–76	4,474	487	11	9.71
1876–77	4,773	384	8	8.53
1877–78	5,074	412	8	8.16
1878–79	5,755	386	7	10.28
1879–80	6,606	410	6	9.83
1880–81	5,456	470	9	10.66
1881–82	6,949	339	5	9.12
1882–83	5,713	511	9	9.13
1883–84	5,682	450	8	9.19
1884–85	6,576	430	7	8.39
1885–86	6,505	546	8	8.06
1886–87	7,047	663	9	8.55
1887–88	6,938	652	9	8.50
1888–89	7,473	704	9	8.55
1889–90	8,653	578	7	8.59

Crop Year	U.S. Crop Harvested[1]	Receipts/Sales in Memphis[2]	Percent Memphis Sales of Total U.S. Crop	Seasonal Average Price Per Pound[3]
1890–91	9,035	723	8	7.24
1891–92	6,700	773	12	8.34
1892–93	7,493	427	6	7.00
1893–94	9,091	488	5	4.59
1894–95	7,162	588	8	7.62
1895–96	8,533	430	5	6.66
1896–97	10,899	562	5	6.68
1897–98	11,278	690	6	5.73
1898–99	9,535	786	8	6.98
1899–1900	10,124	597	6	9.15
2. *1900 to World War I Period*				
1900–01	9,508	677	7%	7.03
1901–02	10,630	680	6	7.60
1902–03	9,851	893	9	10.49
1903–04	13,438	749	6	8.98
1904–05	10,576	984	9	10.78
1905–06	13,274	801	6	9.58
1906–07	11,106	958	9	10.36
1907–08	13,241	750	6	9.01
1908–09	10,649	984	9	13.52
1909–10	11,609	785	7	13.96
1910–11	15,694	921	6	9.65
1911–12	13,703	970	7	11.50
1912–13	14,153	821	6	12.47
1913–14	16,112	1,130	7	7.35
1914–15	11,172	1,071	10	11.22
1915–16	11,448	971	8	17.36
1916–17	11,284	1,336	12	27.09
1917–18	12,018	1,422	12	28.88
1918–19	11,376	931	8	35.34
1919–20	13,429	1,222	9	15.89
3. *The Nineteen Twenties*				
1920–21	7,945	930	12	17.00
1921–22	9,755	957	10	22.88
1922–23	10,140	1,113	11	28.69
1923–24	13,683	926	7	22.91
1924–25	16,105	1,303	8	19.62
1925–26	17,978	2,000	11	12.49
1926–27	12,956	2,349	18	20.20
1927–28	14,477	1,512	10	17.98
1928–29	14,574	1,823	13	16.78
1929–30	13,932	1,995	14	9.46
4. *The Nineteen Thirties*				
1930–31	17,097	1,395	8	5.66
1931–32	13,003	2,092	16	6.52
1932–33	13,047	2,150	16	10.17
1933–34	9,472	1,903	20	12.36
1934–35	10,638	1,442	14	11.09
1935–36	12,399	2,087	17	12.36
1936–37	18,946	2,571	14	8.41
1937–38	11,943	2,719	23	8.60
1938–39	11,481	2,127	19	9.09
1939–40	12,566	3,190	25	9.89

Crop Year	U.S. Crop Harvested[1]	Receipts/Sales in Memphis[2]	Percent Memphis Sales of Total U.S. Crop	Seasonal Average Price Per Pound[3]
5. *World War II Period*				
1940–41	10,744	4,100	38	17.03
1941–42	12,817	3,498	27	19.05
1942–43	11,427	3,300	29	19.90
1943–44	11,838	2,982	25	20.73
1944–45	9,015	3,211	36	22.52
1945–46	8,640	3,547	41	32.64
6. *Post World War II Years*				
1946–47	11,860	2,877	24	31.93
1947–48	14,877	3,994	27	30.38
1948–49	15,419	3,764	24	28.70
1949–50	10,014	5,288	53	40.07
1950–51	15,149	4,459	29	37.88
1951–52	15,139	4,255	28	34.59
1952–53	16,465	4,167	25	32.25
1953–54	12,921	3,478	27	33.85
1954–55	14,721	3,774	26	32.33
1955–56	13,310	4,100	31	31.75
1956–57	10,964	5,130	47	29.65
1957–58	11,512	4,337	38	33.22
1958–59	13,914	2,494	18	31.66
1959–60	14,272	5,441	38	30.19
1960–61	15,634	6,485	41	32.92
1961–62	15,569	3,656	23	31.90
1962–63	14,212	4,000	28	32.33
1963–64	14,055	4,548	32	31.07
1964–65	13,613	4,640	34	29.37
1965–66	9,552	4,854	51	21.75
1966–67	7,997	5,487	69	26.70
1967–68	10,159	4,894	48	23.11
1968–69	11,051	2,749	25	22.00
1969–70	11,155	3,081	28	21.98
1970–71	11,471	4,692	41	28.23
1971–72	12,984	3,719	29	27.3
1972–73	11,970	5,225	44	44.6
1973–74	12,547	4,352	35	42.9
1974–75	8,796	2,733	31	51.3
1975–76	10,914	2,259	21	64.1
1976–77	13,279[4]	2,201	17	51.7[4]
1977–78	n.a.	3,230	n.a.	n.a.

SOURCE: (1) U.S. Bureau of the Census, *Historical Statistics of the United States, Colonial Times to 1870,* Bicentennial Edition, Part 1, Series K550–563; and U.S. Department of Agriculture, *Agricultural Statistics,* 1977 and 1978 editions.
(2) Memphis Cotton Exchange.
(3) U.S. Bureau of the Census, *Historical Statistics,* Series K550–563; and U.S. Department of Agriculture, *Agricultural Statistics.*
(4) Preliminary data.

APPENDIX C

Books of General Interest About Memphis

Baker, III, Thomas H. *The Memphis Commercial Appeal: The History of A Southern Newspaper.* Baton Rouge: Louisiana State University Press, 1971.

Capers, Gerald M., *The Biography of A River Town: Memphis, Its Heroic Age.* New Orleans: by the author, 1966.

Church, Annette E., and Church, Roberta. *The Robert R. Churches of Memphis.* Ann Arbor, Mich.: Edwards Brothers, 1974.

City Planning Commission. *A Comprehensive City Plan, Memphis, Tennessee.* Memphis, 1924.

Coppock, Paul R. *Memphis Sketches.* Memphis, Tenn.: Friends of the Memphis and Shelby County Libraries, 1976.

Crawford, Charles W. *Yesterday's Memphis.* Miami, Fla.: E. A. Seeman, 1976.

Davis, James D. *The History of the City of Memphis.* reprint ed. Edited by James E. Roper. Memphis, Tenn.: West Tennessee Historical Society, 1972.

Gibson, Arrell M. *The Chickasaws.* Norman, Okla.: University of Oklahoma Press, 1971.

Hamilton, G. P. *Beacon Lights of the Race.* Memphis, Tenn.: F. H. Clarke and Brother, 1911.

_____ . *The Bright Side of Memphis.* Memphis, Tenn.: n. p., 1908.

History of Tennessee. Shelby County edition. Nashville, Tenn.: Goodspeed Publishing Company, 1877.

Hutchins, Fred. *What Happened in Memphis.* Kingsport, Tenn.: n.p., 1965.

Keating, J. M. *A History of the Yellow Fever Epidemic.* Memphis, Tenn.: printed for the Howard Association, 1879.

_____ . *History of the City of Memphis and Shelby County, Tennessee, with Illustrations and Biographical Sketches of Some of Its Prominent Citizens.* 2 vols. Vol. 2 by O. F. Vedder. Syracuse, N.Y.: Mason, 1889.

Lee, George W. *Beale Street, Where the Blues Began.* foreword by W. C. Handy. New York: R. O. Ballou, 1934.

McIlwaine, Shields. *Memphis Down in Dixie.* Society in America Series no. 3. New York, N.Y.: Dutton, 1948.

Malone, James H. *The Chickasaw Nation.* Louisville, Ky.: John P. Morton and Co., 1922.

Meeman, Edward J. *The Editorial We, A Posthumous Autobiography.* Memphis, Tenn.: Memphis State University Printing Services, 1976.

Miller, William D. *Memphis During the Progressive Era, 1900–1917.* Memphis, Tenn.: Memphis State University Press, 1957.

_____. *Mr. Crump of Memphis.* Southern Biography Series, Baton Rouge, La.: Louisiana State University Press, 1964.

Plunkett, Kitty. *Memphis, A Pictoral History.* Norfolk, Va.: Donning Company, 1976.

Tucker, David M. *Black Pastors and Leaders: The Memphis Clergy, 1819–1972.* Memphis, Tenn.: Memphis State University Press, 1975.

_____. *Lieutenant Lee of Beale Street.* Nashville, Tenn.: Vanderbilt University Press, 1971.

United States Congress. *Memphis Riots and Massacres.* Elihu B. Washburne, Compiler. House Report 101, 39th Congress, 1st Session. Washington, D.C.: Government Printing Office, 1866.

Williams, Samuel Cole. *Beginnings of West Tennessee: In the Land of the Chickasaws, 1541–1841.* Johnson City, Tenn.: The Watauga Press, 1930.

Young, J. P., ed. *Standard History of Memphis, Tennessee.* reprint ed. West Tennessee Historical Society, 1974.

Notes

CHAPTER 1

1. Gerald M. Capers, *The Biography of A River Town: Memphis, Its Heroic Age* (New Orleans: by the author, 1966), 16.

2. Arthur Preston Whitaker, *The Spanish-American Frontier: 1783–1795* (Gloucester, Mass.: Peter Smith, 1962), 214–216.

3. Charles W. Crawford, *Yesterday's Memphis* (Miami: E. A. Seeman, 1976), 14.

4. Benjamin H. Hibbard, *A History of Public Land Policies* (New York: P. Smith, 1939), 11–12.

5. Bette Baird Tilly, "Aspects of Social and Economic Life in West Tennessee Before the Civil War" (Ph.D. dissertation, Memphis State University, 1974), 43–45.

6. Thomas P. Abernathy, *From Frontier to Plantation in Tennessee* (Chapel Hill: The University of North Carolina Press, 1932), 176.

7. James H. Robinson, "A Social History of the Negro in Memphis and in Shelby County," (Ph.D. dissertation, Yale University, 1934), 20.

8. Samuel Cole Williams, *Beginnings of West Tennessee: In the Land of the Chickasaws, 1541–1841* (Johnson City, Tenn.: The Watauga Press, 1930), 86. This volume contains an extensive review of the negotiations.

9. Francis Clifton, "The Life and Activities of John Overton," (M.A. thesis, Vanderbilt University, 1948), 30.

10. Dallas T. Herndon, *Why Little Rock Was Born* (Little Rock, Ark.: Central Printing Co., 1933), 32–35.

11. Penetrating research on the founding of Memphis has been contributed by Professor James E. Roper, Southwestern at Memphis, in his book, *The Founding of Memphis, 1818–1820* (Memphis: The Memphis Sesquicentennial, 1970), and in his article, "Paddy Meagher, Tom Huling and the Bell Tavern," *The West Tennessee Historical Society Papers* 31 (1977), 5–32.

12. Clifton, "The Life and Activities of John Overton," 102. The ad appeared in the *Nashville Whig*, 7 June 1820.

13. Capers, *River Town*, 34.

14. This interesting transformation is described in the publication, Henry D. Whitney, ed., *Land Laws of Tennessee*, 1893.

15. Williams, *Beginnings of West Tennessee*, 108.

16. *Aldermen of Memphis* v. *Wright*, (Justice Green, 1834).

17. *The Commercial Appeal*, 17 August 1906.

18. Robert W. O'Brien, "Beale Street, A Study of Ecological Succession," *Sociology and Social Research* 26 (May 1942), 431.

19. Memphis historian Paul R. Coppock brings to life the evolution of this venerable thoroughfare in his article, "Pigeon Roost Road: A Chickasaw Trail," *The West Tennessee Historical Society Papers* 18 (1964), 59–69.

20. Memphis *Public Ledger*, 31 December 1878.

21. David M. Hilliard, "The Development of Public Education in Memphis, Tennessee, 1848–1945" (Ph.D. dissertation, University of Chicago, 1946), 28. The *Fourth Annual Report* of the Memphis city schools commented on the difficulty of obtaining good rented accommodations. See *1855–56 Report*.

22. Tilly, "Aspects of Social and Economic Life in West Tennessee," 58.

23. Clifton,"The Life and Activities of John Overton," 40–41.

24. James E. Roper, "Marcus B. Winchester, First Mayor of Memphis: His Later Years," *The West Tennessee Historical Society Papers* 13 (1959), 17. Professor Roper, in this authoritative article gives a detailed account of the relationships between Marcus Winchester and the proprietors. The research undertaken by Roper was extensive. I acknowledge the background information provided in this excellent article.

25. Reported in the daily feature of *The Commercial Appeal,* "News of Bygone Days," in the issue of 8 December 1970. The item was from the issue of that same date in 1845.

26. John C. Mehrling, "The Memphis and Charleston Railroad," *The West Tennessee Historical Society Papers* 19 (1965), 22.

27. J. M. Keating, *History of the City of Memphis and Shelby County, Tennessee, with Illustrations and Biographical Sketches of Some of Its Prominent Citizens,* 2 vols. Vol. 2 by O. F. Vedder (Syracuse, N.Y.: Mason, 1889), 380.

28. O. B. Emerson, "Frances Wright and Her Nashoba Experiment," *Tennessee Historical Quarterly* 6 (December 1947), 299.

CHAPTER 2

1. Hodding Carter, *Lower Mississippi* (New York, Toronto: Farrer and Rinehart, Inc., 1942), 174.

2. Francis B. Simkins, *A History of the South* (New York: Knopf, 1953), 151.

3. Ralph K. Andrist, *Steamboats on the Mississippi* (New York: American Heritage Publishing Co., 1962), 92, 94.

4. George H. Devol, *Forty Years A Gambler on the Mississippi* (Cincinnati: Devol and Haines, 1887).

5. James Hall, *The West: Its Commerce and Navigation* (Cincinnati: Derby, 1848), 304.

6. C. R. Calvert, *Historical Sketch of Traffic on Lower Mississippi River and Tributaries* (Memphis: General Freight Office, Illinois Central Railroad, 1912), 14.

7. Mississippi River Commission, *Flood Control in the Lower Mississippi Valley* (Vicksburg, Miss.: 1964).

8. An excellent description of the military and political conditions of the times as they affected the location of military and naval defense facilities is given in St. George L. Sioussat's article, "Memphis As A Gateway to the West," *Tennessee Historical Magazine* 3 (March 1917), 21–22. See also Capers, *River Town,* 82.

9. Sioussat, "Memphis As A Gateway to the West," 23.

10. A feature article in the *Evening Appeal,* 27 October 1927 describes the community's bitter disappointment in losing the naval installation.

11. This reference originating in the Cincinnati *Railroad Record* is quoted in the publication, *Memphis: An Illustrated Review, 1886.*

12. Robert S. Cotterill, "Early Agitation for a Pacific Railroad, 1845–1850," *Mississippi Valley Historical Review* 5 (1919), 396–397.

13. Frederick A. Cleveland and Fred W. Powell, *Railroad Promotion and Capitalization in the United States* (New York: Longmans, Green and Co., 1909), 240–258.

14. Robert E. Riegel, *The Story of Western Railroads* (Gloucester, Mass.: P. Smith, 1974), 18.

15. U.S. War Department, *Explorations For A Route for the Pacific Railroad,* 12 vols. Serials 791 to 801, and 1054–55 (1855 and 1860).

16. For two excellent articles describing Memphis' role in the Pacific Route question, see Addie Lou Brooks, "The Building of Trunk Line Railroads in West Tennessee, 1852–1861," *Tennessee Historical Quarterly* 1 (1942), 99–124; and Robert S. Cotterill, "Memphis Railroad Convention, 1849," *Tennessee Historical Magazine* 4 (1918), 83–95.

17. David M. Potter, "The Historical Development of Eastern-Southern Freight Rate Relationships," *Law and Contemporary Problems* 12 (Summer 1947), 416–448.

18. John C. Mehrling, "The Memphis and Charleston Railroad," 22.

19. Ibid., 31.

20. Maury Klein, *History of the Louisville and Nashville Railroad* (New York: Macmillan, 1972), 7.

21. Ibid.

22. Memphis *Daily Appeal,* 21 May 1853. Earlier, in the issue of 12 April 1853 this newspaper developed a justification for the Memphis and Little Rock Railroad: "The eyes of the whole Union seem to be on Memphis. Our young city is the central point in this vast Mississippi Valley and it is to our interest that the gateway to the West should be through our city. Here must be the grand gathering point for those who would set out for the lands beyond. We must not curtail our subscription to the Little Rock Railroad, but rather add to it." This was reprinted in the 12 April 1978 issue of *The Commercial Appeal* as a news item of 125 years earlier in this same paper.

23. William E. Hayes, *Iron Horse to Empire, The History of 100 Years of the Progress and Achievements of the Rock Island Lines* (New York: Simmons-Boardman, 1953), 160–161.

CHAPTER 3

1. Roper, "Faddy Meagher, Tom Huling and the Bell Tavern," 5–32.

2. *Memphis Appeal,* 1 December 1878.

3. David L. Cohn, *The Life and Times of King Cotton* (New York: Oxford University Press, 1956), 121.

4. J. M. Keating, *History of the City of Memphis,* 328.

5. Frederick Bancroft, *Slave Trading In the Old South* (New York: Frederick Ungar Publishing Co., 1931), 258.

6. Ibid., 264.

7. Robert A. Starobin, *Industrial Slavery in the Old South* (New York: Oxford University Press, 1970), vii.

8. Data obtained from a search of the City of Memphis Archives.

9. Eugene D. Genovese, *The Political Economy of Slavery* (New York: Pantheon Books, 1965), 23–24; and Clarence H. Danhof, "Four Decades of Thought On the South's Economic Problems," in *Essays in Southern Economic Development,* eds. Melvin L. Greenhut and W. Tate Whitman (Chapel Hill: University of North Carolina Press, 1964), 8.

10. Danhof, "Four Decades of Thought on the South's Economic Problems," 34.

11. H. C. Nixon, "The Changing Political Philosophy of the South," *The Annals of the American Academy of Political and Social Science* 153 (January 1931), 246.

12. Mississippi River Commission, *River Papers, 1845 Memphis Convention;* and Floyd M. Clay, *A Century on the Mississippi: A History of the Memphis District U.S. Army Corps of Engineers 1876–1976* (Memphis: U.S. Army Corps of Engineers, Memphis District, 1976), 11–12.

13. Eighth Census, *Manufactures in the United States in 1860* (Washington, 1865).

14. Clark Porteous, *The First Orgill Century, 1847–1947* (Memphis: Merrill Kremer, Inc., n.d.), 5.

15. Jesse, the "Scribe," edited by James E. Roper, *Chronicles of the Farmers' and Merchants' Bank of Memphis,* Burrow Library Monograph No. 4 (Memphis: Southwestern at Memphis, 1960), n.p.

16. Ibid.

17. *Memphis City Directory* (1859).

18. Paul R. Coppock, "Mid-South Memoirs—In the Days of Grand Hotels," *The Commercial Appeal,* 10 March 1974.

19. Seldon Faulkner, "The New Memphis Theatre of Memphis, Tennessee, From 1859 to 1880" (Ph.D. dissertation, University of Iowa, 1957), 4.

20. Maurice B. Davie, *World Immigration With Special Reference to the United States* (New York: The Macmillan Co., 1936), 63–67.

21. George Potter, *To The Golden Door: The Story of the Irish In Ireland and America* (Westport, Conn.: Greenwood Press, 1973), 140.

22. Ibid., 155.

23. Ibid., 205.

24. Robert Rauchle, "Biographical Sketches of Prominent Germans in Memphis, Tennessee, in the Nineteenth Century," *The West Tennessee Historical Society Papers* 22 (1968), 78–85.

25. Rabbi James A. Wax, "The Jews of Memphis: 1860–1865," *The West Tennessee Historical Society Papers* 3 (1949), 39–89.

26. Richard K. Thomas, "The Residential Distribution of Immigrants in Memphis, Tennessee" (M.A. thesis, Memphis State University, 1970), 33. This thesis covers the time period from before the Civil War through the early 20th century. Mr. Thomas examined Census data thoroughly to develop his residential distribution patterns.

CHAPTER 4

1. Capers, *River Town*, 136.
2. Ibid., 135.
3. Ibid., 136.
4. W. Raymond Cooper, "Four Fateful Years of Memphis, 1858–1861," *The West Tennessee Historical Society Papers* 11 (1957), 66.
5. Civil War Centennial Commission, *Tennesseans in the Civil War* (Nashville, 1964), 1.
6. John D. Milligan, "The Federal Fresh-Water Navy and the Opening of the Mississippi River: Its Organization, Construction and Operations Through the Fall of Vicksburg," (Ph.D. dissertation, University of Michigan, 1961), 238–250.
7. Francis Vinton Green, *The Mississippi*, Vol. 3 of *Campaigns of the Civil War* (New York, 1885), 7.
8. Ernest W. Hooper, "Memphis, Tennessee: Federal Occupation and Reconstruction, 1862–1870" (Ph.D. dissertation, University of North Carolina, 1957).
9. Joseph H. Parks, "A Confederate Trade Center Under Federal Occupation: Memphis, 1862 to 1865," *The Journal of Southern History* 7 (1941), 291–292.
10. Ulysses S. Grant to Henry W. Halleck, 27 June 1862, in *Official Records*, Ser. 1, Vol. 17, Part II, 41.
11. For an excellent account of this war profiteering, see Bertram W. Korn, *American Jewry and the Civil War* (Cleveland: World Publishing Co., 1961), 121. An equally interesting account appears in David L. Cohn's, *The Life and Times of King Cotton*, 128.
12. Harold D. Woodman, *King Cotton and His Retainers* (Lexington, Ky.: University of Kentucky Press, 1968), 221.
13. Ibid.
14. Leo E. Huff, "The Memphis and Little Rock Railroad During the Civil War," *Arkansas Historical Quarterly* 23 (Autumn 1964), 260–270.
15. J. P. Young, *Standard History of Memphis, Tennessee* (Knoxville: H. W. Crew, 1912), 589.
16. Capers, *River Town*, 162.
17. Thomas B. Alexander, *Political Reconstruction in Tennessee* (Nashville: Vanderbilt University Press, 1950), 54. Mr. Alexander quotes from newspaper editorials of the day commenting on the problems of the then recently freed blacks crowding into the cities.
18. Memphis *Argus*, 26 September 1865. See also Howard N. Rabinowitz, *Race Relations in the Urban South* (New York: Oxford University Press, 1978), 346.
19. Joe M. Richardson, ed., "The Memphis Race Riot and Its Aftermath," *Tennessee Historical Quarterly* 24 (Spring 1965), 63–69. See also James G. Ryan, "The Memphis Riots of 1866: Terror in the Black Community During Reconstruction," *The Journal of Negro History* 62 (1977), 243–257. And see also Alexander, *Political Reconstruction*, 56–57.
20. Potter, *Golden Door*, 384.
21. Memphis *Avalanche*, 7 June 1866.
22. United States Congress, *Memphis Riots and Massacres*, House Report No. 101, 39th Congress, 1st Session (Washington, D. C., 1866), 1.
23. W. J. Battersby, *The Christian Brothers in Memphis, 1871–1971* (Memphis: Christian Brothers College, 1971), 6.
24. Elizabeth Avery Meriwether, *Recollections of 92 Years: 1824–1916* (Nashville: The Tennessee Historical Commission, 1958). See the Foreward written by Lee Meriwether entitled, "My Mother" on pp. v-vi. Also, Alexander, *Political Reconstruction*, 184.
25. Hodding Carter, *The Angry Scar* (New York: Doubleday, 1959), 214–216.
26. Alexander, *Political Reconstruction*, 184.
27. Ibid. See also William Goodman, *Inherited Domain: Political Parties in Tennessee* (Knoxville: The Bureau of Public Administration, University of Tennessee, 1954).

28. S. J. Folmsbee, R. E. Corlew, and E. L. Mitchell, *History of Tennessee* (New York: Lewis Historical Publishing Co., 1960), II, 132.

29. One Memphian, black teacher Ida B. Wells, sued the Chesapeake and Ohio Railroad in 1884 for being asked to sit in segregated facilities. A local court upheld her claim and awarded her $500 in damages. The C & O appealed this verdict. See Alfreda M. Duster, ed. *Crusade for Justice–The Autobiography of Ida B. Wells* (Chicago: University of Chicago Press, 1970).

30. George W. Lee, *Beale Street, Where the Blues Began.* Foreward By W. C. Handy (New York: R. O. Ballou, 1934), 240–241.

31. Memphis *Appeal,* 3 July 1870; 1 September 1874. See also *Memphis City Directory,* 1872.

32. Memphis *Appeal,* 1 September 1872.

33. Alrutheus A. Taylor, *The Negro in Tennessee* (Spartanburg, S.C.: The Reprint Company, 1974), 154–155.

34. Ibid.

35. See Walter L. Fleming, *The Freedmen's Savings Bank* (Chapel Hill: University of North Carolina Press, 1927), 36; 146–147; and Taylor, *The Negro in Tennessee,* 162–164.

CHAPTER 5

1. Hooper, "Federal Occupation and Reconstruction," 228–234.

2. For two excellent articles describing civic and public health conditions of this time period, see John H. Ellis, "Business Leadership in Memphis Public Health Reform, 1880–1900," *The West Tennessee Historical Society Papers* 19 (1965), 94–104; and Charles Clotfelter, "Memphis Business Leadership and the Politics of Fiscal Crisis," *The West Tennessee Historical Society Papers* 27 (1973), 33–49.

3. U.S. Department of Commerce, Bureau of the Census, *Historical Statistics* (1960), 127.

4. *The Commercial Appeal,* 1 April 1915.

5. J. Harvey Mathes, *General Forrest* (New York: D. Appleton and Co., 1902), 361–362.

6. U.S. Surgeon-General's Office, *The Cholera Epidemic of 1873 in the United States,* Executive Document No. 95, (1875).

7. Gerald M. Capers in his article, "Yellow Fever in Memphis in the 1870's" in *Mississippi Valley Historical Review* 24 (1937–38), 486 quoted from an 1867 issue of the Memphis *Public Ledger.* See also the description of unsanitary conditions in Memphis in Edward King's, *The Great South* (Hartford: American Publishing Co., 1875), 268–269.

8. Report to the City of Memphis Board of Alderman and the Common Council in joint session, 7 August 1878.

9. Clark Porteous, prominent Memphis newspaperman, wrote this dramatic phrase in *Hardware Age* 212 (4 July 1975), 56; 58.

10. M. J. Stewart, William T. Black and Mildred Hicks, eds., *History of Medicine in Memphis* (Memphis: Memphis and Shelby County Medical Society, 1971), 32.

11. Ibid.

12. Two excellent sources relating day-to-day events, and reviewing Memphis' public health problems are: Mimi White, "Yellow Fever," an 8 page Supplement in *The Commercial Appeal,* 31 October 1978; and J. M. Keating, *The Yellow Fever Epidemic of 1878* (Memphis: printed for the Howard Association, 1879). Keating describes the heroic work of the members of the Howard Association in aiding victims of yellow fever. Many gave their own lives in the battle to save lives.

The Memphis branch of this benevolent organization was one of many such chapters operating in Southern cities during 1878. For an excellent history of this Association which was first organized in New Orleans in 1837, see Anne Marie Falsone, "The Memphis Howard Association: A Study in the Growth of Social Awareness," (M.A. thesis, Memphis State University, 1968).

13. *The New York Times,* 4 December 1879.

14. Capers, *River Town,* 212. The citation for this decision is *O'Connor* v. *the City of Memphis,* 6 Lea 730.

15. For a detailed analysis of the financial plight of the State of Tennessee during the post-Civil War period, see Robert B. Jones, *Tennessee at the Crossroads: The State Debt Controversy, 1870–1883* (Knoxville: University of Tennessee Press, 1977), 192 p.

16. *New York Tribune,* as reprinted in the *Memphis Daily Appeal,* 2 December 1879.

17. Memphis Merchants Exchange, *1894 Annual Report.*

18. William W. Sorrels, "Memphis' Greatest Debate: A Study of the Development of the Public Water System" (M.A. thesis, Memphis State University, 1969), 103–104. The study documents in detail all of the pre and post-Civil War events relating to the water supply problems in Memphis. I acknowledge the background assistance this thesis has provided. It was published by Memphis State University Press in 1970.

19. Ibid., 53–54.

20. Ibid., 65.

21. Ibid., 87.

22. *The Commercial Appeal,* 4 September 1904.

23. William D. Miller, *Mr. Crump of Memphis* (Baton Rouge: Louisiana State University Press, 1964), 46.

24. *Commercial and Statistical Review of the City of Memphis, 1883,* 52.

25. Capers, "Yellow Fever in Memphis," 502. See also E. Merton Coulter, *The South During Reconstruction, 1865–1877* (Baton Rouge: Louisiana State University Press, 1947), 258.

26. *The New York Times,* 9 July 1870.

CHAPTER 6

1. For a comprehensive history of the Cotton Exchange during its 19th and 20th century life, see Forrest O. Lax, "The Memphis Cotton Exchange From Beginning to Decline" (M.A. thesis, Memphis State University, 1970), 133 p.

2. J. V. Paine, *Memphis Cotton Exchange . . . One Hundred Years* (Memphis: Memphis Cotton Exchange, 1973), 2.

3. For two sources of information on the institution of cotton factorage, see Alfred H. Stone, "The Cotton Factorage System in the Southern States," *American Historical Review* 20 (1915), 557–565; and George D. Green, *Finance and Economic Development in the Old South* (Palo Alto: Stanford University Press, 1972), 28–32.

4. W. J. Britton, *Front Street: A Book of Poems* (Memphis: S. C. Toof, 1948), 7.

5. At the turn of the century, the Memphis Industrial League promoted the city's excellent location. When this group languished, the same theme was adopted by the Business Men's Club.

6. Howard A. Hanlon, *Delta Harvest* (Watkins Glen, N.Y.: Watkins Review, Inc., 1966), xiii; 3.

7. Ibid, xiii.

8. Memphis *Appeal,* 1 September 1873.

9. "Manufactures in Memphis," *Old Folks' Record* I (December 1874), 125–126.

10. Broadus Mitchell, *The Rise of Cotton Mills in the South* (Baltimore: Johns Hopkins University Press, 1921) 232.

11. Ibid., 116.

12. Kate Born, "Organized Labor in Memphis, 1826–1901," *The West Tennessee Historical Society Papers* 21 (1967), 63–67; and Baker, *The Memphis Commercial Appeal,* 52.

13. *The New York Times,* 6 February 1884.

14. Memphis *Avalanche,* 22 October 1887.

15. *Harper's Weekly,* 14 May 1892, p. 473.

16. Memphis *Appeal-Avalanche,* 29 April 1892.

17. For a comprehensive review of the origin of the Mississippi River Commission and the responsibilities assigned to it, see Capt. Smith S. Leach, U.S. Engineers, *The Mississippi River: What It Needs, and Why It Needs It* (Washington, D. C.: 1890). This monograph appears in Vol. 2, Mississippi River Commission, *Mississippi River Papers* (1890).

18. Memphis *Avalanche,* 1 September 1883.

19. Memphis *Daily Appeal,* 2 December 1879.

CHAPTER 7

1. Business Men's Club, *Factory Facts and Figures Demonstrating the Superiority of Memphis As A Manufacturing Center* (Memphis, 1910), 64.

2. Ivan Allen, *Atlanta From the Ashes* (Atlanta: Ruralist Press, 1929), 12.

3. Ernest Kirschten, *Catfish and Crystal* (Garden City, N.Y.: Doubleday, 1965 ed.), 428.

4. Carl V. Harris, *Political Power in Birmingham, 1871–1921* (Knoxville: University of Tennessee Press, 1977), 22.

5. William D. Miller, *Memphis During the Progressive Era, 1900–1917* (Memphis: Memphis State University Press, 1957), 59–60.

6. Excellent research has been done on these early railroad terminals by Memphis historian Paul R. Coppock in several articles he prepared for *The Commercial Appeal*. See in particular the issues of 27 January 1967 and 23 April 1972.

7. Keith L. Bryant, Jr. "The Railway Station As A Symbol of Urbanization in the South, 1890–1920," *South Atlantic Quarterly* 75 (Autumn 1976), 499–509.

8. Theodore Saloutos, "The Southern Cotton Association, 1905–1908," *The Journal of Southern History* 12 (1947), 492–510. See also Charles S. Barrett, *The Mission, History and Times of the Farmers' Union* (Nashville: Marshall and Bruce Co., 1909), 419 p.

CHAPTER 8

1. *The Commercial Appeal,* 28 September 1900.

2. The Delta is here defined as the 12 counties in Mississippi which are located totally in the alluvial plain east of the Mississippi River, plus another six Mississippi counties which lie partially within the alluvial plain.

3. Letter from Mayor E. H. Crump to U.S. Congressman Kenneth McKellar, 1 April 1912, in McKellar Papers, in The Memphis Room, Memphis-Shelby County Public Library and Information Center.

4. *The Commercial Appeal,* 6 September 1906.

5. Memphis *Scimitar,* 5 May 1904.

6. *The Commercial Appeal,* 20 July 1901.

7. Memphis *Scimitar,* 5 May 1904.

8. *The Commercial Appeal,* 5 March 1905.

9. Bobby Joe Williams, "Let There Be Light: History of the Development of Public Ownership of Electric Utilities in Memphis, 1933–1940" (M.A. thesis, Memphis State University, 1972), 22.

10. Ibid., 23.

11. For a capsulized history of Memphis utilities, see *The Commercial Appeal,* 24 July 1932.

12. *Memphis Press-Scimitar,* 13 June 1931.

13. Carl W. Condit, *The Chicago School of Architecture: A History of Commercial and Public Building in the Chicago Area, 1875–1925* (Chicago: University of Chicago Press, 1964), 238 p.

14. Mary Ann Connell, "The Peabody Hotel" (M.A. thesis, University of Mississippi, 1971), 6–7.

15. Ibid.

16. George W. Lee, *Beale Street,* 13.

17. Ibid., 25.

18. *Memphis Press-Scimitar,* 22 January 1947. Harris died at the age of 92.

19. *Memphis Press-Scimitar,* 7 October 1953. Turpin was over 70 years of age at death.

20. Memphis historian Paul R. Coppock prepared a profile of Duke Bowers which appeared in *The Commercial Appeal,* 5 December 1971.

21. Memphis Chamber of Commerce, 1921.

22. *The Commercial Appeal,* 8 January 1933.

CHAPTER 9

1. Bureau of Municipal Research, *Memphis: A Critical Study of Some Phases of Its Municipal Government With Constructive Suggestions for Betterment in Organization and Administrative Methods* (Memphis, October 1909), 203 p.

2. Ibid., 51.

3. *The Commercial Appeal,* 26 September 1909.

4. Ibid., 17 October 1954.

5. Miller, *Mr. Crump,* 27–59.

6. W. C. Handy, ed., *A Treasury of Blues* (New York: C. Boni, 1949), 18.

7. *Memphis Press-Scimitar,* 1 September 1949.

8. *The Commercial Appeal,* 19 October 1952.

9. Lamar W. Bridges, "Editor Mooney Versus Boss Crump" (M.S. thesis, University of Wisconsin, 1963), 59–63.

10. Miller, *Mr. Crump,* 113–114.

11. Randall G. Shelden, "Rescued from Evil: Origins of the Juvenile Justice System in Memphis, Tennessee, 1900–1917" (Ph.D. dissertation, Southern Illinois University, 1976), 187. See also Bureau of the Census, *Child Labor in the United States* (1907).

12. Shelden, *Rescued from Evil,* 254.

13. Ibid.

14. Raymond G. Fuller, *Child Labor and the Constitution* (New York: Arno Press, reprinted 1974), 128–129.

15. *The Commercial Appeal,* 14 March 1917.

16. Kate Born, "Memphis Negro Workingmen and the NAACP," *The West Tennessee Historical Society Papers* 28 (1974), 90–107.

17. Grace Elizabeth Prescott, "The Women's Suffrage Movement in Memphis: Its Place in the State, Sectional and National Movements," *The West Tennessee Historical Society Papers* 18 (1964), 87–106.

18. This information appeared in an editorial in *The Chattanooga Times,* 21 November 1912.

19. *The Commercial Appeal,* 10 January 1943.

20. Ibid., 1 January 1940.

21. Ibid., 15 March 1912.

22. Ibid., 7, 8 and 9 January 1909.

23. Statistics taken from *The Spectator* were reported in *The Literary Digest,* 19 October 1912.

24. *The Literary Digest,* 19 January 1918.

25. *The Commercial Appeal,* 15 July 1917.

26. Gerald M. Capers, "The Rural Lag on Southern Cities," *Mississippi Quarterly* 21 (1968), 253–261.

27. *The Commercial Appeal,* 11 September 1918.

28. G. P. Hamilton, *The Bright Side of Memphis* (Memphis: n.p., 1908), 14.

29. *The Commercial Appeal,* 3 June 1916.

30. Ibid., 15 April 1917.

31. Ibid., 8 April 1917.

32. Ibid., 11 March 1919.

33. John Norris, "Park Field: World War I Pilot Training School," *The West Tennessee Historical Society Papers* 31 (1977), 76.

CHAPTER 10

1. *The Commercial Appeal,* Centennial Edition Supplement, 16 May 1919.

2. Frederick Lewis Allen, *Only Yesterday: An Informal History of the Nineteen Twenties* (New York: Blue Ribbon Books, 1931), 370 p.

3. Memphis *Chamber of Commerce Journal,* April 1921.

4. *The Commercial Appeal,* 16 March 1919.

5. Ibid.

6. Ibid.

7. "The New United States III, As Memphis Sees the Future," *The Nation* 108, No. 2801 (19 March 1919), 348–349.

8. *The New York Times,* 8, 9 December 1920.

9. *The Commercial Appeal,* 6 October 1919. See also the articles by David M. Tucker, "Black Pride and Negro Business in the 1920s: George Washington Lee of Memphis" *Business History Review* 43, No. 4 (1969), 437; and Jonathan Daniels, "Men At A Corner," *Virginia Quarterly Review* 31 (1955), 222.

10. U.S. Department of the Interior, Bureau of Education, *The Public School System of Memphis, Tennessee,* Bulletin No. 50, Part I.

11. *Biennial Report of the Public Schools of the City of Memphis, Tennessee,* 1922–1924, p. 5.

12. *The New York Times,* 14 May 1923.

13. *The Commercial Appeal,* 11 November 1927.

14. Ibid., 13 April 1924.

15. Bette Baird Tilly, "Memphis and the Mississippi Valley Flood of 1927," *The West Tennessee Historical Society Papers* 24 (1970), 41–56.

16. Pete Daniel, *Deep 'n As It Come: The 1927 Mississippi River Flood* (New York: Oxford University Press, 1977), 134–135.

17. Professor Ralph Hon of Southwestern at Memphis analyzed these problems as a guest columnist in *The Commercial Appeal,* 14 April 1935.

18. Isaac Reese, "Memphis As A Future Iron and Steel Center," *Memphis Chamber of Commerce Journal* (November 1919), 229.

19. For an interesting series of articles on the Memphis mule market, see *The Commercial Appeal,* 8 April 1903 and 27 June 1951; and *Memphis Press-Scimitar,* 27 December 1947.

CHAPTER 11

1. *Memphis Chamber of Commerce Journal* (July 1922), 11–12.

2. Virginia Phillips, "Rowlett Paine's First Term As Mayor of Memphis, 1920–1924" (M.A. thesis, Memphis State University, 1958). This information was extracted by the above author from *The News Scimitar,* 30 November 1920.

3. City Planning Commission, *A Comprehensive City Plan, Memphis, Tennessee* (Memphis, 1924).

4. *Spencer-Sturla Company* v. *City of Memphis,* 155 Tenn. 70; 290 S.W. 608 (1927).

5. *The Commercial Appeal,* 4 October 1927.

6. Ibid., 15 March 1928.

7. David L. Cohn, *God Shakes Creation* (New York: Harper and Brothers, 1935), 17.

8. Lester C. Lamon, *Black Tennesseans, 1900–1930* (Knoxville: University of Tennessee Press, 1977), 188–196. See also Tucker, "Black Pride and Negro Business," 448–449.

CHAPTER 12

1. George B. Tindall, *The Emergence of the New South, 1913–1945* (Baton Rouge: Louisiana State University Press, 1967), 354–355.

2. Ibid., 359.

3. Letter from U.S. Senator Kenneth McKellar to E. H. Crump, 7 May 1930, in McKellar Papers.

4. *The Commercial Appeal,* 2 June 1930. This ad was placed by the managing director of the Made-in-Memphis Exposition.

5. Ibid., 27 July 1933.

6. *Monthly Labor Review* 36 (April 1933), 769.

7. Baker, *The Memphis Commercial Appeal,* 284–285.

8. *The Commercial Appeal,* 3 September 1934.

9. *Memphis Press-Scimitar,* 21 September 1935.

10. *The Commercial Appeal,* 7 March 1933.

11. Ibid., 27 August 1934.

12. *Monthly Labor Review* 36 (1933), 413.

13. Works Progress Administration, *The Housing Survey of the City of Memphis and Part of Shelby County, Tennessee* (Memphis: Memphis Housing Authority, 1941), 18.

14. O. P. White, "Sinners in Dixie," *Collier's,* 26 January 1935, p. 16.

15. This brief statement was taken from one of the five minute spot radio announcements sponsored by the Mayor's Employment Committee.

CHAPTER 13

1. *The Commercial Appeal,* 16 May 1919, p. 1.
2. Murray R. Benedict, *Farm Policies of the United States, 1790–1950* (New York: Octagon Books, 1966), 307.
3. *Memphis Press-Scimitar,* 5 December 1933.
4. Ibid.
5. *The Commercial Appeal,* 30 November 1934.
6. *The New York Times,* 12 May 1937.
7. *The Commercial Appeal,* 1 January 1934.
8. *Memphis Press-Scimitar,* 8 April 1937.
9. Norris, "Park Field," 76.
10. Memphis Housing Authority, *Annual Report,* 1944–45.
11. Works Progress Administration, *The Housing Survey,* 17.
12. Letter to Mayor Walter Chandler, 5 February 1940, in City of Memphis Archives.
13. *The Commercial Appeal,* 21 September 1941.
14. Letter from Lawrence P. Cockrill, Engineer-Secretary, City Planning Commission to Mayor Watkins Overton, 14 April 1939, in City of Memphis Archives.
15. *Memphis Press-Scimitar,* 1, 2 July 1937 and 19 March 1942; and *The Commercial Appeal,* 25 May 1938.
16. *The Commercial Appeal,* 18 May 1937.
17. *Memphis Press-Scimitar,* 19 November 1935.
18. *The Commercial Appeal,* 8 March 1934.
19. Letter from U.S. Senator Kenneth McKellar to E. H. Crump, 30 December 1936, in McKellar Papers, Memphis Room, MPL.
20. Telegram from E. H. Crump to Senator McKellar, 10 February 1937, in McKellar Papers.
21. B. A. Botkin, ed., *A Treasury of Mississippi River Folklore* (New York: Crown Publishers, 1955), 557.
22. *Memphis Press-Scimitar,* 6 April 1932.
23. *The Commercial Appeal,* 28 February 1943 and 17 July 1947.
24. *Memphis Press-Scimitar,* 21 May 1936.
25. *The Commercial Appeal,* 16 December 1938.
26. Letter from E. H. Crump to Senator McKellar, 17 January 1937, in McKellar Papers.
27. Telegraph from E. H. Crump to Senator McKellar, 15 January 1937, in McKellar Papers.
28. *The Commercial Appeal,* 19 January 1938 and 8 April 1938.
29. *Memphis Press-Scimitar,* 13 November 1939.
30. *The Commercial Appeal,* 22 March 1936.
31. Ibid.
32. *Memphis Press-Scimitar,* 1 October 1938.
33. Ibid., 23 September 1937.
34. Allan Nevins and Frank E. Hill, *Ford: Decline and Rebirth, 1933–1962* (New York: Charles Scribner's Sons, 1962), 133.
35. Tindall, *The Emergence of the New South,* 527.
36. *Memphis Press-Scimitar,* 6 June 1942.
37. Howard Kester, *Revolt Among the Sharecroppers* (New York: Arno Press, 1969), 98 p.
38. *The Commercial Appeal,* 1 January 1940.
39. Ibid., 13 November 1936.
40. Letter from Mayor Watkins Overton to Macon Callicott, 4 December 1933, in City of Memphis Archives.
41. Memorandum from K. C. Larkey, Assistant City Attorney, to Mayor Watkins Overton, 5 March 1935, in City of Memphis Archives.
42. *The Commercial Appeal,* 1 April 1942.
43. *Memphis Press-Scimitar,* 26 January 1941.
44. Ibid.
45. *The Commercial Appeal,* 5 May 1944.

CHAPTER 14

1. *The Commercial Appeal*, 1 January 1940.
2. Ibid., 11 November 1939.
3. *Memphis Press-Scimitar*, 28 March 1942.
4. *The Commercial Appeal*, 8 December 1941.
5. Ibid., 9 December 1941.
6. Memphis Chamber of Commerce, *A Brief Survey of Industrial Opportunities*, revised March 1941.
7. *The Commercial Appeal*, 27 October 1941.
8. Ibid., 12 March 1942.
9. Ibid., 29 April 1942.
10. Letter to Mayor Walter Chandler from Lawrence P. Cockrill, Engineer-Secretary, City Planning Commission, 21 June 1943, in City of Memphis Archives.
11. *The Commercial Appeal*, 1 June 1944.
12. *Memphis Press-Scimitar*, 15 March 1945.
13. *The Commercial Appeal*, 18 March 1972.
14. Ibid., 3 May 1953.
15. *Memphis Press-Scimitar*, 10 August 1946.
16. *The Commercial Appeal*, 27 September 1946.
17. *Memphis Press-Scimitar*, 5 November 1947.
18. *The Commercial Appeal*, 5 March 1950.
19. Letter from E. H. Crump to Senator McKellar, 10 May 1948, in McKellar Papers.
20. *The New York Times*, 17 October 1954.

CHAPTER 15

1. *Memphis Press-Scimitar*, 12 September 1938.
2. *The Commercial Appeal*, 9 June 1954.
3. Ibid., 28 June 1951.
4. *Memphis Press-Scimitar*, 24 February 1953.
5. Ibid., 20 February 1953.
6. Ibid., 29 October 1955.
7. *The Commercial Appeal*, 26, 27 May 1966.
8. Ibid., 17 February 1954 and 23 February 1954.
9. Paul R. Coppock described the history of the annexation of Frayser in a feature article in *The Commercial Appeal*, 27 March 1977.
10. Memorandum from Mayor Edmund Orgill to the City Commissioners, 19 October 1959, in Orgill Papers, The Mississippi Valley Collection, John W. Brister Library, Memphis State University.
11. *The Commercial Appeal*, 2, 3 July 1947.
12. *Memphis Press-Scimitar*, 6 October 1947.
13. Ibid., 6 October 1947.
14. Harland Bartholomew and Associates, *A Report Upon Interstate Highway Routes in Memphis and Shelby County, Tennessee*, prepared for The Board of Commissioners, City of Memphis; Shelby County Commissioners; and Tennessee State Highway Department, August 1955, 73 p.
15. *Memphis Press-Scimitar*, 26 February 1970.
16. 432 F2d 1307 (1970).
17. *The New York Times*, 8 December 1970 and 3 March 1971.
18. *The Commercial Appeal*, 8 March 1972.
19. Office of Planning and Development, *Annual Transportation Report Memphis Urban Area* (Memphis: City of Memphis, 1976).
20. *The Commercial Appeal*, 6 December 1970.

CHAPTER 16

1. *The Commercial Appeal,* 1 March 1953.
2. *Memphis Press-Scimitar,* 28 June 1972.
3. *The Commercial Appeal,* 11 July 1961.
4. Ibid.
5. Ibid., 25 December 1971.
6. *Memphis Press-Scimitar,* 12 April 1969.
7. *The Commercial Appeal,* 25 September 1952.
8. Connell, "Peabody Hotel," 79.
9. *The Commercial Appeal,* 15 December 1965.
10. "Memphis Airport," *Architectural Record* 127 (April 1960), 213–220.
11. Information furnished by the Memphis-Shelby County Airport Authority.
12. Harland Bartholomew and Associates, *Shelby Farms* (Memphis: The Associates, 1970), A–1.
13. Garrett Eckbo and Associates, *Shelby Farms* (Memphis, 1975), 8.

CHAPTER 17

1. Memphis Housing Authority, *Annual Report 1946–1947.*
2. *The Commercial Appeal,* 16 July 1953.
3. Ibid., 15 February 1954.
4. Ibid., 1 March 1977.
5. Ibid., 17 March 1963.
6. Ibid.
7. Ibid., 10 December 1970.
8. Ibid., 21 September 1966.
9. *Memphis Press-Scimitar,* 10 June 1976.
10. *The Commercial Appeal,* 2 May 1951.
11. Ibid., 28 August 1959 and 2 September 1959.
12. Ibid., 31 August 1959.
13. *Memphis Press-Scimitar,* 12 March 1968.
14. Marcou, O'Leary and Associates, *Downtown Memphis: Plan and Program for Downtown Development,* prepared for the City of Memphis, Shelby County and the Downtown Council of the Memphis Area Chamber of Commerce (Washington: Marcou, O'Leary and Associates, 1974), 46 p.
15. *The Commercial Appeal,* 21 June 1974.

CHAPTER 18

1. W. Lawrence Prehn, Jr. and Francis X. Mahady, *Economic Potentials for Memphis* (Dallas: Economic Research Associates, 1978), 17–22.
2. *The Commercial Appeal,* 25 March 1942.
3. *Memphis Press-Scimitar,* 26 September 1972; and *The Commercial Appeal,* 17 July 1975.
4. *Ayer Directory of Publications* (Philadelphia: Ayer Press, 1947 and 1978 editions).
5. *The Commercial Appeal,* 6 May 1958.
6. *Memphis Press-Scimitar,* 7 January 1966.
7. *The Commercial Appeal,* 8 January 1966.
8. Thomas W. Collins and David H. Ciscel, "An Analysis of the RCA Television Assembly Plant in Memphis: Why It Closed," *Mid-South Quarterly Business Review* (1st Qtr. 1976), 3–7.
9. Ibid.
10. Federal Deposit Insurance Corporation, *Summary of Deposits in All Commercial and Mutual Savings Banks,* 30 June 1977.
11. Ibid.
12. Charles Thornton, "The Demise of Memphis' Bond Daddies," *The Commercial Appeal,* 1 October 1972.

CHAPTER 19

1. *Memphis Press-Scimitar,* 18 March 1938.
2. *The Commercial Appeal,* 2 September 1947.
3. Ibid., 18 October 1951.
4. *Memphis Press-Scimitar,* 23 February 1950.
5. *The Commercial Appeal,* 14 February 1968.
6. Frank Cormier and William J. Eaton, *Reuther* (Englewood Cliffs, NJ: Prentice-Hall, 1970), 389.
7. Kay Dunlap Veazey, "Public Employee Unrest May Frighten Industry Away," *The South Magazine* (January 1979), 48–51.

CHAPTER 20

1. *Memphis Press-Scimitar,* 4 November 1966.
2. *The Commercial Appeal,* 2 January 1968.
3. *Memphis Press-Scimitar,* 9 November 1951.
4. *The Commercial Appeal,* 30 January 1956.
5. Memphis and Shelby County Planning Commission, *The Economy of Metropolitan Memphis,* prepared by Hammer, Siler, Greene Associates and the Bureau of Business and Economic Research, Memphis State University (1965), 228 p.
6. *Time,* 12 April 1968, p. 18.
7. *Memphis Press-Scimitar,* 10 March 1969.
8. Ibid., 28 May 1969.
9. Ibid.
10. *Memphis in the 70s* (Memphis: Memphis State University, 1970), 262–263.
11. *The Commercial Appeal,* 26 January 1973.
12. Future Memphis, Inc., *Blueprint for Memphis* (Memphis, 1973), 23–24.

Index

References to illustrations in boldface